A Critical Sense

'Rigorous almost to the point of impertinence, these interviews hold fashionable thought to the highest standard. We watch as these thinkers earn their celebrity, and we can see that they are sexier as thinkers, finally, than they are as celebrities.'
Bruce Robbins, *Rutgers University*

The interviews gathered in *A Critical Sense* bring together many of the leading figures of contemporary radical theory in a single volume. Moving freely between philosophy, politics and cultural studies, they offer a fascinating overview of today's intellectual Left. The thinkers who discuss their work in this collection are:

Judith Butler	Edward Said
Cornelius Castoriadis	Renata Salecl
Drucilla Cornell	Gayatri Chakravorty Spivak
Axel Honneth	Cornel West
Istvan Mészáros	Slavoj Žižek

All the interviews follow the same underlying structure: starting from questions about the interviewee's influences and formative years, they move on, via critical exchanges about key concepts and ideas, to reflections on political issues and recent events. Peter Osborne's introduction situates the interviews within the broader history of the relations between philosophers, academics and public intellectuals.

A Critical Sense offers a welcome introduction to the work of some of today's most important thinkers. The interview format makes their thought accessible without ever sacrificing the intellectual rigour or political implications of their theories. For those already acquainted with the writings of the theorists interviewed here, the broad contextualization, dialogical structure and comparitivist perspective of this collection will throw new – and often surprising – light on familiar ground.

Peter Osborne is Reader in Modern European Philosophy at Middlesex University. He is a member of the *Radical Philosophy* editorial collective and has written widely on philosophy, aesthetics and social theory. His most recent book is *The Politics of Time: Modernity and Avant-Garde* (1995).

A Critical Sense

Interviews with Intellectuals

Edited by Peter Osborne

London and New York

First published 1996
by Routledge
11 New Fetter Lane, London EC4P 4EE

Simultaneously published in the USA and Canada
by Routledge
20 West 35th Street, New York, NY 10001

Typeset in Sabon by Florencetype Ltd, Stoodleigh, Devon

Printed and bound in Great Britain by
Biddles Ltd, Guildford and King's Lynn

British Library Cataloguing in Publication Data
A catalogue record for this book is available from the British Library.

Library of Congress Cataloging in Publication Data
A critical sense: interviews with intellectuals/edited by Peter Osborne.
    p. cm.
    "Radical philosophy."
    Includes bibliographical references and index.
    1. Philosophers–Interviews. 2. Philosophy, Modern–20th century.
    3. Radicals–Interviews. 4. Intellectuals–interviews. 5. Theory
    (Philosophy)–History–20th century. 6. Criticism–History–20th
    century. I. Osborne, Peter, 1958–.
    B804.C79 1996
    109.2–dc20   96–3442
    CIP

ISBN 0–415–11505–1 (hbk)
ISBN 0–415–11506–X (pbk)

Contents

Note on the Texts

The following interviews were previously published in *Radical Philosophy*, as stated: Cornelius Castoriadis, *RP* 56 (Autumn 1990); Slavoj Žižek/Renata Salecl, *RP* 58 (Summer 1991); Istvan Mészáros, *RP* 62 (Autumn 1992); Edward Said, *RP* 63 (Spring 1993); Axel Honneth, *RP* 65 (Autumn 1993); Judith Butler, *RP* 67 (Summer 1994); Cornel West, *RP* 71 (May/June 1995); Drucilla Cornell, *RP* 73 (September/October 1995). The introduction, Slavoj Žižek's postscript to 'Lacan in Slovenia', and the interview with Gayatri Spivak, 'Setting to Work (Transnational Cultural Studies)', are published here for the first time.

Notes on the contributors appear at the beginning of each interview.

The journal *Radical Philosophy* has been published in England by the Radical Philosophy Collective since 1972. Originally appearing three times a year, it has been bi-monthly since issue no. 69 (January/February 1995). It is available by subscription and from selected bookshops in both the UK and USA. For subscription details, write to: Central Books (*Radical Philosophy*), 99 Wallis Road, London E9 5LN or telephone 0181–986 4854. Bookshop distribution in the UK is also by Central Books. Bookshop distribution in the USA and Canada is by Bernard De Boer Inc., 135 East Centre Street, Nutley, New Jersey 07100 (tel. 201–667 9300) and Ubiquity Distributors Inc., 607 Degraw Street, Brooklyn, New York 11217 (tel. 718–875 5491).

Introduction: Philosophy, and the Role of Intellectuals

Peter Osborne

> CRITIC Always 'eminent'. Supposed to know everything, to have read everything, to have seen everything. When you dislike him, call him a Zoilus, a eunuch.
>
> Gustave Flaubert, *Dictionary of Received Ideas*

Interviews are children of opportunity. Creatures of context and occasion, they are nonetheless ultimately the products of the artful edit: careful fictions, conjuring the promise of the actual from the signs of the present. Interviews with philosophers labour under the burden of a dual expectation: of the actuality of philosophy (a restricted if not altogether uninteresting affair) and, more compelling, philosophies of the actual. Philosophy as actuality – such is the heritage of Hegel's struggle to keep the idea of philosophy alive in the face of the multiplication of knowledges. It is still discernible today, however hedged with qualifications, in the work of some of his most stringent critics.

Foucault, for instance, maintains that the question of philosophy is the question of this present which constitutes us. That is why, for him, 'contemporary philosophy is entirely political and entirely historical. It is the politics immanent in history and the history indispensable for politics.'[1] Philosophy as the critique of the present – one does not have to agree with Foucault's particular understanding of this idea to recognize beneath it, as he came to himself, the common ground of a philosophical discourse of modernity. It is through their claims on the present – their ability to expound its actualities and subject them to judgement – that modern philosophies construct their claims to authority, however different their conceptions of this process may be. And what better form in which to capture such claims than the interview, itself a paradigmatically modern genre?

An invention of nineteenth-century journalism, the interview was originally designed for newspapers. Its extension into book form and, more recently, academic publishing, marks the intrusion of the interruptive time of modernity into the *longue durée* of university life; pushing the artifice of up-to-dateness to its limits, while allowing for its subsequent retrieval, as document, once its moment has passed. Many of Foucault's most influential formulations are to be found in interviews. *Politics and Letters,* the massive serial interview with Raymond Williams, is acknowledged to be the best overview of his work; while the (incomplete) list of published interviews *omitted* from Derrida's three collections of interviews, which appears at the end of the latest, 500-page, selection, contains sixty from the period 1982–1992 alone.[2]

However, if there is an affinity between the currency of the interview and modern philosophy's claim on the present, it is not the figure of the philosopher in whom it is epitomized, but that of the intellectual. In today's cultural market place, 'philosophers' remain somewhat removed from reality – sheltered from the demands of the media by the difficulty of their questions, the height of their abstractions and the weight of their traditions. Modern philosophy's claim on the present provides no licence for it to break what Vincent Descombes has called its 'golden rule': namely, 'a philosophy may be "idealistic" or "realistic", dialectical or illuminative, but it cannot allow itself the luxury of not being *difficult*. For who would care about philosophical problems if they were not especially difficult?'[3]

Difficulty is one of the things that alienates philosophy from public discourse, generating the anxiety captured in the imperative to 'snigger at it' which makes up its entry in Flaubert's *Dictionary of Received Ideas* – one of a string ridiculing intellectual activities, in which the laughter ('Always "Homeric"') is as nervous as it is frequent. If philosophers are to make their takes on modernity count, it would seem, they must move beyond the restricted sites and habits to which they have become increasingly confined, back into broader spaces of opinion formation and debate; mitigating the intricacies of their craft through strategic interventions and a more pragmatic attitude towards other modes of speech. Bertrand Russell is a much-cited model here; but also Karl Popper, whose influence on educated popular culture was far greater than in the academy – especially with regard to social thought, where he remained a determined amateur.[4] In doing so, returning to the Socratic origins of their vocation, philosophers find themselves cast in the role of intellectuals. Just what this involves, however, is by no means as clear as it once appeared to be.

Changes in the social structure and economic function of higher education, and the technology and cultural form of the media, have greatly complicated an idea which was always more at home in certain national contexts than others. The very need for the qualification 'public' in recent US debates over 'the decline of the public intellectual', for example, registers a fissure in the classical conception of the role. Yet this has more to do with changes in the forms of publicity than anything originating in the sphere of intellectual production itself. As one commentator has put it:

> The point is not simply that the mass media have helped reinvent the notion of the public as an urban space of aesthetic self-presentation, sociability, theatricality, and pleasure. More pertinently, it is that in so doing, the media bring [a] notion of the public ... which seems to have more to do with aesthetics than politics together with the politically participatory thrust of the 'republican virtue' model ... [P]articipation in the making, exchanging, and mobilizing of public opinion – the defining characteristic of 'republican virtue' – has to some extent been reinvented or relocated ... [It] is now discoverable to an unprecedented extent in the domain of culture.[5]

Hence the importance of the new discipline of cultural studies, and the far greater significance of alternative forms of cultural production. What relationship might be developed between these new discourses and practices and more classical forms of philosophical legitimation and critique is something which remains to be established.

This essay aims to situate the interviews which follow within the nexus of a broader history – of philosophers and intellectuals, socialists and academics – and to draw attention to certain recurring themes within the exchanges themselves. The thinkers in this volume were chosen, in part, for the diversity of their contributions to the theoretical culture of an increasingly fragmented Left. Yet this diversity retains a certain unity – a complexity – which, if not that of anything so securely instituted as a 'tradition', nonetheless marks the continued existence of a common set of overlapping conditions and concerns.

Figures of the Intellect (Classical Traditions)

Classically, 'the intellectual' is the product of a French imaginary in which the abstractly rational element of a (bourgeois) revolutionary tradition appeared in the symbolic form of a concrete social persona. As a noun referring to a particular kind of person, or a person doing a particular kind of work, the word did not come into general usage in English until the early nineteenth century. And it carried with it negative connotations, connected to its association with Jacobinism, from the start; including, ironically, ineffectiveness, as well as the coldness associated with abstraction.[6] In this respect, its history parallels that of 'ideology', which (coined by de Tracy in 1796 to denote a science of ideas) was soon employed by Napoleon in a derogatory sense, to attack proponents of democracy as purveyors of 'ideas'. Marx maintained the negative usage from the standpoint of opposed political beliefs. He may not have written much about intellectuals, but he had plenty to say about 'ideologists'. He thought them idealists, in the sense that their activities depend upon an idealistically misconceived self-understanding – just like philosophers, in fact. Yet he practised his own version of their trade, much as he continued to depend upon the conceptual resources of a supposedly superseded philosophical tradition.[7]

Ineffectiveness is now, of course, routinely ascribed to philosophers as their special preserve. It was not always so. The Enlightenment tradition of the *philosophe* was a profoundly practical one. 'Centuries were needed to know a part of the laws of nature', according to the entry for *philosophe* in Voltaire's *Philosophical Dictionary*, 'but a day is enough for a wise man to know the duties of man.' The ineffectives in this text are all religious hypocrites, fanatics who persecute philosophers, and they live in France. Voltaire optimistically portrayed England as free of them. England took its revenge in the form of Burke, intellectual champion of anti-intellectualism. Burke's displacement of the French Enlightenment image of religion back on to the heritage of the Enlightenment itself, in his *Reflections on the Revolution in France* (1790), laid the foundations for modern conservatism and the political disparagement of intellectuals alike. This position was reinforced during the Cold War (communism the 'God that failed'), when 'intellectuals' and 'ideology' were linked to 'totalitarianism' via 'Marxism' and 'party'.[8] It is a structure of hypocrisy which remains central to right-wing populism, although its influence is more pervasive than that.[9] The projected ineffectiveness of the philosopher is as likely to stem from this broad current of anti-intellectualism as it is from an independent perception of philosophy's specific intellectual function; beyond a vague sense of its abstractness, perhaps. Whether the current resurgence of pragmatism in the Anglo-American academy, as a self-consciously paradoxical 'anti-philosophical philosophy', continues or combats this heritage of anti-intellectualism is one of the things at stake in several of the interviews in this book.

In Germany, on the other hand, the situation is different. The intimate historical connection of philosophy to both nationalism and the state – from Fichte's *Addresses to the German Nation* (1807) to Heidegger's *Rectoral Address* (1933) – alongside the history of German nationalism itself, has left behind an altogether other set of discursive deposits. Enlightenment in Germany produced not the *philosophe* but the philosophy *professor*. Yet this professor's ambitions for his discipline far exceeded anything suggested by its place in the established hierarchy of intellectual genres or university faculties.[10] The combination of universality and publicity elsewhere attributed to the intellectual (in opposition to the specialisms of professionals and university scholars alike) appears within this tradition as a specifically philosophical trait. Philosophy is attributed a unifying power with regard to culture and socialization which makes it the ideal reflexive form of modern culture as a whole. For Schelling, for example, it was nonsensical to conceive of philosophy as containable within a faculty, since: 'Something which is everything cannot, for that very reason, be anything in particular.[11]

This particular universalism has proved open to a range of political interpretations, from liberal cosmopolitanism, through corporatism, to a primarily linguistic nationalism. However, it was its accommodation to fascism during the Third Reich which most profoundly problematized its Enlightenment credentials. The German philosophy of the 1930s exhibited a will to power quite unlike anything to be found in its English, French or North American equivalents.[12] As a result, since 1945, liberal philosophers in Germany have tended self-consciously to reject German philosophy's previous aspiration to a special relationship with state and nation; appealing instead to the democratic responsibility of the individual philosopher as a citizen, like any other. This stance, which has its origins in Jaspers's immediate post-war writings,[13] is epitomized by Habermas when he insists: 'Philosophers are not teachers of the nation. . . . if they want to design just institutions for a certain type of society under given historical circumstances, philosophers can only join those who are involved in the democratic process as citizens or serve as assistants with a certain expertise.'[14]

For Habermas, the activities elsewhere bundled together under the category of the philosopher-intellectual should be carefully separated, into a strictly cognitive or specifically intellectual component (where philosophy holds sway) and a public-democratic responsibility or function, shared equally by all. This has some odd consequences: such as the denial that Rawls's *Theory of Justice* is a philosophical work, since it elaborates specific principles of justices, rather than restricting itself to 'clarification of the general grounds or rules under which moral claims can be justified'. Conversely, it involves the disavowal of a philosophical dimension to 'the common business of political discourse among citizens'.[15] Yet in this case, it is unclear how such business might benefit from philosophers serving as 'assistants' or what the relevance of their particular 'expertise' might be.

In practice, however, through his journalism and interviews, Habermas has played precisely that role of the philosopher as intellectual, the validity of which he has so strenuously denied; and never more significantly than when it has been questions of national identity or the structure and role of the state which have been at issue – from the conflicts over student protest and the democratization of the universities in the 1960s, via the arguments about terrorism in the 1970s and the Historians' Dispute of the 1980s, to more recent debates about German reunification and the Gulf War.[16] Thus, while German history has special lessons to teach us about 'the entwinement of myth and enlightenment' within the practice of philosophy itself, the suggestion that it constitutes a decisive argument against the public role of the philosopher is unconvincing. In fact, Habermas's fear of the philosopher as a political figure is connected to his *acceptance* of a central tenet of the tradition he is concerned to combat: namely, its identification of philosophy with the absolutely binding power of certain sorts of argumentation. It is as if, once mixed with the social, philosophy cannot but demand power over it. This logicist abstraction (and feared false concretion) of the claims of reason, in relation to the social forms in which they exist, is precisely what is questioned by both most contemporary French and much recent Anglo-American philosophy. Such questioning is reinforced by the image of the intellectual as a literary figure.

The absence of a discourse on intellectuals from Habermas's writings on the task of philosophy derives from both the national and the literary provenance of the idea in its dominant form. German debates about the social function of philosophy take us back, fairly swiftly, to the politically ambiguous heritage of Plato – the *Republic*, rather than anything by Nietzsche or Heidegger, was the most widely read work on political theory among Nazi philosophers.[17] Most contemporary writing about intellectuals has its origins rather closer to home: in Julien Benda's *Trahison des Clercs* of 1927. This is the book which laid down the terms with which Western debates about the responsibility of intellectuals have thenceforth grappled: the moral universalism of a heroic individualism, rejecting all national particularism and social partisanship, practised in the name of the service of humanity as a whole. These terms are epitomized today in the figure of Chomsky.[18]

A product of the conscience-stricken liberal humanism of the crisis-strewn years between the wars in Europe – its philosophical framework a barely secularized Christianity – Benda's idealistic view of intellectuals as a corporation of individuals with universal responsibilities (an adaptation of the nineteenth-century Russian tradition of the 'intelligentsia') survived the context of its birth to become the baseline of a tradition which remains hard to shake.[19] Subsequent writers (most notably Sartre) have contested both its theoretical and its political terms, rejecting its abstract humanism in favour of an existential discourse on intellectual freedom, connected to a political discourse of rigorous partisanship or 'commitment'. But they have stuck with its distinctive aspiration to universality, making the intellectual an *exemplary* figure for humanity as a whole. It is this aspiration to exemplification which produces the intellectual as a paradigmatically literary (indeed theatrical), as well as a moral, persona. For, as Habermas points out, the bourgeois public sphere, privileged site of intellectual activity, came about historically through a political refunctioning of the space of a pre-existing literary culture.[20]

Habermas associates this development with the demise of what he calls 'representative publicness', which he identifies with the corporate culture of the Middle Ages. For Benda, on the other hand, the intellectual is the moral exemplar of the spirit of publicness itself. A sociological version of this view, in which intellectuals 'play the part of watchmen in what otherwise would be a pitch-black night', was outlined in Germany around the same time as Benda's book, by Karl Mannheim in *Ideology and Utopia* (1929).[21] Notoriously, for Mannheim, the relative classlessness of intellectuals as a 'stratum' produces a 'free-floating intelligence' (frei-schwebende Intelligenz) capable of 'subsum[ing] in itself all those interests with which social life is permeated'. 'Bearers of synthesis', intellectuals turn out to be the sole representatives of the 'total perspective' corresponding to 'interest in the whole'.[22]

This kind of corporate universalism of the intellectual function is more central to the liberal tradition in Germany than Habermas's history of the public sphere allows; extending the authoritarianism of the 'mandarin' tradition, reconstructed by Ringer, beyond its more conservative roots.[23] A sociological extension of Hegel's account of the state bureaucracy in the *Philosophy of Right* (1821), in the context of a Nietzschean epistemology, Mannheim's work was particularly influential in the technocratic context of the reconstruction of the 1950s, in both a Germany in flight from 'ideology' and an England (to which Mannheim fled from the Nazis) in which it was able to feed into the Fabian tradition, as a positivist infusion into its ideology of social planning by experts. It was vigorously attacked by Adorno, for upholding the 'innocuous scepticism' of a standpoint which 'calls everything into question and criticizes nothing'.[24] Yet one should not forget what Mannheim and other corporate-universalists share with Marxism, via Hegel. Just as Marx carried over much of the conceptual structure of Hegel's logic into his account of the German proletariat as a universal class, so something of Hegel's corporatism is to be found in Gramsci's work on intellectuals, albeit once again translated into class terms.[25] The dilemmas of intellectual representation (thinking the particular from the standpoint of the universal, and vice versa) are not so easily dispelled as Adorno's critique of the pseudo-universalism of Mannheim's corporatism implies.

It is corporatism (in both its particularistic and its moral-universalist forms) which Habermas is reacting against in his work on the public sphere, in the name of the democratic extension and transformation of a bourgeois model which has more in common with a nineteenth-century US tradition than with the model of eighteenth-century Britain from which it ostensibly derives. However, if the general problem with a corporatism of intellectuals concerns their claims to power (the representative publicness of the feudal lord was the result of the exclusion of other estates from *res publica*), the representative publicness of Benda's lay clerisy derives precisely from its remoteness from formally constituted power, its political powerlessness. For his is an essentially individualistic vision. The moral power of the intellectual's pen depends here, not only on public institutions of writing and reading (the means of representation), but also, paradoxically, on the rhetorical force of the image of powerlessness: right within the bounds of reason alone. 'One does not arrest Voltaire', as de Gaulle is reputed to have remarked with respect to Sartre; although as a matter of fact, if expediency demands, one usually does.

In this respect, the familiar figure of the intellectual as moral hero, fashioned in France during the defence of Dreyfus at the end of the nine-teenth century, and reworked during the Cold War into the figure of the dissident, is deeply ambivalent towards politics. Exclusion from power is its life-blood.[26] Yet how, then, is the intellectual to effect change with the public demonstration of his or her individual moral worth, once we discount appeals to enlightened political absolutisms of the kind presumed by Kant's original formulation of the problematic?[27] The exceptional historical circumstances which propelled the unhappy Havel to the Presidency of Czechoslovakia (later the Czech Republic) reinforce rather than resolve the problem, since the power of the powerless was quickly transformed into the powerlessness of a formal political authority in the face of structural social change. In this situation, resignation, not resistance, is the price of authenticity, since there is no other con-stituted authority to hold responsible and address. Melancholy replaces protest as the intellectual's characteristic existential mode. Czech Heideggerianism becomes the apposite ideology of ex-dissident intellec-tuals in post-communist states.

Power and Representation

Two main responses to the question of power stand out in recent writing about intellectuals. One involves a modified reassertion of the aspiration to a democratic public sphere, within which the intellectual might play a special role in political will-formation, without being compromised by his or her relations with established (or alternative) political authorities, in the context of a complex multiplicity of audiences and constituencies. The other is based upon a more radical rejection of the intellectual's aspiration to universality, in favour of the enhanced practicality and supposed greater oppositional credibility of his or her provision of 'specific knowledges' to specific, local groups. The first approach is associated with the belated English-language reception of Habermas's work on the public sphere, in the context of the political debates of the 1980s, although it is not restricted to it. The latter derives directly from Foucault. Both aspire to move beyond the individualism of Benda's abstract moral universalism, yet each remains in danger of succumbing to more or less Bendaesque tendencies.

In the first case, the now widely accepted pluralization of the notion of the public sphere, whereby Negt and Kluge's Marxist critique of

Habermas is extended to include the full range of contemporary social movements, the universality of 'the' public is recognised as being subject to multiple, competing claims. Yet the aspiration to (and necessity for) the projection of some such universality – however illusory, merely regulative, or ideal – is maintained, alongside a belief in the power of social integration of the public sphere itself.[28] This is a theoretically uncertain, but politically productive, development of civic republicanism for more highly differentiated societies, in a state of constant interaction and internal flux (commonly misnamed 'postmodern'). Its dilemmas may be illustrated with reference to Edward Said's *Representations of the Intellectual* – a text which, whilst not dependent on Habermas, is nonetheless reliant upon a similar notion of the public sphere for its account of the intellectual's political role.[29]

For Said, it is the special duty of the intellectual, as an individual 'endowed with a faculty for representing, embodying, articulating a message, a view, an attitude, philosophy or opinion to, as well as for, a public', to use this faculty to address 'the constituted and authorized power of one's own society', in public, on issues of freedom and justice. Intellectuals 'speak the truth to power' in order 'to induce a change in the moral climate'. To do this, they require independence from power and authority. Yet, as Said acknowledges, there is no getting around the intellectual's relationship to power and authority. Independence must thus be constantly wrested by the individual intellectual from his or her circumstances in order to keep the public realm alive. Said's collective name for the 'values and prerogatives' of such individual struggles is *amateurism*.[30]

This is essentially a more sociologically knowing, activist updating of Benda. It presents particular commitments (such as Said's own advocacy of the Palestinian cause) as an enrichment of, rather than a challenge to, universalism. Yet its continuing individualism and concomitant moral idealism remain problematic. For if the effectiveness of the intellectual in the public sphere is dependent on his or her ability to 'intervene *on behalf of* rights that have been violated and truths that have been suppressed'[31] – on the ability, in Said's terms, to 'represent' what will always be already partially constituted interests and beliefs – what, then, of the relationship of the intellectual to those whose interests are represented? What of the cultural power and authority of intellectuals themselves?

It is characteristic of the self-reflection of intellectuals to exaggerate their marginality and emphasize their lack of power. As Said remarks, their exile is not only often actual, it is also a metaphorical condition.[32] Yet one cannot but be sceptical of Chomsky's stated belief that 'within the intellectual community, anybody who is a dissident is not going to have any status' (leading as it does to such hyperbole as: 'There's probably no human being more vilified than Bertrand Russell');[33] or worry about the equivalence in Said's view between the threats posed to intellectual independence by established authority and oppositional organizations alike. The Cold War provenance of the figure of 'the dissident' is a warning about the politics of such determined individualism, as is the ease with which discourses of 'marginality' have been transformed into the stakes of academic competition in the humanities in recent years.[34] The rhetoric of marginality and independence is quite capable of accompanying conformity in other spheres, as the political history of the famous 'New York intellectuals' shows. For all his antipathy to professionalism, Said still sees the Western university as a 'quasi-utopian space'; and his concept of amateurism – 'entering and transforming the merely professional routine' – is spiritual, not economic.[35] There is a form of *cultural power* inherent in the representative function of the institutions of the public sphere which remains unaddressed here. It is a libertarian desire to be freed of such a complicity with power, while maintaining a sociological realism about the intellectual function in capitalist societies (professional specialization), which leads to the alternative approach: Foucault's rejection of the aspiration to universality, in favour of the enhanced practicality and oppositionality of the notion of 'specific' intellectuals.

Foucault's approach to intellectuals is distinctive in treating the issues of power, representation and professionalism together as aspects of a single practical field.[36] It has three main components: a critique of the traditional representative function of intellectuals as a part of the system of power; an outline of an alternative conception of oppositional professionalism as the provision of specific knowledges to specific groups; and an indication of the problems which remain for the new view. The first, critical dimension follows from Foucault's general idea of the will to truth as one of 'the three great systems of exclusion which forge discourse': a distinct historically produced and developing regulative system of power/ knowledge.[37] The classical conception of intellectuals' responsibility for discourse make them *agents* of this system of power. The so-called 'public' sphere (in actuality, a system of exclusion) names the sites of this agency. Once this is recognized, Foucault argues, the intellectual's role can no longer be 'to place himself "somewhat ahead and to the side" in order to express the stifled truth of the collectivity'. Rather, it must be 'to struggle against the forms of power that transform him into its object and instrument in the sphere of "knowledge", "truth", "consciousness" and "discourse"'. This struggle takes the reflexive form of the production of 'analytics of power'.[38]

Moreover, in order to avoid arriving at 'a new disposition of the same power with, at best, a change of masters', such analytics must refuse the totalizing drive characteristic of the dominant will to truth, in favour of a notion of theory as both irreducibly 'local and regional' – not directional. The intellectual is no longer cast in the role of an 'adviser', rather: 'The project, tactics and goals to be adopted are a matter for those who do the

fighting. What the intellectual can do is provide instruments of analysis . . .
a topological and geological survey of the battlefield – that is the intellectual's role.' What Foucault calls 'counter-discourses' – discourses which contest the prevailing system of power, but which are not strictly speaking
'about' it – must be produced by the 'subjected' objects of that system itself.[39]
The intellectual carriers of this new 'politics of truth' are thus no longer the
writers, generalists or amateurs of old – let alone the 'philosophers', with
their will to representation and totality – but professionals with specific
instrumental functions within the existing regime of truth or power/
knowledge: biologists, physicists, social workers, doctors, lawyers, etc.

The difficulty is that if the pervasiveness of power is characterized by
the unity of discourses ('regularity in dispersion'), which are irreducibly
multiple in their sites and modes of operation, what is to correspond to
this unity at the level of the multiplicity of oppositional struggles? Foucault
cites the 'failure of integration' of oppositional strategies as the reason
for the return, in the politics of the 1960s and 1970s, of the romantic
anarchist themes of the late nineteenth century, in terms of which his own
work has often (not unreasonably) been read.[40] Yet he offers no political
alternative. Nor is this the only problem. For when one examines the
structure of Foucault's appeal to intellectuals, it looks suspiciously like a
new version of the *trahison des clercs*: the exposure of a particular type
of intellectual's complicity with power, a power that is exercised at the
expense of the people.[41] Furthermore, once the motif of the 'integration
of strategies' is pursued a little further, it begins to look as if the universal
intellectual might not actually have been banished at all, so much as
reformed and rethought. For while what generality there is to piecemeal
struggles may be strictly negative (since it 'derives from the system of
power itself', rather than any positive common features of resistances),
Foucault nonetheless acknowledges that this is enough to link each specific
struggle to 'the general functioning of an apparatus of truth'. It thus turns
out that the position of the specific intellectual '*can* take on a general
significance'; that his/her local struggle '*can* have effects and implications
which are not simply professional or sectoral'; even that the intellectual
'*can* operate and struggle at the general level of that régime of truth which
is so essential to the structure and functioning of our society'.[42] Indeed,
how else is the political dimension of Foucault's own intellectual work to
be understood? Or the intellectual component of his political practice?[43]

Moreover, since the struggle is not over a truth to be 'discovered' or
'uncovered', but over '*the ensemble of rules* according to which the true
and the false are separated and the specific effects of power attached to
the true',[44] it would seem to have a specifically 'philosophical' dimension.
('Clarification of the rules under which claims can be justified' is one of
Habermas's descriptions of philosophy.) The distinction between
'universal' and 'specific' intellectuals thus begins to crumble, leaving

behind an ineliminably philosophical dimension to intellectual activity. Once this is recognized, Foucault's sociological insights can be fed back into the newly pluralized model of the public sphere, diversifying it further. Such is the basic tendency of Said's work, in fact. However, important differences remain between the two approaches concerning both the concept of power and the politics of professionalism in universities, especially in the humanities.[45]

Academics, Critics and Theorists

It is common on both Left and Right to bemoan the state of the universities in capitalist democracies, as part of a more general narrative of the decline of public intellectual life.[46] The story comes in various versions, but it usually gives a central role to the increased power of the media and the rise of professionalism among academics. Thus, for example, in his account of the three ages of intellectual power in France, Regis Debray argues that the social site of intellectual influence has moved successively from the university, via publishing, to the media; and that this progression follows a single historical law of increasing symbolic immiseration.[47] Said, on the other hand, dismissing what Debray describes as 'almost entirely a local French situation' (an exaggerated reaction to the belated erosion of the power of French universities, given exceptional autonomy under the Third Republic), insists that it is not 'the appalling commercialism of journalism and publishing' which is the threat to intellectual life, but 'what is considered to be proper, professional behaviour – not rocking the boat, not straying outside the accepted paradigms or limits, making yourself marketable and above all presentable, hence unpolitical and uncontroversial and "objective"'.[48] Yet the two positions are less opposed than Said thinks, since 'making yourself marketable and above all presentable' must surely be understood, at least in part, in terms of media-defined conceptions of marketability and presentability.

However, neither perspective does justice to the complex combination of change and continuity characteristic of university education in the West over the last fifty years. For all the national variation, there is a remarkable structural similarity among advanced capitalist states. The demographic expansion of university systems after 1950, from an average rate of enrolment of around 4 per cent of national populations to what is now past 40 per cent, constitutes an extraordinary democratic achievement. Only the most jaundiced conservative could believe this to be offset completely by the increase in the cultural power of the media which has accompanied it. For despite their power, the mass media do not, and seemingly cannot, constitute themselves as an independent source of authority on intellectual matters. To a large extent, the university 'acts as a licensing authority for other cultural institutions, recognizing and/or regulating the extent and demarcation of their various claims to knowledge and endowing them with something of its own accumulated prestige'.[49] What is sometimes called the 'crisis of the universities' should thus not be interpreted as a loss of power, but rather, as Foucault argued, as 'a multiplication and re-enforcement of their power-effects as centres in a polymorphous ensemble of intellectuals who virtually all pass through and relate themselves to the academic system'.[50]

This expanded circulation of intellectuals here is no more a threat to the academic system than it is restricted to the kind of conservative adaptation of the *status quo* detected by Mulhern as the cunning of British continuism: 'the doyen of Oxford history on prime-time television'.[51] The development of mass media and the partial reinvention of the public as 'an urban space of aesthetic self-presentation and theatricality'[52] which it involves – viewed unequivocally by Habermas as a threat to the democratic functioning of public space – enlarge the scope and reform the aesthetics of established models of public intellectual activity. They impose new restrictions, creating new challenges, but they do not destroy the terrain. A similar point can be made about professionalism. Tensions between specialization and the broader cultural functions of intellectual life have been around since the foundation of modern universities at the beginning of the nineteenth century. (They were the object of Heidegger's proposed reforms at the University of Freiburg in the 1930s, for example, as well as of the organization of interdisciplinary labour in the Frankfurt Institute for Social Research.) As circumstances have changed, these tensions have played themselves out in new ways, pulling the idea of the intellectual in opposite directions at once: outwards, away from the limited horizons of the academy, towards those wider social spaces and fields of interest now, apparently, dominated almost exclusively by 'the media'; and inwards, towards a redefinition of the social function of education in the humanities in what are increasingly recognized as 'multicultural' capitalist societies.[53]

Such changes are better seen as the result of an ongoing negotiation of purposes and boundaries than any sudden fall from publicity into professionalism. For 'professions *are* public', as Robbins puts it in *Secular Vocations*, his interesting attempt to rethink the academicization of intellectual life in North America, insofar as they are vocations which are regulated and licensed by the state.[54] However, while this means that public responsibility 'belongs within rather than outside professionalism', in general, the point applies to professional work in the humanities in a more specific, extended sense. For it was literary criticism which, in the Anglo-American context, took over the Romantic notion of culture as a redemptive whole, which developed in Germany mainly via the philosophical tradition. Given the ground of this notion in a critique of the division of labour, this has the curious consequence that, once literary criticism developed into a specialized discipline, anti-professionalism became an essential part of its ritual of professional legitimation.[55] A similar structure can be detected in strands of institutional philosophy – in the figure of Wittgenstein, for example. But academic philosophy this century has largely abrogated the task of cultural synthesis (taken over from religion) to literature. Said's affirmation of the spirit of amateurism against professional routine is in this respect in the mainstream of his professional tradition. As Robbins reminds us, R. P. Blackmur called criticism 'the formal discourse of the amateur'.[56] This is one reason why it was in literary studies that the main advances were made by the Left in the US academy in the 1970s. As Jameson put it, it became the role of literary criticism 'to keep alive the idea of a concrete future'.[57]

However, this should not be taken to imply that the responsibilities of criticism, in the romantic sense, can be discharged within the sites of professional literary activity alone. On the contrary, the boundaries of both discipline and institution must be constantly crossed, if they are to maintain their legitimacy. In the Anglo-American context, the intellectual is a critic in the broadest sense; often a professor, for sure, but a professor-journalist or some such, rather than someone whose activities are confined to the academy. And as Foucault saw, in common with Marxism, the politics of these activities will be mainly determined by their relations to other institutions and social groups, already engaged in the articulation of social interests. The 'problem' of the professionalism of criticism, as it is sometimes called, is in large part a product of the transformation of these relations.

The fundamental changes which have occurred in intellectual life over the last thirty years reflect the political changes which have occurred internally to both Left and Right, as well as the changing (weakening) position of the Left within the field of politics as a whole, and longer-term structural changes inherent in the development of capitalism. The rise to prominence of questions of race, gender, sexuality and religion has highlighted precisely those issues which were previously excluded from serious political consideration by the constitution of the public sphere.[58] Unsurprisingly, perhaps, liberal traditions in the humanities have made some universities a less hostile environment for the intellectual representation of these so-called 'minority' interests than the mainstream institutions of the public sphere, where the political stakes are higher. But they no more originated there than any other social interest, and their sustenance depends upon their continuing interaction with alternative cultural institutions (especially newspapers and journals) and other forms of social support. Meanwhile, the profile of the intellectual within the university has shifted. He or she (usually he) used to be a critic; nowadays, he (and increasingly also she) is more likely to be a theorist. Received ideas will have to be rethought.

Increasingly, it is neither 'philosophy' nor 'criticism' which performs the totalizing, socially integrative critical intellectual function central to the definition of the humanities, but a generalized, interdisciplinary and internationalized 'theory'. In Western universities, 'theory' is the discourse which first philosophy, then criticism, and briefly Marxism once were, but have failed to continue to be. And like the intellectual, theory is quintessentially 'French'; especially when it is outside France, even though it is probably German. In their passage through France in the 1960s, the Nietzschean and Heideggerian traditions of German philosophy acquired startlingly new disciplinary and political forms and meanings. These were further transformed on arrival in North America in the 1970s, in the context of the rightward lurch of US politics. 'Theory', one might say, is the product of a derealization inherent in the international circulation of ideas, which achieved theoretical self-consciousness in the 'anti-discipline' of semiotics in the 1960s, and institutional reality in the US academy of the 1970s and 1980s.[59]

There are several things to note about this process. The first is that the pantheon of intellectual heroes whose writings make up the theoretical canon (Althusser, Barthes, Deleuze, Derrida, Foucault, Kristeva . . .) held, or hold, only marginal positions within the French university system. As such, Bourdieu has argued, their work may be seen to share 'a sort of anti-institutional mood homologous in its form to that of a considerable fraction of students: they are inclined to react impatiently to the discrepancy between their already considerable fame in the outside world, that is, outside the university and also outside France, and the subaltern status which is accorded them inside the French university world.'[60] This sustains an image of marginality and exclusion, even though their writings are far better known than those of their academic superiors. Second, this work represents a distinctive response to the threat posed to philosophy by the development of the social sciences. At once an affirmation of philosophy's dethroning and a recuperation of aspects of its tradition, 'theory' is in many ways an ambiguous, displaced continuation of philosophy by other means – generally, without the burden imposed by a responsibility to the classical, emphatic conception of truth. Finally, despite its often anti-Marxist character, this work developed within the field of Marxism, as the hegemonic intellectual discourse of the day. It was from their antagonistic relation to the Marxism of the French Communist Party, in the context of its Left-libertarian critique, that the theories in question derived their political meaning in France. (This was true even of Althusser, who was a loyal member of the Party.) The *anti*-institutional impetus provided by these three factors was transformed into the *alternative* institutional project of the Left within the US academy, in the context of a quite different set of goals and concerns, and in far greater isolation from mainstream politics and institutions alike.

At its best, 'theory' plays the role of the absent discourse of totality, opening up individual disciplines to broader intellectual and political scrutiny and accountability, fashioning not just new objects of study, but 'new publics, new instances of judgment, new collective viewpoints'.[61] The emergence of queer theory, an innovative discourse on gender and sexuality, out of the reception of Foucault in gay and lesbian circles in North America, is a case in point. So too is the ongoing transformation of the discipline of comparative literature, under the combined pressure of postcolonial theory and cultural studies.[62] At its worst, though, 'theory' can be little more than a jargon of aspiration, obfuscating and effacing, rather than crossing or reworking, disciplinary boundaries and conceptual histories. It is then as a reminder of its terms and difficulties that its philosophical and political pre-histories become most important. If philosophy can no longer play the role of a self-sufficient discourse of legitimation, if philosophy is no longer a tribunal, it nonetheless survives as a set of conceptual resources and a form of critical intent which, as we see in this volume, remain central to all the major forms of contemporary theory: from Marxism, through psychoanalysis and Frankfurt critical theory, to feminism, queer theory, colonial discourse analysis, pragmatism, deconstruction and cultural studies. What the philosophical significance of these various discourses is, and how it shapes their political meanings, are two of the main things which the interviews in this book are about.

All of the thinkers interviewed in this book identify themselves with the broad tradition of socialist politics; all have been influenced by Marxism, to a greater or lesser extent; all have made distinctive contributions to theoretical debates; above all, each has played an important part in the dissemination of new ideas across disciplinary boundaries into the increasingly fluid network of Left intellectual culture. Yet there is clearly no single tendency, theoretical or political, of which they might be considered a part. Indeed, they are often in strongest disagreement with one another when they are disputing the meaning of a common source: as in the case of the differences between Žižek's and Butler's understanding of Lacan's account of sexual difference, or Spivak's and Cornell's readings of the philosophical status of deconstruction. Their work derives from a multiplicity of national and disciplinary contexts and it registers a variety of generational experiences. Nonetheless, it makes claims upon a common field insofar as it attempts to give theoretical articulation to the most general features of social experience, signification and practice in an historically informed way. If there is a single thematic thread that runs throughout, it is a tension between the historicist, deconstructive and pragmatist tendencies characteristic of the theory of the last two decades and the residual metaphysical elements of the paradigms of Marxism and psychoanalysis which continue to provide such theory with a crucial part of its conceptual content.

The interviews were conducted between early 1990 and late 1994 and they appear here in chronological sequence. Each has the same broad tripartite structure: questions about biography, formation and generational experience; theoretical issues raised by the subject's published writings; and more immediate political topics. They are intended to provide contextual elaborations, more accessible formulations, and critical extensions of the theoretical and political views of their authors – as a way into, rather than a substitute for, their other writings. Together, they make up a snapshot of part of the current international scene of radical theory, allowing the reader to uncover affinities and disjunctions, continuities and juxtapositions, between the participants, enlivening our sense of the complexity of their work and, hopefully, providing fresh stimulus to return to the denser bodies of other texts.

London, October 1995

Notes

1 Michel Foucault, 'Power and Sex', trans. David J. Parent, in Lawrence D. Kitzman (ed.), *Michel Foucault: Politics, Philosophy, Culture: Interviews and Other Writings, 1977–1984*, Routledge, New York and London, 1988, p. 121.

2 Raymond Williams, *Politics and Letters: Interviews with 'New Left Review'*, Verso, London, 1979. Jacques Derrida, *Points ... Interviews, 1974–1994*, trans. Peggy Kamuf et al., Stanford University Press, Stanford, 1995.

3 Vincent Descombes, *The Barometer of Modern Reason: On the Philosophies of Current Events*, trans. Stephen Adam Schwartz, Oxford University Press, New York and Oxford, 1993, p. 7.

4 See Jerry Ravetz, 'Last of the Great Believers', in the 'Symposium on Karl Popper, 1902–1994', *Radical Philosophy* 70 (March/April 1995), pp. 4–6.

5 Bruce Robbins, 'Introduction: The Phantom Public Sphere', in Bruce Robbins (ed.), *The Phantom Public Sphere*, University of Minnesota Press, Minneapolis, 1993, p. xix. This book is particularly useful in confronting the debate over the public sphere provoked by the belated translation of Habermas's early text, *The Structural Transformation of the Public Sphere: An Inquiry into a Category of Bourgeois Society* (1962), MIT Press, Cambridge MA, 1989, with a more recent literature on culture and the media.

6 See Raymond Williams, *Keywords: A Vocabulary of Culture and Society*, Fontana, London, 1976, p. 141.

7 See Marx/Engels, *The German Ideology* (1845), in Karl Marx and Friedrich Engels, *Collected Works*, vol. 5, Lawrence and Wishart, London, 1976. It is important to distinguish what Marx explicitly says about 'philosophy', 'ideology' and 'ideologists', in *The German Ideology* and elsewhere, from the conceptions which are most consistent with his theoretical practice as a whole.

8 See, for example, György Konrad and Ivan Szelényi, *The Intellectuals on the Road to Class Power*, trans. A. Arato and Richard E. Allen, Harvester, Brighton, 1979.

9 See John Carey, *The Intellectuals and the Masses: Pride and Prejudice among the Literary Intellegensia*, Faber and Faber, London, 1982; and Paul Johnson, *Intellectuals*, Weidenfeld and Nicolson, London, 1988. For a sociological equivalent to the perspective of Konrad and Szelényi, applied this time to the West, see Alvin Gouldner, *The Future of Intellectuals and the Rise of the New Class*, Seabury Press, New York, 1979.

10 See Immanuel Kant, *The Conflict of the Faculties* (1798), trans. Mary J. Gregor, University of Nebraska Press, Lincoln NE and London, 1992.

11 F. Schelling, *Lectures on the Methods of Academic Studies* (1802), quoted by J. Derrida in 'Mochlos; or, The Conflict of the Faculties' (1980), in Richard Rand (ed.), *Logomachia: The Conflict of the Faculties*, University of Nebraska Press, Lincoln NE, 1992, p. 26. Schelling is explicitly taking issue with the contradictions of Kant's position; contradictions which are intensified by Derrida's deconstructive reading.

12 See Hans Sluga, *Heidegger's Crisis: Philosophy and Politics in Nazi Germany*, Harvard University Press, Cambridge MA, 1993, chs 6 and 7.

13 See Anson Rabinbach, 'The German as Pariah: Karl Jaspers' *The Question of German Guilt*', *Radical Philosophy* 75 (Jan./Feb. 1996, pp. 15–25).

14 Jürgen Habermas, 'Life-forms, Morality and the Task of Philosophy', in Peter Dews (ed.), *Habermas: Autonomy and Solidarity: Interviews with Jürgen Habermas*, Verso, London, 1986, pp. 204–5. This interview was conducted in 1984.

15 Ibid.

16 See Jürgen Habermas, *Towards a Rational Society: Student Protest, Science and Politics* (1969), trans. Jeremy J. Schapiro, Polity Press, Cambridge, 1987; *Observations on 'The Spiritual Situation of the Age': Contemporary German Perspectives* (19xx), MIT Press, Cambridge MA, 1984; *The New Conservatism: Cultural Criticism and the Historians' Debate*, trans. Shierry Weber Nicholson, Polity Press, Cambridge, 1989; 'What Does Socialism Mean Today? The Rectifying Revolution and the Need for New Thinking on the Left', *New Left Review* 183 (Sept./Oct. 1990); and *The Past as Future* (1991), trans. Max Pensky, Polity Press, Cambridge, 1994. This last is a book of interviews, the German edition of which carries the subtitle 'The Old Germany in New Europe?'

17 Sluga, *Heidegger's Crisis*, p. 175.

18 Julien Benda, *The Treason of the Intellectuals* (1927), trans. Richard Aldington, rpt. Norton, New York, 1969; Noam Chomsky, 'Intellectuals and the State', in his *Towards a New Cold War: Essays on the Current Crisis and How We Got There*, Pantheon, New York, 1982. Cf. Ernest Hello's description of the critic, from 1914, applauded by Apollinaire: 'The domain of criticism

is broader than people generally think. The critic is not a gardener who culti-
vates only one kind of flower: all nature is his domain. Wherever there is a
great man in danger, there the critic must be. ... Standing next to the man
of genius who is waiting for his day, the critic must begin to play the role of
humanity and serve as a prelude to the choruses that his descendants will sing
at the tomb of the man of genius.' Quoted by Apollinaire in 'The Task of
the Critic', in *Apollinaire on Art: Essays and Reviews, 1902–1918*, trans.
Susan Suleiman, ed. by Leroy C. Breunig, Da Capo Press, New York, n.d.
(rpt. of 1972 edition, Viking Press, New York), pp. 419–20. Benda's intellectual, one might say, must be genius and critic *at once*.

19 See Francis Mulhern, 'Introduction' to Regis Debray, *Writers, Teachers,
Celebrities: The Intellectuals of Modern France*, trans. David Macey, Verso,
London, 1981, pp. vi–xxvi.

20 Habermas, *The Structural Transformation of the Public Sphere*, pp. 51–6.
When he finally writes about intellectuals in the classical sense, in the context
of a discussion of their absence from Germany prior to 1945, it is 'politically
committed writers', rather than philosophers, whom Habermas takes to be
exemplary; although he continues to depict the public sphere as a space where
'attitudes are to be changed through arguments', *rather than* via rhetoric or
aesthetic form. Jürgen Habermas, 'Henrich Heine and the Role of the
Intellectual in Germany' (1986), in *The New Conservatism*, pp. 92–3. This
uncertainty about the status of writing reflects a more general tension within
Habermas's work between a methodological and a more fully pragmatist
conception of truth as validity.

21 Karl Mannheim, *Ideology and Utopia: An Introduction to the Sociology of
Knowledge*, Routledge and Kegan Paul, London, 1936. Only parts II–IV of
this volume represent the original text. The quotation about watchmen is from
p. 143.

22 Ibid., pp. 136, 140, 143–4.

23 Fritz Ringer, *The Decline of the German Mandarins: The German Academic
Community, 1890–1933*, Harvard University Press, Cambridge MA, 1969.

24 Theodor W. Adorno, 'The Sociology of Knowledge and its Consciousness', in
Prisms, trans. Samuel and Shierry Weber, Neville Spearman, London, 1963, p. 53.

25 See Antonio Gramsci, *Selections from the Prison Notebooks*, trans. Quintin
Hoare and Geoffrey Nowell Smith, Lawrence and Wishart, London, 1971,
pp. 5–23.

26 See Vaclav Havel, 'The Power of the Powerless' (1978), in his *Open Letters:
Selected Prose, 1965–1990*, Faber and Faber, London, 1991.

27 Immanuel Kant, 'An Answer to the Question: "What is Enlightenment?"'
(1784), in his *Perpetual Peace and Other Essays on Politics, History and
Morals*, trans. Ted Humphreys, Hackett, Indianapolis, 1983.

28 See Oskar Negt and Alexander Kluge, *Public Sphere and Experience: Toward
an Analysis of the Bourgeois and Proletarian Public Sphere* (1972), trans. Peter

Labanyi et al., University of Minnesota Press, Minneapolis and London, 1993; Nancy Fraser, 'Rethinking the Public Sphere: A Contribution to the Critique of Actually Existing Democracy', in Craig Calhoun (ed.), *Habermas and the Public Sphere*, MIT Press, Cambridge MA, 1991 – a collection containing several important contributions to the debate.

29 Edward W. Said, *Representations of the Intellectual: The 1993 Reith Lectures*, Vintage, London, 1994. See also Said's remarks about intellectuals in his interview in this volume (pp. 78–81) and Cornel West's criticisms of his view (pp. 139–40).

30 *Representations of the Intellectual*, pp. 72, 9, 13, 69, 74, 71, 62, 61. See also Edward Said, 'Swift as Intellectual', for some reflections upon the dialectic of proximity and marginality to power characteristic of Swift's career as an intellectual at the beginning of the eighteenth century, in Edward W. Said, *The World, the Text, and the Critic*, Vintage, London, 1991, ch. 3. Said's self-consciously anachronistic application of the category of the intellectual to Swift reveals the idealism inherent in Habermas's historical deployment of a categorical distinction between 'literary' and 'political' public spheres. For the literary public sphere was already political in the early eighteenth century, albeit in a different way from that in which it would be later.

31 Habermas, *The New Conservatism*, p. 73; emphasis added.

32 *Representations of the Intellectual*, p. 39.

33 'Noam Chomsky: An Interview', *Radical Philosophy* 53 (Autumn 1989), pp. 35–6.

34 See Gayatri Chakravorty Spivak, 'Marginality in the Teaching Machine', in her *Outside in the Teaching Machine*, Routledge, New York and London, 1993, ch. 3.

35 *Representations of the Intellectual*, pp. 61–2.

36 Just as Mannheim reworks Hegel, and Said reworks Benda, so Foucault takes Gramsci's conception of the 'organic' intellectual and inscribes it into his own 'post-Marxist', 'disciplinary' discourse on power.

37 Michel Foucault, 'The Order of Discourse' (1971), trans. Ian McLeod, in Robert Young (ed.), *Untying the Text: A Post-Structuralist Reader*, Routledge and Kegan Paul, London, 1981, p. 55. Cf. 'Truth and Power' (1977), in Michel Foucault, *Power/Knowledge: Selected Interviews and Other Writings, 1972–1977*, ed. Colin Gordon, Harvester Wheatsheaf, Hemel Hempstead, 1980, p. 133: '"Truth" is to be understood as a system of ordered procedures for the production, regulation, distribution, circulation and operation of statements. "Truth" is linked in a circular relation with systems of power which it induces and which extend it.'

38 'Intellectuals and Power: A Conversation Between Michel Foucault and Gilles Deleuze' (1972), in Michel Foucault, *Language, Counter-Memory, Practice: Selected Essays and Interviews*, ed. Donald F. Bouchard, Cornell University Press, Ithaca, 1977, pp. 207–8.

39 'Intellectuals and Power', p. 216; Michel Foucault, 'Body/Power' (1975), in *Power/Knowledge*, p. 62; 'Intellectuals and Power', pp. 209–11.

40 'Truth and Power', p. 130.

41 Cf. Karlis Racevskis, *Michel Foucault and the Subversion of the Intellect*, Cornell University Press, Ithaca, 1983, p. 126.

42 'Intellectuals and Power', p. 217; 'Truth and Power', p. 132; emphases added.

43 For which, see David Macey, *The Lives of Michel Foucault*, Jonathan Cape, London, 1993, chs. 12 and 15. During the 1970s, Foucault often found himself on committees of intellectuals alongside Sartre; including his involvement with the Information Group for Prisons (GIP), where the stated object was 'to create conditions that permit the prisoners themselves to speak' ('Intellectuals and Power', p. 206). In the second half of the 1970s, in line with the Atlantic drift of French libertarianism more generally, he became increasingly involved in the politics of Eastern European dissidents. For an (unsuccessful) attempt to take dissidence as the model for a new kind of intellectual, parallel in certain ways to Foucault's specific intellectual, see Julia Kristeva, 'The Dissident: A New Type of Intellectual' (1977), trans. Sean Hand, in Toril Moi (ed.), *The Kristeva Reader*, Blackwell, Oxford, 1986, ch. 12.

44 'Truth and Power', p. 132, emphasis added.

45 For Said's views about Foucault, see Edward W. Said, 'Foucault and the Imagination of Power', in David Cousins Hoy (ed.), *Foucault: A Critical Reader*, Blackwell, Oxford, 1987; and 'Michel Foucault, 1926–1984', in Jonathan Arac (ed.), *After Foucault: Humanistic Knowledge, Postmodern Challenges*, Rutgers University Press, New Brunswick, 1988.

46 See Russell Jacoby, *The Last Intellectuals: American Culture in the Age of Academe*, Basic Books, New York, 1987; Allan Bloom, *The Closing of the American Mind: How Higher Education Has Failed Democracy and Impoverished the Minds of Today's Students*, Simon and Schuster, New York, 1987.

47 Debray, *Writers, Teachers, Celebrities*, pt 2. This is also, of course, the predominant view of the Frankurt School.

48 *Representations of the Intellectual*, pp. 50, 55.

49 Mulhern, 'Introduction', in Debray, *Writers, Teachers, Celebrities*, p. xviii. The reference is to Britain, but the point can be generalized.

50 Foucault, 'Truth and Power', p. 127.

51 Mulhern, 'Introduction', p. xviii.

52 See note 5.

53 This latter process is most developed in the USA; and probably least so in Germany. For the residual strength of the classical tradition, see Jürgen Habermas, 'The Idea of the University: Learning Processes', in his *The New Conservatism*, ch. 4.

54 Bruce Robbins, *Secular Vocations: Intellectuals, Professionalism, Culture*, Verso, London and New York, 1993, p. 21. Robbins draws upon John Ehrenreich's *The Altruistic Imagination* (Cornell University Press, Ithaca, 1985), a history of the professionalization of social work, which he takes to parallel that of university teachers.

55 Ibid., pp. 79, 77, 74.

56 Ibid., p. 73.

57 Fredric Jameson, *Marxism and Form: Twentieth Century Dialectical Theories of Literature*, Princeton University Press, Princeton, 1971, p. 416.

58 For the location of such exclusions within Kant's founding definition of the public use of reason, see Jane Flax, 'Is Enlightenment Emancipatory? A Feminist Reading of "What is Enlightenment?"', in Francis Barker et al., *Postmodernism and the Re-reading of Modernity*, Manchester University Press, Manchester, 1992, pp. 232–49.

59 See Pierre Bourdieu, *Homo Academicus* (1984), trans. Peter Collier, Polity Press, Cambridge, 1988, p. xv; John Mowitt, *Text: The Genealogy of an Antidisciplinary Object*, Duke University Press, Durham NC, 1992. See also Edward Said, 'Traveling Theory', in *The World, the Text, and the Critic*, ch. 10.

60 *Homo Academicus*, p. xix.

61 Robbins, *Secular Vocations*, p. 117.

62 See the interviews with Judith Butler, Edward Said and Gayatri Spivak below. For the current state of comparative literature, see Charles Bernheimer (ed.), *Comparative Literature in the Age of Multiculturalism*, Johns Hopkins University Press, Baltimore and London, 1995 – a series of responses to Bernheimer's 1993 Report to the American Comparative Literature Association, 'Comparative Literature at the Turn of the Century'.

I am grateful to Peter Dews and Francis Mulhern for their comments on the draft version of this introduction.

1
Institution and Autonomy
Cornelius Castoriadis

Cornelius Castoriadis is a leading figure in the thought and politics of the postwar period in France. Throughout the 1950s and early 1960s he was a member of the now almost legendary political organization *Socialisme ou Barbarie*, along with other currently well-known figures, such as Claude Lefort and Jean-François Lyotard. Unlike some of his contemporaries, however, he has remained firm in the basic political convictions of his activist years.

Castoriadis is notable for his effort to rescue the emancipatory impulse of Marx's thought – encapsulated in his key notion of 'autonomy' – from what he takes to be the rigid and dogmatic structures of Marxism itself. From very early in his career he unfashionably combined a forceful critique of Communist bureaucracy with an unwavering commitment to the radical Left. Castoriadis has also played an important role in a range of debates in the philosophy of science, social theory, political philosophy and the interpretation of Freud. The major statement of his social thought is *The Imaginary Institution of Society*, which appeared in France in 1975 (English translation, Polity Press, 1987). His collected *Political and Social Writings* are available in two volumes from the University of Minnesota Press (1988). A selection of more recent pieces, *Philosophy, Politics, Autonomy,* was published by Oxford University Press, New York, in 1991.

Since the late 1970s Cornelius Castoriadis has been practising as a psychoanalyst in Paris. He is close, theoretically, to the 'Quatrième Groupe', a group of senior Lacanian analysts who broke with Lacan in 1969, over his downgrading of clinical concerns and his bizarre innovations in training procedure. Castoriadis is also a Professor at the Ecole des Hautes Etudes en Sciences Sociales, where he teaches a seminar. The *Revue Européenne des Sciences Sociales* has published a multilingual *Festschrift for Castoriadis* (vol. XXVII, 1989, no. 86), which provides a valuable range of critical perspectives on his work.

RP What were the fundamental experiences which brought you to philosophy and politics, and to the exploration of the relation between the two?

Castoriadis To begin with, there was always an intellectual curiosity for which I am indebted to my family. I came into contact with philosophy very early on, at a ridiculously early age in fact, at 13. I came to philosophy through classical manuals; to politics through Communist publications in Greece, around 1935, and then immediately afterwards, through the works of Marx. The two things have been always there – in parallel. What attracted me to Marxism, as I saw it at the time, was a very strong feeling about the absurdity and injustice of the existing state of affairs.

RP What was the political situation in Greece at that time?

Castoriadis 1935 was the eve of the Metaxas dictatorship which lasted throughout the war and the occupation. At that time, in the last year of my secondary education, I joined the Communist Youth, which was underground, of course. The cell I was in was dissolved because all my comrades were arrested. I was lucky enough not to be arrested. I started political activity again at the beginning of the occupation. First, with some comrades, in what now looks like an absurd attempt to change something in the policies of the Communist Party. Then I discovered that this was just a sheer illusion. I adhered to the Trotskyists, with whom I worked during the occupation. After I went to France in 1945/46, I went to the Trotskyist party there and founded a tendency against the official Trotskyist line of Russia as a workers' state. We split in 1948/49 and started *Socialisme ou Barbarie*, which went on until 1965 (the journal) and 1967 (the group).

RP Is it true to say that you never really accepted Trotsky's interpretation of the Soviet Union? Or did you accept it for a short time?

Castoriadis For a very short time, yes. As soon as I moved out of Stalinism, the very first thing to grasp was the idea that the revolution had degenerated and that there was a bureaucracy which was just a parasitic stratum. But I soon started to reject this. You must realize that under the Metaxas dictatorship all left-wing books were burnt. And then there was the occupation. So one was not really in touch with the literature. Still, in 1942/43 in Greece, I had the good luck to find copies of Trotsky's *The Revolution Betrayed*, Victor Serge, Ciliga's book and Boris Souvarine's *Stalin* – a wonderful book which has been re-issued now in France. And it was already clear in *The Revolution Betrayed* that Trotsky was contradictory.

RP In what way contradictory?

Castoriadis Well, he says, for instance, that Russia is on socialist state groundings because all property belongs to the state. But he goes on to say that the state belongs to the bureaucracy. So therefore property belongs to the bureaucracy. If one is logical, one asks, 'What has all of this to do with the workers' state?' The means of production belong to the bureaucracy. As I discovered afterwards, this idea had been around for some time already. One can see it among the inmates of the Russian concentration camps in 1926/27: the idea that the bureaucracy was becoming a new ruling stratum and exploiting class. What reinforced me in this conviction was the first Stalinist attempt at a coup d'état in Greece in December 1944. There really was something there, with the masses struggling under the leadership of the Communist Party; and for me it was crystal clear. If the Stalinists had gained power at that time, they would have installed a regime similar to that of Russia. I said so and wrote so at the time. It was the only time I was in disagreement with an elder militant, Spiros Stinas, who I had worked with all this time, and who, in a certain sense, was my political teacher.

How could one account for this on the basis of the Trotskyist theory of the Russian regime, that is, a proletarian revolution which has degenerated? Bureaucracy was appearing as a quasi-autonomous historical force attempting to establish a regime for its own interest and outlook. The whole development of my political conceptions about bureaucracy – and in contra-distinction to this, what is socialism? – started at this time. If socialism is not nationalized property, not just a bureaucratic method of central planning, then what is it? Immediately, the idea of autonomy arose. Socialism as self-government in production and political life; that is, collective organization and self-determination at all levels.

RP How did your move away from Trotskyism affect your understanding of the Russian revolution? As I understand it, *Socialisme ou Barbarie* was quite closely identified with the ideas of the Left Opposition in the Soviet Union? Did you identify politically with the Left Opposition?

Castoriadis In a certain sense, yes. But they didn't go far enough. Later on, I wrote a text about Alexandra Kollontai's paper on the Left Opposition of 1921, and its limitations. But this is not our problem now. The defects are obvious there: about the role of the party, the role of the trade unions and so on. Of course, Kronstadt was the last mark of some independent activity of the masses, which was crushed by the Bolshevik party. But once I started the critique of bureaucracy, it evolved quite rapidly into a critique of lots of things: of the Leninist conception of the party, and then of Marxian economics. I had started working as an economist at this time, and was working on *Das Kapital*. I couldn't make much sense of it in relation to actual developments. I couldn't make much sense of it theoretically, either. Here starts all my criticism of the theory of value, which finds its final form in the text about Marx and Aristotle which appears in *Crossroads in the Labyrinth*. Next came the critique of the Marxian conception of what socialism is all about, the bad utopian aspect of all this: the elimination of the idea of politics, the sort of paradisiac state depicted in the early manuscripts, where in the morning you are a fisherman, in the afternoon a poet, etc. – I don't know what you are after dark! There is also the idea, absolutely central to Marx, that labour is slavery and freedom is outside the field of labour. Freedom is leisure. This is written in so many words. Labour is the field of necessity.

RP That's more characteristic of the older Marx, isn't it?

Castoriadis It is in *Das Kapital*. The kingdom of freedom can be built only through the reduction of the working day. During the working day, you are under necessity. This is diametrically opposed to any idea of self-management by producers, and of production itself – once it is radically changed, and once technology is also changed – as a field of exercise of human capabilities and human freedom.

RP There is also the idea of labour becoming 'life's prime want'.

Castoriadis That's in the early manuscripts. But this is abandoned in the system. Next came the critique of what one can call Marxist economism. The imaginary signification of the centrality of production and economy throughout history. This is obviously a retrojection of capitalist imaginary significations throughout the whole of human history. Then there was the philosophical work, which is thère in 'Marxist Thought and Revolution', the first part of *The Imaginary Institution of Society*, which was published in the last five issues of *Socialisme ou Barbarie* in 1964/65.

Socialisme ou Barbarie

RP Could you say something about the experience of *Socialisme ou Barbarie*? What was the political context in which you operated? And how, given your critique of the Leninist conception of the party, was the group organized, internally? How were its interventions made? What do you think are its enduring achievements?

Castoriadis Well, the famous organizational problem was there all the time. After an initial period during which there were strong residual elements, including in myself, in favour of the Leninist conception of the party (which I gave up about 1950), there was still an internal divide concerning the problem of organization, between people who were saying that no organization is needed (the proletariat will do everything, we are just a group trying to work out some ideas) and others, like myself, who insisted, as I still would insist, that a political organization is necessary. Not a vanguard party, certainly, but some sort of political organization. Political activity is collective activity, and it ends up with concrete acts, be it a publication or whatever. You have to take decisions. And so you have to have some rules about how you take decisions. Say, majority rules. Obviously, you allow the minority to express themselves, even publicly. But there are some points at which decisions have to be taken, and they have to be univocal. Some coordination of the general activities is necessary. But I said very early on that the only way to do this is on the basis of the idea of some sort of collective self-government. Also, the political organization could play the role, not of a model, but of a sort of exemplary activity, showing people that they can organize collectively; that they can rule their own affairs.

RP It sounds quite Luxemburgian.

Castoriadis If you wish. In a certain sense, yes. From this point of view, certainly. This led to splits with Lefort. He was against any formal organization – 'We are an intellectual group, we publish a magazine, that's all.' You must remember the circumstances at the time. The Cold War started about 1947 and in Europe, especially in France, the Stalinists were almost all-powerful, even if they did leave the government in 1947. All the Left was with them. Remember the stories of Sartre and others, the fellow travellers? We were absolutely isolated. There was a period when, after the outbreak of the Korean war, we were less than a dozen in the group. And the audience was extremely limited, residual ultra-leftist groups. We cleared the ultra-left ground. Whatever was really of worth there came to *Socialisme ou Barbarie* – not the Trotskyists, of course. But the situation was extremely hard. Later, after 1953, with Stalin dead, the Berlin revolt, the Czechoslovakian strikes in 1954, then Hungary and Poland in 1956, the atmosphere started changing, and the review gained some audience – never very important. At the time we were selling about 1,000 copies of the magazine, which were read around. Then came the Algerian war, and the stand we took against the Algerian war. There was a kind of renaissance amongst the student youth at that time. People started coming and the group grew. Some time in 1958/59, in the whole of France, including the provinces, we were about 100. By 1962, 1963, 1964 we could hold public meetings in Paris with, say, 300 or 400 people. But all of this, as you see, was extremely limited. Of course, after 1968 lots of people said they were in *Socialisme ou Barbarie*. To which I have answered that if all these people who say that they were in *Socialisme ou Barbarie* had really been in *Socialisme ou Barbarie*, we probably would have grasped power in France some time around 1958.

RP So you disbanded as an organization just before that moment, in the later 1960s, when the left began to open up and expand as a result of changes in the political and economic situation more generally?

Castoriadis Yes. We had some people in the Renault factories who were producing a paper specifically for Renault workers. This was not a subsidiary of *Socialisme ou Barbarie*. It was produced by workers and so on. But all this was extremely limited. There was much more under-ground influence, unknown, anonymous; and it sprung out in 1968 in lots of people, including, for example, Dany Cohn-Bendit.

RP Why did *Socialisme ou Barbarie* come to an end?

Castoriadis This was a decision which I pushed very strongly. First of all, there had been a split, a second split, between 1960 and 1963. In 1960 I wrote a text called 'Modern Capitalism and Revolution', which was the most thorough critique of the classical Marxist position at this time: of the idea that the proletariat has a privileged role to play, of the idea that economic problems are the main problems, and so on and so forth. It argued that the problem of the transformation of society is a much more general problem. There is the question of youth, the question of women, of the changing character of labour, of urbanism, and of tech-nology – changing technology. All this created a strong reaction from part of the group, for which the theoretical representative was Lyotard, who at the time was playing the adamant Marxist. This led to a split in 1963 which weakened the group. We were the majority. We kept the magazine, they kept the monthly journal, *Workers' Power*. It was the first paper of this name. Later, the Italians published *Potere Operaio*. This was part of the underground influence. In Italy, lots of these people had been reading *Socialisme ou Barbarie*. But the group was weakened.

Public influence was expanding, as I have said. We were selling more and more. People were coming to the meetings, but they would not actively participate. They were passive consumers of the ideas. And this was reflected on the review, because to produce a magazine the main problem is the collaborators – the people who write. It's very funny. We never had money, but publishing *Socialisme ou Barbarie* was never a financial problem. We always managed. The problem was the contents. Not enough people were coming into the group. Also, my own personal collaboration was beginning to take a different form. I was digging deeper and deeper into the theoretical underpinning, both of Marxist theory and of what we needed for a new conception. This was the first part of *The Imaginary Institution of Society*.

RP You were still working as an economist at this time?

Castoriadis Yes. I was working at the OECD. The review was taking the bizarre aspect of a theoretical-philosophical magazine which was also pretending to be a revolutionary organ. It was the first in France, and all over Europe, for instance, to produce an extensive account of the Berkeley events. The review anticipated the movements of the 1960s. It is there, about the students, the women and so on. It is written down. But this was not enough. And so at some time in 1966, we said, 'For the time being, the thing has become meaningless. We had better stop and begin again later.' And two years later, of course, came 1968. I don't know what would have happened if we had still been a group in 1968. But 1968 very quickly fell under the spell of Maoists and Trotskyists and so on – not at the beginning, I mean the great period, but very quickly. One can't rewrite history.

RP Did you have any relations with the *Arguments* group, the people who left the Communist Party in 1956?

Castoriadis Yes. But the relations were bizarre. Edgar Morin published a paper in which he both recognized the role of *Socialisme ou Barbarie* and criticized it very strongly, saying that we were obsessed with bureaucracy and making a sort of panacea or shibboleth out of self-management. There were answers in *Arguments* on our part. But there was not very much contact, except on some personal levels. Later on, when *Arguments* had stopped, Morin participated in some of our public meetings. He wrote a paper in *Socialisme ou Barbarie*. But there was never a close collaboration. From the beginning, *Arguments* took itself as being a review by intellectuals for intellectuals. We never abandoned the idea that we aim at the general public, and not at intellectuals.

Philosophy and Imagination

RP Perhaps we could switch the topic back to the issue of your intellectual formation. What were the main intellectual sources of your move away from Marxism? What did you draw upon to fuel your development away from an orthodox communist politics? You have defined your relationship to Marxism negatively, in terms of the things that you gradually gave up until finally more or less the whole thing had been given up and you embarked upon an independent intellectual project. Who inspired you in this second stage?

Castoriadis It is quite difficult for me to answer your question in a modest way. I would say that the main source was the immanent critique. It does not work, this system which had fascinated me as a 13-year-old boy: the idea that you have a coherent picture of human history and the world – that that's how it works – and it's going to reach a happy final stage.

RP You mentioned Aristotle . . .

Castoriadis Yes, but that was 1975. In the whole of my writings for *Socialisme ou Barbarie*, which have been published in paperback now in France, there is, I think, in all one mention of Plato, and one mention of Thucydides. That's all. Before the first part of *The Imaginary Institution of Society* (1964/65), there is no mention of any philosopher whatsoever. It's not that I didn't want to mention one. It was because this was an immanent critique. The main thing that fuelled it was contemporary experience: the experience of working-class movements. The theme was the critique of capitalism, the critique of the development of capitalist economies – the nonsensical character of the aims proposed by the capitalist economy, which were more or less shared by Marxism: let's increase material wealth and so on. Then, after a point, the questions became for me: 'What is history?' and 'What is society?' The work about the institution began here, in 1959. There are already seeds in a 1953 article criticizing Marxist economics and speaking about creativity in history; and even before, in 1950/51, speaking about creativity and autonomy. The idea was there, but it was not elaborated.

RP It wasn't drawn from Merleau-Ponty?

Castoriadis No. Merleau-Ponty had nothing to do with it. There is no idea of creation or creativity in Merleau-Ponty, as far as I can see. I had been interested in philosophy since my adolescence, but I kept the two things separate. This is perhaps a bizarre personal trait. I didn't want to mix political thinking and political activity with philosophy. Not for practical or pedagogical reasons – you don't go to the workers telling them to read the *Third Critique* – but this is a position which I still have. I don't think you can draw directly from philosophy, as such, political conclusions.

RP Yet in your more recent writings you see philosophical reflection as quite central to the project of autonomy – not the whole of that project, but very central to it . . .

Castoriadis That's true. But my ontology is an ontology of creation: creation and destruction. Creation can be democracy and the Parthenon and Macbeth, but it is also Auschwitz, the Gulag and all that. These are fantastic creations. Politics has to do with political judgements and value choices.

RP For which you can't find an ontological ground?

Castoriadis No. I don't think there is an ontological basis for value judgements. Once you enter the field of philosophy, you have already made a value judgement, Socrates' value judgement: the unexamined life is not worth living (and the unlived life is not worth examining, as you say in Essex – this is true as well). But this is already a stand you have taken. In this sense, the decision to enter the reflexive domain is already a sort of grounding decision, which can't rationally ground itself. If you try to rationally ground it, you use what is the result of the decision. You are in a vicious circle.

RP So how do you draw people into the reflexive life? Through examples?

Castoriadis Yes, through examples and through consequences. But you can't force somebody rationally to be rational. There is no demonstration of the kind: if you don't philosophize, you are absurd. Because the other says, 'I don't care about being absurd', or 'I have to be absurd, otherwise I am not a true Christian.' *Credo quia absurdum*. You can't 'refute' Tertullian.

So, for a long time, I tried to keep politics and philosophy separate. They joined in the first part of my article of 1964/65, 'Marxism and

Revolutionary Theory'. Once I had reached the idea of institution, of the imaginary creation of history, I started re-reading philosophy with a different eye. And what I encountered there as forerunners in this field – but only at the level of the subjective individual imagination, of course – was Kant and Fichte. Later, I took up Aristotle, much later. That is the first place you find an examination of the problem of *phantasia*: the genius discovering the thing, and the limitations and impossibilities the discovery of *phantasia* creates for the Aristotelian ontology. Then another development starts. I had never stopped busying myself with philosophy. I came to France to do a Ph.D. thesis in philosophy. (The theme of the thesis was that any attempt at a rationally constructed philosophical system leads to blind alleys, to aporias and to antinomies. Mostly, what I had in mind was Hegel, but not only.) This remains an unfinished manuscript. So I was reading things and scribbling and jotting all the time, but not systematically. It was only after *Socialisme ou Barbarie* that I took this up again systematically. Even then my main sources of inspiration have never been, properly speaking, in the history of philosophy. They have been much more problems arising out of, say, psychoanalysis; out of the analysis of the social-historical; out of the state of contemporary sciences – the crisis of foundations in mathematics, the aporias of contemporary physics, or problems in biology – the emergence of living things: what is a living thing? What is the biological closure of an organism?

As far as the problem of imagination is concerned, the main difference is that for both Aristotle and Kant, as for all philosophers, imagination is looked at uniquely from the point of view of the subject: the transcendental imagination in Kant, the imagination of the Transcendental Ego in Fichte, etc. There is nothing corresponding to the social-historical. The same is true of Heidegger. There is no substantial relation of *Dasein* to history; to society even less. If I have made a contribution, it is this: what I call the radical imaginary, the instituting imaginary, as a social-historical element.

I accuse all philosophers of ignoring the ontological status of, for instance, language. Language is institution. It is a fantastic paradigm of institution. The philosophers think – they think, therefore they talk, they use language, but they don't care to say what language is and how it came about. And when they do say, they say, like Heidegger: the gift of Being. Everything is a gift of Being – including death, of course. If one envisages the institution of language, one has to envisage a creative possibility which actualizes itself in the anonymous collective, which is the instituting imaginary, which posits language, which posits rules, and thereby enables the singular human being – which is unfit for life qua singular human being, a biological monstrosity – it enables it to survive. I am very much attracted by some philosophers. There is no problem about it. I'm very much attracted by the Great Four – Plato, Aristotle, Kant and Hegel. I always find food for thought there.

RP You've referred to your classical predecessors, but someone looking at French intellectual history in the twentieth century can see a very strong thematics of the imagination. For example, there is one of Sartre's first books, *L'Imaginaire*. When you arrived in Paris, you attended a course given by Bachelard, for whom the notion of the imagination is absolutely central. Then there is Lacan, of course, as well. You do seem to fit into a twentieth-century French tradition of reflection on the problem of the imagination. Are there really no influences here?

Castoriadis I think I come from a completely different direction. Sartre's imaginary or imagination is purely negative. It is the possibility of envisaging that something could not be. It's a negativizing faculty of the ego. For me, it's just the opposite. It's the capacity to posit something which is not there.

RP Isn't the philosophical structure of that process actually the same, with one side rather than the other being emphasized?

Castoriadis But there is no given without imagination. In this respect, my view of imagination is much nearer to Kant. It's constitutive, absolutely constitutive. The difference from Kant is that my imagination is creative in a genuine sense. The Kantian imagination, the transcendental imagination, always has to imagine the same thing. If the Kantian imagination started really imagining, the world would collapse. It has to posit the same forms, otherwise it's just what he calls empirical imagination. We remain in the realm of the subject. Lacan's imagination is a very bizarre thing. Vulgarly speaking, it is the illusion. Nothing more than that; the reflection in the mirror; the image in the mirror, and the image the other sends to me of myself. Lacan's imaginary is the optical illusion.

RP Is it not also connected to the lack? Isn't it a more dynamic process – the filling of a lack? You make it sound very empirical, this notion of reflection . . .

Castoriadis The attempt at filling a lack is desire. Lacan doesn't link it to the imaginary as such, which, for him, has to do with what he calls 'demand'. It's another realm. You have the lack, you have desire, you have the Law – which imposes the lack in a certain sense. But the imaginary is not a result of the desire – or of 'demand'. It is exactly the other way round. Cows do not desire, for they have no imagination – not in the human sense. Bachelard is another thing. I followed Bachelard when I arrived in Paris, for half a year, because he was the only one worth following. Then he stopped. That year, he was engaged in discussing some aspects of science from the point of view of his own epistemological conceptions. It was interesting, but it didn't go very far. I read Bachelard much later, but if you know his work you'll see the differences. It's imagination in a very loose sense. It's not constitutive in character. And certainly, it's not a social element.

RP But there is that sense of creativity there?

Castoriadis There is, in a certain sense, a sense of creativity in Bachelard. That's true. But I was never really attracted to his work.

RP What about surrealism?

Castoriadis I knew a bit about it because there were some Greek surrealists, and I was very fascinated by them. Then, when I came to France, I learnt much more. I was extremely fascinated by Breton and everything he had to say. At that time, the interest of Breton for me was the poetic dimension. Twenty-five years later, I said 'creation is poesis', and I gave another meaning to poesis. It's very difficult to make one's own intellectual biography in a thorough and honest way. You are exposed to influences all the time that you don't even know about; or you don't know the way they are going to work through you, perhaps much later. But among the people who for me were the most important in France at that time was Breton. And then Benjamin Peret, who came later to *Socialisme ou Barbarie*, and published a text in the journal; and a younger surrealist called Jean-Jacques Lebel who was in the group and very much in touch with us.

RP We were thinking on a more theoretical plane, about your interpretation of the Freudian unconscious. One can read Freud in a very deterministic way, but the notion of the creativity of the unconscious is obviously there, if you read between the lines. It seems that it was the surrealists who picked up on that.

Castoriadis They picked it up, yes; but they never theorized it. They used it. They interpreted it this way. It is the fantastic part of Freud, the Freud who is always talking about imagination but never names the thing. But what else are the phantasies? The positivistic streak in him is very strong. After all, this is Vienna at the end of the nineteenth century, and there are problems of scientific respectability. He was already creating havoc by saying that children are polymorphous-perverse people. If in addition he had said, 'Whatever I tell you, it's just the imagination of the subject . . . ', he would have been even more laughed out of court than he was at the beginning. Around 1911 he signed a manifesto calling for the establishment of a Society for the Diffusion of Positivistic Thinking, with Petzold, Hilbert, Einstein and some other people. He was a very contradictory character.

Autonomy

RP You have said that your notion of the imagination is not related back to the subject, at least not only to the subject – individuals are formed within the context of a particular institution of society; and you have written about the heteronomous institution of society as that which has obtained historically; and about autonomy as a political value. Yet if the process of institution is not in some sense the outcome of collective activity, but is the matrix within which all activity takes place, how could there be an autonomous institution of society? It seems as though institution always already precedes the empirical activity of human beings.

Castoriadis This is the problem of the politics of autonomy, of the establishment of an autonomous society. I think that you can have, you can imagine, you can devise – and you do have, up to a certain point, you did have, in the Western world – institutions which are not just institutions of closure. If we have institutions which not only allow but further the creation of individuals who are capable of discussing, or putting into question, if we create a public space where discussion is genuinely made possible, where information is available, etc., this is already something completely different, completely other, from the state of classically heteronomous societies, where you have to think what the institution of society tells you to think.

RP But doesn't the philosophical structure of the concept of institution mean that, at an ontological level, it is tied up with heteronomy in a way that suggests that when one is speaking of autonomy and heteronomy politically one is actually talking about something else?

Castoriadis We are working under the weight of inherited thought here. Behind what you say, there is a conception of autonomy which I would call metaphysical freedom, in the derogatory sense.

RP Some Kantian notion?

Castoriadis Kantian, or perhaps even, to be obscene, Sartrean. That is, one would be autonomous if one were absolutely outside any external influence and fully spontaneous. Now, this is just nonsense. This is a philosophical phantasy. Philosophy has put up this phantasy, and it judges reality against this phantasy. It doesn't exist. Autonomy, as I understand it in the field of the individual, is not a watertight frontier against everything else, a well out of which spring, absolutely spontaneously, absolutely original contents. Autonomy is an ongoing process, whereby you always have contents which are given, borrowed – you are in the world, you are in society, you have inherited a language, you live in a certain history. You have been *geworfen*, as Heidegger says. You have not chosen to be born in 1952, or whenever, neither have you chosen to be born in England. This just is the case. You will never know the great philosopher of the year 2100, who might have changed your way of thinking. It is in this world that we have to have a workable and effective concept of autonomy. Autonomy does not mean I am totally separated from everything external. And, in relation to my own contents, which are 99 per cent borrowed, have come from outside,

I have a reflective, critical, deliberative activity, and I *can* to a significant degree say yes and no. I can also allow my own radical imagination, my flux of representations and ideas – we are talking about thinking now – to well up, and there to choose again; because my radical imagination may produce nonsense, or absurdities, or things which do not work. It is this ongoing process which I call an autonomous subjectivity.

RP So the radical imagination is a kind of pure source?

Castoriadis It is the permanent welling of representations, desires and affects which, in heteronomous societies, are practically 100 per cent repressed and appear only in Freudian slips, dreams, maladies, psychoses and transgressions. It is always with us, and can be freed; not that we would accept all its products. But it could be free to supply contents, new contents, upon which our reflective and deliberative activity can work. So if we consider the relation to the collectivity, the idea that I'm not free because the others are there, or because the law is out there, only really makes sense against this traditional phantasy. Others, and the existence of the law, are not just constraints. They are also sources of freedom. They are sources of possibilities of action. They are sources of facilitation. They are riches.

RP So what you understand by the project of autonomy is the maximization of the possibilities of reflection, self-reflection and deliberation? Is this an Idea in the Kantian sense?

Castoriadis No, it's not an Idea in the Kantian sense.

RP So it's realizable, then, your concept of autonomy? It's philosophically constituted in such a way that it is a possible object of historical realization. It must be materially possible?

Castoriadis Yes. It must be materially possible. It's not a utopia. And it's not a Kantian Idea. It's not at an infinite distance. It's not the polar star.

RP And yet it's not already implicit within history, in the way that some people understand Marx to have thought.

Castoriadis No. It's an historical creation, an historical creation which is up to now unfinished.

RP But if it's not implicit in history, if it is to be created in an open history, how do we know it's actually going to be realizable?

Castoriadis We don't. We work for it, but we don't know in advance.

Market and Plan, System and Lifeworld

RP Perhaps we could turn more directly to politics. It has become prevalent on the Left to say, 'If the plan doesn't work, then we've got to go back to the market. In a complex modern society we have to have impersonal forms of mediation, impersonal forms of collective regulation' – in Habermas's terms, the distinction between system and lifeworld. Habermas argues that, although systems should ultimately be under the democratic control of the lifeworld, we can't abolish the systems as such. The market and some forms of administrative–bureaucratic regulation of society must remain. This is the basis of his critique of Marx: that Marx has some notion of collapsing all social relations back into the immediacy of the lifeworld. It seems that a lot of your inspiration comes, albeit indirectly, from the early Marx. Where does your concept of autonomy place you in this debate?

Castoriadis Marx was certainly wrong in thinking that all impersonal mediations have to be abolished. This appears in his critique of the commodity, and also of money. I repudiated this as early as 1957 in a text called 'The Content of Socialism' which is in my *Political and Social Writings*. For me, it's quite obvious: you can't have a complex society without, for instance, impersonal means of exchange. Money has this function, and is very important from this point of view. It's another thing to deprive money of one of its functions in capitalist and pre-capitalist economies as an instrument for the personal accumulation of wealth and the acquisition of means of production. As a unit of value and as a means of exchange, money is a great invention, a great creation of humanity. We are living in societies; there is an anonymous collectivity; we express our needs and preferences by being willing to spend that much on that item, and not on anything else. This doesn't, to my mind, create any problem. The real problem starts when you say 'market'. Again, in this text from 1957, I said that the socialist society is the first society where there's going to be a genuine market, because a capitalist market is not a market. A capitalist market is not a market, not only if you compare it with the manuals of political economy, where the market is transparent and where capital is a jelly which moves from one field of production to another instantaneously because profits are bigger there – all that is nonsense – but because prices have nothing to do with costs. In an autonomous society you will have a genuine market in the sense both of the abolition of all monopolistic and oligopolistic positions, and of a correspondence of the prices of goods to actual social costs.

RP Will you have a market in labour power?

Castoriadis This is a problem. My position is that you can't have a market in labour power in the sense that you can't have an autonomous society if you persist in the differentiation of salaries, wages and incomes. If you do have this differentiation, then you keep all the motivations of capitalism, of *homo economicus*, and all the old hodge-podge starts again.

RP Won't this undermine the market?

Castoriadis I don't see why. There are no economic and rational grounds on which I can say, 'One hour of this man's work is worth three times that of some other man.' This is the whole problem of the critique of value theory, and the critique of what underlies value theory, which is the idea that you can impute the result of production to this and that other factor, in a definite way. But in truth, you cannot do this imputation. The product is always a social product and an historical product. You have to take into account that whatever imputation of costs you do, it's a relative imputation, geared to social needs and geared to the future – which has, of course, to have some relation to historical costs and reality. But you cannot have differential labour costs based on any rational or even reasonable justification. That's a very hard point to swallow.

RP So you don't think that there is any rationality to the capitalistic distribution of social labour through the wage relation, in terms of productivity? It's purely political?

Castoriadis It's purely political. The present distribution of income, both between groups and between individuals, is the sheer outcome of a struggle of forces. Nothing more. This creates problems in relation to work discipline. If the work collective is not capable of establishing enough solidarity and discipline, in order to have everybody working according to some accepted collective rules, we reach the political hard core of the problem. Then there is nothing to do; no more than there is in the field of political democracy, if people are not willing to be responsible for the decisions of the collectivity, to participate actively and so on. This doesn't mean that you have to maintain bureaucratic and hierarchical structures in production – on the contrary. The division of tasks is not the same as the division of power.

I spent a lot of my time trying to analyse the functioning of capitalist factories. I found that the capitalist planning of production in the factory is half of the time absurd. The factory works because the workers transgress the capitalist organization of production. They work against the rules, or at a distance from the rules, so production can go on. If they were to apply the rules, production would stop immediately. The proof is that 'working to rule' is one of the most efficient ways of breaking everything down. So much for the capitalist organization of hierarchy. As soon as you have hierarchy, you have this fundamental opacity in the production sphere, because you have the division between executives and directors: people who manage and people who execute. By virtue of their position, the workers have to hide what is going on from the eyes of the directors. This reaches delirious proportions in a fully bureaucratic society, but is the case practically everywhere. The collective has to take the basic decisions. It can delegate, but it elects and it can revoke.

RP This will entail very high levels of political culture and activism.

Castoriadis Yes, high levels of responsibility between people. That's certain. You cannot have a truly democratic collectivity, not only self-management and production, but on the sheer political level, unless people are really active. But we shouldn't fetishize this: one can think of institutions which facilitate this participation. Today, to be responsible, to attempt to participate, you would have to be heroic twenty-four hours a day. We have to create a situation whereby you can participate without being heroic twenty-four hours a day.

RP This would mean a reduction of working time.

Castoriadis Certainly. But there are other considerations. What is working time spent on? During the war in America production doubled between 1939 and 1942. And the workers were actually working for only about four hours in the factory. They were playing the numbers, or they were playing cards, or they were 'working for the government', as the Americans say – 'Leave me alone, I'm working for the government.' That meant he was doing something which he would take home. What is the English expression? – moonlighting. In France they call it 'la perruque'. And in Russia, you know the tremendous extent of it. I would argue that present output under different conditions of participation of the workers could take place in four hours or six hours instead of eight.

RP Would it be true to say that you are in favour of what is sometimes called indicative planning, via some general democratic framework at a social level?

Castoriadis More than indicative. I don't think there is contradiction between market and planning in this respect. In an autonomous society one must have a true market, not just with consumer freedom, but with consumer sovereignty: which specific items are produced for consumption must be decided by consumers in the day-to-day vote of their purchases *where everybody has equal vote*. Today, the vote of Mr Trump is worth one million votes of the average American. That's not what I mean by a true market. But you have to have general decisions about at least two things: the partition of national product, or national income, between consumption in general and investment in general; and the share of the mass of consumption between private consumption and public consumption – how much society decides to devote to education, to roads, to erect monuments, to all public endeavours; and how much it decides that individuals are free to spend as they want. You need a collective decision about this. You have to have proposals and discussions, and bring forward the implications of decisions before the eyes of the people.

In this sense, you have to have a planning, because the implications of the decision about investment and consumption have to be foreseen. If you decide that you will have so much investment, these are more or less the consumption levels you can count upon in the coming years. If you want more investment, then you will have to consume less. But maybe you will be able to consume more in five years time. If you want more education, you can't have it for nothing. You will have to devote resources to education, and you have to decide where you take these resources from. Do you take them from private consumption? Or do you take them from investment, that is, from the future growth of productive facilities? Do you care about any future growth of productive facilities, or do you just want to renew the existing capital? All this has to be brought forward, and it cannot be reasonably decided by market forces.

RP This sounds like the kind of debate currently taking place in the Soviet Union.

Castoriadis In a sense, yes. But I don't accept this idea of Habermas's that because you have to have the system you have to accept a degree of alienation or heteronomy. I don't say that you can be master of everything. You can't control everything. That's not the problem. The point is that you can always look back, always change things, and establish mechanisms whereby the function of society is made controllable by people, though certainly not fully transparent.

Events in Eastern Europe

RP You draw a contrast between *fragmented* bureaucratic capitalism and *totalitarian* bureaucratic capitalism which makes it look as though the Eastern European societies were a more closed, more extreme form of the same sort of society which we have in the West. Yet they have revealed a fragility which was quite unexpected. Do you think that your interpretation of bureaucracy and capitalism needs to be revised in the light of recent events? And, given that what perhaps the majority of Eastern Europeans seem to want at the moment is simply to exchange the plan for the market, in what sense was 1989's 'Springtime of Nations' a manifestation of autonomy?

Castoriadis Eastern Europe is different from Russia. It had an imposed and an imported regime, which never had the same roots and the same strength as it had in Russia. I don't think the events in Eastern Europe, or even in Russia, have changed the characterization of the regime as it was. The regime was a form of bureaucratic totalitarian capitalism. But it was subject to deep internal antinomies, which I have analysed for a long time. From the time of the Hungarian revolution, and even before, people were resisting passively, but they were resisting fantastically, even in Russia. In Russian factories they were resisting fantastically. But this totalitarian regime, this bureaucratic totalitarian capitalism, is not a timeless essence. It has a history. Already after Stalin's death, it was obvious that it couldn't go on as it had before. You had Khrushchev, and the period under Brezhnev, which I characterized as stratocracy, in the sense that the regime had become totally cynical. Nobody believed in any ideas in this regime. The only objective was sheer force. Brute force for the sake of brute force. The maximum possible social resources were put into the military sector. What we know now about what was going on proves that, if anything, my analysis fell short of the reality. The degree of the suppression of the civilian economy for the sake of the military was even bigger than I had originally reckoned at the time, in 1981.

The Polish and Afghan events played a very big role in the change, in the sense that the Russian leading groups realized that they were confronted with an impasse. They didn't intervene militarily in Poland, they intervened in an indirect way through Jaruzelski. And in Afghanistan they failed. What nobody had foreseen, me as little as anybody else, was the emergence of Gorbachev and the reforming group. This was totally unforeseeable. A big part of the thing is Gorbachev's role as a civilizing autocrat. But it's not just that. He also happened to be a very clever and able politician. And he certainly could not have risen to power without the support of the army and the KGB. That's quite clear. They realized that there was an over-extension of Russia's attempts to be a world power. This unleashed a series of events which culminated in Eastern Europe. There, people hated the regime and were ready to act, as soon as they were sure that the Russian tanks would not enter.

I gave an interview to *Esprit* in 1982 called 'The Hardest and Most Fragile of All Regimes' in which I argued that, as long as the thing holds it appears to be like steel, but in fact it is extremely fragile – like glass – and could be pulverized from one day to the other. This is what happened. This amazed people, because all these organizations, these steely Stalinist people – 'We are the vanguard of humanity' – became sand from one day to the next. But the same thing is not happening in Russia. Which proves that there the thing has much more important roots. Up to now the process is much slower. You have ethnic strife, and you had this fantastic miners' strike in the summer of 1989, with demands which were not just economic but also political, but demonstrations by the people are only beginning. But Gorbachev is overrun by events, both in the ethnic field and the general field – that's why he retreats constantly in external relations. I wrote in 1977 that of all the industrialized countries Russia is the first candidate for a social revolution. Up to now, the social revolution hasn't appeared, but . . .

RP Are you hopeful?

Castoriadis No. If the social revolution happens . . . that's another point. We will probably have to pay the legacy of Marxism-Leninism for years from now. It's true that in Eastern Europe at the moment, people can't think of anything else except a liberal capitalist society. Almost everything else has disappeared from the horizon. As an Hungarian friend of mind was telling me some months ago: in Hungary you can't even pronounce a word which starts with 'S' – enough of it. Any word. This is the negative side of it. They are under the understandable delusion that the West is a utopia, a cornucopia. In actual fact, they are not even going to have that. They are going to have a very miserable situation. Even in the political field it's not clear that anything resembling a parliamentary regime in the West will be easy to establish; except perhaps in Czechoslovakia or Hungary. We are confronted with history in the process of creation.

RP Are there no grounds for hope, then?

Castoriadis I don't much like to talk about 'grounds of hope'. I think that you have to do what you have to do – and hope for the best. If you take the rich, ripe capitalist countries, we certainly should not renew the discourse about insurmountable internal contradictions. Yet there are at least two facts which make it extremely difficult to believe in an indefinite reproduction of the present state of affairs. The first is the ecological limit, which we are nearer and nearer to. The second concerns the present state of capitalist society, but is somewhat analogous to the ecological question. Everybody is lauding the extraordinary efficiency of capitalism in the field of economic production. This is true. But up till now this has been achieved through the irreversible destruction of a capital of natural resources which had been accumulating for three billion years (or at least 700 million years). This has been thrown away, destroyed, over fifty years or a hundred years. There were sediments of forests, of land, of oxygen, of ozone, of a variety of living species, etc. But the same is true on the anthropological level. Capitalism can function – could function – because there was a capitalist entrepreneur who was fascinated and impassioned by producing things, and setting up new machines. Very often he was, if not an inventor, at least a quite clever design engineer – Edison and Ford, for example. This type is disappearing. More and more, you make money by playing in the casino, not by setting up production facilities. Capitalism also presupposes anthropological types – the bureaucrat, the judge, the educator – which are pre-capitalist products. If the prevailing philosophy and system of values is that you try to earn as much money as you can, and to hell with the rest – one doesn't see why you should have judges, or university professors, or even schoolteachers. You will have them, but they will do their job in the worst possible way: trying to get away with as much as they can; being corrupt, if corruption is materially feasible, and so on. In this respect, capitalism is living by exhausting sediments of previous norms and values, which become meaningless in the present system. Absolutely meaningless. But this is not a 'ground' for hope. An ecological catastrophe, for instance, could very well lead to a series of quasi-fascist dictatorships – 'The holiday is over. This is your ration for the coming month: ten litres of oxygen, two gallons of petrol, etc. That's all.'

Interviewed by Peter Dews and Peter Osborne
Essex University, February 1990

2
Lacan in Slovenia

Slavoj Žižek and Renata Salecl

One notable result of the political ferment in Central and Eastern Europe since 1989 has been the emergence of new theoretical currents, often combining strands of thought which – to West European eyes – appear as starkly incompatible. Nowadays, one can meet young Soviet philosophers whose interest in the Frankfurt School, and in deconstruction, is matched by their keen advocacy of neo-liberal economics, and East European sociologists whose Foucauldian critique of Marxism and the one-party state is tempered by deep scepticism about the politics of privatization.

One of the most intriguing of these new syntheses is the 'Lacanian-Hegelian-Marxism' which has been developed by, among others, Slavoj Žižek, Senior Researcher at the Institute for Social Sciences, University of Ljubljana in Slovenia – the westernmost republic of the old federal state of Yugoslavia and the first to declare its independence, in 1991. Philosophically, Žižek's work is distinguished by its novel psychoanalytical interpretation of Hegel, which stresses the dimension of contingency in this thought and – against a more fashionable postmodernism – highlights the subjective resistance to closure it finds in the structure of his dialectic. (See, for example, *The Sublime Object of Ideology*, Verso, 1989, and *Tarrying with the Negative: Kant, Hegel, and the Critique of Ideology*, Duke University Press, 1993.) More generally, it is notable for its application of Lacanian psychoanalytical theory to the study of popular culture – film, in particular: from *For They Know Not What They Do: Enjoyment as a Political Factor* (Verso, 1991) and *Looking Awry: An Introduction to Jacques Lacan through Popular Culture* (MIT Press, 1991) to *Metastases of Enjoyment: Six Studies on Women and Causality* (Verso, 1994) via *Enjoy Your Symptom: Jacques Lacan in Hollywood and Out* (Routledge, 1992). His most recent work is

The Indivisible Remainder: An Essay on Schelling and Related Matters (Verso, 1996). These studies have been accompanied by essays published so far only in journals, reflecting upon the respective fates of liberalism and nationalism in Eastern Europe.

It is this aspect of the Slovenian school's thought which has been taken up by Renata Salecl, a colleague of Žižek's, and explored in the context of feminism in her book *The Spoils of Freedom: Psychoanalysis and Feminism After the Fall of Socialism*, published by Routledge in 1994. A Researcher at the Institute for Criminology, University of Ljubljana, she is also a Visiting Scholar at the New School for Social Research, New York. Her more recent works include *Politik des Phantasmas* (Turia and Kane, 1995).

RP Perhaps you could begin by saying something about the history of Lacanian theory in Ljubljana, Slovenia. How did it come to develop? And what role has it played?

Žižek It was contingent, an absolute exception. In each of the big republics of Yugoslavia – Slovenia, Croatia, Serbia – there is an entirely different theoretical tradition which predominates. In Serbia, it is a kind of analytical philosophy, but not a good one – not one that I have found interesting – but rather the most boring kind of philosophy of science, now linked to some kind of new liberalism – Hayek, that kind of thing. In Croatia, it is the old Praxis School which predominates. In Slovenia since the beginning of the 1970s the big conflict, the big philosophical struggle, was between some kind of Western Marxism, which was more or less official philosophy, and Heideggerianism and phenomenology as the main forms of philosophical dissidence. This was the struggle. And then we, the younger generation, precisely as a third option – to be a dissident but not a Heideggerian – we were a reaction to both of these.

In Slovenia, this opposition – Critical Theory versus Heideggerianism – had a totally different investment from that in Croatia. In Croatia, Western Marxism was the great dissidence of the 1960s. So the Heideggerians, who were their opponents there too, were the official philosophers. In Croatia, people would lose their jobs during the 1970s for dissidence, but their dismissal would be articulated in Heideggerian terms. There were extreme obscenities, such as a Party official saying that, for example, some Praxis philosopher does not understand some Heideggerian twist – that the essence of self-management is the self-management of essence – that kind of thing. There were extremely perverse things: a pragmatic political power structure of self-management legitimized in purely Heideggerian terms. There was even a general who became chief of staff who had been under the influence of Heideggerians as a student who wrote an article (you know that the

Yugoslav notion is the self-defence of the people) saying that the essence of self-defence was the self-defence of the essence of our society. Meanwhile, in Slovenia, you had people being dismissed because they hadn't grasped Adorno's *Negative Dialectics*. The two positions which usually in Eastern Europe are associated with opposition to existing power structures (Heideggerianism and Western Marxism) were the two official positions in different parts of Yugoslavia.

RP So there was no Soviet-style dialectical materialism in Yugoslavia?

Žižek No, it doesn't exist in Yugoslavia. You can mark the point, 1960, at some great philosophical event, when there was a last stand. But the idea of dialectical materialism was defeated. There are some pockets of resistance, but even the power structure itself does not rely on them. They are marginalized, although not in opposition. During the last ten to fifteen years, there has been a de-ideologization of power, and Marxists have usually been more dissident than non-Marxists. What was never reported in the West was that the people who benefited from this were the analytical philosophers in Belgrade, who were definitely not Marxists. You had a communist regime openly supporting analytical philosophy of science. Their message to the power structure was clear: 'We are doing instrumental scientific research. We are no danger to you. You leave us alone and we will leave you alone.'

Salecl But the Lacanian movement in Slovenia was always on the side of the opposition. In the early 1980s when new social movements began to develop in Slovenia, it was really only Lacanians who gave theoretical support to these groups.

Žižek What you need to understand, to understand the philosophical background to the different dissidences, is that the split which is now becoming visible in, for example, Poland, between the populist right-wing nationalism of Walesa and the market liberalism of Michnik – this split was present from the very beginning in Slovenia. The opposition movement in Slovenia has two quite distinct origins. On the one hand you have a nationalist intelligentsia, nationalist poets writing about national roots, etc. Their philosophical reference is Heidegger. On the other hand, you have the remnants of an old New Left connected to new social movements – peace, human rights movements, etc., – and, extremely important, a punk movement. The band Laibach, for example. It is precisely through punk that the pluralist opposition reached the masses. It was a kind of political mass education, and we supported it.

RP But how did Lacanianism come to have this resonance within Slovenian political culture in the first place? After all, to a lot of people, Lacan's theory doesn't look like an emancipatory theory at all. It is a theory of perpetual lack, of inescapable alienation in the signifier, and so forth.

Žižek Here, you have already produced an answer. For this was precisely the point with respect to self-management. In Yugoslavia, it was an extreme form of alienation, a totally non-transparent system that nobody, including those in the power structure, could comprehend. There were almost two million laws in operation. No one could master it. This was the paradox: this is what you get when you want total disalienation or pure transparency. This was how we experienced Laibach, for example.[1] Their fundamental cry, for us, was 'We want more alienation.' The paradox in Yugoslavia was that we had a Communist Party bureaucracy which ruled in the name of an ideology the basic premise of which was that the greatest danger to socialism was the rule of an alienated Party bureaucracy. It saw itself as the main enemy. This worked very nicely. They even succeeded in integrating the Praxis philosophers, up to a certain point. The trick was that if you wanted to criticize the system . . .

Salecl . . . it was already all the time criticizing itself.

RP It sounds like Marcuse's old notion of repressive tolerance.

Žižek Yes, but a special version of it.

Salecl It produced a special kind of Newspeak. They changed 'business' to 'organization of associated labour'. 'Workers' became 'direct producers'. Directors were called 'individual business organs'. The idea was that with this demystification of language self-management could be portrayed as a form of direct democracy.

Žižek On this point, we agree with Habermas: the price of modernity is that you must accept a certain division, alienation, etc. But I disagree with the way in which Habermas understands this in relation to the postmodernism debate. For me, it is modernism which insists on the utopian idea of disalienation, while postmodernism is precisely the recognition that you accept a certain division as the price of freedom. In this specific sense, Habermas is a postmodernist without knowing it.

RP A certain strand of postmodern thought – one thinks of Foucault in the 1970s for example – wants to reach the ultimate equation: emancipation = non-emancipation, emancipation = repression, without qualification. But you, via Lacan, seem to want to do something rather more complex. In your book *The Sublime Object of Ideology*, you describe Lacan as a thinker of the Enlightenment. It seems that for you the project of emancipation doesn't always equal repression, but somehow we do have to reassess the project. By repudiating a certain conception of what the project of emancipation should lead to we somehow preserve the project. Is that a fair description of your position?

Žižek Absolutely. This is why I insist so much on the split between Foucault and Derrida, on the one hand (despite all their differences), and Lacan. If we understand modernism in terms of the urge to demask an illusion, etc., then deconstruction is itself a most extreme form of modernism. At this general level, despite all their differences, Habermas and Lacan move in the same direction in accepting certain limits and renouncing certain utopian conditions on the possibility of freedom. The way these divisions have been made should be reformulated.

RP The question of the limits of enlightenment is already there in Kant's essay 'What is Enlightenment?' in the distinction between the public and private use of reason. To the extent to which you agree with Habermas, aren't you just reinstituting a more classically Kantian notion? Isn't your 'postmodernism' just a pragmatic enlightenment?

Žižek In a sense, yes. Let's look at the process that Lacan calls 'la passe': how as an analysand you become an analyst. The basic idea is that you choose two of your colleagues, not analysts, and you tell them about the experience of your analysis, and they must be able to retell it to someone else. At this point, at which you are able to make your experience totally transmissible to a third by the intermediary of the second, this is the sign of success. Here, in the heart of Lacan, you can see the idea of making it public. This is enlightenment. You must be able to externalize your innermost experience.

Hegel, Freud, Lacan

RP Perhaps we could turn to your interest in Hegel. You combine an interest in Hegel with one in Lacan in a rather unusual way. Is there not a basic irreconcilability between Hegel and Lacan that your reading covers over? After all, there would seem to be some kind of *telos* of reconciliation in Hegel. You seem to read Hegel very much through the *Phenomenology*.

Žižek No, it is through the *Logic*. I think that Hegel wrote a book called *Logic of the Signifier*, and that by historical accident the second part of the title fell out. More seriously, take the category of reconciliation. People talk of a *telos* of reconciliation in Hegel as if this meant some kind of radical transparency. Look at the place in the *Phenomenology* where Hegel introduces the term: towards the end of the chapter on spirit, just before the chapter on religion. Reconciliation comes about from the breakdown of the condition of the beautiful soul. It means that the beautiful soul must recognize the irrationality of the world as a kind of positive position. It must accept it. There is no freedom, no acting in the world, without renouncing your narcissistic self, without accepting some basic 'irreconcilability'. When you want to actualize your non-alienated project and you are confronted with some limit, disalienation does not consist in annihilating the limit, but in seeing how this limit is the positive condition of your very activity.

It is the same at all crucial points of Hegelian theory. For example, in the logic of judgement where after the judgement of necessity you get the notional judgement (*Begriffsurteil*). You would expect a triad, but there is a fourth type of judgement. This one reintroduces contingency.

It is interesting that even poststructuralist critics, such as Gasché in *The Tain of the Mirror*, when they criticize Hegel come up with positions which are already within Hegel. Take the idea of reflection. It is not the simple idea that I reflect myself, I am a property of the object, etc. Reflection is always redoubled with Hegel. There is a certain point in the object where the subject cannot recognize itself – a blind spot. But it is precisely this blind spot where the subject is inscribed. What the Derrideans, with such effort, try to produce as the blind spot of Hegelian dialectic: this is the fundamental mechanism of Hegel. The monarch in the *Philosophy of Right*, for example. If you want the state to be a rational totality, it must have a certain totally irrational excess or surplus, a totally idiotic presence – the King. Without it, totality cannot exist.

It is these dimensions of Hegel's thought which were opened up for me by Lacanian notions of lack in the Other, of how the final moment in analysis is your acknowledgement of your lack as the correlate of the lack of the Other, etc.

RP But is this Lacan really Freudian? There is a whole philosophical background in Lacan – the interest in intersubjectivity, the theory of the subject – which is missing in Freud. The concept of the subject doesn't really occur in Freud's work, does it? Is Lacan explicating what is implicit in Freud or is he establishing a new theory?

Žižek Lacan only interprets Freud *if* you conceive the idea of interpretation the way Lacan does. In the early seminars, he is close to some phenomenological approaches when he says that interpretation is not just the rediscovery of something that already exists. You are confronted in interpretation with a lot of inconsistent traces – Lacan's notion of the unconscious is a kind of creationist one – and you construct what retroactively will have been. Freud was an inconsistent author. Lacan showed one way to retroactively construct a consistency. There was a certain fundamental theoretical traumatism, an impossibility, ultimate contradiction, which generated Freud's inconsistencies. The point is not to flatten Freud out.

RP So it's in Freud's texts, it's not in Freud?

Žižek If you like. You can put it that way, yes. It is what's in the text which could not be written there.

RP Perhaps we could return to the reception of Lacan in Slovenia. You spoke earlier of Slovenian Lacanians giving theoretical support to new social movements. Is there any particular articulation of Lacanianism with gender issues involved here? As you probably know, in England, the reception of Lacan has been very closely tied up with feminism.

There is a certain type of feminist theory which is very Lacanian. It articulates its sexual politics through Lacan. Is there any equivalent to this in Slovenia?

Žižek There are two issues here: the reception of Lacan in England, and the question of feminism in Slovenia. On the first one, I must make some comradely criticisms. The Lacan received in England in film theory and women's studies was already a reduced version of Lacan, mediated in part by Foucault and Kristeva. Let us take two central notions: 'suture' and the gaze. The way the idea of suture operates here is incredible. It is precisely the reverse of Lacan. It is used to mean the bad thing, the representation, the closure. Lacan's point is much more dialectically refined. For him suture is not just the moment of closure but also that which sustains openness. Take the phallic signifier, for example. For Lacan this is not just the signifier which closes the field of unlimited polymorphous perversity, it is the signifier that opens the field of plurality. The paradox of Lacan is that to have a certain field open there must be a certain closure (it is like Hegel on reconciliation). To de-suture a field you must always have another mega-suture. Take the notion of nation. The nation functions to de-suture traditional societies, but it de-sutures them by finding another central point.

The problem of the gaze is, I think, an even bigger one. The way the Lacanian problematic of the gaze works here in England is mediated through Foucault's work on the panopticon: for the male gaze, the woman is reduced to an object, etc. Whereas for Lacan it is the opposite: the gaze is the object, it is not on the side of the subject. In this way, for Lacan, it is woman who occupies the place of the gaze. If there is something totally alien to Lacan it is the idea that the male position is that of the gaze that objectifies woman.

Salecl With regard to the other side of your question, it is important to note first of all that there is no women's movement in Slovenia. As elsewhere in Eastern Europe, this lack of a feminist movement is very problematic, with the emergence of a new 'moral majority' in the opposition movement – on questions of abortion rights, for example. We do have some small groups that call themselves feminist, and their view is that psychoanalysis is very anti-feminist. But it was the Lacanian movement in Slovenia that first raised the issue of the newly emerging moral majority there. The small feminist groups which exist are dealing with the question in a very old-fashioned way, saying that all is male chauvinism, etc. They are not locating the issue properly; they are not connecting it up to the nationalist threat, for example, which we think is behind the obsession with 'morality'. The main struggle for feminists in Croatia and Slovenia, we believe, is an anti-nationalist one.

Žižek It is a fight for the very formulation of the problems. The nationalist parties in government in Slovenia and Croatia don't accept contraception and abortion as women's problems. All that exists for them are problems of the family and low birth rates. For us, on the other hand, the 'problem of the family' doesn't exist as such. The problems are those of women's rights, rights of children, etc.

Salecl When they say we must prohibit abortion, they do not say it for Christian moral reasons. They openly say that it is to preserve the nation. And you must not forget that they were very much a part of the old opposition movement, anti-totalitarian, etc. So they present their new morality as part of the fight against communism: freedom to abort as a brutal totalitarian intervention by the state into private life! We want to keep the old legislation on abortion.

Politics in Yugoslavia

RP Slavoj, you recently stood as a candidate for the five-man presidency of Slovenia as a member of the newly formed Liberal Party. Could you explain the current layout of the political parties in Slovenia, and in particular the nature of the Liberal Party to which you belong?

Žižek Along with the old Communist Party, the Liberal Party is now part of the opposition bloc. But what defines the distinctive role of the Liberal Party is our opposition to the rise of this national-organic populism in Slovenia, of which we have already spoken.

RP For people used to the ideological distinctions of West European politics, it may appear strange that the Liberal Party emerged from the youth wing of the Slovenian League of Communists; especially since, in the information bulletins of the Ljubljana Press Centre, your party is described as affiliating to the classical traditions of liberalism. Could you explain more precisely where the Liberal Party stands ideologically?

Žižek Our aim is to promote pluralism and an awareness of ecological issues, and to defend the rights of minorities. This is the kind of liberal tradition we represent. Not the purely capitalist values of the free market, not Friedrich von Hayek.

Salecl We took the name 'liberal' as a symbol of opposition to the national-organic populist tradition. In order to defend the rights of minorities, one has to reject emphatically this notion of the primacy of the nation, of the need for self-sacrifice for the sake of the nation, the idea that you can only find your place as an individual within the organic community of the nation.

Žižek To put it in terms of Ernesto Laclau's theory of hegemony, we were engaged in a struggle for the re-articulation of this floating signifier, 'liberalism'. The term was associated, throughout Slovenia, with the idea of freeing ourselves from Communist domination. It was extremely important who should succeed in occupying this ideological terrain, and in fact the right-wingers were furious. We managed to force them on to the defensive, because they were then obliged to explain why *they* were also in favour of liberties, individual human rights, and so on. I think it was the proper mode of attack, which – to use the Leninist phrase – accorded with the concrete analysis of the concrete situation. It was the right gesture to make.

RP The Liberal Party is the second biggest party in the Slovenian parliament. But what about the Party of Democratic Renewal, the former League of Communists?

Žižek Personally, they are quite nice guys. There are a lot of younger people, and former Party dissidents. So you might ask, if they are such nice guys why didn't we in the youth wing simply stay with them? The problem was – and here I think that Foucault's analysis of 'micropowers' has some bearing – that the general power of the Party remains intimately linked to the extremely corrupt local power structures. This was simply too much for us.

Salecl Our crucial failing was connected with the role of the Green Party, which is rather strong. The Green Party is part of DEMOS, the ruling Centre-Right coalition, but this catastrophic development was purely the result of personal struggles and animosities. Formerly, the Greens were linked with the youth organization of the Communist Party. About five months ago they started moving towards DEMOS – three months before the election. The leading members of the Greens are ex-communists, and in many cases ex-hard-liners.

Žižek They are all personal enemies of mine. They attacked me about ten years ago – they threw me out for not being enough of a Marxist. It was these long-standing personal enmities which were crucial in the decision of the Greens to join DEMOS. To use Ernesto Laclau's jargon again, the Green problematic – as you know – has a peculiarly floating status within the ideological field. You can inscribe it into the field of pluralism, of new social movements and so on; or you can inscribe it into the chain of equivalences: 'pollution of the environment' equals 'pollution of our minds through cultural degeneration' and so on. This ideological shift of the Greens was a real tragedy, because without them DEMOS would not have an absolute majority – in other words, they would not have been able to form a government without us, and there would be a much stronger leftist and pluralist influence in current Slovenian politics.

Salecl It should be remembered that the Greens allied themselves with the nationalists when it came to reopening the questions of abortion, women's rights and so on.

Žižek However, those who now form the Liberal Party also bear some responsibility for the current situation, because we didn't take DEMOS seriously enough – I would say that even DEMOS didn't take itself seriously enough! Until the fall of the regimes in East Germany and

Romania towards the end of 1989, the aspiration of DEMOS was to be strong enough to be taken seriously as an opposition. It was only after these events that they themselves saw that there was a real possibility of winning power. Neither ourselves, nor the Communist Party, foresaw that this might happen – and now the real political problem is simply to stay alive.

What I mean by this is that up till now there has been some kind of state support for all political parties. But DEMOS – arguing demagogically that we are a small, poor country – have radically reduced this money. And although they promised that being a member of parliament would become a professional occupation, they have not professionalized it. For example, even the general secretary of the Communist Party of Slovenia has a post in a university. What this means is that there are ten or fifteen professional ideologists of DEMOS, who have ministerial posts, and nothing in between them and the common people – all the intermediary structures are being dissolved. So maybe eight or ten people get together at somebody's house and they make all the crucial decisions.

Salecl So we have the same system as we had before!

Žižek Furthermore, about half a year ago the nationalists began to make a great noise about how Slovenians were in danger of becoming an extinct race. They tried to calculate the date when there would be no more Slovenians! Very cleverly, they reckoned around 2040 to 2050 – not so far away as to appear unrealistic, and not so near as to make people feel insecure. Other calculations claim that by around 2050, half of Yugoslavia will be populated by Albanians.

RP This seems an appropriate point to move on to the national question in Yugoslavia more generally. In your view, will the Federation be able to hold together?

Žižek I think the maximum that can be hoped for is a confederation. In Slovenia, this is not such a great problem because – to use a rather racist term – we are 'ethnically pure'. The real problem is not only Albania, but in Bosnia also. This is because, if a new confederation were established, the Serbs would want to change borders. They would want to incorporate parts of Bosnia and possibly also Croatia, where there are two to three million Serbs. However, I do not believe that there is any real danger of a restoration of Serbian domination, of the kind which characterized Yugoslavia before the revolution – it is too late for that. Slovenia and Croatia – the two richest republics – have now held democratic elections, and in order to reverse this situation half of Yugoslavia would have to occupy the other half – it's simply not conceivable.

Salecl In my view, the chance for Yugoslavia to survive will depend on the outcome of the free elections which will be held in every republic before the end of this year. Strong republican governments will have to be formed, and then, hopefully, these governments will be able to agree on a new type of confederation. The problem is, however, that in republics such as Serbia and Montenegro, the Left and Liberal opposition hasn't really had time to organize. This opposition is based in small groups centred on the universities. The real opposition consists of far right-wing nationalists – without too much exaggeration they could be described as 'chetniks'.[2]

Žižek The miracle of Milosevic, the populist leader of the Communist Party in Serbia, was that he managed to synthesize some unthinkable combination of fascism and Stalinism. He promoted typically Stalinist values, but with elements which up till now were considered to be typically fascist, such as the setting-up of a violent vigilante movement, the obsession with the nationalist enemy . . .

RP You suggest these are not characteristic of communist dictatorships, but what about Romania under Ceausescu?

Žižek Romania was a totally 'closed' society, to use the categories of the unfortunate Karl Popper, whereas Serbia under Milosevic is more reminiscent of fascist Italy, where there was a certain degree of freedom, but if you dissented from the regime you were excluded, marginalized . . .

Salecl I would say that Milosevic's success consisted in being able to play in two ideological registers at the same time – on the one hand defending a strong federal Yugoslavia, with a democratized and market-oriented society, but, on the other hand, behind this, always aiming – for example – to crush the Albanians in Kosovo province, and to promote the Serbian domination of Yugoslavia, without ever openly renouncing the legacy of Tito. People knew what he was aiming at, there were whole series of fantasies which he didn't have to spell out. But now there are parties of the nationalist Right operating openly, and Milosevic is branded as the guy who doesn't go far enough.

Žižek As Fred Jameson would say, a vanishing mediator . . .

Salecl Milosevic is now under attack from both sides – from the right-wing 'chetnik' movement which we have been describing, and from the small, emergent democratic parties. What is unifying these two blocs is that they are both anti-communist – Milosevic still has that albatross round his neck. His charisma is already broken.[3]

Žižek But what is also fascinating here is what we Marxists call the 'material force of ideology'. For example, according to the official statistics, which as we know always present an upbeat picture, purchasing power in Yugoslavia has declined by between 40 and 50 per cent over the last decade. But despite all this, the issues dominating the elections in Croatia and Slovenia, and this will also apply to the elections in Serbia, have not been economic but nationalistic.

RP This raises the question of the relation between these nationalist movements and the new liberal economics of marketization.

Žižek The way it works is that the general economic crisis is reinterpreted through a nationalistic perspective. All would be well at home on the economic front, if we didn't have to help to support the other republics, and so on.

RP But what about concrete policies for economic restructuring?

Žižek People are not yet thinking on that level. Even for the Communist Party, the main economic points of reference are Thatcher, the Chicago School. Personally, I'm a pragmatist in this area. If it works, why not try a dose of it? But one should at least recognise that neo-liberal economics is not a neutral technical instrument – to use Lacan's terms, there are certain subject positions inscribed within it. We Liberals are the only political force opposed to this – the supposed 'de-ideologizing' of the economy through the application of 'neutral', technically efficient measures. The tragedy is that even the communists perceive this kind of Thatcherite or Friedmanesque economics as something ideologically neutral, as not involving any class- or subject-positions.

Salecl Now we are facing the issue of the privatization of publicly owned property. Overnight, managers, who were formerly connected with the communist regime and the secret police, are becoming owners. So you have this problem of former communists who are becoming capitalists.

Lacanian Theory and Social Analysis

RP We would like to conclude by shifting back from politics towards theory. More specifically, we would like to raise some epistemological issues about your use of psychoanalytic categories in social and political analysis. For example, you have described the basic structure of capital accumulation as 'hysterical', because it is characterized by insatiable demand, irrecuperable excess. But what is the status of this description? Is it analogical? It often looks as though you are simply projecting psychoanalytic categories on the social level, without paying sufficient attention to the specificity of *social*, as opposed to *psychological*, processes.

Žižek I am definitely not using these categories merely analogically, because Lacan is always talking about structures of discourse. I would try to avoid the very terms of your question. For me hysteria is always already a structure of discourse, in other words, a certain structuring of the social bond. Hysteria is not some kind of private psychological state. For Lacan 'discourse' is not simply another fashionable term – you know how people refer to the 'discourse' of Foucault, Derrida, etc., when all they really mean is their books or their texts. For Lacan 'discourse' refers to the social bond – 'le lien social'. In order for someone to be a hysteric, the whole intersubjective space must be structured in a certain way – it is in this sense that one can say that capitalism is 'hysterical'.

RP But this raises a whole series of problems – because psychoanalytical terms derive their primary semantic charge from their role within a certain therapeutic relation between individuals. But what would the political correlate of the practice of analysis be? How could one 'psycho-analyse' the hysteria of capitalism in general?

Žižek My reply would be that for Lacan the relation between 'hysteria' and 'historia' is not just a play on words. Hysteria is an eminently historical notion. Let us suppose that an Althusserian notion of inter-pellation gives us the main form of subjectification – we must see that this form is always historically specified, even though Althusser didn't stress this himself. Hysteria just means that the identification which should be produced through interpellation fails. What Americans now call a 'borderline case' is not something radically new – it is just another form of the failure of identification, that is to say of hysteria. To say that the structure of capitalism is hysterical is just to say that this failure of identification is built into it, as was first perceived by Max Weber in his study of the Protestant ethic.

RP But doesn't this mean that you fall into the same kinds of difficulties that one finds in the work of some contemporary discourse theorists – discourse becomes an undifferentiated category which is supposed to exhaust the ontology of the social. From a more traditional Marxist perspective, one might object that, although we may talk about the 'material force of ideology', it is necessary to distinguish different levels of materiality within the social. There seems to be a kind of hyper-trophy of ideological analysis implied by the concept of discourse. If one can't make a distinction between different levels of the social, for example in an Althusserian way, the relation of such discourse analysis to political practice becomes seriously problematic. Political practice, surely, is not *just* a matter of ideological struggle.

Žižek My reply would be that in the most classical forms of Marxism, indeed in *Das Kapital* itself, notions such as 'class struggle' occupy precisely such an unspecified place. As you know, after three volumes, the manuscript ends with the promise of a chapter on classes. If you read *Das Kapital* retrospectively from this point you can see that it is not simply an objective theory of production. It becomes apparent that in concepts such as that of 'surplus-value' class struggle is already at work. The whole point is to retain this refined dialectic: not to reduce everything to class struggle, but at the same time not to reduce class struggle simply to one of the 'instances', to say we have objective rela-tionships, and then class struggle.

RP This is a persuasive account. But could we press you again on the affinities between your work and that of the contemporary discourse analysts, for whom politics often seems to be reduced to a matter of transforming personal identities, or of finding the right ideological 'chain of equivalences'? After all, you have written a sympathetic review of Laclau and Mouffe's *Hegemony and Socialist Strategy*.

Žižek I cannot emphasize enough my admiration for Laclau and Mouffe, but I do perceive a danger in the idea of radical democracy. It seems like a slip into commonsense wisdom: 'you must not be unilateral, you must listen to as many viewpoints as possible, etc. . . .' I think the condition of being active politically is precisely to *be* unilateral: the structure of the political act as such is 'essentialist'. Furthermore, to say that we must not give centrality to any particular site of struggle represents a kind of legerdemain, since the real upshot of Laclau and Mouffe's book is an interpretation of all struggles, social, economic, and so on, as extensions of *democratic* struggles.

RP Could we perhaps put our basic question in one final form. For Marx, there are certain institutions and processes – money for example – which are constituted sheerly through social recognition. However, there are also for Marx other processes, such as capitalist production itself, which are not simply constituted through such recognition. Do you acknowledge the existence of this distinction?

Žižek On this point, I think I would be willing to describe myself as a 'postmodernist'. I would say that as soon as you are within a spoken language, within a certain universe of meaning, you are automatically caught within a certain ideology. There is a certain basic misrecognition. This makes possible – on the social level – certain experiences which Lacan describes as 'traversing the phantasy', 'identifying with the symbol'. For example, the kind of discourse which emerged after Chernobyl, in which various leftist groups began proclaiming that 'we all live in Chernobyl'. This is a kind of phenomenon which the ruling ideology would like to dismiss as some marginal misadventure: the fact that people recognise something as a symptom, as precisely the exception where the repressed truth of the totality emerges.

But to return to your point, I would say that my type of analysis doesn't exclude, but rather requires a concrete social and economic analysis. Let's return to Marx's notion of class struggle. A direct attempt to explain everything in terms of class struggle would end up explaining nothing. But neither is it enough to say that class struggle is simply a *result* of objective conditions. We might say that – retroactively – class struggle comes to be seen as what is essential. But this retroactive standpoint is never fully available in the present – it is always the standpoint of the future perfect.

Interviewed by Peter Dews and Peter Osborne
London, July 1990

Notes

1 'Laibach' is the German word for Ljubljana. The band sought to provoke the regime through the wearing of fascist insignia, etc.

2 'Chetniks' was the name applied to members of the Second World War resistance group in Yugoslavia which was led by General Mihailovic, Minister of War in King Peter's government in exile. It found its main support in Serbia. Soon after its formation it came into conflict with Tito's predominantly communist Partisans, and a three-way struggle developed between the Germans, the chetniks and the Partisans. The Allies supported Tito. Mihailovic was executed by the new Yugoslav regime in July 1946, on a charge of treason.

3 This turned out to be a serious underestimation of Milosevic's capacity for survival. In the elections of 9 December 1990, he secured a substantial majority, bucking the trend in Eastern Europe for former Communist Party bosses to lose their credibility in the new political climate. The old Serbian Communist Party renamed itself the Serbian Socialist Party (SPS).

Postscript

RP When we last met, just over three ago, the situation in former Yugoslavia was very different. The break-up of the Federation was on the horizon, it was expected, but nobody predicted that it would occur so violently, so destructively, or that the leadership in Serbia would resort to war so quickly. You identified Serbian claims on parts of Bosnia and Croatia as a stumbling block to a new confederation, but you didn't believe that there was any real danger of a restoration of Serbian dominance, once Slovenia and Croatia had undertaken democratic elections. Do you still believe that now?

Žižek I thought that Milosevic's charisma was already in decline – that he'd lose the elections in 1990 – but the war saved him. Without this conflict, Milosevic would have been lost. When did the conflict erupt in Croatia? A couple of weeks after big anti-Milosevic demonstrations in Belgrade. The army had to send in tanks to pacify the situation. Later, it turned out that there had been a secret meeting of the entire Milosevic leadership where the connection was discussed quite openly: they were in a crisis and the only way to save the situation was to proclaim the Serbian nation itself as in danger and to create a new emergency state.

RP The war saved him, but you are going so far as to say that there was a war *in order* to save him?

Žižek Yes, that's my analysis. It was overdetermined, it was more complex, but I think that was ultimately the decisive factor. The key ingredient in the Yugoslav crisis is the survival of the Serbian regime. Up until the summer of 1991 – until the brief, ten-day conflict in Slovenia – there was only a very vague coalition between Milosevic and the Yugoslav army. Milosevic was mainly a Serbian nationalist but the army's idea was to keep the whole of Yugoslavia together, at any price. So there were differences. The result of the Slovene conflict (the loss of

Slovenia) was that Milosevic and the army closed ranks on a new political platform, which was no longer to defend the entire Yugoslavia, but only 'Greater Serbia'. That was the plan: let's leave Slovenia and the majority of Croatia, but let's still have Bosnia and even Macedonia. It was a big shift. It bonded Milosevic and the Yugoslav army together.

RP So the war saved Milosevic, but will he survive the peace – assuming that there will be some kind of peace in the former Yugoslavia in the foreseeable future?

Žižek No, in the longer term he definitely cannot survive the peace. On the other hand, contrary to those who think that the disintegration of Yugoslavia was some kind of Western plot, there is already pressure – Western pressure – to provide some new unity in the old Yugoslav space. It is a part of the fundamental tendency in today's capitalism to seek a clear line of demarcation between inside and outside, between those who are included (meaning social security, human rights, etc.) and those who are excluded. This is a structural line of separation which is getting stronger and stronger, not only between nations but more and more within nations. It's the problem in LA, for example. It's also what lies behind all this talk in Eastern Europe about who really belongs to Western civilization. It's about who will be allowed in. It's a desperate struggle.

RP You have spoken about Eastern Europe in terms of a struggle over the floating signifier of 'liberalism'. Is that what's at stake here? Are there no other political discourses with a purchase on these events?

Žižek Well, the fundamental axis of opposition is still liberal openness against some kind of nationalist closure. The tragedy is that the Left hasn't yet succeeded in articulating its own proper agenda. Back-to-the-roots organic nationalist movements are an inherent reaction to liberalism and as such a part of it. The only serious political question today is: Is the liberal-democratic horizon the ultimate horizon? Must we accept the liberal-democratic way, and just widen it a bit by including gay rights, minority rights, etc., or is it possible, at least in the long term, to place it in question? And the way to place the liberal-democratic horizon in question, for me, is definitely not through some kind of neo-conservative corporatism. That's just a reaction of the same kind as nationalism.

Marxism is still valid in its belief in a fundamental antagonism pertaining to today's liberal democracy, but the antagonism has assumed a new form. It is no longer capitalists versus proletarians, but those who are inside the system versus those who aren't. It's written into the very notion of liberal democracy, this inherent splitting, but it cannot be reproduced endlessly. There is a limit to it, and where that limit is, is for me the only serious question. This is why I am suspicious of Laclau's concept of radical democracy, because basically it's simply a more radical version of the standard liberal-democratic game – which is why he is uncannily silent about capitalism. That's his scarecrow. The moment you mention the words 'capitalism' or 'world system', you get a panicky reaction: it's fundamentalism, essentialism, etc. Well, it's not necessarily so.

Going Through Phantasy

RP You have reworked Laclau's notion of antagonism in terms of the Lacanian analysis of identity claims as sites of phantasmic identification; more specifically, you offer us a theory of social antagonism as the 'theft of enjoyment'. Isn't this psychologization of social antagonism still too generalizing? It may give you an interpretive framework, but it doesn't account for any particular social antagonisms. It doesn't seem to be *socially* explanatory.

Žižek I agree. I'm very autocritical at this point: there is a danger of over-quick universalization, of a kind of false, bad or abstract universal, in the Hegelian sense. Instead of a concrete analysis, you simply apply the universal. Nonetheless, I insist, you must take into account the fundamental level of a traumatism of enjoyment. Take the example of violence against immigrants, which is common in so many parts of Europe today. What is the reason for the violence?

I read some so-called 'in-depth' interviews with German skinheads responsible for beating immigrant workers. To begin with they gave explanations at the level of what can quickly be translated into psychoanalytic terms as 'ego evil': acts of the ego as the agency of rational utilitarian reasoning. That is to say, they attack immigrants because from their perspective immigrants steal their work, their women, etc. At a deeper level, you then had certain ideological rationalizations. They said: we want to protect Western civilization, etc. We might call this 'superego evil': evil done in the name of some kind of principle, ideological 'fanaticism' or whatever. However, what Hans Magnus Enzensberger claims, and from my experience I agree, is that once you go a little bit deeper, they themselves really don't take these explanations seriously. Their ultimate answer corresponds much more closely to what Freud and Lacan have conceptualized as a type of pleasure, a falling body of traumatic enjoyment. Its basic terms are: 'we cannot assimilate them', 'they bother us', 'we must throw them out', etc. Exactly the same words occur in Freud's account of the most elementary relationship of the ego to traumatic enjoyment in *The Ego and the Id*, and in Lacan. The other two levels – the utilitarian notion of interests being threatened by foreigners, and the more basic level of ideological attachment – don't work. You are left with the fundamental level of a threat to enjoyment. It's a very elementary matrix. I think that we can also use it to explain anti-abortion campaigns, for example.

How are we to counteract it? One of the options – and I'm not saying that this is a general answer – is exemplified by Laibach, our famous post-punk rock group in Slovenia. They don't try to take a critical distance, or to establish some kind of a dialectical mediation, they go the opposite way, through overidentification. Ideology always involves a kind of self-splitting, an unacknowledged support in phantasies which must remain unacknowledged. Even in Nazi Germany during the extermination of the Jews, the physical brutality of it was not part of the public discourse. There was a splitting between what was publicly acknowledged and what was inferentially present, but never talked about. My point is that if you bring this unspoken under-side into the light of the day, maybe you can block the functioning of the ideology. That's what Laibach were doing, by staging totalitarian rituals. It wasn't irony. They were saying: 'This is what you really desire but are not yourselves prepared to acknowledge.' The problem concerns the enthusiasm of the passive observers. Although they condemn the violence, condemn the violent minority, at a deeper level they already accept their problematic. They agree that the minority are overdoing it – 'okay, it's horrible' – but they still think 'there really is a problem of immigrants', 'we must do something', etc. It's these observers who are the true problem.

RP This notion of publicity, of bringing into discourse the things which are repressed, your social equivalent to the cure, is the Habermasian side of Lacan to which you referred last time. In the section at the beginning of *Seminar I*, 'Overture to the Seminar', Lacan talks about the ideal of analysis being 'to render the subject capable of sustaining the analytical dialogue'. You seem to be extending this idea to polit-ical life. How does it differ from the Habermasian ideal of undistorted communication?

Žižek Lacan is even more Habermasian later on, in his idea of how you should become an analyst. He wants to avoid any kind of initiation in the relationship between student and teacher. You become an analyst if you are able to externalize your innermost rules in the public medium. But things get more complicated with the problematic of phantasy. It is here, I think, that there is a difference from Habermas.

According to Lacan, when you approach, let us say, the hard core of your phantasy, there, this kind of interpretive argumentation or translation into discourse, it doesn't work. You must accomplish a shift at a different level: what Lacan calls 'going through phantasy'. It's not that you must accept your phantasy – you cannot do anything about it – but you must suspend the control of your phantasy over you; and not through interpretation. The other crucial difference concerns the whole Lacanian problematic of the inconsistency of the field of language. Language moves in a vicious circle, it's inconsistent.

That's why it needs some kind of phantasy support – in order to render this lack invisible.

The Foucauldian Challenge (Late Capitalist Subjectivities)

RP Lacan's emphasis on phantasy has been a powerful influence on feminist work on sexual difference. Recently, however, this work has come into conflict with a more Foucauldian tendency in feminist theory. From this point of view, Lacan's location of the (sexed) structure of phantasy in a lack inherent in language itself appears far too monolithic and ahistorical to be either empirically credible or politically useful – indeed, it appears as an *expression* of patriarchy. I am thinking of Judith Butler's recent work, in particular, here (*Bodies That Matter*) – its undermining of the distinction between the imaginary and the symbolic – but it represents a wider tendency towards the historicization of theoretical discourses. In this particular instance, there is a definite political point: namely, that if what Lacan calls 'the symbolic' is merely a hegemonic form of the imaginary, the outcome of an ongoing sexual-political struggle, then we can wage counter-hegemonic struggles against its phallic form in the name of alternative structures of desire. In this context, your own emphasis on what Lacan calls 'the real', and your critique of over-hasty historicizations of psychoanalysis, is in danger of appearing as an attempt to shore up the existing symbolic space, to defend the old hegemonic symbolic: the priority of the castration complex. It looks like a conservative reaction to an historically produced crisis of sexual identity, the very existence of which undermines the terms of your Lacanian defence. How do you respond to this kind of criticism?

Žižek I'm not familiar with Butler's latest book yet, although I do know *Gender Trouble*, in detail. My counterattack will be on two levels. First, for me, the best way to analyse somebody is to ask, not what he or she asserts, but what is the image of the enemy that the work implies? In *Gender Trouble*, the enemy is somebody who can be called identitarian, patriarchal or phallocentric. My point is very simple: this is not the enemy today. To put it in Marxist terms, the form of subjectivity which is produced by late capitalism is no longer patriarchal-identitarian. The predominant form of ideology today is precisely that of multiple identities, non-identity and cynical distance. This includes even sexual identities. If we play this game – not male, not female, but assume all the possibilities – this is the late capitalist game. These Foucauldian practices of inventing new strategies, new identities, are ways of playing the late capitalist game of subjectivity.

Take a typical example of capitalist mass media in the USA, like *Newsweek* or *Time Magazine*. Isn't it deeply suspicious that the common denominator of all those they attack – Arabs, terrorists, etc. – is that they are designated as 'fundamentalists': the ones who over-identify? This is my first line of attack, not only on Judith Butler but on the whole late Foucauldian idea of multiple identities and an aesthetics of existence: it simply describes the conceptual structure of late capitalist subjectivity.

Now, to return to Lacan, I can give you a more detailed answer here: *there is no elementary imaginary.* Lacan is quite clear: the big enigma of the mirror stage is that in order for identification with the alienated image of the body to take place, a certain depth must already be there, and this depth is symbolic. Furthermore, when Lacan speaks about the failure of identification, he doesn't mean that there is a certain ideal symbolic structure that you never can live up to. His point is far more radical. His point is that there is a certain fundamental deadlock – the Lacanian real, why not call it 'gender trouble'? – and the putative subject formulates different symbolic constructs to avoid this deadlock.

Let me put it in another way. What struck me about *Gender Trouble* was that the first two parts of the book show very nicely how all symbolic attempts to cope with sexual difference fail. I agree with Butler that there is always trouble with gender. My point is that suddenly, in Part Three, gender trouble disappears. Where is the gender trouble there? She moves from saying that the symbolic is a hegemonic imaginary, to saying that everything is imaginary, therefore we can imagine anything!

Now, regarding the real, I agree that if you understand the real as some kind of persisting traumatic kernel you have a problem. This rude way of saying 'that's real, this is symbolic' depends upon a purely symbolic distinction. Drawing a clear line between the real and the symbolic is a symbolic operation *par excellence*. So Butler is radically opposed to this kind of substantialization of the real. I agree with her on this point, but I think it's a misreading of Lacan. It's not Lacan himself, but a certain rank appropriation of Lacan. Let's not forget the famous problem of feminine enjoyment. The real does not refer to some substantial, positive entity beyond the symbolic, resisting symbolization. Lacan says quite clearly that not all of woman is subordinated to the phallic function, but at the same time there is nothing in woman which eludes the phallic function. So what Lacan calls 'the real' is nothing beyond the symbolic, it's merely *the inherent inconsistency of the symbolic order itself.*

Still, not everything is cultural, that's the paradox. Although you cannot pinpoint a moment which is pure nature, which is not yet medi-ated by culture, in spite of this you must not draw the conclusion that everything is culture. Otherwise you fall into 'discursive idealism' – let's use the horrible Marxist term, why not? It is the Lacanian notion of the real that I miss in *Gender Trouble* which produces its political problems. It is because of this that Butler's political project remains entirely within a liberal-democratic frame.

RP Surely the attempt to historicize the psychoanalytical account of sexual identification has some validity. Your own talk of 'over-hasty' historicization suggests that *some* kind of historicization is legitimate, if not the Foucauldian, absolutizing one. At what level are you prepared to historicize questions about sexual identification?

Žižek The kernel that resists historicization is not a positive one, it is not notions like father, authority, Oedipus. The kernel that resists historicization can be defined only in the terms of a certain impossibility, a deadlock, in purely negative ways. That would be my point. When the classical repressive patriarchal sexual ideology was breaking down, there was a certain opening, but as soon as these new forms of sexuality were integrated, this deadlock became invisible again.

RP But have these new forms of sexuality really been 'integrated'? It doesn't seem enough to claim that they form part of the subjectivity of the latest forms of capitalism. From a Marxist standpoint, the historical status of social forms within capitalism presumably has to be viewed dialectically, in the sense that all kinds of things have developed within capitalism – have required capitalism in order to develop and have even been essential to the reproduction of capital – which one hopes will outlive it, historically, albeit in new forms.

Žižek Precisely, let's take a concrete analysis. Do you know that some religious fundamentalists were among the most raucous critics of the Vietnam war? Somebody who can be quickly labelled a fundamentalist can play a far more progressive role. This is the concrete dialectic.

RP What you have to show is not the 'correspondence' of the new forms of sexual subjectivity to today's capitalism – since in some sense that will always be so, in a capitalist society – but that they impede progressive forms of social transformation; that they are a *barrier* to the construction of political subjectivities which are anti-capitalist. That seems rather harder.

Žižek Precisely, that would be my point. I think they do function as a barrier in this way. You put it in a very precise way. This is for me the whole problem of political correctness. It has a blocking effect. This can be shown in an empirical way. On the other hand, I tend to agree with Laclau when he says that there is no guarantee of the political meaning of any movement in advance. It is open. That is what the struggle for hegemony is all about. The struggle is open, in the Hegelian sense of the mediation between particular and universal. However, there are only no limits to this openness so long as we remain at the level of symbolic articulation What I try to isolate is the level of phantasy – that's what limits it. This is where I disagree with Laclau. The element that limits this boundless parade of symbolic reinscriptions is the level of phantasy enjoyment. These are not just symbolic differentials, they exist as historical traumas, registered by the real.

Intellectuals in Eastern Europe

RP Perhaps we could end by talking a little about the role of intellectuals. Do you think that the intellectuals have had their public moment in Eastern Europe now, that it is past?

Žižek This might be a traditional opinion, but unfortunately I would say 'yes'. The last years under communism were a kind of magical period, not only for intellectual life, but for underground culture more generally. We had a regime which did not believe in itself – an ideal situation for intellectuals – a regime which did not believe in its own legitimacy. They were extremely receptive to every kind of criticism. What we had next, however, in the first generation of the new, so-called democratic regimes, was a group with an exaggerated belief in their legitimacy. In Slovenia, they used a special term, 'inner party opposition'. They said: 'Yes, you did play a certain role in the fight for democracy, but you were allowed to play that role because you were an inner party opposition. If you continue with your critical attitude now, though, you will be replaying the culture of the ex-communist oppressors.' So those who were the victims first time around are being victimized again by the new populist parties playing the cards of the ex-opposition.

So, yes, our time is over, but one should not accept this too easily. There are differences between countries of the same political type. After all, in America, intellectuals are more or less strictly confined to the ghettos, but in a country like France incredible things happen. When Foucault died, when Lacan died, it was the front page of *Libération*, with a whole eight-page special supplement. With the Gulf War, every big intellectual not only had a position, but felt a need to take a stance in public. We stand a fair chance in Slovenia, as they do in Poland, that we will not fall back into the American situation; that there will still be *some* role for public intellectuals, if only a small one. Eastern Europe is far from being a one-dimensional capitalist space. We still have a lot of tensions where there are spaces for different intellectual traditions. It's likely that intellectuals will play a much larger role than they usually do in the West.

RP Currently, you play a role in two quite different intellectual spaces: in Slovenia and the American academy. Do you see yourself continuing to move between these two situations, or are you likely to drift increasingly towards the American scene?

Žižek No, definitely not. Firstly, for contingent reasons, because I have a pure research job. This is a nice case of a dialectical inversion. What was meant under communism as a way of isolating subversive intellectuals – because we all wanted to have contacts with students – is now the best possible formula. In Western terms, it is a permanent sabbatical. You do whatever you want. I can play popular culture here and then politics there, but I firmly believe that the two sides are mediated. In ex-Yugoslavia, reference to popular culture, especially underground culture, has a very precise and, I claim, an extremely progressive political potential. We must not forget that. When I was attacked by some American academics after a lecture a year or so ago, saying: 'My God, your country is dying in flames, and you speak about Hitchcock', I said, 'Yes, we are dying in flames because we don't have enough Hitchcock.' That is the best antidote to nationalism. On the other hand, I have a very traditional Marxist belief that the new liberal-democratic order cannot go on indefinitely, that there will be a moment of explosion, probably caused by some kind of ecological crisis or whatever, and that we must prepare ourselves for that moment.

Interviewed by Peter Osborne
London, September 1993

3
The Legacy of Marx

István Mészáros

István Mészáros left Hungary after the Soviet invasion of 1956. After periods in Italy and Canada, he settled in England. In the late 1980s he retired from a Chair in Philosophy at the University of Sussex. He established his reputation in the English-speaking world with his widely translated *Marx's Theory of Alienation* (1970), which was awarded the Isaac Deutscher Memorial Prize. His other works include Lukács's *Concept of Dialectic* (1972), *The Work of Sartre* (vol. 1, 1979) and *The Power of Ideology* (1989). He received the Lukács prize in 1992. His work has been particularly well received in Latin America.

Mészáros's thought is characterized by a fiercely combative Marxism and, in contrast to the development of those of Lukács's former followers who once made up the Budapest School, a socialist commitment undiminished by recent events. He has continued developing his ideas about the theory and practice of the transition to socialism in *Beyond Capital: Towards a Theory of Transition* (1995), nominated in the US for the Michael Harnington Award. He was elected a member of the Hungarian Academy of Sciences in 1995.

RP How did you get interested in Marxism?

Mészáros Amazingly by picking up books in a bookshop, fairly small things like *The 18th Brumaire*, *Communist Manifesto*, and so on, brochures which one could buy for pennies, and then later Engels's *Anti-Dühring*, and later still I got to Marx's major works. At the same time I got interested in Lukács. I found a book of his about Hungarian literature, which I knew; I liked it so much that a week or two later, after reading it, I sold all my precious possessions, like my penknife and fountain pen, to buy his very expensive books. I was about 15 or

16 at the time. After reading those, that was when I decided I wanted to work with him at the University in Budapest.

RP What was it like when you met him? Was he interesting as a man, or as a colleague?

Mészáros Very interesting. I started at the University in September 1949, and attacks on Lukács had started in July 1949 and they were very savage attacks. I almost got expelled from University because of my frequenting his seminars. In fact at that time the attacks on Lukács were so savage his Institute was almost completely deserted, so he had a very small seminar only. This went on for two years and in 1951 things had become very dangerous even for him. There was a time when Fadeyev, who was a very old adversary of Lukács's, attacked him in the Soviet Union, and at that point he feared that he might be arrested.

RP What sort of personal impression did Lukács make on you? What was it like to encounter him as a human being?

Mészáros In this period I got to know him very well, very closely, and I liked not only his intellectual way of approaching problems but also his sense of humour. He had a wonderful sense of irony and I can illustrate it with a story. He told me once that he was in hospital with a stomach complaint, for general investigative tests, and the professor who conducted these investigations, these medical tests, when he saw the X-rays, became very excited and said 'This is wonderful, this is an extraordinarily rare condition, I must show these to my students at the University', and Lukács remarked, 'At last I have become teaching material'; because, in the period between 1949 and the mid-1950s, his books were banned, they were taken out of public libraries and so on, people couldn't even have access to them. This shows he always had a nice story if he wanted to illustrate something. Like on the question of what should be the role of the writer, the intellectual in general: should it be tied to the Party in the way in which the politicians and the ideologues of the Party maintained it should? Lukács's position was no, it shouldn't. This is the difference between the foot soldier of the army and the partisan, the guerrilla fighter. The role of the partisan is to act autonomously. The overall aim and objective may be identical, to win the war, but the way in which one can do it is quite radically different. He was a good man, a man of tremendous moral integrity and a good friend.

RP What was it like in '56 generally, in the University, in the Petöfi circle, and all this ferment?

Mészáros As you can imagine it was very dramatic because it was coming out of a period in '55 when Rákosi and company tried to clamp down, quite savagely really, on whatever opposition was coming forward. The Hungarian Writers' Association was a very influential body that was in the forefront of debates and moving against Rákosi and his clique. In that way it was even anticipating what happened at the twentieth Congress in Russia; and as you know in October '56 that's when Rákosi was eventually spirited away: I mean he wanted to refuse to go, and the Russians simply had to drag him away from the country. But then they imposed Ernö Gerö who was very much a Stalinist himself. Then of course events unfolded. 23 October 1956 was the uprising, and November 4th the second Russian intervention, and that put an end to a period of great expectations and hopes in the Petöfi circle. The Petöfi circle grew step by step and when Rákosi authorized it, he made the cynical remark, 'Well, we'll let them talk and then we hit them on the head.' It didn't quite work out like that because this talking generated an enormous popular echo and some of the meetings, especially towards the end, were attended by 5,000-6,000 people.

RP Did Lukács show any reluctance to take a job with the Nagy government or was he pleased to do that?

Mészáros He took a job with the Nagy government, making it clear that he would do it strictly for a very limited period until things worked out and then he would return to writing, because he was extremely keen to write not only his *Aesthetics* but also the *Ethics* which in the end turned out to be his *Ontology of Social Being*. He was always dreaming about writing an ethical work which in the end he could not write.

RP Why did you go into exile? Was it in accordance with Lukács's advice?

Mészáros Neither on his advice or against it. At the time when I decided, Lukács was under arrest, but I decided really a bit earlier, at the time of the second Russian intervention, because I became convinced that there was no hope for socialist transformation in Hungary. They repressed what was actually far from being counter-revolutionary. It was a very promising upheaval to start something new, and in no time at all workers' councils were constituted all over the country; the question of turning towards the capitalists was never envisaged.

RP You have written a lot on Lukács. How would you sum up his historical significance? What's his importance for Marxism?

Mészáros I consider it very great. He's one of the outstanding philosophical figures of this century and he was a highly successful and important philosopher before he even embraced Marxism. He has written a number of works which no Marxist can ignore and it goes beyond that, because he has in some way theorized the historical experience of the Russian revolution and its aftermath. That is probably his most important achievement as a thinker. While I don't think that *History and Class Consciousness* is his best book, it doesn't mean that in its own place it's not an immensely important, and representative, book in which this experience, this historical experience, has been representatively theorized.

RP Do you think there is any influence from Simmel in *History and Class Consciousness*?

Mészáros A bit of influence from Simmel, more from Weber, and of course more than anything else from Hegel. Under the circumstances it enabled him to work out a historical view of what was going on and how to in a sense pull ourselves up by our bootstraps – a revolution which aimed to be a socialist revolution when the relation of forces was extremely in favour of the other side.

RP If that isn't his best book which is his best book?

Mészáros There are several. For instance *The Young Hegel* is an outstanding work. I remember when I was appointed in St Andrews, and T. M. Knox, who was at that time the Vice-Chancellor of St Andrews University, to my astonishment (he was a good Hegelian and certainly Marxism didn't taint him in the slightest) said to me that he learnt more from Lukács's *The Young Hegel* than from all the other books on Hegel put together. It was quite a compliment from a great Hegel scholar.

RP Some people argue that at an intellectual level, because of Hegel's stress on reconciling one to the present, this admiration for Hegel represents Lukács's reconciliation with Stalinism.

Mészáros I think that would be a very simplifying way of putting it because he was not – as documented through his own history, his own development – he was not at all reconciled with Stalinism. If you like, he *survived* Stalinism, that is something quite different. But precisely the book, *The Young Hegel*, shows that it is nonsense to say that he simply reconciled himself with Stalinism, because that book was written explicitly against a Stalinist line on Hegel. Stalin's line on Hegel was that it is an aristocratic reaction against the French Revolution, and Lukács demonstrates that it is an enthusiastic embracing of the French Revolution. In fact there couldn't be even a dream of publishing it in the Soviet Union at the time when Stalin's line prevailed against Hegel.

RP Was it first published in Hungary, then?

Mészáros It was published in Austria, that's where it was published, in Vienna in '47 and much later on in Germany and also in Hungary. You know he told me the story that in 1941 at the outbreak of the war he was living in a big tenement. The caretaker of that tenement house once stopped him because the Central Committee of the Soviet Party passed a resolution against Hegel, and when you pass a resolution every Party cell has to debate that resolution. The caretaker's Party cell duly debated it and, knowing that Lukács was a professor, he stopped him after this discussion at the door and said, 'This Hegel, this wretched Hegel, he should be shot forthwith', to which Lukács replied in his rather angelic way: 'That would be a little difficult because he has been dead for 110 years.' The fact that the Central Committee of the Soviet

Party had nothing better to do at the outbreak of the war than to pass a resolution against Hegel gives the lie to 'Lukács's accommodation with Stalinism'. What is problematical in his horizon in that period is that basically he accepted the vision of socialism in a single country. This he maintained to the end of his life, and of course in as much as that was Stalin's political line you have a commonality.

RP You recently wrote a critical article on Lukács about his inadequacies on the theory of value (in *Critique* 23, 1991). I have just read Lukács's *Process of Democratisation* which he wrote in 1968. It is generally good, but has this incredibly wrong theory of value where he simply identifies value with labour, and surplus value with surplus labour. I was very surprised.

Mészáros That is very problematical, in fact it's totally unacceptable. And also there you find that the idea of socialism in one country is still haunting him in the background. That is where you have the historical limits of Lukács who was very much in that vision of what happened after the revolution, that's what he identified himself with. I remember when he was not even a quarter of the way through his *Aesthetics* he was dreaming about writing the *Ethics*. That's what he had wanted to write since 1910 or thereabouts. I was very sceptical. I said to him he would never be able to write it because it is impossible to write a systematic work on ethics without a radical critique of politics. There is no ethical work in the history of philosophy from Aristotle to Hegel which doesn't go hand-in-hand with an equivalent theorization of politics, and under the conditions of Stalinism, in whatever form, even the form of so-called de-Stalinization, politics remained a taboo. It was always handed down from above and therefore it was impossible under the circumstances to undertake that radical critique of politics which is necessary, and I said to him that under those circumstances he could only write about the most abstract dimensions and abstract problems of ethics because there is an inherent and integral relationship between ethics and politics. That's what happened because years later when I asked him how the *Ethics* was proceeding he wrote to me that he couldn't proceed because it became necessary to write a long introduction. At that time he called it an introduction on social ontology, and that long introduction turned out to be a very nearly 3,000-page work which is full of references to an *Ethics* to be written. He continued to dream about writing that *Ethics* but for that it would have been necessary to undertake a radical critique of the whole social and economic framework in which politics functioned, which of course he could not do. You have to see the historical limits under which thinkers have to operate. You can't jump out of that, and certainly he couldn't, and it would be very naive to say that this work on democratization solves the problem in that respect. It came unfortunately too late for him. Today he could do both.

Sartre's Alternative

RP You met Sartre in 1957. Why did you decide to write a book on him?

Mészáros I always felt that Marxists owed a great debt to Sartre because we live in an age in which the power of capital is overbearing, where, significantly, the most commonplace platitude of politicians is that 'there is no alternative' – whether you think of 'Tina', Mrs Thatcher, 'there is no alternative', or Gorbachev who endlessly repeated the same until he had to find out, like Mrs Thatcher, that after all there had to be an alternative to both of them. But it goes on and on and, if you look around and think of how Conservative or Labour politicians talk, they always talk about 'there is no alternative', and the underlying pressures are felt everywhere. Sartre was a man who always preached the diametrical opposite: there *is* an alternative, there *must be* an alternative; you as an individual have to rebel against this power, this monstrous power of capital. Marxists on the whole failed to voice that side. I don't say that you have to become therefore an existentialist or a politically-committed existentialist in order to face it, but there is no one in the last fifty years of philosophy and literature who tried to hammer it home with such single-mindedness and determination as Sartre did: the necessity that there has to be a rebellion against this wisdom of 'there is no alternative' and there has to be an individual participation in it. I don't embrace his ideas but I embrace the aim. How you realize that aim is up to you in the context of your own approach, but the aim is something without which we won't get anywhere.

Sartre today in France is a very embarrassing person even to mention. Why? Because what happened is that in the name of Privatism and Individualism they have totally sold out to the powers of repression, a capitulation to the forces of 'there is no alternative', and that's why Sartre is a terrible reminder. When you also look into the background of the people we are talking about, postmodernists of a great variety, they very often were politically engaged people. But their engagement was skin-deep. Some of these people, around '68, were more Maoist than the extreme Maoists in China, and now they have embraced the Right in a most enthusiastic way; or they were in the 'Socialism or Barbarism' group and have become the peddlers of the most stupid platitudes of postmodernity. What these people have lost is their frame of reference. In France intellectual life used to be dominated in one way or another by the Communist Party. That goes also for Sartre who tried criticizing it from outside and pushing it in a direction which he embraced until he had to come to the conclusion that 'work in collaboration with the Communist Party is both necessary and impossible', which is a terrible, bitter dilemma. He said this at the time of the

Algerian War when the role of the Communist Party was absolutely disgraceful. That's what made it necessary, because you need a movement to oppose the repressive force of the State; and impossible, because look what that movement is like. What happened, of course, was the disintegration of the Communist Party like several other parties of the Third International in the last two decades. And with the sinking of this big ship in relation to which all these intellectuals defined themselves in one way or another, here are these intellectuals left behind; the ship has disappeared and they find themselves in their self-inflated rubber dinghies throwing darts at each other. Not a very reassuring sight; and they are not going to get out of it by simply fantasising about some individuality which doesn't exist; because true individuality is inconceivable without a community with which you relate yourself and define yourself.

Marxism Today

RP You have lived in various countries. Why did you settle in England? Surely English culture is not very congenial to your kind of thought?

Mészáros Well, I beg to differ because I had actually quite a long relationship to English-speaking culture way before I left Hungary. I had been a great admirer of a certain line of thought from Hobbes to the great figures of the English and Scottish Enlightenment and these really meant a hell of a lot to me, because they had a great message for the future and have to be an integral part of your own work. Another reason was that I was always a great admirer of English and Scottish poetry from Shakespeare to the present. And the third reason which I found equally important is that I always thought of England as the country of the Industrial Revolution which went with a working class with tremendously deep roots, and that remains despite everything. I think you have to relate yourself to something; political and social commitment cannot be in thin air or in a vacuum. I am deeply committed to the working class, and that is how I think of the future intellectually. Theoretically there must be points of reference; there cannot be social transformation without an agency and the only agency conceivable under the present condition to take us out of this mess is Labour – Labour in the sense Marx was talking about and which we have to rediscover for ourselves under our present conditions.

RP Your most recent book is *The Power of Ideology*. The last part has some interesting criticisms of Marx. What do we have to rethink in Marx's legacy?

Mészáros Well, we have to relate him to his time which does not mean we have to in any way abandon the framework of his theory. The framework of Marxian theory remains the overall horizon also of our activity, our orientation, because it embraces the whole epoch, this epoch of capital in crisis and the necessity of finding a way out of it. However, historical circumstances change and some of the things about which I wrote in *The Power of Ideology* show that he had to take short-cuts. For well over ten years I have tried to draw attention to a passage in which Marx talks about this little corner of the world. Europe is after all only a little corner of the world. What is it for us social-ists, what is the meaning of it, that capital on a much larger terrain, the rest of the world, not this little corner of the world, is in its ascen-dancy? He decided to put that on the side and proceed from the horizon and perspective of the little corner of the world which Europe was. And that was a conscious choice for him.

RP In recent papers on socialist transformation, you have introduced an important distinction between capital and capitalism. Can you explain this distinction and its significance for socialist struggle?

Mészáros Well, in fact this distinction goes back to Marx himself. I pointed out several times that Marx didn't entitle his main work 'capi-talism' but *Das Kapital, Capital*, and I also underlined that the subtitle of Volume One was mistranslated under Engels's supervision, as 'the capitalist production process', when in fact it is 'the production process of capital', which has a radically different meaning. What is at stake of course here is that the object, the target, of socialist transformation is overcoming the power of capital. Capitalism is a relatively easy object in this enterprise because you can in a sense abolish capitalism through revolutionary upheaval and intervention at the level of politics, the expropriation of the capitalist. You have put an end to capitalism but you have not even touched the power of capital when you have done it. Capital is not dependent on the power of capitalism and this is important also in the sense that capital precedes capitalism by thousands of years. Capital can survive capitalism hopefully not by thousands of years, but when capitalism is overthrown in a limited area, the power of capital continues even if it is in a hybrid form.

The Soviet Union was not capitalist, not even state capitalist. But the Soviet system was very much dominated by the power of *capital*: the division of labour remained intact, the hierarchical command structure of capital remained. Capital is a command system whose mode of func-tioning is accumulation-oriented, and the accumulation can be secured in a number of different ways. In the Soviet Union surplus labour was extracted in a political way and this is what came into crisis in recent years. The politically regulated extraction of surplus labour became untenable for a variety of reasons. The political control of labour power is not what you might consider an ideal or optimal way of controlling the labour process. Under capitalism in the West what we have is an economically regulated extraction of surplus labour and surplus value.

In the Soviet system this was done in a very improper fashion from the point of view of productivity because labour retained a hell of a lot of power in the form of negative acts, defiance, sabotage, moonlighting, etc., through which one could not even dream of achieving the kind of productivity which is feasible elsewhere, and which undermined the *raison d'être* of this system under Stalin and his successors – politically forced accumulation. The accumulation part of it became stuck and that is why the whole system had to collapse. I published in Italy a long essay in Spring of 1982, in which I explicitly stated that, whereas the old US policies for the military-political rollback of communism were not likely to succeed, what was happening in Eastern Europe is likely to lead to the restoration of capitalism. I also found for the same reason the idea of market socialism a contradiction in terms, because it would, in a wishful concept, want to wed the two modalities: of the economic extraction of surplus labour with the politically regulated extraction – so that was why it was always a non-starter really.

What is absolutely crucial is to recognize that capital is a metabolic system, a social-economic metabolic system of control. You can overthrow the capitalist but the factory system remains, the division of labour remains, nothing has changed in the metabolic functions of society. Indeed, sooner or later you find the need for reassigning those forms of control to personalities, and that's how the bureaucracy comes into existence. The bureaucracy is a function of this command structure under the changed circumstances where in the absence of the private capitalist you have to find an equivalent to that control. I think this is a very important conclusion, because very often the notion of bureaucracy is pushed forward as a kind of mythical, explanatory framework, and it doesn't explain anything. The bureaucracy itself needs explanation. How come that this bureaucracy arises? When you use it as a kind of *deus ex machina* that explains everything in terms of bureaucracy; if you get rid of bureaucracy then everything will be all right. But you *don't* get rid of bureaucracy unless you attack the social economic foundation and devise an alternative way of regulating the metabolic process of society in such a way that the power of capital at first is curtailed and is of course in the end done away with altogether. Capital is a controlling force, you cannot control capital, you can do away with it only through the transformation of the whole complex of metabolic relationships of society, you cannot just fiddle with it. It either controls you or you do away with it, there is no halfway house between, and that's why the idea of market socialism could not conceivably function from the very beginning. The real need is not for the restoration of the capitalist market, under the name of an utterly fictitious 'social market', but for the adoption of a proper system of *incentives*. There is no social production system which can function without incentives, and who are the people to whom these incentives have to be related? Not abstract collective entities but individuals. So if people as individuals are not interested, not involved in the production process, in the regulation of the social metabolic process, then sooner or later they assume a negative or even an actively hostile attitude towards it.

RP Are we talking about moral or material incentives?

Mészáros It can be both. The opposition between moral and material incentives is often a very rhetorical one, an abstract and rhetorical one, because, if the result of this intervention and participation in the social processes is a better production, an increasing productivity, activation of the potentialities of the individuals involved, then it becomes a material incentive. But in as much as they are in control of their own life processes, it is also a moral incentive, so the two go hand-in-hand. Material and moral incentives have to go hand-in-hand. It is a question of control of the processes of this social economic system in which the activation of the repressed potential of the people is also an incentive. Material incentives in our society as presented to us always divide people against one another. You can see this everywhere, in every profession, teaching, university, every walk of life: the incentives work on the presumption that we can divide people from one another in order to control them better; that's the whole process. Now if you then reverse this relationship and say that people are in control of what they are involved in, then the divisiveness doesn't work any longer because they are not the suffering subjects of that sort of system. So material incentives and moral incentives can also be egalitarian in character. That is the tragedy of the Soviet-type development. When they talk about the collapse of socialism in relation to that, it's a grotesque misrepresentation of the facts, because socialism was not even started, not even the first steps have been taken in the direction of a socialist transformation whose target can only be to overcome the power of capital and to overcome the social division of labour, to overcome the power of the state which is also a command structure regulating the lives of the people from above.

Mickey Mouse Socialism

RP You talk about challenging the power of capital and I wondered if you could say a bit more about the practical implications, the implications for socialist struggle of your distinction between capital and capitalism.

Mészáros First of all the strategy which you have to envisage has to be spelled out in those terms. Socialists cannot carry on with the illusion that all you have to do is abolish private capitalism – because the real problem remains. We are really in a profound historical crisis. The process of the expansion of capital embracing the globe itself has been more or less accomplished. What we have witnessed in the last couple of decades is the structural crisis of capital. I always maintained that there is a big difference from the time when Marx talked about crisis in terms of the crisis that discharges itself in the form of great thunderstorms. Now it doesn't have to discharge itself in thunderstorms. What is characteristic in the crisis of *our* time is precipitations of varying intensity, tending towards a depressed continuum. Recently we started to talk about double-dip recession, soon we will talk about treble-dip recession, maybe even one day quintuple-dip recession. What I am saying is that this tendency towards a depressed continuum, where one recession follows another, is not a condition which can be maintained indefinitely because at the end it reactivates capital's internal explosive contradictions with a vengeance and there are also some absolute limits which one has to consider in that respect.

Remember, I am talking about the structural crisis of capital, which is a much more serious problem than the crisis of capitalism because one way to get out of the crisis of capitalism in principle was a state regulation of the economy, and in some respects on the outer horizon of the Western capitalist system you can allow for its possibility. State capitalism can arise when the Western capitalist system is in deepest trouble, but again I would say it's not a tenable solution in the long run because the same kinds of contradictions are reactivated, namely the contradiction between the political and the economic extraction of surplus labour. I'm not talking about fictitious future events – think of fascism, think of the Nazi system which attempted this kind of corporate state regulation of the system in order to get out of the crisis of German capitalism at that given time of history. Therefore what we are considering here is that all those ways of displacing temporarily the internal contradictions of capital are being exhausted. The world as a whole is very insecure. The overwhelming majority of humanity lives in the most abominable conditions. Whatever happened to the modernization of these countries? It has taken such forms of robbery and extraction and mindless refusal to consider even the implications for the survival of humanity – the way in which these territories and the population of these territories have been treated – that the whole thing has been totally undermined, and today you find a situation in which nobody believes any more in the modernization of the so-called 'Third World'. And that is why that depressed continuum is, in the long run, an untenable situation and for that reason a social transformation must be feasible. But it is not feasible through the revitalization of capital. It can only be done on the basis of a radical departure from the logic of this accumulation-orientated mindless destructive control.

This tremendous crisis I am talking about saw not only the virtual extinction of the communist parties, the parties of the Third International, but also the extinction of the parties of the Second International. For about a hundred years those who believed in the virtues of evolutionary socialism, and reform, were talking about the transformation of society which leads towards socialist relations of humanity. This has gone totally out of the window even in terms of their own programmes and perspectives. You have seen recently that the socialist parties of the Second International, and their various associates, have suffered quite devastating setbacks and defeats in every single country: in France, in Italy, in Germany, in Belgium and in the Scandinavian countries, and now recently also in England, the fourth successive defeat for the Labour Party. It was quite appropriate that this serial defeat in all these countries coincided with the celebratory opening of Euro Disneyland because what these parties themselves have adopted in this historical period, in their response to the crisis, is some kind of Mickey Mouse socialism, and this Mickey Mouse socialism is totally incapable of intervening in the social process. That is why it is not accidental that these parties adopt the wisdom of capital as an irreplaceable system. The leader of the Labour Party once declared that the task of socialists is the better management of capitalism. Now this kind of preposterous nonsense is in itself a contradiction. It is a contradiction in terms because it is extremely presumptuous to think that the capitalist system would work better with a Labourite government. The problems continue to become more severe, and the political system is incapable of responding because the political system operates under the ever-narrowing constraints of capital. Capital as such doesn't allow any more margin for manoeuvre. The margin of manoeuvre for political movements and parliamentary forces was incomparably greater in the nineteenth century or in the first third of the twentieth century. Britain is already part of Europe and there is no way in which you can unwind that process, in the sense that little England will be capable of solving these problems.

But that immediately also raises the question, how do we relate ourselves to the rest of the world? – With what happened in the East, in the Soviet Union? A new fundamental problem has arisen on the horizon. In the case of Russia I read recently that, in addition to the twenty five billion dollars which exist in the form of promises from the West, Russia will need this year alone another twenty billion. Where are we going to find these billions which Russia needs for this process when the American debt itself is quite astronomical? The problems of this world are becoming so intertwined, so enmeshed with one another, that you can't think of partial resolutions to them. Fundamental structural changes are needed. The two and a half decades of expansion after the Second World War were followed by deepening malaise, the collapse of the earlier cherished strategies, the end of Keynesianism, the appearance of monetarism, etc., and all of them leading nowhere. When self-complacent people like John Major say socialism is dead, capitalism works, we must ask: capitalism works *for whom* and *for how long*? I read recently that the directors of Merrill Lynch received, one 16.5 million, another 14 million, and another ten or fifteen of them, 5.5 million dollars each, as annual remuneration. It works very well for them, but how does it work for the people in Africa, where you see them every day on your television screen? Or in vast areas of Latin America, or in India, or in Pakistan, or in Bangladesh? I could continue and name the countries where you are talking about thousands of millions of people who can hardly survive.

RP The agent of change in this situation, the revolutionary subject, is still in your view the working class?

Mészáros Undoubtedly, there cannot be any other. I remember there was a time when Herbert Marcuse was dreaming about new social agents, the intellectuals and the outcasts, but neither of them had the power to implement change. The intellectuals can play an important role in defining strategies, but it cannot be that the outcasts are the force which implements this change. The only force which can introduce this change and make it work is society's producers, who have the repressed energies and potentialities through which all those problems and contradictions can be solved. The only agency which can rectify this situation, which can assert itself, and find fulfilment in the process of asserting itself, is the working class.

The Problem of Organization

RP What about its form of organization? Do you think new forms of organization are needed? Some people say the old-style political party is irrelevant.

Mészáros Yes, I would completely agree with that. The old-style political party is integrated into the parliamentary system which itself has outlived its historical relevance. It was in existence well before the working class appeared on the historical horizon as a social agency. The working class had to accommodate itself and constrain itself in accordance with whatever possibilities that framework provided and consequently it could produce only defensive organizations. All organizations of the working class which have been historically constituted – its political parties and trade unions have been the most important of them – all of them were defensive organizations. Now they worked up to a point and that was why the reformist perspective of evolutionary socialism was successful for so many years, because partial improvements could be gained. The working-class standards of living in the G7 countries have risen enormously in this period. When Marx was saying in the *Communist Manifesto* that the working class only has chains to lose, that is certainly not true of the working class of the G7 countries today or even yesterday. They have been very successful in improving their standard of living throughout this historical period until the last decade or so. What happened in the last decade or decade and a half was the coming to an end of this process because capital can no longer afford to grant benefits and significant gains to the working classes. Capital never gave anything away. If it was in tune with its own internal logic of expansion, self-expansion, then those gains could be provided. In fact they became dynamic factors in this self-expansionary process. That is not the case now. That's why we are in the situation that the health service is in crisis, the education system is in crisis, the welfare state as a whole is in crisis. So the historical end of this process reopens the question: if the working class cannot obtain defensive gains any longer, through what strategies can it transform society?

RP What I had in mind is more the extra-parliamentary parties like Lenin's Bolsheviks or the Chinese Communist Party which succeeded in destroying capitalism. Are they historically outmoded?

Mészáros Yes, completely. Even those parties remained constrained by the perspective of parliamentarianism, and Lenin himself was in favour of these parties operating within the parliamentary framework. So what is of course an immense problem for the historical agency of transformation is that capital is, by definition, and very effectively in its mode of acting and functioning, an extra-parliamentary force *par excellence*. And the working class on the other side has no politically effective extra-parliamentary force. The extra-parliamentary force would be the trade unions, but the trade unions identified themselves with the reformist parties, and that constrained them. There will be no advance whatsoever until the working-class movement, the socialist movement, is re-articulated in a form capable of offensive action, through its appropriate institutions and through its extra-parliamentary force. The parliament, if it is to become meaningful at all in the future, has to be revitalized, and can only be if it acquires an extra-parliamentary force in conjunction with the radical political movement that can also be active through parliament.

RP What do you think of the current state of Marxist philosophy?

Mészáros I think Marxist philosophy in general finds itself in a very difficult situation precisely for the reasons we are talking about, because we are in a major historical crisis, and disorientation is the rule of the day, and what happened in the East has greatly affected socialists and Marxists in the West and understandably so. It has to go through a process of revaluation and heart searching and redefinition of all kinds of things. I find the situation in Latin America, for instance, much more interesting, the kind of intellectual ferment which is going on there is much more interesting for the time being than what I could point to here. But I don't think this is a permanent condition, and I am the last to suggest that a radical socialist transformation can come out of these areas alone. In fact I am paradoxically convinced that the future of socialism will be decided in the United States, however pessimistic this may sound. I try to hint at this in the last section of *The Power of Ideology* where I discuss the problem of universality. Either socialism can assert itself universally and in such a way that it embraces all those areas, including the most developed capitalist areas of the world, or it won't succeed.

The world is one. I always rejected the notion of a 'Third World': there is only one world. I am convinced that a revival of Marxist thought in the future will also come here in response to the problems and demands of the age – especially when some of the mystifications of the past are swept away. For how much longer can people be fooled with the idea that if they wait long enough then, through social democratic processes of reform and evolutionary socialism, one day their problems will be solved? I don't think that many people believe this today and there was plenty of evidence in the elections all over Europe that this idea has been profoundly discredited. When parliamentary expectations are bitterly disappointed, people move in the direction of taking action. We had a very dramatic case in the recent past with the opposition to the poll tax and the defeat of Margaret Thatcher who was considered permanent, undefeatable, through that process. And now, after the British general election, in Scotland people are talking about direct action, even civil disobedience, in order to assert what they consider to be their legitimate interest of securing their own parliament or even their independence. So these are the kind of social events, social movements, in relation to which Marxist philosophy, Marxist thought in general can redefine itself.

RP   Presumably what needs to happen is that the workers in the United States form links and make common cause with workers in the 'Third World'? But how can they? These workers are to some extent living on a transfer of value from these same countries.

Mészáros   This is one of the problems and that's where also a critique of Marx has to be indicated, because the working class itself is fragmented, is divided, there are so many contradictions. In the United States in the last ten years the standard of living of the working class has gone down. So we are talking about a process, we are not talking about wish objects but realities which are happening in our times. In January 1971 I gave the Isaac Deutscher Memorial Lecture – *The Necessity of Social Control*

– and I indicated there the beginning of structural unemployment. Now unemployment at that time in Britain was well under one million. Today, even after twenty three times of falsifying the true unemployment figures, it is officially around 2,740,000. And no commitment even from the Labour Party to a return to full employment. That is the measure of the changes that are taking place. It is a massive contradiction when you declare a very large portion of the population superfluous. This portion of the population is not going to remain always meek and compliant and resigned to the conditions to which it is condemned. So things are happening, things are changing. But these changes will have to go deeper and I am convinced that they will.

Interviewed by Chris Arthur and Joseph McCarney
London, April 1992

4

Orientalism and After

Edward Said

Edward Said is Professor of Comparative Literature at Columbia University, New York. Best known academically for his book *Orientalism: Western Conceptions of the Orient* (1978), which was a milestone in the redefinition of the concerns of literary studies, he is most widely known for his tireless representations on behalf of the cause of the Palestinian people. His writings span the areas of literary criticism, politics and music. His works include *The Question of Palestine* (1980), *Covering Islam* (1981), *The World, The Text, and the Critic* (1983), *After the Last Sky: Palestinian Lives* (1986), *Musical Elaborations* (1991) and *Culture and Imperialism* (1993). Nurtured by the literary humanism of the 1950s, Said's career spans the period of the radicalization and subsequent transformation of the humanities in North America. This has recently given rise to heated debates over the canon, the curriculum, and the character of liberal education in multicultural capitalist societies, in which Said has been an active participant. His latest book, *Representations of the Intellectual* (1994), derives from his delivery of the prestigious Reith Lectures in Britain in 1993.

RP Perhaps we could begin by asking you to say something about your intellectual and political background in the late 1950s and 1960s. How did you identify yourself politically in relation to the civil rights and student movements in the USA during the period when you were a young member of faculty at Columbia? What from that period of your life was a formative influence on your later work?

Said Well, in the 1950s I was a student and by 1957 I had finished my undergraduate education. I then went back to the Middle East for a year, basically to play the piano. And then in '58 I came back to graduate school, at Harvard, and I just plunged into that. I did really nothing else but study for five years. My family remained in the Middle East and moved from Egypt, where they had come after 1948, to Lebanon. My entire family became refugees in 1948. One member of my family, in particular, whom I saw in Cairo in those years, was very active in Arab politics, as a Palestinian. This is the period of Nasserism. He was there because Nasser was bringing into Egypt a lot of these revolutionary types from the Arab world. His name was Kamal Nasir, and although he was a Baathi at the time he was also a Nasserite. Later he became a spokesman for the Palestinian movement in Amman in the late 1960s. Then he moved to Beirut, after Black September, and in 1973 he was one of the three leaders assassinated by the Israelis in April of that year – I had seen him that very night actually. So that was going on. But I was largely oblivious of it, in the sense that I was focused on my studies. I got my Ph.D. in 1963 and moved to New York where I took up a position at Columbia in English. Then, too, I was pretty focused on that and writing my first book, on Conrad.

With the emergence of the civil rights movement in the middle 1960s – and particularly in '66–'67 – I was very soon turned off by Martin Luther King, who revealed himself to be a tremendous Zionist, and who always used to speak very warmly in support of Israel, particularly in '67, after the war. In 1968 the Columbia revolution occurred, but I was away for that academic year! It was the revolution I missed. I was like Fabrice del Dongo looking for the Battle of Waterloo. I was on leave at a research centre in the Middle West, and I got a telegram from the President of the University saying, 'There's a faculty meeting on such and such a day.' So I trekked all the way back to Columbia, and when I got there, they wouldn't let me in the meeting, although I was a member of the faculty, because I didn't have an up-to-date ID card. So I stood outside while this momentous event was taking place.

When I returned to Columbia in the fall of '68, I got quite involved in the anti-Vietnam campus activities. Many of the students who had been involved in the revolution were students of mine. But it was the period when the emergence of the Palestinian movement was also occurring. And for the first time in my life I got involved in Palestinian politics, as did some of my family and school friends. A contemporary of mine from Harvard, for example, gave up his position at the University of Washington and went to Amman to become a full-time cadre. He was killed in 1976, during the Lebanese war, in rather obscure circumstances. He was a very important figure in the movement, and there is still a question-mark over who killed him and why. He was the one who introduced me in 1972 to Jean Genet, who was in Beirut. He was the man who took Genet around. He's referred to in Genet's last work, *Prisoner of Love*, as Abu Omar.

Anyway, I went to Amman in 1969 and got involved in the movement – not to stay there, but as an expatriate. I began to write about
politics for the first time in my life, to be published in America, and
to appear on television and radio. This was all in the aftermath of the
'67 war, which was the great event of my political life. I was in Amman
during the summer of 1970 right up until the fighting broke out. I
simply had to go back to my teaching. I was there for the National
Council meeting. (I wasn't a member then. I became a member in 1977.)
That was the first time I ever saw Arafat, in 1970, in Amman. Then,
after Black September, the movement drifted into Beirut. My mother
lived in Beirut, so I would go to Beirut a great deal. That year I married
a Lebanese woman, and for the next twelve years, 1970 to 1982, I was
very involved in Palestinian politics in Beirut, as an expatriate. I always
tried to steer clear of the inter-party fighting. I was not interested. For
a time people thought I was – as indeed I was, in the early days –
sympathetic to the Democratic Front. But I was never a member, and
I never got involved in the disputes between them. Arafat made use of
me, in a way, because I was in America. They came to the United
Nations in '74, and I helped with the speech: I put it into English.

Then, of course, during the Carter Presidency, I was useful to
the movement because some of my classmates were members of the
Administration. They were people I'd gone to school with. One has to
remember that I grew up as an Establishment figure in America. I went
to boarding school, I went to Princeton, I went to Harvard. They were
things I could draw on, although they were frequently misinterpreted
by the Palestinians – some of them, I mean – who thought I 'represented' America. When my book *The Question of Palestine* appeared,
for example, the Popular Front weekly magazine ran a tremendous
attack on me because I was supposed to be a representative of bourgeois this and that – all that formulaic bullshit. In any event, I was
plunged totally into politics, simultaneously with my academic work,
which was going on in parallel. They were joined, in a certain sense,
in the middle 1970s when I wrote *Orientalism*. The book married the
two things I was most interested in: literature and culture, on the one
hand, and studies and analyses of power, on the other. From then, it
continued pretty much unbroken until the autumn of 1991, when I
resigned from the National Council.

Orientalism and Humanism

RP Perhaps we could ask you something about the character of this
marriage of concerns in *Orientalism*. *Orientalism* is often read as a kind
of counter-history of the European literary tradition, an exorcizing of
the political ghost of high literary humanism. On the other hand, the

literary quality of the texts which are criticized politically is emphasized and affirmed. This has led some people to detect an ambivalence towards literary humanism in the work. After all, this is a tradition which not only affirms literary values, but has often gone so far as to identify them with human values. Is there still an ambivalence in *Orientalism* towards literary humanism?

Said Yes. The heroes of the book, insofar as there are heroes (I can't think if there are any heroines, particularly), the heroes are basically the novelists. People like Flaubert, like Nerval, some of whom were poets as well. There is an ambivalence, however. As Orwell said about Salvador Dali, it's possible to be a disgusting human being and a great draftsman, which Salvador Dali was. So you could be an imperialist and an orientalist, and also a great writer. That's really what I'm interested in, the co-existence of these two things. What does one do in the face of that? My own profession has been pretty consistent. The tradition has been to separate them completely, and to say, 'Well, we're not going to talk about this, we're just going to talk about that.' More and more I'm perceived as having become shrill about talking about them together.

RP Isn't the mainstream position rather to *suppress* the politics in the name of the human side?

Said Exactly.

RP It's not really a separation . . .

Said . . . no, it's not separating all the time . . .

RP . . . an overriding, perhaps . . .

Said . . . overriding. Yes. But it is a *form* of separating, in the sense that you won't talk about *this*, because *that's* much more important. I mean, even Raymond Williams, for example – Raymond Williams, as you know, I revere and loved, he was a great man – has this long chapter in *Culture and Society* on Carlyle. How can you read Carlyle the way he did? Even if it was 1950 or whenever. Carlyle wrote *The Nigger Question* in the 1840s, and it was an appalling piece of racist horror. If you look through his work it's everywhere. The same is true of Ruskin. For all that he was a great influence on people like Gandhi and Tolstoy, Ruskin was a profound imperialist. He really thought that England should colonize the world – and actually said so! So it's not a question of looking for it. It's there. You just have to read it. So you're right. The overriding of one discourse by another is what it's all been about. And I'm interested not only in the way the two co-exist, but the way in which you can read the works with these concerns in mind and, by a process of what I call contrapuntal reading, transform the works into the enabling conditions of a decolonizing critique.

This is what I try to do more explicitly in my new book, *Culture and Imperialism*. It becomes possible, for instance, to read *Mansfield*

Park from the point of view of the Antigua plantation of the Bertrams, instead of reading it from the point of view of Mansfield Park. And we can see in that reading the origins not only of the slave revolt in Santo Domingo, but the whole tradition of Caribbean writing that comes out of it: the work of C. L. R. James and Lamming and Eric Williams. At this point, in my opinion, *Mansfield Park* becomes an even more interesting novel, even greater for containing within itself this possibility of reaccommodating it to something else, to another kind of reading, to a different interest. It becomes part of another trajectory, which is not that of the English novel. It becomes part of the Caribbean thing.

RP Yet *Mansfield Park* remains the novel to read. In other words, you stick with the canonical works.

Said Yes, of course, because I'm culturally very conservative. There are good books, and there are less good books.

RP But there could be several reasons for that. One could say that these books are the books in which certain historical experiences are most significantly sedimented, and put forward a purely strategic defence of them: these are the books which constitute the canon in this culture, and so this is the place we're going to start to unravel it. But you want to say something rather stronger than that it's a strategic starting place?

Said Yes. *Mansfield Park*, while not my favourite Austen novel, is a remarkable piece of work in its own right. That's where the stakes are highest, in the argument from quality. Because Austen was profoundly implicated in her own society, or a segment of it, it enabled her to see – by virtue of that very limited vision – the necessity of an empire. In my opinion, in an uncompromising way. And that is consistent; despite the fact that Jane Austen has been reclaimed by feminists. The feminism of Fanny Price in *Mansfield Park* is totally untroubled by the slavery and by the sugar plantation. I think one has to note that.

RP But is the quality of the book intrinsically connected to the possibility of its contrapuntal reading?

Said I think so, but it would obviously require more than just asserting it to prove this sort of thing. One doesn't have time to do everything. Take *Heart of Darkness* as another example. *Heart of Darkness*, whatever you think about it politically, is *the* novel about Africa. Many African novelists, including Chinua Achebe, who attacked it so, felt the need to engage with it. Not because it's a racist text, but because it is the most formidable work of the imagination by a European about Africa. It has that quality. It's strategically central because it has that quality. The same is true of *The Tempest*. And what one should add at this moment is the word 'pleasure'. It's not just strategy, it's not just quality, but it is a work in which one can take aesthetic pleasure. Perhaps for some of those reasons, but also because it's a wonderful

counterpunctual → punctuated
different
Thomas J had 8 slaves
but how does that

70   Edward Said

book to read. I don't by any means put down or denigrate or minimize the role of the enjoyment of the work. One of the arguments I make in my new book about such works as *Kim* – why they're so important by the end of the nineteenth century – is that Kim, the character, is an instrument for Kipling to enjoy being in India. Nevertheless, you can't remove from that the imperial quality: that he's there in the service of the British Empire. In the end, he becomes a loyal servant in the Great Game. But up until that point the major quality, I think, of *Kim* for Kipling is enjoyment – a certain kind of imperial pleasure.

RP The imperial pleasure is to be able to move across boundaries. So isn't it a pleasure that's intrinsically politically implicated?

Said True, but other people can also move across boundaries. You'd be surprised. What is interesting is that Kipling is enjoying the pleasures of the Empire in such a way that he is completely blind to what is taking place at the time: namely, the emergence of an Indian national movement. He is blind to this other factor, this other element, forming, emerging, and ultimately overcoming the Empire.

RP One could say that the subtleties of the text are precisely where it's not blind to the emergence of the national movement.

Said There are two places in the novel where Kipling talks about changes in India; most of the time he represents a changeless India. One of them is the episode with the old soldier about the Great Mutiny. And he represents it as a temporary madness that came over the Indians. So he saw it, he transformed it into something else, and off he went. He saw it, but he didn't take note of it – as what it was. The second place is later on, when one of the women, the widow of Shamlegh, says that we don't want these new English people who are coming. (It's a reference to the educated young colonial hands, like Forster's Ronnie Heaslop, twenty-five years later.) We prefer the old style. There is a sense in which, according to Kipling, the Indians prefer traditional orientalists, like Colonel Creighton. So he registers a sense of what the Indians may want, but he doesn't linger over it, and he transmutes it into something else, and off he goes. I don't think there are any other subtleties there, of that sort, that openly refer to the political situation.

RP So it's an opposite example to *Mansfield Park*? There you were saying there's a place in the text from which you can reread the text, but here there isn't another place.

Said No, there is another place. There is a national movement. For example (it's an important detail), this old soldier who was in the English Army, whom Kim and the Lama visit, is described by Kipling as revered in his village. Now, to my way of thinking, given my own background, somebody like that who collaborated is very likely *not* to be revered. He's likely to be an outcast. So one focuses on that.

RP *Orientalism* drew upon a Foucauldian perspective, but that was framed by a Gramscian theory of hegemony. Are there not great differences and tensions between these respective theorizations of power?

Said Very much so.

RP Have you continued to maintain that dual perspective?

Said No. I won't say I abandoned Foucault, but I'd say I'd gotten what there was to be gotten out of Foucault by about the time *Discipline and Punish* appeared, in the mid-1970s. The discovery I made about Foucault, about which I wrote in a small essay called 'Foucault and the Imagination of Power', was that, despite the fact that he seemed to be a theorist of power, obviously, and kept referring to resistance, he was really the *scribe* of power. He was really writing about the victory of power. I found very little in his work, especially after the second half of *Discipline and Punish*, to help in resisting the kinds of administrative and disciplinary pressures that he described so well in the first part. So I completely lost interest in his work. The later stuff on the subject I just found very weak and, to my way of thinking, uninteresting.

I was one of the first in America to teach Gramsci, but there are problems in teaching and talking about Gramsci. First of all, the English translation of the *Prison Notebooks* was based on a corrupt text, and conveyed a very false impression. Even when I was working on *Orientalism* I discovered mistakes in it. Secondly, and perhaps more importantly, since it's now possible to read a very good text – the Gerratana four-volume critical edition of the *Prison Notebooks* with a huge apparatus – Gramsci was an inveterate note-writer. He never wrote a consistent piece, except the *Southern Question*, which I make great use of in my new book. It's very hard to derive from Gramsci's work a consistent political and philosophical position. There's a bit of this, a bit of that – mostly, I think, in the tradition of Vico and Leopardi, a kind of Italian cosmopolitan pessimism; along with his tremendous involvement in the Italian working-class movement. But beyond that, methodologically it's very difficult to 'use' him.

RP The concept of hegemony is of use, perhaps . . .

Said Yes, it has a kind of gross fascination, a gross applicability, which I still make use of. But as to exactly what it means . . . ? Its most interesting quality is the idea of mutual siege. Hegemony and what is required to mount a counter-hegemonic movement. But that can't be done theoretically; it has to be part of a large political movement, what he called an ensemble. That I find tremendously useful. But beyond that it's difficult to make instrumental use of him.

RP In left political culture, there have been at least two quite different uses of Gramsci. One based on a cultural reading of him, the other on what one might call the Turin Gramsci, which is about organic intellectuals, working-class organizations, etc. Are you drawing on both of these?

Said I think one has to. For example, in the *Southern Question*, he draws attention to the role of somebody called Gobetti, who was a kind of northern intellectual who became a southern activist. What that's all about is overcoming political and geographical divisions between states, between actualities. What Gramsci was doing was improvising in a highly particularized local situation (Italian politics in the early 1920s) in order to put together a counter-hegemonic movement of some sort. That's what interests me most about him. In my opinion, the central thing about Gramsci's thought, which hasn't really been focused on enough, is that it's basically geographical. He thinks in terms of territories, in terms of locales, which is tremendously important to me. Maybe I got it from Gramsci. I was struck by the difference between Gramsci, with his focus on geography, and Lukács's focus on temporality, where the Hegelian tradition is so strong. The materialist tradition, the pessimistic materialist tradition in Italy, is all about place. It's tremendously undogmatic, tremendously unabstract. You can always find applications to the Italian situation. Most of the theoretical stuff that one reads in left periodicals today – and for the last ten years, maybe more – is so vague, so out of touch with any political movement of any consequence.

RP The way you're talking about Gramsci here seems to be in tension with the kind of things you were saying earlier in relation to Austen, about the qualities of the humanist literary tradition.

Said Why? Gramsci was a literary humanist. His training was in philology and he was passionately interested in Italian and other forms of literature. He read omnivorously. I think there's been a mistake of putting in opposition the humanistic and the political, or radical, or whatever. There's a much longer tradition of the two feeding off each other. If you look at Thompson's *The Making of the English Working Class*, for example, running throughout are example after example of people like Blake, of poets and writers, of the radical movements' use of Shakespeare. I don't think there's this necessary opposition, which goes back, in my opinion, to some phony or factitious Althusserian opposition. It's possible to imagine a literary humanism that is not mandarin, disembodied, or scornful of politics. One can see it actually very much involved in politics. There's a whole tradition of Caribbean writing which, as C. L. R. James says, never had any other background. We're not talking about Africa, we're talking about the Caribbean – it's a transported population. This is its background: precisely these Western humanistic – and political – ideas. So it doesn't trouble me, what you call this tension.

RP Foucault and Gramsci provided you with alternative theoretical approaches to literary objects that go beyond certain methodologically narrow stances towards the text. They make different kinds of

theoretical bridge between texts and their contexts, readings and practices, etc. However, when you come to reject the Foucauldian position
because of its problematic, all-pervasive view of power, and you say
that Gramsci is to be read only tactically – he doesn't give you a
theoretical framework – this seems to open up something of a methodological vacuum. Do you worry about this? Or do you think that other
people are worrying too much about having the right theoretical framework?

Said Yes, I think so. Theory has become a substitute. From my perspective,
theory is really not interesting as a subject in and of itself – to write
endlessly refined accounts of some theory or other. (I make exceptions.
Adorno strikes me as interesting for his own sake, for reasons that none
of the books on Adorno have ever touched, namely because of his
grounding in music. That's what's great about Adorno. Not so much
what he has to say about administered society, or the conquest of
nature.) But what's happened, in the years since I wrote *Beginnings* in
the early 1970s, is that theory has become a subject in and of itself. It
has become an academic pursuit of its own. And I am totally impatient
with it. Why? Because what has been neglected in the process is the
historical study of texts, which to me is much more interesting. Firstly,
because there are many more opportunities for genuine discovery; and
secondly, because political and cultural issues can be made much clearer
in terms of comparable issues in our own time. The question of oppression, of racial oppression, the question of war, the question of human
rights – all these issues ought to belong together with the study of
literary and other forms of texts; as opposed to the massive, intervening,
institutionalized presence of theoretical discussion.

Orientalism and Feminism

RP Sticking with *Orientalism*, one critic, Jane Miller, in *The Seductions
of Theory*, has pointed to the way in which you use all those terms
with feminine associations in the discussion of *Orientalism*, and they
are critical terms. Feminism does have a very ambiguous presence in
the book here.

Said Yes, it does. There's no question about it. What I was doing in
Orientalism, twenty years ago when I was writing it, was pointing out
two things: the extraordinary degree to which the Orient had become
feminized by male writers in Europe; and the way in which the women's
movement in the West was hand in glove with the imperialist movement.
It was not a deterrent. It's only very recently – I would say in the last
four or five years – that the questions of race and gender have been
joined, in a historical and theoretical way – as opposed to just gender.
That's an ongoing discussion, which at the time of *Orientalism* I didn't

feel to be a part of the subject that I was dealing with. I think Miller is absolutely right, but it's very interesting that those critiques of *Orientalism* which are now being made were not made then! What is the role of feminism in the orientalism of a field like music or anthropology, for example? It's very complicated, very troubling, and it's only just come up: I would say in the last three or four years, in discussions at the American Anthropological Association, and various other places. The engagement's only just begun.

RP Recent feminist scholarship directly related to *Orientalism* has supported either a cultural nationalist position or a women's rights position. What do you make of these kinds of arguments?

Said For me, they've become very interesting recently, in the last year. Just looking at the Middle East, there's been a sudden efflorescence of quite complex and interesting work on, for example, women's role in Islam and Islamic society. A new book by Leila Ahmad, which was published by Yale three or four months ago, has not yet received a single review in the USA. Nobody wants to touch it, it's too complicated, quite a troubling view of the whole question. A mass of material is now coming out. In the past we had Nawal al-Saadawi and a few others. But very little. Then of course there are the anthologies – *Let Women Speak*, *Islamic Women Speaking* – and the translation of women's texts from the part of the world I know best – the Islamic and Arab world. However, most important of all for me are not these theoretical questions, but the emergence here and there of a serious, politically effective, women's movement. That's what it's all about in the end. There is a movement and there is a literature now in the Middle East itself as part of the general struggle against the status quo – which is appalling – in places like Saudi Arabia, Algeria, Tunisia, Lebanon, and, from my point of view, especially in Palestine. The role of women in the Intifada is extraordinarily avant garde. So the situation is changing. It's very different from what it was ten years ago, certainly twenty years ago. And for me it's mainly interesting because of the oppositional quality of the women's movement, asserting a set of rights for women essentially denied them by authorities who purport to use the arguments of the Sharia, the Quran . . .

RP Do you feel that you've taken on board these kinds of discussion in your new book?

Said Well, I was very interested. But the literature is still small. You get into another problem: what is the relationship between the women's movement and nationalism? In the early days of the national movement in places like Indonesia, India, Egypt, where there were pioneering women's movements, these were basically nationalist movements. They were thought of as part of the general struggle against the white man. I had a striking illustration of the difference between that and the present movement when last year I went to South Africa. I was invited by the University of Cape Town to give a lecture called The Academic Freedom Lecture. Because of the boycott, I had to be cleared by the ANC, which I was, and I gave a seminar at the ANC headquarters and at various other places. In Johannesburg, the first talk I gave was at an Islamic centre in Linasia, which is an Asian township, mostly Muslim. I gave a talk about Palestine, which is what they wanted to hear about. Then I was told, 'We've listened to you, now you listen to us.' Which I thought was a fabulous notion, since usually visitors give a lecture and leave. So I heard somebody who spoke about schooling, about legal changes, violence, prison conditions, etc. There was a woman who stood up, whose name I'll never forget, Rohanna Adams: a Muslim name and a Christian last name – fantastic. She was the only one not to use the *Bismil-rahimrahmanulrahim*, which is the statement of faith which Muslims use, and which in South Africa and throughout the Islamic world is some-times a revolutionary, sometimes a reactionary, thing to say. In the former case, you're saying, 'Islam is my guide against you, the oppressors, apartheid,' etc. In places like Saudi Arabia it means loyalty to the king. In Algeria it was used against the French: Islam as a political force. She was the only one not to do that. It was her way of not getting sucked into the struggle against apartheid again. She said, 'All right, we're struggling against apartheid, but there's still the problem of women. You haven't addressed it, any of you.' (Pointing to them all, accusingly.) 'You try to put us to one side,' and indeed they did. They had the hall arranged so that the women were on one side and the men on the other – talking against apartheid. She said that we have to deal with this.

So, it's a completely different type of women's movement where there's a veering off from nationalism. There's a general discovery – and the women's movement is one of the places where this discovery has occurred – that nationalism has become the catch-all for the *oppression* by the new class of minorities: women, religious and ethnic groups, and so on and so forth. The great virtue of the women's movement in the Occupied Territory in Palestine is that it's not only against the Israelis, but against the so-called Islamic Arab oppression of women. But it's only beginning now to do that. It's changing.

After *Orientalism*

RP Our final question about *Orientalism* concerns your relation to some of the work that it provoked, which goes under the heading of 'colonial discourse theory'. People often identify *Orientalism* as the founding text of a new theoretical genre. But that genre is now frequently articulated in terms of poststructuralist theory, which is quite different in many ways from the theoretical assumptions and practices of your book.

Said Absolutely.

RP It is also associated, at times, with a political tendency with which, rather surprisingly, you have occasionally been associated by your critics: 'orientalism in reverse', or a simple inversion of the hierarchical relationship between the West and its other. What these two things have in common is a fixation on the binary opposition between the West and its 'other', and a tendency to homogenize both categories, thereby losing any kind of historical or geo-political specificity: in the first case, by refusing to go beyond the pure negativity of the deconstructive stance; in the latter, by politically lumping together all kinds of very different colonial relations. What is your view of these developments?

Said Where I think *Orientalism* was useful was in those works that looked at the cultural component of forms of domination as giving rise to Africanist, Indianist, Japanesist, etc. types of discourses; as having, in a very narrow sense, played an important constitutive role in talking about those places. You could no longer look at, say, descriptions by nineteenth-century explorers of Africa as if they were just seeing what they saw. There was the notion of a collaborative enterprise having to do with the domination of a region. *Orientalism* gave rise to studies of that sort, which I think were salutary. However, it also gave rise to a bad thing, which I didn't intend, and which I thought I had dealt with, but obviously didn't: the problem of homogenization. For example, in the Arab world I'm read by many people as a champion of Islam, which is complete nonsense. I wasn't trying to defend Islam. I was simply talking about a very specific form of activity: representation. The problem then becomes (as some have suggested): you didn't say what the true Orient really was. So what I try to do in my new book (which I didn't do in the other one) is to talk about not only imperialism, but also decolonization, and the movements that emerged from the Third World – all kinds of opposition and resistance.

There is a focus on what I view as the opposition within the nationalist movements – nationalism versus liberation. There's nationalism which leads to the national bourgeoisie, separatist, statist, national security: the problem of the pathology of the Third World state. But there's always the opportunity for the alternative, what I call liberation. 'There's room for all at the rendez-vous of victory' (C. L. R. James quoting Césaire) is a very important phrase for me. It's impossible to talk about the sides of the opposition between oriental and occidental separately. I talk about what I call overlapping areas of experience. The whole point is that imperialism was not of one side only, but of two sides, and the two are always involved in each other. That's where the contrapuntal method comes in. Instead of looking at it as a melody on top and just a lot of silly accompaniment down here, or silence, it's really like a polyphonic work. In order to understand it, you have to have this concept of overlapping territories – interdependent histories, I call them. That's the only way to talk about them, in order to be able to talk about liberation, decolonization, and the integrative view, rather than the separatist one. I'm totally against separatism.

As for orientalism in reverse, there's a literature on this throughout the Islamic world – 'Occidentosis': all the evils in the world come from the West. It's a well-known genre that I find on the whole extremely tiresome and boring. And I've separated myself from it and from what I call nativism. I'll give you a perfect example of it. In 1962 or 1963, Soyinka, an advanced intellectual, publishes a withering critique of the great nativist concept of negritude. He attacks Sengor, saying that Sengor's idea is really a way of giving in to the concept of the inferior black man. It's the other half of the dialectical opposition. Excellent. In 1991, in his own magazine, *Transition*, which has been re-established in America with Skip Gates, he writes a tremendous attack on the African political scientist Ali Mazrui, who is a Muslim from Kenya. The essence of the attack on Ali Mazrui is that he is not a pure African. He's an Islamicised and Arabized African. So the integrative liberationist African, twenty years later, in Nigeria, has become a nativist, attacking a man for not being black enough! – the man who had attacked negritude. Those reversals are part of the political situation.

The same thing operates in the Salman Rushdie case. In the Islamic world I've been vociferous in attacking the banning of the book. It's the result, firstly, of the absence of any secular theory of any consequence that is capable of mobilizing people, that is understandable by the people who are laying their lives on the line; and secondly, of the absence of organization. There is no effective secular organization, anywhere, in the fields in which we work, except the state. I mean secular political organization. That's part of the failure which I lament so much. So there is this tremendous thing about authenticity and ethnic particularity. The politics of identity is the problem: the failure to take account of, and accept, the migratory quality of experience; that everybody is a migrant or an exile. In England, for example, the people who have been most vociferous against *The Satanic Verses* are migrants who want to assert their authenticity in an environment which has been basically hostile to them. Rather than saying, 'Our experience is very much like that of the Palestinians, very much like that of the Bangladeshis'; instead of seeing it as something beyond the binary oppositional thing, 'us versus them', and therefore being able to see it in different terms, there's this obsession about returning to yourself: only in the community, and the purer form of the community, is my salvation – which is, I think, a form of perdition. It's the end of the best things about our civilization, and it's something that I completely oppose. The marginalization, the ghettoization, the reification of the Arab, through orientalism and other processes, cannot be answered by simple assertions of ethnic particularity, or glories of Arabic, or returning to Islam and all the rest of it. The only way to do it is to get engaged, and to plunge right into the heart of the heart, as it were. That's the only answer; not these retreats.

Intellectuals and their Constituencies

RP The idea of secularity plays an important role in your work, particularly as a way of defining intellectual practice. Do you think the term 'secular intellectual' bears enough critical force in the current situation? It seems an almost nineteenth-century category, insofar as it sets up the oppositional role of the intellectual solely in terms of a division between the theological and the secular. Secularity seems to define a space, an intellectual space which is oppositional to those who won't allow you to occupy it, but inside the secular space many different oppositional positions would seem to be possible. Is there a specific oppositional content here beyond the secularity?

Said As you said, it goes back to the secular versus the religious. That's clear. And the space is the space of history as opposed to the space of the sacred or the divine. The second point I take from Gramsci. He wrote a letter, I think it was in 1921, where he says that the great achievement of his generation, partly acting under the aegis of Croce, was that they were involved in the conquest of civil society, taking it away from mythological ideas of one sort or another: he called it the secular conquest of civil society. What interested me was that he also makes the point that the conquest is never over. You keep having to reappropriate as much as possible, which is otherwise going to be taken back. It's a constant re-excavation of public space. Beyond this, we have to describe functions of the secular intellectual. (I don't want to get into the whole question of general versus specific, which is, I think, a phony set of categories invented by Foucault. I reject that.)

Instead, I prefer various functions, of which one, for example, is bibliographical: where the role of the secular intellectual, in opposition, is in relation to approved sources and documentation. The role of the secular intellectual is to provide alternatives: alternative sources, alternative readings, alternative presentation of evidence. Then there is what I call an epistemological function: the rethinking of, let's say, the whole opposition of 'us' versus the Islamic world, or 'us' and Japan. What does 'us' mean in this context? What does 'Islam' mean in this context? I think only intellectuals can fulfil these functions, in opposition, that is to say, in contravention of the approved *idée reçue*, whatever that happens to be. Then I see a moral function, a dramatic function:

the performance in particular places of a type of intellectual operation that can dramatize oppositions, present the alternative voice, and so on. So it's by no means an open category. It encompasses a plurality of particular things and activities.

RP So the secular intellectual is inherently critical and oppositional? Yours is a Sartrean position ...

Said Yes, exactly.

RP ... but not so close to Gramsci, where the distinction between 'traditional' and 'organic' intellectuals is central?

Said No, I think it is. Part of the problem is that the categories of organic and traditional intellectuals in Gramsci are fantastically unclear, and difficult to make clear. The categories are simply not stable categories. At one time you could say that Matthew Arnold was an organic intellectual. When he wrote *Culture and Anarchy* in 1869, he had an affiliation with a particular class. But by the end of the century, he had become a traditional intellectual. People read his work as a kind of apology for culture, without any connection to anything except the Church.

RP But with Gramsci, one has the sense of a particular audience; that he is addressing a specific audience, an ideal audience, even.

Said Yes, all of this has to do with an audience, when I talk about a dramatic function. The difference is that I feel we all have different audiences in different constituencies. Just performing acts of routine solidarity, or mindless loyalty, strikes me as not interesting, not important. Although there may be a time for it. The great problem in essentially administered societies, the Western democracies, is precisely the drowning out of the critical sense. That has to be opposed by the secular intellectual and the critical sense revised for various audiences, various constituencies.

RP This question of intellectuals and their constituencies has been raised quite acutely in the American academy in recent years in ways that relate directly to some of the issues we have discussed regarding the reception of *Orientalism*: namely, in the debates about political correctness and the canon. These are debates about exclusion, about boundaries, about what is to be excluded and what included. The position you have taken in these debates looks like a fairly traditional liberal humanist one, of opening up the space, including more texts, but defending canonicity. There are two questions here. The first is that if the way the state works culturally is through exclusion (as you suggest), can you really expect the existing state to open itself up to all these things? The pure liberal state is a fiction of political theory. The second question derives from a piece you wrote in the *THES* where you ask: 'Who benefits from levelling attacks on the canon?' and reply: 'Certainly not the disadvantaged person or class, whose history, if you bother to read it at all, is full of evidence that popular resistance to injustice has always derived immense benefits from literature and culture *in general*, and very few from invidious distinctions between ruling class and subservient cultures.' This is a strong defence of the oppositional political possibilities of 'great texts'. But are such distinctions *always* invidious?

Said I've never felt the canon to be imposing a set of restrictions on me. It never occurred to me that in either reading or teaching the canon I was like a servant at work in the orchard of some great ruling-class figure who employed me to do that. I took it as requiring a certain kind of attention, a certain kind of discipline. Because I didn't feel that restriction, I felt the whole question of the canon – whether it was raised by its defenders or its opponents – to be a very limited one. Secondly, everything I said in that article, and thereafter, concerned not the role of the canon in the state, in the context of the state, but in the university. Now, in my view, the university is one of the last quasi-utopian spaces in modern society. And if it becomes a place for displacing one set of categories in order to put in their place another set of categories, if we're going to read aggressively one set of texts that were forbidden in the past and that are now possible, and we're going to forbid the texts that we read in the past in order to read these texts, I'm against the practice. That's not the answer. In America, the vogue might be for Afrocentrism to replace Eurocentrism. In the Islamic world it is to not read Western texts in order to read Islamic texts. I don't have to make that choice. If that's what it's all about, I'm off. I'm ag'in them both. Just as I'm against William Bennett and Bernard Lewis, and all these who keep telling us that we should only read Homer and Sophocles, I'm against the other ones who say, you'll only read texts by black people.

The question is: Are there open categories? That's really your question. I think there are. But they're not out there, they're what you do. That's what it's all about. It's not about somebody saying: 'OK, Said, you can do anything you like.' That's not interesting. What is, is what you do in your individual practice as a teacher, a writer, an intellectual. What are the choices you make? Now, if your attitude is venerative, then that's stupid. I'm against that. I've spent a lot of time trying to show the limitations of that. If, on the other hand, your attitude is critical, I think that's what education is all about – to instil a critical sense, a kind of nasty, demanding, questioning attitude to everything that's put before you. But that by no means exempts you in the end from making judgements, from deciding what is good versus what is better, what is excellent, what is lousy. Questions of taste are very important. I don't derive the same pleasure reading a novel by a great novelist and a political pamphlet. It's a different kind of thing. So in the end it's not the categories that are open, it's the possibilities of political and intellectual work that are relatively open, if one knows how to take advantage of them.

RP Can we return to your own position as a Palestinian working and living in the USA? In the introduction to a discussion with Salman Rushdie about your book *After the Last Sky*, you talked about the dangers of being a 'cultural outsider'. Is that how you see yourself, as a cultural outsider?

Said Yes, I do, without necessarily feeling alienated, if you see what I mean. You could be an outsider, and become more of an outsider, and cultivate your own garden, feel paranoia, all the rest of it. I've never felt that. I've felt discriminated against, but I've never felt that my situation was hopeless; that I couldn't do something to lessen my feelings of marginality. I've never lacked for opportunities to speak and write. Sometimes it hasn't been very good. A couple of years ago I was under a death threat, when some group was trying to kill me. I had to change the way I lived. And it's been very hard for me constantly to be on the defensive in a public situation, in the media, or even socially, in a place like New York, where people look at me and say, 'Oh yes, PLO terrorist.'

RP Has that got worse since the Gulf War?

Said No, it's pretty much the same. Just before the Gulf War, there was a horrific attack published in *Commentary* called 'The Professor of Terror' – it was completely libellous – which tried to prove that I plotted the murder of Jewish children and all this sort of thing. It was clearly reckless, designed to provoke me into starting a libel suit, which would tie me up for ten years, and prevent me from doing anything else. So I didn't even reply. Those things happen all the time. But you go on, and that's important. In the Arab world, I feel alienated for political reasons. I haven't been to Jordan or Lebanon in over ten years, for reasons that are entirely political. Most of these places have changed beyond recognition. So my own past is irrecoverable, in a funny sort of way. I don't really belong anywhere, but I've resolved that that's the way it is. It's OK. I don't mind so much. You don't have much choice

Palestine, Politics and the Gulf War

RP Is it this sense of alienation from the Arab world that led you to resign from the National Council?

Said I began to be dissatisfied with the tendencies of the Palestinian movement, in particular the PLO, to which I've always been loyal as an overall political authority, several years ago. During the summer of 1991, I was very involved in the preparations for the Madrid Conference. I knew a lot of the people on the West Bank, and since

America became central, it was thought that my input would be useful. I thought the emphasis in the Arab world, and above all in the Palestinian movement, on the United States, which was the last super-power, was scandalous, a slavish kind of fawning, almost desperate, cap-in-hand, 'Help us, we rely on you', etc. When the United States has been the enemy of our people! I thought it was scandalous. It was very confusing to people, this sudden tilt towards America after the Gulf War. Because of the stupidities of what the PLO did during the Gulf War, there was a sudden dropping in the lap of America and accepting everything that they wanted, openly saying 'Only America can rescue us!' It confused people a great deal. They suddenly thought, 'What are we struggling about?' What happened after Madrid was that the situation on the West Bank and Gaza got *worse*, and it's getting worse every day. I was also unhappy with the Mafia-like quality of the PLO, and I thought that Arafat, whom I've always been loyal to – he's a friend – I thought that his tenure had been too long. It's not been good for us. I began my critique in Arabic about three years ago, in 1989. They don't know where they're going. It's too in-grown.

RP Inevitably, perhaps?

Said Perhaps. But it's also important for independents, such as myself, to say openly what the problems are. One last point I want to make is that talking about negotiations over the West Bank and Gaza really didn't affect me in a way, because I'm not from the West Bank and Gaza. I'm from what used to be called West Jerusalem. And there was no role forecast for those of us who are exiles. Four million Palestinians (many of them stateless) have no place to go. There are many hundred thousands in Lebanon, Syria, etc. They're not included in these nego-tiations. It's just about residents on the West Bank and Gaza. So it's their problem. Fine, they're doing a great job – let them go on doing it. And the third reason I stopped, which was very important to me, is that since I discovered I have an insidious and chronic blood disease, I decided I would like to visit Palestine. I tried to go once in 1988 and Shamir refused entry, because I was a member of the National Council. So the resignation makes it possible for me to do that. And in fact I'm going the day after tomorrow. I'm on my way, for the first time in almost forty-five years.

RP When you go to the Arab world, do you see this as some kind of returning home, or is America now your home?

Said No, I'm totally at home in both places. But I'm different, in a way. In the American context, I speak as an American and I can also speak as a Palestinian. But in neither case do I feel that I belong in a proprietary sense or, let us say, in an executive sense, to the central power estab-lishment. I'm in the opposition in both places. And of course it means quite different things. If you're in opposition in Palestine, in the

Palestinian context, it means that you support and help shape an emerging national consensus. I played, I thought, a relatively important role in 1988 at the National Council meeting in Algeria where I helped to draft some of the statements and involved myself in a lot of the discussions, pushing towards recognition of the Israelis (UN resolution 242) by two states, all of that – I was for that, because it seemed to me logical, because we had no ally, no strategic ally, and because I thought it was right. The Soviet representative had absolutely nothing to say. In fact he was very discouraging. He didn't want us to do that. He said, 'Lie low', etc. But I thought it was important to do that. So I did all of that. And as I said, I support the national consensus. On the other hand, I certainly didn't feel it something that I could deny myself. That if I felt something was wrong I should say it, and I said it.

For example, I've felt for almost fifteen, sixteen, seventeen years, that Palestinian policy in the United States is badly organized. The USA is not like an Arab country. It's not even like a European country. And they've taken no steps to deal with that. The important thing becomes how you pursue your criticism. The venue becomes central. I would never speak to a Western press person, because, in that context, it is interpreted as an attack on the national movement, which I wouldn't do. But in the Arabic press, in Arabic, I would do it. But rarely without having spoken to Arafat first. In America I'm totally in the opposition. It's true, in effect, I've become some kind of Mister Palestine to a lot of commentators. But I have never been on television, or in the press, or any sort of forum in America, without always being on the defensive, or in the minority.

I was on a big Sunday morning programme once – I think it was the Brinkley show – and it was one of the key moments of the Intifada. People were getting killed and beaten and all the rest, and they actually showed a tape of it. The first question to me after the tape was: 'When are the Palestinians going to stop terrorism?' But when I give lectures now, political ones, since the Gulf War, and even during the Gulf War, I very rarely get hostile questions. It's quite extraordinary. Opinion has changed so much. The standard official Israeli position has simply nothing to recommend it any more. We've gone all the way, we've recognized them. We've said we want co-existence, we're willing to talk peace. Why then does the occupation continue? Why does the systematic persecution and oppression of Palestinians continue? That's been a tremendous change.

RP Do you think the Gulf War was the turning point?

Said No. During the Gulf War, I took a position which was very much against Saddam, but I was also opposed to American troops. I've always been against Saddam. The only time I ever went to Kuwait was in 1985 and I had a huge semi-public fight with a local luminary who was blathering on about what a great man Saddam was. This was in the middle of the Iran-Iraq War. And I said, 'Saddam's a murderer and a pig and a tyrant and a fascist, and you're criminals, and fools,' and all the rest of it. And they said: 'Ah, we're giving them billions' – and they did, they gave him fifteen billion dollars. And I told them that he was going to be the end of them. During the first weeks after the Gulf Crisis the same luminary called me up and abused me over the phone, because he said people had told him that I had appeared on English television, and I hadn't been strong enough in defence of Kuwait. And I said, 'Of course I've defended Kuwait. I've been opposed to the occupation, I've been opposed to Saddam, but I won't take the position that Saudi Arabia and your morally and politically bankrupt government and the Americans should now send troops in and start a war. There are many moves that can be made before that.' Two weeks later, he wrote a column in the leading Saudi paper, published in London, in which he wrote in Arabic: 'Why I invited the prominent Arab intellectuals to commit suicide.' And he mentioned me. He said, 'Said should commit suicide because he's been a traitor to the Arabs and to Kuwait.'

During the Gulf War, my position was very different from the so-called official Palestinian position, such as it was. Basically, I opposed Iraq, I opposed the depredations of the Kuwaiti regime, I opposed Saudi policy, and I opposed the American position. I opposed the war. But I refused to fall into the position taken by people like Fred Halliday and Hans-Magnus Enzensberger – that in the war between imperialism and fascism you back imperialism. I was against them both. I think that was the honourable and only serious position to take. It could have been taken by more intellectuals in the West, but to their shame – partly because of anti-Arabism and anti-Islam, and the sort of things I talk about in *Orientalism* – they didn't. It's a scandal. It's a great block. What has the war accomplished? Saddam is still there, he's still killing Kurds, Shiites, he's killing everybody. And he may even be supported by the Saudis now. At the same time as they're supporting his overthrow, they're trying to buy him off, as they do everywhere throughout the Arab world.

RP So your position was to maintain sanctions?

Said Yes, to maintain UN sanctions, but also to maintain uniformity and consistency of positions, everywhere, not just with regard to Palestine. What about Cyprus? There are any number of UN resolutions on the Turkish invasion and partition of the country. One of the reasons I was very upset about the US position during the so-called peace process, the Madrid phase, was that it said the Palestinians should strip themselves of their right to representation. No liberation movement in history has ever done that. They nominate. They say: We pick the people, and not you, not the enemy. Secondly, I thought it was a classic mistake, typically imperial, that the United States should make this *its* peace process, with the Soviet Union. You notice – if you look at the letter of invitation to the Madrid Conference – the United Nations is specifically cited as excluded. The United States will oppose any initiative from the United Nations. So suddenly the United States, which had used the United Nations in the Gulf War, had banned it from the peace process! All of these things have to be said.

RP In a television interview with you and Chomsky, during or immediately after the war, you talked about the persistence of orientalist attitudes. At the time, that explanatory framework seemed to miss the precision of the West's economic and military motives. The reference to orientalist discourses appeared almost superfluous in the face of that kind of precision.

Said Maybe I'm overly sensitive to it, but I don't think a war like that could have been fought, paid for by Arabs against other Arabs, with contempt towards the whole procedure of negotiating, without orientalism. This was not a war about aggression or anything like that. It was a war about cheap oil, and only Arabs have cheap oil: that combination has a particular kind of racial tinge to it. Nobody said – certainly not the Americans – that this is Arab oil for the Arabs, not just for the Kuwaiti royal family. These states – Saudi Arabia and Kuwait – are owned by families. There's no state in the world that's designated like Saudi Arabia – it's the House of Saud – they actually own the country. All of these anomalies were only possible, it seems to me, and produced contradictory and lying discourses about justice and aggression and all the rest of it, *because* they're Arab.

The United States has never supported human rights in the Arab world. I made a study of it. Every US position of importance, whether political or economic or military, in the Arab world has always been taken against human rights. They've opposed human rights for Palestinians, they've opposed human rights in the Gulf, they've opposed human rights in places like Syria, and so on and so forth. So I think you can't not talk about what we might call cultural attitudes. There was a kind of contempt. The other discourse – what you call economic and military – is not precise enough without this component. There was a massive campaign on the media in the United States: an anti-Arab and racist campaign, the demonization of Saddam. In many ways, Iraq is the cultural centre of the Arab world. You didn't know that from the television screen, which just showed those smart bombs going in over Baghdad. Saddam is not Baghdad. And to this day, not a word, not even a word about the people killed. This could only have been done with Arabs.

RP Do you think that the American anti-war movement did enough?

Said What anti-war movement? Of course not. I don't think it would have been hard to do it. I think there was a lot of popular ambivalence about the war. The left position was ambiguous. Not enough was made about the human catastrophe visited upon Iraq and the Gulf generally. Not enough was known about it, you see. A leading article in *Foreign Affairs* in December, just as the United States was about to go to war, began: 'Saddam is from a brittle country which has no connection to ideas, books, or culture.' This is a description of the country they're going to war against ... 'camel jockeys' and 'towel heads', whether they're for us or against us. The same kind of scorn was heaped on the Saudis, and they were the 'good Arabs' in this war. This was considered to be a war good for Israel, because Iraq was touted as the country most threatening to Israel. So there was really very little in the way of protest. To call it a movement would be wrong. It could have been a movement.

RP What would it have needed?

Said It would have needed organization. Don't forget, this is the period after the collapse of socialism, of the Left. There is no Left in America, like there is a European Left, or a British Left.

RP The British Left was itself very confused.

Said Well, if you were confused, what about America, where there is no real Left? There are people who are sort of vaguely Left, who are Left by virtue of sentiment and providence – people like Irving Howe, for example, or Michael Walzer – who are great gurus of the Left. Walzer was for the war. He thought it was a just war. The media was completely in cahoots with the government. It was one of the great satanic collaborations between the media and the government. You couldn't get on. Radio, however, was very important during the war, National Public Radio and a few of the national networks carried a lot of stuff. But it doesn't have the power of television. It was a television war.

RP In Baudrillard's terms?

Said What did he say? Probably not.

RP Baudrillard said it was a hyper-real non-event.

Said Good old Baudrillard! For that I think he should be sent there – with a toothbrush and a can of Evian, or whatever it is he drinks.

Interviewed by Anne Beezer and Peter Osborne
London, June 1992

5
Critical Theory in Germany Today
Axel Honneth

Axel Honneth is Professor of Sociology and Philosophy at the University of Frankfurt. He is the author of *The Critique of Power: Reflective Stages in a Critical Social Theory* (1985; English translation, MIT Press, 1991) and *Struggle for Recognition: The Moral Grammar of Social Conflicts* (1992; English translation, Polity Press, 1995) – books which have placed his work at the centre of debates in Germany within the Frankfurt School tradition.

Setting out from Habermas's reorientation of Critical Theory away from the philosophy of consciousness towards a paradigm of linguistically mediated intersubjectivity, Honneth makes three important new moves. First, by returning to the source of the paradigm in Hegel's early work, he recovers the dimension of *struggle* central to its original formulation. Second, reconstructing its legacy in a tradition of social theory which includes Sorel and Sartre alongside Marx and Mead, he restores the connection of *moral* struggle to empirical work in the social sciences. Finally, differentiating between three main forms of recognition in modern societies, he has begun the elaboration of a formal theory of the good life.

RP We'd like to begin with a question about your background. What was it like going through university in Germany in the late 1960s and early 1970s? What were your formative experiences, theoretically and politically?

Honneth I started to study in 1969, after the birth of the student movement, in very conservative surroundings, at the University of Bonn. Neither in philosophy nor in literature (which I studied at that time) was there anything of interest there for someone who had already been influenced by the student movement. In philosophy, a kind of neo-Kantianism was still hegemonic, which was typical of German

universities at the time. It was oriented towards German Idealism in an
enlightened way, but for the most part it was very boring. It had nothing
to do with the questions of the political movements. The same was true
in literature, where a very conventional form of literary history was
prominent. The only point of contact between the two was Gadamer's
hermeneutics. It was the bridge between literature and philosophy in
the University. There was nothing left from the original generation of
the 1950s in Bonn, to which the young Habermas and Karl Otto Apel
belonged. They were both in Bonn as either students or assistants of
Erich Rothacker, who was oriented towards philosophical anthropology, and they learned to combine Heidegger with a certain
anthropological theory there. The early pragmatism of that generation
was born in Bonn, but there was nothing of it left by the time I arrived,
and it was not my reason for studying there. What influenced me at
the beginning was logical positivism. It was the methodological counterpart to Bonn's strange combination of neo-Kantianism, hermeneutics,
and German Idealism; a methodological standpoint from which we
could criticize these boring conservative orientations which we found
at the university. That took a year or two, no longer. The first person
whose work allowed me to build a bridge between my political interests
and what was going on in my theoretical studies was Adorno. Like a
lot of young students in philosophy, I was totally influenced by Adorno.
I had this tendency to just imitate him. It's awful to read now, the
imitation of his language, using arguments which, if you don't really
deepen them, if you don't have the background to place them philosophically, sometimes seem very silly.

At the same time, I wasn't very active in the student movement in
Bonn. The real places for the student movement were Berlin and
Frankfurt, maybe Heidelberg. That's where the interesting and intellectually far-reaching debates were. In Bonn, the student movement didn't
really occur in the classroom, but only through some happenings on
the street. I had no connections to this. I came from a much closer and
much safer world, and I felt quite distanced from it. That changed when
I went to the University of Bochum, which is huge.

RP Which year was that?

Honneth 1971. In philosophy, it's an interesting place because of the
Hegel archive. They are preparing and editing the new Hegel edition,
and they are very careful. The leading figure at that time was Otto
Pöggeler. Being there changed my philosophical orientation in two ways.
Firstly, I could see that there was something in German Idealism which
is not, let's say, simply to be killed by logical positivism. There are
some speculative ideas which we should take much more seriously.
Secondly, I read Habermas for the first time. This was of unbelievable
importance to me because he started out from an immanent critique of

logical positivism, and an immanent critique of what was happening in the conventional German university. If you read some of his early things in *Theory and Practice*, you can see how it was related by way of immanent critique to what was left over from Max Scheler and Nicolai Hartmann, and that kind of German philosophy of the 1920s and 1930s. There was a chance for me to bring my different interests together.

This was also the way I came into contact with Marxism. Maybe that's strange, for a student in a German university at that time to come into contact with Marx via Habermas, and not the other way round. My political orientation had changed insofar as I had become a member of the USOS which is the youth organization of the SPD, and which was quite radical at that time – although not as radical as most of the groups in the student movement. And I had become interested in a critique of capitalism from the standpoint of workers' movements. I began to see how one could formulate philosophical and theoretical questions in such a way that they have a certain relation to these movements. That was a very fruitful experience for me, even though the philosophical debates in Bochum were not relevant to this.

RP What was the reception of Heidegger like in this period? We ask because of the more recent debates about the politics of Heidegger's philosophy. Heidegger's role in German philosophy is obviously much more complicated than these debates suggest. So I wonder, was there any Heideggerian influence?

Honneth As far as I can remember, none at all. Most of us had read Adorno's Heidegger critique, and that was all. The fact that Habermas and Apel had a certain closeness to Heidegger in their early period – and you can see that when you read the very first articles, especially Apel's – was always something very strange for me. We did not even read *Being and Time* then. It was simply outside the debate of the philosophically-oriented members of the student movement.

RP Gadamer wasn't viewed as a Heideggerian?

Honneth No, Gadamer was the big person in Germany philosophy, formulating a hermeneutical position which had, we thought, quite conservative elements. But that was a book we read. One was very familiar with this book. It started to have a very big influence. It was already clear that there was an interesting confrontation brewing between Habermas and Gadamer. Gadamer's hermeneutics on the one side, and the developing theory of Habermas on the other, were the two poles between which we lived.

RP At this time, was Habermas seen to represent an extension of the Frankfurt School tradition?

Honneth No. Not at all. Never during my whole educational career was he ever seen as that.

RP Was Habermas viewed primarily as a philosopher or as a social theorist?

Honneth More or less a social theorist, I would say. The influence of Marxism and critical theory started in sociology. But he had a very hard time, because he was totally isolated from the student movement. He was even seen as an enemy in the circles of the student movement, because of his use of the phrase 'Left fascism'. The movement was becoming more and more orthodox. Around 1973, when I wrote my *Magisterarbeit* (on Habermas, mainly his interpretation of psycho-analysis), the interesting people of my age started to orient themselves towards either communism in the Leninist sense or a certain Maoism. Only a very few people remained unorthodox in the sense that they were simply oriented to the critical theory of the Frankfurt School, or had a strong interest in Krahl. Krahl was a young, intellectually brilliant member of SDS, who combined a strong interest in Hegel with an enormous knowledge of the tradition of Western Marxism – something like a young Lukács in the student movement. He played a very decisive role in all discussions. He died in 1969, but he was an adversary of whom you really took notice. For myself, the move away from philosophy towards sociology was decisive. I started to study sociology, I came into contact with people who did empirical research on the class structure in Germany, and I learned a lot about empirical research.

Two other things should be mentioned. One is the growth of small groups reading *Capital*. I was a member of one of these private groups. It was a very typical event in these years. Everyone who had an interest in Critical Theory and in the critique of capitalism was in one way or another a member of such a group. This was interesting because the group I was in was not too orthodox. We had objections to either the methodology of Marx, or the content of the first volume of *Capital*. The other big experience was the opening up of a whole repressed tradition of Left thinking. I started to read Lukács, I was even influenced by Bloch in a certain way, and Karl Korsch. The unorthodox tradition of Western Marxism was a big influence.

RP Did Althusser have any influence in your *Capital* reading group?

Honneth At that time, no, not at all. That's something I was confronted with for the first time in Berlin. That was the next decisive step in my development. I got an offer to go with Jaeggi to the Free University in Berlin. He had written a book on capital and labour in the Bundes-republik – an empirical study, which was very influential both among the unions and the student movement – and he invited me to go with him to the Institute of Sociology. That was an incredible break in my intellectual development because in Berlin there was a totally different atmosphere. It was overpoliticized in every class.

The Institute of Sociology was very orthodox, in the sense that most of the members believed either in Marx or in some other tradition in a very uncritical way. There were a lot of Leninists there at the time, a lot of people oriented to Maoism, and a growing interest in Althusser. Althusser was someone producing a new form of social theory and it was my luck or my fate, I'm not sure which, that the person I had come to Berlin with decided to establish an Althusser group. This group was totally convinced by Althusserianism. (One has to say that Althusser played a very minor role in Germany.) I had a very hard time because I was already a totally convinced Habermasian, and there were very few of us at that time. We were seen by members of the student movement and the growing parts of orthodox movements as reformists, absolutely reformists, betrayers of the goals of the movements; and for the very few conservative people in the humanities at the Free University we were too left-wing.

So I was in the strange situation of defending my Habermasian approach against a growing belief in Althusser. On the one hand, I was very frightened by these orthodox tendencies, I felt very alone; on the other, I developed a real interest in a critique of Althusserian orthodoxy. It forced me to write an article against Althusser which was strongly attacked by all the other members of the group.[1] That was something like a first chance to formulate my own position. I wasn't an orthodox Habermasian in a strong sense, although everyone took me for one. I already had certain objections against Habermas especially in connection with his notion of work. I had problems with the way he reduced the Marxian notion of work to instrumental action because I was influenced by sociological studies on the experience of work. I always had a feeling that it is a much broader field of experiences than it is possible to reduce to instrumental action.

The critique of Althusser gave me the chance to make my own approach much clearer. At the time, this meant starting out from something like a philosophical anthropology. So I was greatly interested in Marx's early writings. This also had something to do with the early Habermas and the early Apel. I found out that at the Free University, in my own Institute, there were people with a strong interest in philosophical anthropology. I came into contact with them and I started to work with Hans Joas. We wrote a book together on philosophical anthropology. There were some interesting people who were interested in philosophical anthropology. There was Gehlen, a conservative anthropologist, and Plessner, who played a very interesting role. We could connect this with certain tendencies in international Marxism, especially the Budapest School around Agnes Heller and György Marcus. They had a special interest in anthropology via Lukács's development. So I could locate myself in a new and interesting way. I could see that there were certain bridges to developments in unorthodox Marxism, and on the other hand, to developments around Habermas in Frankfurt.

This was a strange point in my intellectual development. I started to come closer to philosophical anthropology at the precise moment at which Habermas became convinced that he had to give it up, for methodological reasons – because the propositions of an anthropology are too strong. They can't be falsified. He switched to the theory of language which was to replace philosophical anthropology in his approach. My own development was in opposition to that. I thought of philosophical anthropology as a very fruitful and helpful tradition. It's a very German tradition. Much later I saw that, in Charles Taylor, for example, there was a similar development. But at that time I took it as a German tradition which had something to do with the early Marx. So my approach was in total opposition to the Althusserians, and to what was happening at that time in the hegemony of intellectual thinkers in Berlin.

RP In turning to the empirical, in a sense Habermas was more in line with the Althusserians: rejecting philosophical anthropology in the name of positive science – not the same positive science, but nonetheless . . .

Honneth Yes, one could say so. I wouldn't formulate it in that way, but I can see that one could say that. The orientation towards social theory, concentrating on the inner logics and mechanisms of development, one could understand it as a development in the same direction that the Althusserians took in concentrating on the late Marx and the inner logic of *Capital*. But I was strongly opposed to this development. At the same time, what was going on politically isolated me from any political move-ment. The youth organization of the SPD became a more and more unfruitful form of orthodoxy – what was called Stamocap theory (State Monopoly Capitalism) – believing in the essentially capitalist character of the state. On the other side of the student movement there was a lot of debate about the importance and the moral legitimacy of terrorism. The colleagues I had were either orthodoxly oriented toward Leninism or, if they were unorthodox, they were oriented towards what I would call an orthodox Adornism. Adorno played a very decisive role at the Free University. But because I had separated from Adorno, via Habermas, I also felt isolated from this kind of thinking: something like a totalizing critique of capitalism, as we know it from Adorno. This approach was used in every field of research, not only in the philosophical debates, but also in the different branches of sociology in which I was working at that time. I had split my work into a philosophical part and a sociological part, doing studies on the experiences of workers' children. I had dedicated a lot of my own work to the socialization processes of working-class youth. This was a very helpful empirical period of my own research and development, but again I felt quite isolated in this area. I was living in different worlds in Berlin. The only shared orientation I had was towards philosophical anthropology.

Critique of Power

RP Perhaps we could move on to talk about some of the positions you adopt in your book *The Critique of Power*. The thing that strikes the British reader immediately is the way you place Foucault in the Frankfurt tradition. Habermas and Foucault are usually constructed in a binary, antagonistic way, whereas your book assumes from the very beginning that Foucault is part of the Frankfurt tradition. Why is this?

Honneth It has to do with my experiences in Berlin. Foucault was read by people who were formerly interested in Adorno. He was taken as a kind of extension of what Adorno did. The interest in poststructuralism came from people who were oriented towards Adorno. They switched from Adorno to Foucault. That was the intellectual situation in which I started to think of a book which would be a critique of the present situation of Critical Theory, taking Foucault as a part of it. I wanted to distance myself from approaches like those of Adorno and Foucault, in order to show that neither has the means or the potentiality to build a social theory which could compete with the complexity of theories like Parsons's and the tradition of Durkheim. That was my interest at that time. It was strongly located in a field of social theory, not so much in philosophy. I wanted to find a way to develop the necessary means to construct a social theory. So I started to give lectures on Adorno, on Foucault, and on Habermas.

RP Could you say something about your understanding of the category of the social here? The book hinges around quite a strong claim that there is no such category as the social in Adorno and Foucault. Now, of course, in one sense that's quite explicit in Adorno in the essay called 'Society', but in other ways it's not so clear. Could you say something about this missing category? At what level is it constructed? Is it a transcendental category, or what?

Honneth It had to do with the influence of philosophical anthropology combined with my growing interest in the French tradition of sociological investigation – Durkheim, but also Lévi-Strauss. I also started to read Bourdieu at that time. I took all these approaches to be investigations into the inner structure of the social – what Durkheim had in mind when he spoke of the collective consciousness, that binding force which is the only power to integrate a society. One could say that I meant what David Lockwood described as social integration as opposed to system integration.

RP And this would be a more differentiated, and more empirically open way of doing what the Marxist category of ideology does, or something like that, would it?

Honneth Yes, but without the immediately negative undertone which the notion of ideology has. Today, I would say it was a very Durkheimian step to concentrate on the social as those mechanisms of social integration which have to do with a certain amount of social consent in a society. I always had the feeling that neither Adorno nor Foucault had the right means to describe these mechanisms.

RP Some people would put Foucault in the Durkheimian tradition of French social theory ...

Honneth Yes, but that's a question of how to interpret Durkheim. If you take Durkheim as someone who was only describing mechanisms of ideological integration, like Althusser, maybe. If you take Durkheim from this side, it is easy to show that Foucault is in the tradition of Durkheim. But I took Durkheim much more from the concept of social consent: we don't have the methodological possibility of separating *a priori* an ideological consent from a true consent. On the other hand, I saw some big advantages in Foucault's approach over Adorno's. I had a very bad feeling about what Adorno had produced in the intellectual atmosphere of the German Left. It was my conviction that his critique of the sociological tradition had cut us off from a fruitful body of work, especially in my Institute. There is a biographical background to this feeling. I had the impression that my colleagues were not really able to read Durkheim or Parsons or Bourdieu, because they had internalized Adorno's critique of ideology. It put them in the position of not taking this approach seriously enough.

RP This leads us to the question of how you conceive your book in relation to what might be called the Frankfurt tradition. Would you now say that Habermas is in that tradition? And are you? At the Walter Benjamin conference in London last summer you were introduced as a member of the third generation of the Frankfurt School, but you immediately denied it by saying that there is no third generation. Is this really so? Alternatively, is there even a second generation?

Honneth On the question of the second generation, I always answer positively. I once wrote an article on the linguistic turn in Critical Theory, quite similar to the article by Wellmer (we both wrote articles separately on the same topic) showing that all the decisive elements of Critical Theory could be saved on a methodologically higher level by Habermas's linguistic turn. That means that the decisive element of Critical Theory, the broad tradition of, let's say, the unorthodox Western Marxist critique of capitalism, is retained.

RP That's much broader than Frankfurt Critical Theory ...

Honneth Yes, that's broader. I would prefer a broader notion of Critical Theory. One that doesn't reduce it to Adorno and Horkheimer, but includes the young Lukács and Korsch. Habermas is still interested in a critique of capitalism as a reified form of social life. That interest is shared with the tradition, but he uses totally different methodological means. From the beginning, I thought this to be a better formulation of Critical Theory than the orthodox one I came to know in Berlin.

The problem with the idea of a *third* generation is that I can't see anyone who will reformulate Adorno's and Horkheimer's critique of capitalism in the horizon of the early Critical Theory. There is a lot of interest again now in Adorno in Germany. But all I see is an increasing interest in aesthetics, and in the critique of identity – an interest in the methodology of philosophy. I don't see a new way of bringing back the critique of capitalism in my generation. Therefore I wouldn't say there is a third generation.

RP But this is to define the third generation in terms of the first, rather than as a development out of the second.

Honneth Yes. This is the other part of my answer. It's difficult to say whether those who are trying to develop an immanent critique of Habermas, bringing some motives of the early tradition back into Habermas, should be thought of as a third generation. The person who is doing that on the highest level is Albrecht Wellmer, who has a certain relation to Adorno, and tries to reformulate certain ideas of Adorno in the framework of Habermas. It's an open question. It really would be a third generation if we were able to reformulate some of the stronger notions of the critique of capitalism which Adorno and Horkheimer had, in a totally new framework, using a lot of Habermas but making the critique of capitalism much stronger. Then one could speak of a third generation.

Moral Struggle and Recognition

RP In the linguistic reformulation of earlier motifs in the critique of capitalism, like reification, in the move away from political economy, there is a much closer relationship to classical liberal thought, in a Kantian mode. Now, one of the things that seems to be distinctive about your own work is an emphasis on the conflictual aspect of communicative action. This picks up some of the non-liberal motifs in Critical Theory, because of the notion of struggle. But it is formulated as moral struggle. Could you say something about this category of moral struggle, specifically in relation to whether the term 'moral' here has primarily Kantian or Hegelian implications?

Honneth To answer the last part of your question first, I would say that it plays in between them. We can see this in all the productive approaches of Critical Theory: it's always an ongoing tension between Kant and Hegel. I would say that the most productive element – one of the most productive elements of the Critical Theory tradition – is to be unable to decide which side you are on here. The notion of moral struggle became more and more important to me in order to criticize the more liberal elements in Habermas. That's one of the backgrounds for it. The theoretical background is an interest in a more Durkheimian reading of Foucault; a reading in which the notion of struggle, which is very decisive for Foucault, is given another interpretation: struggle is *morally* motivated in a very broad way, not only by questions of injustice, but by all forms of disrespect, indignation, and so on. So I think the background for my notion of moral struggle is more Hegel than Kant: they are not only struggles for a just legal order, they are struggles for the recognition of the special value of your own life form. Charles Taylor is going in a quite similar direction. He has just published a book on multiculturalism, which has as a subtitle 'The politics of recognition'. He is making the same step of describing struggles with the help of the notion of recognition. This is a distancing from Habermas, to see in struggle, I would say like Marx, the real productive force in society.

RP In your latest book, *Struggle For Recognition*, you go back once again to the origins of the paradigm shift to an intersubjectivistic theory of recognition – namely, to the young Hegel – in order to question anew the scope and direction of the theory of communicative rationality, and its normative implications. Could you say a little bit about the motivation for this attempt to actualize the insights of the young Hegel anew? In what respect does your attempt to reconstruct a formal theory of the good life differ from Habermas's attempt to offer normative foundations for Critical Theory by means of the concept of communicative rationality?

Honneth The young Hegel is a motivating power for so many people. Everyone who has an interest in a critique of the modern world – the capitalist world – at a certain moment returns to the young Hegel. I really can't describe why that is. Perhaps it is because this young Hegel is very open and very direct, and not so controlled (like the later Hegel) by his own system. The young Hegel is one of the richest thinkers of the last two hundred years. There are romantic motives in him, there are certain influences of Kant in him. Everything is working towards him at a certain tangent. More specific was my conviction, which was influenced by certain studies in Germany, that in the young Hegel we can find a much broader notion of recognition than we can find in the later Hegel, who was used by Habermas. In the young Hegel we can see a threefold conception of recognition: *love*, something like a relation of rights, *legal relations*, and a third dimension which I would call *solidarity*, a word Hegel never used. He wrote *Sittlichkeit*, ethical life, a kind of community of shared values.

In relation to Habermas, this means two things. First, it means that we can ground Critical Theory not in a linguistic theory, but in some form of philosophical anthropology. I'm not sure whether that's the right word or category, but it is a much broader conception of human life than is allowed by linguistic theory. This allows me to bring in disciplines or motives which Habermas is forced to exclude more and more – like psychoanalysis, concentrating on prelinguistic experience, and so forth. So that's the first step, the first difference. The other difference is with reference to the normative foundation of Critical Theory. More and more I have the impression that if you have a broader notion of recognition you also have a broader concept of the normative background of Critical Theory. That's what I call a formal concept of the good. This is working together with certain trends in American philosophy, like Martha Nausbaum, and also some approaches in Germany. In normative questions you don't reduce yourself to the moral standpoint of a just society, but to the formal standpoint of identifying aspects of a good society. My impression is that the concept of recognition allows one to formulate some quite abstract conditions for every form of a good human life. That gives me the hope of reconstructing some of the deep insights of the early Frankfurt School. But in this respect I'm still very unclear, and I have to work on that. The situation is as follows. The early Frankfurt School never had anything like a normative theory. There were, without question, some normative insights, some normative criteria, which they used to criticize capitalist society. But they never tried to work this normative background out in reference to what was going on in ethical theory, or in moral theory, at that time. You can find Horkheimer's article on morality, but there is no explicit contribution to the question of the normative background of Critical Theory there.

RP One thing that is striking about your recent article on the young Hegel[2] is that in constructing an opposition between a Hobbesian/ Machiavellian tradition of self-preservation and the Hegelian concept of recognition you connect up with the early Horkheimer's book on the bourgeois philosophy of history, which is very much concerned with this tradition of self-preservation. (Think also of the centrality of the concept to *Dialectic of Enlightenment*.) So in a sense you are tracing the problem of a lack of normative foundations right back to there.

Honneth It was always my conviction that it would be easier to go back to the early Horkheimer than to the middle period Adorno.

RP Habermas himself begins by trying to go back to the early Horkheimer. There seems to be a whole series of overlapping returns here . . .

Honneth Going back to early Hegel, going back to early Horkheimer, yes.

RP Going back to early Habermas!

Honneth Yes. Maybe there is a systematic background for this: the early stage of a thinker is the methodologically more naive one, but the theoretically more productive one; the early stage of a thinker is the richest

Honneth and normative forms of life

one in the sense that the most normative and creative ideas are formulated in a direct way in the first period. After that, there are certain tendencies to the systematic reduction of these early insights. I hope that it is possible via the reconstruction of the formal theory of the good, to make clear the normative background of the early Frankfurt School, which could then be redescribed in terms of normative criteria about the conditions of a good life for human beings. I would guess that, for example, in *Minima Moralia* you can find a negativistic form of such a theory. Adorno would like to show, via a negativistic method, what forms of human life exist, from which we can all see that they do not belong to a good form of human life; and then via this negativistic route to show indirectly some preconditions of a good human life. If that is possible, it would mean that I would have a broader, but methodologically *more disputable* foundation for a critical theory; not so universalizable as the normative criteria Habermas is looking for, by reducing all normative criteria to the question of a just society. That is a difference, a difference from the liberal tradition. To go back to philosophical anthropology instead of linguistic theory means to have a broader approach to certain transcendental features of human beings. The only anthropological propositions Habermas would maintain nowadays are those describing mechanisms of understanding in human beings via language. Going back to philosophical anthropology is a necessary step if you want to have a stronger foundation, a broader foundation, for the normative critique of our present society.

RP But isn't there a problem here? Any philosophical anthropology will already have normative assumptions about the most appropriate form of human existence built into its basic theoretical orientation. You would seem to be involved in a circle. Can philosophical anthropology ever be foundational in the way in which Habermas wants universal pragmatics to be?

Honneth This is a very difficult question. I think that philosophical anthropology has to be understood in the same falsifiable way as universal pragmatics. This means that it follows exactly the same methodological rules: in order to find out whether there are any universal constraints on the process of human individuation, we have to collect as much empirical data as possible. My hope is that there is sufficient convergence between psychoanalysis, theories of moral development and sociological studies on personal concepts of injustice to show that the process of human individuation presupposes certain demands for recognition. It is clear that this anthropological hypothesis is not separable from the normative assumptions we have about the most appropriate forms of human existence. But as long as this hypothesis is not falsified empirically, this seems to me a legitimate presupposition.

RP In *Struggle For Recognition* you use the psychoanalytic theories of Donald Winnicott – who is still relatively unknown in Germany – to provide an account of the intersubjective foundation of personal identity in childhood experience (Hegel's dimension of love). Why did you find the work of Winnicott in particular useful for these purposes?

Honneth In the first place, Winnicott is one of the leading figures in object-relations theory. In my view, this is a much more convincing and promising approach than orthodox psychoanalysis because it understands the psychic development of the individual as something which is internally dependent on emotional relations with other people. What is most interesting about Winnicott's approach, however, is the way in which, almost like Hegel, he sees the intersubjective process of individuation as a struggle for recognition: namely, as a struggle between two people on the edge between fusion and demarcation. Jessica Benjamin was the first person to make this implicit relation to Hegel clear to me, in her analysis of female masochism in her book *The Bonds of Love*.

RP The project of a critical social theory has been radically challenged in recent years, both by the lack of utopian energy within society and at an intellectual level. What role do you think critical social theory has to play within modern society? Can we still conceive of an utopian drive for radical democratization and a substantial redemption of the claims to a good life, or is Critical Theory confined to a level of critique which first and foremost concerns the distribution of goods and rights within the modern welfare state, as it would seem to be for Habermas?

Honneth There is a certain tendency to reduce the potentialities of Habermasian theory in respect of his own political and normative insights. If you take his new book, *Faktizität und Geltung*, which just came out in Germany, and which has started to be discussed there now in the academic world, you can see that in respect to his book on communicative action he is not taking a step in the direction of accommodation, but in the direction of radicalization. He's taking back some of his claims about the inviolability of systems. Nowadays, in this book, he sees a certain chance for the democratization of what he previously called the political system, which was taken as a given. That was Tom McCarthy's criticism: in using systems theory for describing the political-administrative system Habermas was reducing himself to the conviction that no further democratization of the political world is possible. In this new book he is much more radical in this respect, because he is again thinking of ways of democratizing the administrative system. On the other hand, it's clear that you could say that immanent critiques of capitalist societies, hinting at a certain increase of democracy, without taking into view the possibilities of other forms of economy, or the working life, are too narrow. In this respect I am in a difficult position, because I can see the empirical justification for that. We are in a position in which we can't see a clear alternative to certain mechanisms of the capitalist economy. All over the world there is a certain apathy of Marxists and Leftists with respect to these economic questions.

On the other hand, I'm not sure whether we should put the question of the reconstruction of the economic system at the centre of our concerns today. Maybe it is more productive to ask what the preconditions are for a good life in our present situation, and then to ask how to reorganize society in order to fulfil this. I would strengthen some criticisms of the capitalist organization of everyday life, and then ask myself, in a second step, what are the societal means to fulfil these normative conditions we think of when we criticize the capitalist organization of everyday life in our time. I don't know whether we should call that utopia. There are certain utopian elements in it, but that is not what is decisive. If you think of the young Lukács, or the young Adorno, they are not utopian thinkers. They had a very strong idea about what reification is, and to describe something as reification we need some standards or criteria in mind about what a non-reified human life is. But maybe that's enough today. Maybe that's an utopian background which you don't have to spell out.

Politics in Germany

RP Perhaps we could move on to some more immediately political issues. Could you give us some indication of the way in which the German Left is responding to current events in Europe, particularly concerning nationalism, in relation to German reunification, on the one hand, and European integration on the other? What's most striking from the standpoint of the Left in Britain is what looks like a peculiar resonance between certain views of the German Left and views on the Right of the Conservative Party in Britain. What they seem to share is an incredible distrust of Germany as a reunified nation in Europe. From the standpoint of the British Left that looks like a very British chauvinism. Yet in some respects it's held even more extremely by people like Günther Grass in Germany. So a certain German Left position looks very much like a certain British Right position.

Honneth I'm not sure that's the right description. I have to say, there is a certain lack of interest in questions of European unity on the Left in Germany. Everyone is concentrating on the question of German unification and on the social results of this unification, in terms of the economic situation – in which there is now a strong discrepancy between East and West in Germany – the new right-wing movements, and racism in Germany. The Left and the Right are both concentrating on Germany even though the Left wants to be non-nationalistic. I would say that the big mistake in this situation is this over-concentration on Germany, on both sides – the negativist nationalists and the positive nationalists. I see this tendency even in Habermas: overstressing nationality in a negativist way, struggling all the time against German nationalism, instead of thinking of a productive route to European unification. Leftists are in a familiar position because, on the one hand, we see that without any doubt European unification is the best way, as a next step in the political development of Europe; on the other hand, we see all the mistakes of the Maastricht treaty: the centralization of Europe in a single financial system, the over-concentration of all political and economic power in one system. That is the main problem of the Maastricht treaty. The task of the future should be to think of new forms of federalism: new intelligent constructions of complex systems of local democracies, hanging together in a federalist way, so that we can speak of a unified Europe. That hasn't even started in Germany. Interestingly enough, the liberal thinkers are the only ones who are concentrating on this question. I can't see any interesting leftist approach to it. Even people like Dahrendorf are thinking of these questions in Germany, but not the Leftists.

RP There is a piece by Adorno from 1959 in which, reflecting on the question of 'working through the past', he writes: 'I consider the continued existence of National Socialism within democracy potentially much more threatening than the continued existence of fascist tendencies against democracy.' This defines a very specific Frankfurtian position. How do you view that distinction, given the current situation? Does it still make sense, this way of thinking about capitalist democracy and fascism such that in some sense fascism isn't 'outside' the system? Or is this a completely anachronistic way of thinking?

Honneth It belongs to the tradition of the political theory of the Frankfurt School concerning which I have many doubts, for liberal reasons. I see a strong difference between a *Rechtsstaat* and a totalitarian state. In this respect, there is a certain relevance to Hannah Arendt's separation between democracy and totalitarianism. Adorno and Horkheimer always wanted to undermine this differentiation, but I would say that all the experiences we have speak for Arendt instead of Adorno and Horkheimer.

RP In a recent speech Manfred Frank went so far as to draw an analogy between the bowing to popular xenophobic sentiment on the part of the German political establishment and Goebbels's populism. Was Frank's analogy therefore misplaced? You don't think there is a danger within the political treatment of recent events which might reflect a new kind of cynicism in Germany's cultural consciousness of its past?

Honneth I would be much more cautious than Frank, because what I hate at the present moment in Germany is this kind of instinctual reaction you have to use traditional words like 'fascism'. We are still living in this schema of being either fascist or a good Leftist. So I have many doubts about Frank's analogy. The question of whether there's a new cynicism with respect to the past is one on which I'm quite optimistic regarding the cultural state of Germany. Maybe I'm wrong. Maybe I'm much too optimistic, but I think that even the conservatives, most of them, are quite aware of Germany's broken past. Even Kohl is aware of the moral debt we have. The difficulty that the conservatives have in debating the question whether German troops should join the UN troops shows how aware they are of this past. The only danger I see for a new cynicism is when the element which one finds in the young generation of skinheads has an influence on other generations and other groups. Then we have the cynical perspective on German history. That could be a danger. You can see it in certain elements of German cultural life. It is an intellectual reaction going back to the 1930s. In this respect, I am quite worried sometimes that there could be a new conservative Right. Interestingly enough, it is not in the conservative party as such. But that kind of cultural elitism does keep coming back.

RP Do you regard the current situation in Germany – social disturbances, riots, strong reactionary sentiments, etc. – as simply a side effect of the reunification process, likely to disappear according to the logic of a democratic learning process? Or are they perhaps due to more substantial insufficiencies within the contemporary political and societal formation, which make it hard to conceive of a frictionless development of German society?

Honneth I would like to say two things. The first is I don't think that the events in Germany are correctly explained using the Left–Right schemata to describe them. What's going on in these teenage riots, for example, is very hard to describe with the notions we are still using in the German debate of 'fascism' versus 'Leftism'. In Germany we are much too quick in using fascism as the key word for describing what's going on. It has a lot to do with the situation of jobless youth, a generation which has no other cultural means to find an identity than using certain symbolic elements of the German past, which they know can produce certain provocations. That has to do with the cycles of cultural demarcation in the last thirty years. There was a whole generation using leftist symbols, even though we can see now that not all of them were morally convinced Leftists – they were simply using the symbols. Now the members of the youth generation are in a situation in which their opposition to what's going on in Germany can only be made by using some protest materials in this way. It sounds as if I'm making the situation look much nicer than it is, but one has to respect that there is a cultural element there. On the other hand, it has to be said that there is also a big revival of small radically right-wing groups, even fascist parties, trying to exert an influence on the skinhead scene. The danger is without doubt this convergence between the symbolic and cultural forms of the young skinheads and the ideological content of the right-wing parties. It could happen that the fascist explanations make a more consistent, biographically more convincing, sense of the cultural symbols that the younger people are using.

RP There does seem to be something specific about the West German state here, concerning immigration laws, for example, and the way that immigrant communities have been formally dealt with by the state in terms of their political rights. The move towards European unity is likely to make the German model the standard European model. Do you have any views about the political rights of *Gastarbeiter*?

Honneth Germany is in a special position because we were never under the real pressure of an immigrant country. Now we are coming under this pressure, and we simply have to learn from the big immigrant countries. That means learning in a political respect and in a cultural respect. That's a learning process that has to be undertaken not only by the younger generation of skinheads, but by every other generation now living in Germany as well. It sounds very easy when the Left is saying we have to become a multicultural country, but I'm not sure whether we are all prepared for that. There is a lack of the cultural democratization which other countries simply had to learn. Something like the introduction of a right to dual nationality would be a very helpful legislative means to force us into such a learning process.

RP Is this why there is this distorting concentration on the concept of nationalism? Does it mark a resistance to these issues?

Honneth Yes, on both sides: on the positive and the negative side of nationalism. Taking the rights of cultural traditions seriously, the rights of groups coming into Germany, and taking them as a normal part of our life, would destroy both sides of nationalism.

RP So you would agree with Habermas's idea of post-traditional identities?

Honneth Yes, but it has to be filled out. And I'm not sure whether I would agree with Habermas there, because I don't know whether this post-traditional identity really has to be a post-national identity. It may be a more open nationalism.

RP How does this relate to the retributive side of German unification? By which I refer not only to such matters as the trial of the East German intelligence chief, Markus Wolf, but in particular to the treatment of intellectuals from the old East Germany, the vast majority of whom have lost their academic jobs, and presumably have little hope of acquiring new ones. As a member of the German Left, how do you view this process?

Honneth With very mixed feelings. On the one hand, there is the feeling that there should be sanctions (if not legislative, then moral) against all those who helped the totalitarian system to reproduce itself ideologically. On the other hand, I have strong doubts as to whether we, the West Germans, are the right ones to judge these intellectuals. We do not have enough knowledge about the everyday routines of this system, we are not in the hermeneutic position to understand the hopes, the ambivalences and the fears these intellectuals had at the time. There is still this tragic feeling that something is wrong when someone who spent years in a fascist prison is now the victim of a trial organized by the West German judiciary. I can't avoid seeing in all this a colonization process which has given birth to a system of unequal exchange of moral power. In my view, what would have been best was a very open, public moral debate in the former GDR – a chance we have gambled away.

Interviewed by Peter Osborne and Stale Finke
Essex University, February 1993

Notes

1 A translation of this piece, 'History and Interaction: On the Structuralist Interpretation of Historical Materialism', appears in Gregory Elliott (ed.), *Althusser: A Critical Reader*, Blackwell, Oxford, 1994.
2 Axel Honneth, 'Moral Development and Social Struggle: Hegel's Early Socio-Philosophical Doctrines', in Honneth et al., *Cultural-Philosophical Interventions in the Unfinished Project of Enlightenment*, MIT Press, Cambridge MA, 1992.

6
Gender as Performance

Judith Butler

Judith Butler teaches in the Rhetoric Department at the University of California, Berkeley. Her first book, *Subjects of Desire: Hegelian Reflections in Twentieth-Century France* (1987) traced the dialectic of pro- and anti-Hegelian currents in French theory across the writings of a wide range of thinkers. She is best known, however, for her second book *Gender Trouble: Feminism and the Subversion of Identity* (1990), which has proved as influential as it is controversial in its analysis of 'sex', 'gender' and 'sexuality' as forms of enforced cultural performance. In particular, it has been read by many as standing at the forefront of the new 'queer theory' – a tendency within gay and lesbian studies which foregrounds same-sex desire without specifying the sex of the partners, in the hope of escaping the theoretical constraints of gender difference.

Gender Trouble calls into question the need for a stable 'female' identity for feminist practice, and explores the radical potential of a critique of categories of identity. It argues that gender identities acquire what stability and coherence they have in the context of the 'heterosexual matrix'. In this discursive chaining of gender to sexuality, it is suggested, subversive possibilities arise for making 'gender trouble'. In her recent book, *Bodies That Matter: The Discursive Limits of 'Sex'* (1993), Butler addresses some of the misconceptions which have accompanied both the popularity and the notoriety of *Gender Trouble*. Concentrating this time on what is meant by the materiality of the body, she looks at the forcible production of 'sex', at heterosexual presumptions, and how they can contribute to their own subversion.

RP We'd like to begin by asking you where you place your work within the increasingly diverse field of gender studies. Most people associate your recent writings with what has become known as 'queer theory'. But the emergence of gay and lesbian studies as a discrete disciplinary phenomenon has problematized the relationship of some of this work to feminism. Do you see yourself primarily as a feminist or as a queer theorist, or do you refuse the choice?

Butler I would say that I'm a feminist theorist before I'm a queer theorist or a gay and lesbian theorist. My commitments to feminism are probably my primary commitments. *Gender Trouble* was a critique of compulsory heterosexuality within feminism, and it was feminists that were my intended audience. At the time I wrote the text there was no gay and lesbian studies, as I understood it. When the book came out, the Second Annual Conference of Lesbian and Gay Studies was taking place in the USA, and it got taken up in a way that I could never have anticipated. I remember sitting next to someone at a dinner party, and he said that he was working on queer theory. And I said: What's queer theory? He looked at me like I was crazy, because he evidently thought that I was a part of this thing called queer theory. But all I knew was that Teresa de Lauretis had published an issue of the journal *Differences* called 'Queer Theory'. I thought it was something she had put together. It certainly never occurred to me that I was a part of queer theory.

I have some problems here, because I think there's some anti-feminism in queer theory. Also, insofar as some people in queer theory want to claim that the analysis of sexuality can be radically separated from the analysis of gender, I'm very much opposed to them. The new *Gay and Lesbian Reader* that Routledge have just published begins with a set of articles that make that claim. I think that separation is a big mistake. Catharine MacKinnon's work set up such a reductive causal relationship between sexuality and gender that she came to stand for an extreme version of feminism that had to be combated. But it seems to me that to combat it through a queer theory that dissociates itself from feminism altogether is a massive mistake.

RP Could you say something more about the sex–gender distinction? Do you reject it or do you just reject a particular interpretation of it? Your position on this seems to have shifted recently.

Butler One of the interpretations that has been made of *Gender Trouble* is that there is no sex, there is only gender, and gender is performative. People then go on to think that if gender is performative it must be radically free. And it has seemed to many that the materiality of the body is vacated or ignored or negated here – disavowed, even. (There's a symptomatic reading of this as somatophobia. It's interesting to have one's text pathologized.) So what became important to me in writing *Bodies that Matter* was to go back to the category of sex, and to the problem of materiality, and to ask how it is that sex itself might be construed as a norm. Now, I take it that's a presupposition of Lacanian psychoanalysis – that sex is a norm. But I didn't want to remain restricted within the Lacanian purview. I wanted to work out how a norm actually materializes a body, how we might understand the materiality of the body to be not only invested with a norm, but in some sense animated by a norm, or contoured by a norm. So I have shifted. I think that I overrode the category of sex too quickly in *Gender Trouble*. I try to reconsider it in *Bodies That Matter*, and to emphasize the place of constraint in the very production of sex.

RP A lot of people liked *Gender Trouble* because they liked the idea of gender as a kind of improvisational theatre, a space where different identities can be more or less freely adopted and explored at will. They wanted to get on with the work of enacting gender, in order to undermine its dominant forms. However, at the beginning of *Bodies That Matter* you say that, of course, one doesn't just voluntaristically construct or deconstruct identities. It's unclear to us to what extent you want to hold on to the possibilities opened up in *Gender Trouble* of being able to use transgressive performances such as drag to help decentre or destabilize gender categories, and to what extent you have become sceptical about this.

Butler The problem with drag is that I offered it as an example of performativity, but it has been taken up as the paradigm for performativity. One ought always to be wary of one's examples. What's interesting is that this voluntarist interpretation, this desire for a kind of radical theatrical remaking of the body, is obviously out there in the public sphere. There's a desire for a fully phantasmatic transfiguration of the body. But no, I don't think that drag is a paradigm for the subversion of gender. I don't think that if we were all more dragged out gender life would become more expansive and less restrictive. There are restrictions in drag. In fact, I argued toward the end of the book that drag has its own melancholia.

It is important to understand performativity – which is distinct from performance – through the more limited notion of resignification. I'm still thinking about subversive repetition, which is a category in *Gender Trouble*, but in the place of something like parody I would now emphasize the complex ways in which resignification works in political discourse. I suspect there's going to be a less celebratory, and less popular, response to my new book. But I wanted to write against my popular image. I set out to make myself less popular, because I felt that the popularization of *Gender Trouble* – even though it was interesting culturally to see what it tapped into, to see what was out there, longing to be tapped into – ended up being a terrible misrepresentation of what I wanted to say!

RP Perhaps we could help to set that right here, by asking you what you mean by 'performativity' – by describing gender as performance. What's the ontological status of performativity, for example? And how does it fit into the Foucauldian discourse about regulatory norms which you deploy? Is performativity the generic category of which regulatory norms are historically specific instances, or what? Are you offering us a kind of pragmatism?

Butler First, it is important to distinguish performance from performativity: the former presumes a subject, but the latter contests the very notion of the subject. The place where I try to clarify this is toward the beginning of my essay 'Critically Queer', in *Bodies that Matter*. I begin with the Foucauldian premise that power works in part through discourse and it works in part to produce and destabilize subjects. But then, when one starts to think carefully about how discourse might be said to produce a subject, it's clear that one's already talking about a certain figure or trope of production. It is at this point that it's useful to turn to the notion of performativity, and performative speech acts in particular – understood as those speech acts that bring into being that which they name. This is the moment in which discourse becomes productive in a fairly specific way. So what I'm trying to do is think about performativity as *that aspect of discourse that has the capacity to produce what it names*. Then I take a further step, through the Derridean rewriting of Austin, and suggest that this production actually always happens through a certain kind of repetition and recitation. So if you want the ontology of this, I guess performativity is the vehicle through which ontological effects are established. Performativity is the discursive mode by which ontological effects are installed. Something like that.

The Body in Question

RP And what about the body? You see bodies as forcibly produced through particular discourses. Some might say that you haven't adequately addressed the biological constraints on bodies here. Take the female body's capacity for impregnation, for example. Why is it that male bodies don't get produced as child bearing? There are certain constraints coming from the body itself which you don't seem to register. Shouldn't you be talking about the constraints *on* discourse as well as 'the discursive limits of "sex"'?

Butler Yes, but doesn't everybody else talk about that? There's so much out there on that.

RP But if you don't say anything about it, people will think you don't accept any limits.

Butler Yes, there will be that exasperated response, but there is a good tactical reason to reproduce it. Take your example of impregnation. Somebody might well say: isn't it the case that certain bodies go to the gynaecologist for certain kinds of examination and certain bodies do not? And I would obviously affirm that. But the real question here is: to what extent does a body get defined by its capacity for pregnancy? Why is it pregnancy by which that body gets defined? One might say it's because somebody is of a given sex that they go to the gynaecologist to get an examination that establishes the possibility of pregnancy, or one might say that going to the gynaecologist is the very production of 'sex' – but it is still the question of pregnancy that is centring that whole institutional practice here.

Now it seems to me that, although women's bodies generally speaking are understood as capable of impregnation, the fact of the matter is that there are female infants and children who cannot be impregnated, there are older women who cannot be impregnated, there are women of all ages who cannot be impregnated, and even if they could ideally, that is not necessarily the salient feature of their bodies or even of their being women. What the question does is try to make the problematic of reproduction central to the sexing of the body. But I am not sure that is, or ought to be, what is absolutely salient or primary in the sexing of the body. If it is, I think it's the imposition of a norm, not a neutral description of biological constraints.

I do not deny certain kinds of biological differences. But I always ask under what conditions, under what discursive and institutional conditions, do certain biological differences – and they're not necessary ones, given the anomalous state of bodies in the world – become the salient characteristics of sex. In that sense I'm still in sympathy with the critique of 'sex' as a political category offered by Monique Wittig. I still very much believe in the critique of the category of sex and the ways in which it's been constrained by a tacit institution of compulsory reproduction.

It's a practical problem. If you are in your late twenties or your early thirties and you can't get pregnant for biological reasons, or maybe you don't want to, for social reasons – whatever it is – you are struggling with a norm that is regulating your sex. It takes a pretty vigorous (and politically informed) community around you to alleviate the possible sense of failure, or loss, or impoverishment, or inadequacy – a collective struggle to rethink a dominant norm. Why shouldn't it be that a woman who wants to have some part in child-rearing, but doesn't want to have a part in child-bearing, or who wants to have nothing to do with either, can inhabit her gender without an implicit sense of failure or inadequacy? When people ask the question 'Aren't *these* biological differences?', they're not really asking a question about the materiality of the body. They're actually asking whether or not the social institution of reproduction is the most salient one for thinking about gender. In that sense, there is a discursive enforcement of a norm.

The Heterosexual Comedy

RP This leads us to the question of heterosexuality.

Butler I don't know much about heterosexuality!

RP Don't worry, it's a theoretical question. You have argued that one thing the gay/lesbian pair can give to heterosexuals is the knowledge of heterosexuality as both compulsory system and inevitable comedy. Could you say more about why it's *inevitably* a comedy? If we understand heterosexuality as repetitive performance, why does the performance always fail? What is it that makes it fail, that means it can only ever be a copy of itself, a copy of something it can never fully be?

Butler Maybe there's a relationship between anxiety and repetition that needs to be underscored here. I think one of the reasons that heterosexuality has to re-elaborate itself, to ritualistically reproduce itself all over the place, is that it has to overcome some constitutive sense of its own tenuousness. Performance needs to be rethought here as a ritualistic reproduction, in terms of what I now call 'performativity'.

RP But what creates this tenuousness?

Butler Why is it tenuous? Well, it's a fairly funny way of being in the world. I mean, how is it – as Freud asked in the *Three Essays on the Theory of Sexuality* – that you get this polymorphous, or at least minimally bisexual, being to craft its sexuality in such a way that it's focused exclusively on a member of the opposite sex, and wants to engage with that person in some kind of genital sex?

RP So you'd give a psychoanalytical answer. We thought you might have a more Foucauldian response. Does the above apply to all social categories?

Butler No, it applies to all *sexual* positions. It's not just the norm of heterosexuality that is tenuous. It's all sexual norms. I think that every sexual position is fundamentally comic. If you say 'I can only desire X', what you've immediately done, in rendering desire exclusive, is created a whole set of positions which are unthinkable from the standpoint of your identity. Now, I take it that one of the essential aspects of comedy emerges when you end up actually occupying a position that you have just announced to be unthinkable. That is funny. There's a terrible self-subversion in it.

When they were debating gays in the military on television in the United States a senator got up and laughed, and he said, 'I must say, I know very little about homosexuality. I think I know less about homosexuality than about anything else in the world.' And it was a big announcement of his ignorance of homosexuality. Then he immediately launched into a homophobic diatribe which suggested that he thinks that homosexuals only have sex in public bathrooms, that they are all skinny, that they're all male, etc., etc. So what he actually has is a very aggressive and fairly obsessive relationship to the homosexuality that of course he knows nothing about. At that moment you realize that this person who claims to have nothing to do with homosexuality is in fact utterly preoccupied by it.

I do not think that these exclusions are indifferent. Some would disagree with me on this and say: 'Look, some people are just indifferent. A heterosexual can have an indifferent relationship to homosexuality. It doesn't really matter what other people do. I haven't thought about it much, it neither turns me on nor turns me off. I'm just sexually neutral in that regard.' I don't believe that. I think that crafting a sexual position, or reciting a sexual position, always involves becoming haunted by what's excluded. And the more rigid the position, the greater the ghost, and the more threatening it is in some way. I don't know if that's a Foucauldian point. It's probably a psychoanalytic point, but that's not finally important to me.

RP Would it apply to homosexuals' relationship to heterosexuality?

Butler Yes, absolutely.

RP Although presumably not in the same way . . .

Butler Yes, there's a different problem here, and it's a tricky one. When the woman in the audience at my talk said, 'I survived lesbian feminism and still desire women', I thought that was a really great line, because one of the problems has been the normative requirement that has emerged within some lesbian feminist communities to come up with a radically specific lesbian sexuality. (Of course, not all lesbian feminism said this, but a strain of it did.) Whatever you were doing in your sexual relations with women had to be very much between women. It could have no hint of heterosexuality in it. In the early days that included a taboo on penetration. More recently, there have been questions about relations of domination and submission, about sado-masochism, questions of pornography, of exhibitionism, of dildos, and any number of fetishistic displays. The question is: are these practices straight, or can they be made gay? And if they can be made gay, can they be radically and irreducibly gay? Because we don't want to be seen as somehow borrowing from, or copying, or miming heterosexual culture.

I guess this is my Hegelianism: one is defined as much by what one is not as by the position that one explicitly inhabits. There is a constitutive interrelationship. Lesbians make themselves into a more frail political community by insisting on the radical irreducibility of their desire. I don't think any of us have irreducibly distinct desires. One might say that there are heterosexual structures that get played out in gay and lesbian scenes, but that does not constitute the co-option of homosexuality by heterosexuality. If anything it's the reterritorialization of heterosexuality within homosexuality.

RP It's interesting that you refer to your Hegelianism here. To what extent would you be prepared to characterize your work as 'dialectical'? Most people who use Foucault and Derrida, for example, in the way you do, would want to resist the notion of dialectic.

Butler I don't know if I resist the notion of dialectic. I certainly think that it has to be supplemented. I would say that in the construction of any binary – when we take masculine and feminine as a binary, for example – what's interesting is not just how the masculine presupposes the feminine, and 'is' the feminine in the Hegelian sense, or the feminine presupposes and 'is' the masculine, but how a field is produced in which there are these two mutually exclusive and mutually defining possibilities, and only these two. There are a set of exclusions that are made in the production of any binary, and those exclusions never make their way into intelligent discourse. That's where the notion of the abject comes in. I accept the Derridean notion that every dialectical opposition is produced through a set of exclusions, and that what is outside the dialectic – which is not a negation – cannot be contained by the dialectic. This provides the opportunity for an important critical reflection on the limitations of dialectical opposition.

RP Speaking of binaries, it is interesting, isn't it, the quite pivotal role which discussions of lesbian sexuality have had in feminist approaches to sexuality since the 1970s. Amber Hollibaugh said that at one point all feminists were trying to have sex the way they thought dykes were doing it. Then later on, in response to the puritanism which some feminists ended up adopting because of this, it was lesbian discussions that introduced a new sexual radicalism. All the way through feminist discussion of sexuality, discussions about lesbian sexuality have been in the vanguard of how to think about sex.

Butler Yes, some of the romanticizing of lesbianism is a consequence of heterosexual guilt, which is the corollary of the phenomenon that I'm talking about. If what is radically lesbian is over here, untainted by heterosexuality, then heterosexuality is constructed as a phenomenon that can only be staining or hurtful. And when it emerges within lesbianism, it is the selling out of lesbianism. And for the straight or bisexual woman, this opposition reconsolidates guilt. This has kept us from really thinking through the comedy of heterosexuality – the compulsory and comic character of heterosexuality – because that means in some sense to own it. On the other hand, I think it's impoverished our analyses of lesbianism and bisexuality as well. The other way this logic works is to make bisexuality into a sell-out position or a traitorous position, or a duplicitous position. That's a horribly moralizing and unfruitful way to think about it.

RP You yourself have made quite a move, haven't you, from over a decade ago, when you contributed to the book *Against Sadomasochism* ...

Butler No, that wasn't me, that was someone else with my name!

RP It wasn't you?

Butler Okay, it was me, but I disavow it. I was really young! I was really guilt-tripped by feminism. That essay is very ambivalent about the notion that sexuality and power are co-extensive, but I didn't yet know how to reflect on that ambivalence in a non-moralizing way.

Psychoanalysis and the Symbolic

RP Perhaps we could go back to psychoanalysis at this point. *Gender Trouble* contains a fairly severe critique of the psychoanalytical perspective on sexual difference. Yet psychoanalysis has since come to play an increasingly central role in your work. How useful do you find psychoanalysis for your theorization of gender?

Butler I probably misled you earlier. I don't actually accept Freud's postulation of a primary bisexuality or polymorphousness, although I do think that any given sexual arrangement is peculiar, and not necessary. The problem I have with Freud's articulation of bisexuality is that it is actually heterosexuality. There's the feminine part that wants a masculine object, and the masculine part that wants a feminine one. Swell, we have two heterosexual desires and we're going to call that bisexuality. So I reject that.

I also think that polymorphousness is a fantasy: the minute you're born into the world you're interpolated in various ways. But this is where I would stop – this is where I would depart from both a structuralist psychoanalysis and a more developmental object-relations one. Because at that moment they're going to start saying: 'You're subject to the law of sexual difference from the minute you're born in the world.' And that law becomes unalterable. There are various relationships to it that can be taken, but the law itself remains unalterable. Or there's a developmental trajectory, differentiation from the mother, etc., which leads to certain kinds of object formations, or formations of attachment. This is where I want to take these models apart, because I feel that's the moment at which a certain kind of heterosexual norm is re-established.

I think there's a really strong heterosexualizing imperative in the Lacanian account of the Oedipal phase, the Oedipal scene, one should say. And I also think that in object relations theory lesbianism is almost always figured as a certain kind of fusion, which I find extremely problematic. On the other hand, there is much in psychoanalytic perspectives that is very valuable. It is the best way we have of understanding how sexual positions are assumed. It is the best account of the psyche – and psychic subjection – that we have. I don't think one can offer an account of how sexuality is formed without psychoanalysis. But I also think that the psychoanalytic sciences are part of the forming of sexuality, and have become more and more part of that forming. I'm with Foucault on that. They don't simply report on the life of the infant, they've become part of the crafting of that life.

RP We'd like to turn to your critique of the tripartite Lacanian division of the imaginary, the symbolic, and the real at this point. One thing we found particularly interesting was the way you criticised Lacan's division between the imaginary and the symbolic by arguing that the role of the phallus in making that distinction is homologous to the role of the bodily image in the mirror phase. So entry into the symbolic is actually merely an extension of the imaginary, and what Lacanians call the symbolic, and reify into the law of the father, is in fact only a *hegemonic* imaginary.

Butler Yes.

RP We have two problems with this. The first is that, as we understand Lacan, the imaginary is always-already symbolic, so 'entry' into the symbolic is simply the point at which the symbolic character of the imaginary becomes clear. Secondly, although your critique dethrones the phallus from its position of psychic absolutism in the Lacanian symbolic, on the other hand what you call the 'heterosexual matrix' stands in for it. So although the phallus is no longer king by virtue of some kind of psychic law, there's a Foucauldian, historicist equivalent to it, which is equally absolute. It may be socially and historically produced, but you treat it as being just as absolute within the present.

Butler Good question. Two responses. One is that although I would accept the notion that every speaking being is born into a symbolic order that is always-already-there, I think the Lacanians describe that order, and the status of its always-already-thereness, in too static a way. The symbolic is repeatedly produced, reproduced, and possibly derailed. I agree with Derrida here in his analysis of structure in 'Structure, Sign and Play' in *Writing and Difference*. A structure only becomes a structure by repeating its structurality. Iterability is the way in which a structure gets solidified, but it also implies the possibility of that structure's derailment. So I do think the symbolic is always-already-there, but it's also always in the process of being made, and remade. It can't continue to exist without the ritualistic productions whereby it is continuously reinstalled. And it gets reinstalled through an imaginary idealization which is rendered as symbolic, as necessary and as immutable. The symbolic is the rendering immutable of given idealizations.

RP And where does this come from – the rendering immutable?

Butler It's what Lacan gives us as the mirror stage. When we're talk about the operation of the imaginary, we're talking about a misrecognition by which an idealized version of oneself is taken to be oneself.

RP So you believe in the mirror phase?

Butler Believe in the mirror phase! I think it allegorizes a certain kind of idealizing move that continuously misrepresents and idealizes the ego.

And I think the phallus is precisely such an idealization. Now, if that's true, and if the mirror stage is part of the imaginary, then the phallus is nothing other than an imaginary and impossible idealization of the masculine. The symbolic gets reproduced by taking imaginary projections and recasting them as law. That's much more of a Freudian approach than a Lacanian one. But I don't mind that. I'm probably closer to Freud than I am to Lacan. There's more leeway, more complexity, in Freud.

RP And slightly less authoritarianism?

Butler Well, at least he throws up his hands every once in a while and says, 'I have no idea what I'm doing here'! At least he models a certain self-questioning. As for your second point – the heterosexual matrix – I think you're right about *Gender Trouble*. The heterosexual matrix became a kind of totalizing symbolic, and that's why I changed the term in *Bodies That Matter* to heterosexual hegemony. This opens the possibility that this is a matrix which is open to rearticulation, which has a kind of malleability. So I don't actually use the term heterosexual matrix in *Bodies That Matter*.

RP Presumably, the dependence of coherent genders on a 'compulsory' heterosexual framing couldn't be universalized, anthropologically, could it?

Butler Well, you could probably make an argument that gender positions within culture are in some ways related to positions within reproductive relations. But it would be a bit of a leap to claim that those reproductive relations involve compulsory heterosexuality, since there are cultures that accommodate reproductive relations without mandating heterosexuality.

There's a very specific notion of gender involved in compulsory heterosexuality: a certain view of gender coherence whereby what a person feels, how a person acts, and how a person expresses herself sexually is the articulation and consummation of a gender. It's a particular causality and identity that gets established as gender coherence which is linked to compulsory heterosexuality. It's not any gender, or all gender, it's that specific kind of coherent gender.

RP Psychoanalytically, this leads us in the direction of the Lacanian 'real'. One way that someone like Zizek would respond to your erosion of the fixity of the Lacanian symbolic by the fluidity of imaginary identifications would be to appeal to the 'real' as the ultimate bedrock of a compulsory construction of this kind of coherent gender. How would you respond to that?

Butler That's where I get scared. He wants make it permanent, and we're the permanent outside. It's as if we've got girls, we've got boys, and then we have the permanent outside. No way! We've got lots of people rolling around the streets who are the 'outside' to girls and boys who Žižek is naming as the impossible real. It's a hell of a thing to live in the world being called the impossible real – being called the traumatic, the unthinkable, the psychotic – being cast outside the social, and getting named as the unlivable and the unspeakable. This worries me. What he's doing is consolidating these binaries as absolutely necessary. He's rendering a whole domain of social life that does not fully conform to prevalent gender norms as psychotic and unlivable.

RP You find a moralizing compulsion in Žižek's Lacanianism?

Butler The line between psychosis and the social and sexual positionalities that have been rendered abject or unthinkable in our society is very fuzzy. The structural rigidity of the symbolic in Žižek's work runs the risk of producing a domain of psychosis that may well be a social domain. One of the problems with homosexuality is that it does represent psychosis to some people. Many people feel that who they are as egos in the world, whatever imaginary centres they have, would be radically dissolved were they to engage in homosexual relations. They would rather die than engage in homosexual relations. For these people homosexuality represents the prospect of the psychotic dissolution of the subject. How are we to distinguish that phobic abjection of homosexuality from what Žižek calls the real – where the real is that which stands outside the symbolic pact and which threatens the subject within the symbolic pact with psychosis?

The Lesbian Phallus

RP Could you say something about what you mean by the 'lesbian phallus'? Presumably, it's part of your counter-hegemonic struggle against the phallus itself . . .

Butler I thought it was kind of funny. People get a little worried about it!

RP Some people take it literally and say: 'I know just what it is, I keep three of them in my drawer.'

Butler Yes, that's unfortunate, an unfortunate literalization! I wouldn't exclude it, but it would be a problem for me if the lesbian phallus were reduced to the notion of the dildo. That would ruin its speculative force.

So, what does it signify? Well, in the first place, it's a contradiction in terms for most people who talk about the phallus, to the extent that 'having' the phallus and 'being' the phallus within the Lacanian framework correspond to a masculine position and a feminine position, respectively. In the lesbian the having and the being are in relation to one another (although of course Lacan would say this is not a relation at all). To claim that the lesbian either has or is the phallus is already to disrupt the presumptive alignment of masculinity with having and femininity with being, and, with that, the relation in which they are conceived.

However, I wanted to do more crossings than that. I wanted to suggest that having and being are not mutually exclusive positions, and that there are a variety of identificatory possibilities that get animated within homosexuality and heterosexuality and bisexuality, which cannot be easily reduced to that particular framework. Of course, there's also a joke in 'The Lesbian Phallus' because to have the phallus in Lacan is also to control the signifier. It is to write and to name, to authorize and to designate. So in some sense I'm wielding the lesbian phallus in offering my critique of the Lacanian framework. It's a certain model for lesbian authorship. It's parody.

RP Could there also be the female heterosexual phallus?

Butler Yes, but that's been around for a while. The female heterosexual phallus has been the phallic mother. The way it usually works is that when the woman has it she becomes the phallic mother, and she becomes absolutely terrifying.

RP Couldn't one have it without being the mother?

Butler That's the question: why is it that when the woman is said to have the phallus she can only be the terrifying engulfing mother? What would it mean to separate the heterosexual woman who has the phallus from the phallic mother? It's an important thing to do.

Transgression and Recuperation: Queer Politics

RP Perhaps we could move on to the politics of queer theory, and in particular to the ideas of subversive repetition and transgressive reinscription, which we touched on earlier when we asked you about drag. Alan Sinfield has suggested that the problem with supposedly subversive representations of gender is that they're always recuperable. The dominant can always find a way of dismissing them and reaffirming itself. On the other hand, Jonathan Dollimore has argued that they're not always recuperable, but that any queer reading or subversive performance, any challenge to dominant representations of gender, can only be sustained as such *collectively*. It's only within critical subcultures that transgressive reinscriptions are going to make a difference. How do you respond to these views on the limits of a queer politics of representation?

Butler I think that Sinfield is right to say that any attempt at subversion is potentially recuperable. There is no way to safeguard against that. You can't plan or calculate subversion. In fact, I would say that subversion is precisely an incalculable effect. That's what makes it subversive. As for the question of how a certain challenge becomes legible, and whether a rendering requires a certain collectivity, that seems right too. But I also think that subversive practices have to overwhelm the capacity to read, challenge conventions of reading, and demand new possibilities of reading.

For instance, when Act Up (the lesbian and gay activist group) first started performing Die-ins on the streets of New York, it was extremely dramatic. There had been street theatre, a tradition of demonstrations, and the tradition from the civil disobedience side of the civil rights move-ment of going limp and making policemen take you away: playing dead. Those precedents or conventions were taken up in the Die-in, where people 'die' all at once. They went down on the street, all at once, and white lines were drawn around the bodies, as if they were police lines marking the place of the dead. It was a shocking symbolization. It was legible insofar as it was drawing on conventions that had been produced within previous protest cultures, but it was a renovation. It was a new adumbration of a certain kind of civil disobedience. And it was extremely graphic. It made people stop and *have to read* what was happening.

There was confusion. People didn't know at first, why these people were playing dead. Were they actually dying, were they actually people with AIDS? Maybe they were, maybe they weren't. Maybe they were HIV positive, maybe they weren't. There were no ready answers to those questions. The act posed a set of questions without giving you the tools to read off the answers. What I worry about are those acts that are more immediately legible. Those are the ones that I think are most readily recuperable. But the ones that challenge our practices of reading, that make us uncertain about how to read, or make us think that we have to renegotiate the way in which we read public signs, these seem really important to me.

The Kiss-ins that Queer Nation did at various shopping malls were quite outrageous. There had been Kiss-ins in front of the Supreme Court when gay statutes were being discussed. I think that was the first one, actually, the Kiss-in at the Supreme Court building. (I was invited but I didn't go, because I didn't want to kiss just anybody!) They worked for a while, but they always run the risk of becoming tropes. Once they've been read, once they're done too often, they become deadened tropes, as it were. They become predictable. And it's precisely when they get predictable, or when you know how to read them in advance, or you know what's coming, that they just doesn't work any more.

RP So they're most subversive when the subculture itself is still struggling over them? When one group of lesbians, for example, are trying to smash up the screen and rip the film out of the projector, while the other ones are saying, 'Yes, this is a really usefully rethinking of female sexuality, look how it undoes the heterosexual reading by placing the lesbian couple differently within the scenario', etc.?

Butler Right. Some people would say that we need a ground from which to act. We need a shared collective ground for collective action. I think we need to pursue the moments of degrounding, when we're standing in two different places at once; or we don't know exactly where we're standing; or when we've produced an aesthetic practice that shakes the ground. That's where resistance to recuperation happens. It's like a breaking through to a new set of paradigms.

RP What are the relations of this kind of symbolic politics to more traditional kinds of political practice? Presumably, its function is in some way tied to the role of mass media in the political systems of advanced capitalist societies, where representations play a role they don't necessarily have elsewhere.

Butler Yes, I agree.

RP Yet at the same time, it is a crucial part of this role that the domain of representation often remains completely cut off from effective political action. One might argue that the reason a politics of representation is so recuperable is precisely because it remains within the domain of representation – that it is only an adjunct to the business of transforming the relationship of society to the state, establishing new institutions, or changing the law. How would you respond to that?

Butler First of all, I oppose the notion that the media is monolithic. It's neither monolithic, nor does it act only and always to domesticate. Sometimes it ends up producing images that it has no control over. This kind of unpredictable effect can emerge right out of the centre of a conservative media without an awareness that it is happening. There are ways of exploiting the dominant media. The politics of aesthetic representation has an extremely important place. But it is not the same as struggling to change the law, or developing strong links with political officials, or amassing major lobbies, or the kinds of things needed by the grassroots movement to overturn anti-sodomy restrictions, for example.

I used to be part of a guerrilla theatre group called LIPS – it stood for nothing, which I loved – and now I'm contemplating joining the board of the International Gay and Lesbian Human Rights Commission. There's nothing to keep me from doing one rather than the other. For me, it does not have to be a choice. Other people are particularly adept working in the health care fields, doing AIDS activism – which includes sitting on the boards of major chemical corporations – doing lobbying work, phoning, or being on the street. The Foucauldian in me says there is no one site from which to struggle effectively. There have to be many, and they don't need to be reconciled with one another.

Democracy at Large

RP Do you see the success of these kinds of sexual politics as depending on their connection to broader Left–liberal alliances? Or do you view them more autonomously, more defensively perhaps, as part of a separate sphere which will have to look after itself, since its agenda is treated with such suspicion or contempt by the mainstream?

Butler I don't think that I could make the gay arena into the fundamental one, and then approach questions of racism or feminism, for example, within the context of the gay movement. I understand myself as a progressive anti-Zionist Jew. I think my Jewish background is more formative than anything else – which is probably why I can't write about it. My agony and shame over the state of Israel is enormous, and the kind of contributions I make in that domain have very little to do with my being queer. They may have something to do with being a woman, but they're more closely related to certain kinds of anti-racist views that I have.

I don't believe that states ought to be based on race. It puts Israel on a par with South Africa. I'm willing to make that analogy, and I'm also willing to talk about the economic and military arrangements that those two countries have between them. So I feel left of the Jewish Left in this particular way. I was touring recently in Germany. I was supposed to be talking about gender, but I ended up only talking about race. I started writing about racism and responsibility in the German press. (There's a debate going on about the relationship between the Turks, as the new Jews, and German guilt, and how guilt relates to responsibility.) It's a whole other venue for me.

It's extremely important to find ways to work between these various struggles. The absence of a common grounding on the Left has been very problematic. It's produced new forms of identity politics without developing a vocabulary for making connections. Unfortunately, there are people from the New Left in the United States, mainly white men who are feeling a little left out of things, who are more than happy to supply the ground. I know that some people have worried about Cultural Studies offering itself as an umbrella organization for this kind of realignment within the academy. But it depends what they're talking about. Cultural Studies in the United States is very different from what it is in Britain. It's often at some distance from the kind of global political analyses offered by Stuart Hall.

RP Perhaps we could return, briefly, to your Foucauldianism here. Implicit in what you have been saying (and it was explicit in your talk at the ICA) is a distinction between enabling and regressive practices and inter-pellations – although, of course, some practices might be both enabling and regressive at the same time. The question that immediately arises is: what's the criterion for the distinction? What are the grounds for affirming some norms and rejecting others?

Butler The trouble with the question of theoretical grounds is that it presupposes that we live outside these norms, that we can witness them and engage them by a set of standards that are not inherent in the practices that we're analysing. What worries me most is that form of rationalist imperialism that thinks it has access to a set of principles extracted from practices, that it can then apply to other practices. The Habermasian recourse to normative grounds is nothing other than an extraction of a contingent set of norms from practices – abstraction and decontextualization – and then a re-application of those norms universally. It strikes me as circular and politically wrong. There's a really problematic circularity in that notion of normativity.

When I say 'enabling', I would admit, sure, there's a normative direction in my work, but I would hope that there is no normative ground. I don't think that in order to have a viable normative direction you need a ground. If I want to claim and describe certain ways of producing gender as restrictive or cruel, that entails that I have some more expansive or complex view of what gender might be. I'm willing to say that without filling in the content of what that's going to be, or prescribing an ideal norm for what that's going to be. I am in favour of opening up certain kinds of practices, be they sexual or gender practices, as sites of contestation and rearticulation. In one sense, that is enough for me. I see that as part of a democratic culture.

RP The refusal to foreclose rationalistically the results of conflict?

Butler Yes, and the opening up of spaces for a certain kind of democratic contestation, or more locally, for a contestation of gender.

RP But doesn't the very notion of a democratic contestation itself imply a norm of some kind of equality of input to the contest? That would be the Habermasian point, I suppose.

Butler Except that the Habermasians tend to impose an exclusionary norm in constructing the notion of the subject whose 'input' would count.

RP We'd like to end by asking you how you see the future of feminism.

Butler Catharine MacKinnon has become so powerful as the public spokesperson for feminism, internationally, that I think that feminism is going to have to start producing some powerful alternatives to what she's saying and doing – ones that can acknowledge her intellectual strength and not demonize her, because I do think there's an anti-feminist animus against her, which one should be careful not to encourage. Certainly, the paradigm of victimization, the over-emphasis on pornography, the cultural insensitivity and the universalization of 'rights' – all of that has to be countered by strong feminist positions.

What's needed is a dynamic and more diffuse conception of power, one which is committed to the difficulty of cultural translation as well as the need to rearticulate 'universality' in non-imperialist directions. This is difficult work and it's no longer viable to seek recourse to simple and paralysing models of structural oppression. But even here, in opposing a dominant conception of power in feminism, I am still 'in' or 'of' feminism. And it's this paradox that has to be worked, for there can be no pure opposition to power, only a recrafting of its terms from resources invariably impure.

Interviewed by Peter Osborne and Lynne Segal
London, October 1993

7
American Radicalism

Cornel West

[handwritten: existentialist absurdity]

Cornel West is Professor of Philosophy of Religion and Afro-American Studies at Harvard University and one of the most influential of a new generation of black intellectuals in the United States. Best known academically for his history of American pragmatism, *The American Evasion of Philosophy* (1989), his work spans the fields of philosophy, political studies, cultural criticism and legal theory. His recent book *Race Matters* (1993) was a best-seller. His other works include *The Ethical Dimension of Marxist Thought* (1991), *Breaking Bread: Insurgent Black Intellectual Life* (with bell hooks, 1991) and *Keeping Faith: Philosophy and Race in America* (1993). His two-volume collection *Beyond Eurocentrism and Multiculturalism* was awarded the 1993 American Book Award.

RP Perhaps we could begin by asking you about the role of religion in your intellectual and political development. How important was the Church to you in becoming an intellectual, becoming a radical?

West For me, the issues on which religious discourse has traditionally focused, such as death and dread and despair and disappointment and disease – the existential issues, the existential dimension of the human condition – have always been fundamental. So, for me, the role of religion, and not just religion, but also music – religion and music – is fundamental. It's a reflection of being a New World African and having to deal with the absurd: both the absurd in America and America as the absurd. There was a need to come up with ways of imposing some kind of sense on the chaos coming at one, the chaos of a certain kind of white supremacist ideology, with its assault on black beauty and black intelligence, black capability and so on.

It is part of the response to being perceived as sub-human in a particular historical epoch, the age of Europe. Coming from a people who

[handwritten margin notes: "The dilemma of the black intellectual", "radical contingency of human action"]

have had to make and remake themselves, a modern people beneath modernity, requires a very strong accent on existential issues. So when I first emerged out of the context of the black Church, in which the problem of evil and the confrontation with social misery is central – to moan, to groan, to wrench and cry, the struggle with madness, suicide and so forth – it was Kierkegaard, it was Chekov, it was the late nineteenth-century Russian writers who were dealing with these kinds of issue, who I read.

RP How did you come across those writers? Given your background, that was quite unusual, wasn't it?

West Oh, very much so. It was a pilgrimage. We lived in a segregated part of Sacramento, California, so we didn't have a library. But we did have a bookmobile and they had some Kierkegaard there. I first began to read Kierkegaard when I was about 13 – 13 or 14 – I guess. It introduced me to a Hegelian tradition, because I saw all the references to Hegel. I didn't get a chance to read Hegel at the time, but I had a sense in which Kierkegaard was responding to a larger backdrop. But it was his struggle over what it means to be human, over how you come to terms with despair and dread, that was inescapable.

RP In your essay 'The Dilemma of the Black Intellectual', you write about routes to becoming a black intellectual, and you say that it normally involves two things. One is that it's a conversion-like experience, the discovery of a world; the other is that there's often an individual figure, a teacher, who sparks it off. Was this true for yourself?

West Yes, to some extent. For the most part I grew up like most young black boys. Willie Mays and James Brown were my heroes. I wanted to be either an athlete or an entertainer. I had the Church background dealing with the problem of evil, issues of social misery, but I didn't think of the life of the mind or an intellectual vocation until I went to college, at Harvard. There, the impact of Martin Kilson and Preston Williams was quite strong. They were black professors. In fact, there were a number of figures who made a difference. My first tutor, Bob Nozick, was wonderful, and there was Hilary Putnam, John Rawls, Roderick Firth, and Israel Sheffler. Later on, Stanley Cavell was very important to me. Terry Irwin had a great impact on me too!

RP So it was the Philosophy Department at Harvard in the early 1970s, that extraordinary array of figures?

West Yes, but I had already been exposed to the Black Panther Party, so I considered myself as part of a Marxist tradition early on. The Black Panther Party was located right next door to our Black Baptist church in Sacramento, so the Black Panther newspaper was something I was reading all the time. I was going off and reading a little Fanon, a little Cabral, a little Nkrumah. The struggle against the absurd, in the form of the struggle against white supremacy, has its existential dimension,

but at that particular moment, the late 1960s, it had an important political dimension as well, a communal one. By the time I got to Harvard
I was hungry for some kind of sociological tradition that took freedom
struggles seriously. Barrington Moore was there and he made a difference, in terms of his work. Michael Walzer introduced me to *Dissent*
magazine, which opened up a whole new world. Peter Camejo was an
old Trotskyite who used to lecture at Harvard at night. I attended every
lecture of his that I could. He wasn't at Harvard, he was just using
Harvard space as a leftist. So I was also part of a left subculture, because
they seemed to be interested in struggles against white supremacy.

RP This is the early seventies, so it's after the peak of the civil rights
movement?

West 1970 to 1973. It's a black nationalist moment, the moment of black
power and its legacy. But being influenced by the Panthers, who were
internationalists and universalists, of course, or *revolutionary* nationalists, I was never willing to become part of the dominant black nationalist
tendencies. They always struck me as too narrow, too parochial,
provincial – later on, I would learn, patriarchal and homophobic too.
I recognized what black nationalists were after – black self-love, black
self-affirmation, black self-respect – but it struck me that analyses of
the economic situation, capital accumulation and the rule of capital,
the various class divisions, were either overlooked or downplayed by
them. For me, that was always a starting point. The starting point for
me was the way in which my existential concerns were shaped by the
various modes of capital accumulation and the way in which the rule
of capital imposes such constraints on the life-chances of black people
and their relations to working people more generally. The Marxist
tradition was and remains for me the 'brook of fire' through which one
must pass.

RP You have spoken of the importance of existential issues, but what
about existentialism as a philosophical position? Were you attracted to
it, or were you more of a pragmatist from the outset, once you discovered philosophy?

West I came to pragmatism a little later. As an undergraduate, it was
Sartre who had a strong influence on me. I read him voraciously, and
Wittgenstein. Wittgenstein was my hero for a while. He struck me as
a philosopher who was not simply highlighting the limits of analytical
philosophy but, to use Cavell's language, was refusing philosophy philosophically. He was accepted by a philosophy department, but he struck
me as someone who was pulling the rug from under so much of what
they were doing. I was impressed by the contextualism that I detected
in the *Philosophical Investigations*. It opens itself on to a broader
historical reading, even though Wittgenstein himself didn't do it. I read
Marcuse on Wittgenstein, and I thought, 'No, Herbert, you've got him

wrong. He's much more continuous with you. He's talking about praxis. It's just that he doesn't have the sociological apparatus to flesh out the way in which the structures of practices are related to one another in economic, political and social spheres.'

RP Later, when you discovered pragmatism, did you read Wittgenstein as a pragmatist?

West Yes, very much so, under Rorty. Rorty had a tremendous impact on me once I went to Princeton. I didn't seriously encounter the pragmatic tradition until I went to Princeton. I took a course on pragmatism at Harvard, where I read Mead, some Dewey, some James, a little C. I. Lewis, actually, but I didn't take it seriously. I just read the texts, got my B+ and kept moving. Under Rorty it began to develop into a much broader view. Then I read Sidney Hook and I saw the ways in which it was continuous with certain of Marx's views, and I saw how Rorty connected the later Wittgenstein to Dewey, and things began to fall into place for me. But I never became a philosopher, professionally speaking. I've never taught in a philosophy department. I went straight from graduate school in philosophy to teaching at the Union Theological Seminary (for eight years) and then the Yale Divinity School (for another three).

RP Why was that?

West By choice. In part, it was because of the tremendous influence of Reinhold Niebuhr and of Paul Tillich, whose very deep commitment to democratic socialist politics as a Christian thinker was exemplary for me. I didn't enter the secular academy until I went back to Princeton, in the Departments of Religion and Afro-American Studies, eleven years later. Even now that I'm going to Harvard, it's to teach philosophy at the Divinity School and Afro-American Studies. There are still philosophical discourses within the academy that I find worth engaging, but I've chosen to avoid philosophy departments because I've wanted to do so many other things: study popular culture, write on music, architecture, painting . . .

Pragmatism and Anti-Foundationalism

RP Let's talk about pragmatism. *The American Evasion of Philosophy*, your history of pragmatism, has contributed to a moment in which the history of philosophy in America is being rewritten as part of a search for a distinctively American philosophy. This looks to be connected to larger-scale, global changes in international relations. What are your views about the search for a distinctively American philosophy?

West There is something distinctively American about pragmatism. There's no doubt about that. But there are a number of things going on in my book. One is that my motivations were thoroughly Gramscian.

That is to say, I wanted to try and understand the historical specificity of the development of American civilization through a particular philosophical discourse. The question became: What are the intellectual resources upon which one can draw for a radical democratic project? To what degree does pragmatism, which is distinctively American, provide both strengths and weaknesses, both blindnesses and insights vis-à-vis the regeneration of a radical democratic, a democratic socialist, project? In going back, I discovered a lot of strengths and a lot of weaknesses. I discovered some real virtues and vices in this tradition. So even though I think you're absolutely right – there is a certain kind of Americanism in the life of the mind being promoted which falls into easy parochial traps – on the other hand, the American intelligentsia, and especially the American Left, has still not seriously excavated and recuperated certain progressive resources within American history. We look toward Europe, toward Germany, toward France and so on. Remember, I was writing this text at a moment in which most of my fellow interlocutors, especially the Western ones, were looking to Paris or Frankfurt. That's fine, but I said: 'Let's see what's in the US tradition, and then work out some of the elective affinities with what's happening on the Left Bank, what's going on in the Frankfurt School, and so forth.'

RP Does this explain your changing attitude to Rorty? You began as his student, then, in your piece in *Post-Analytical Philosophy*, you produced a scathing political critique of his work. Yet when you came to reconstruct the history of pragmatism, placing him in a broader context, and placing yourself after him, you were much more sympathetic to him once again.

West That's true, because in the *Post-Analytical Philosophy* text, I'm talking solely about the politics. It's a very short essay. Rorty and I have always had certain friendly disagreements about politics. He's very much an incrementalist, even though he tilts in a social-democratic direction, whereas I'm more Raymond Williams-like: the long revolution, the march through the institutions, which actually is still revolutionary. I'm aware of the limits and illusions of reformism, but I still think that it's worth talking about the fundamental transformation of society. Hence, I hit Rorty very hard on politics. In the larger narrative, he looks much better because he makes anti-foundationalist moves and he recognizes what I take to be so important for radical democratic politics. This is the *jazz-like character of American culture*, which is not just market-driven but is open to experimentation and improvisation, and a certain malleability of class structure. Race is more difficult, of course, and patriarchy's more difficult. But those themes are there. And for me, they are very important for any kind of radical democratic politics. Rorty himself was quite open to these themes and motifs.

RP But is his kind of anti-foundationalism compatible with the kind of knowledge about society required by the politics you support? My impression of the radical theory which is influential in the American academy at the moment is that it is a very generic anti-foundationalist historicism. It could be neo-pragmatist, it could be deconstructive, it could be Foucauldian – they're all modes of anti-foundationalism, they're all historicist, but the space that they occupy is primarily defined negatively. Now, one of your criticisms of neo-pragmatism concerns its lack of social theory. It opens up a space for social analysis, but it doesn't have any sociological concepts. Yet the kind of social theory which you acknowledge that it needs is associated with a very different set of assumptions, epistemologically, from any of these tendencies. Isn't there a contradiction here?

West I would hope not. A serious analysis of the rule of capital, or white supremacy, or male supremacy, can be done in an experimental spirit. One doesn't have to clash with anti-foundationalism or historicism. Now it's true that Rorty, for example, says: 'Cornel, you claim to be anti-foundational, but when it comes to social theory you fail. You become foundationalist. You invoke Marx and Weber and Lukács and Simmel and Du Bois. You've got foundationalist claims being made, causal explanatory claims being made.' And I say: 'No, not at all.' For me, the choice is never between foundationalism and some kind of empty anti-foundationalism. Mine is a historicism that is contextualist and revisionist, in the sense of recognizing that any causal explanatory claim is open to revision. But these claims are indispensable weapons in any serious struggle for radical democracy and freedom. They must be deployed to the best of our ability. Maybe there is a tension, but I don't see it as a contradiction.

One of the paradoxes of American civilization is that, on the one hand, you have the valorizing of the improvisational, experimental and jazz-like character of the culture; and on the other hand, you have a fixity and a solidity of the rule of capital – economic growth by means of corporate priorities, the sacred cow of the civilization, the business civilization as it is. You also have a deep entrenchment of white supremacy, which sits at the very centre of American civilization: a profound hatred of black folk, in subtle or not so subtle forms. Then there's the patriarchal core and the homophobic overlay. So, on the one hand, you have this valorization of improvisation; on the other, you have this fixity. Now there's not a lot of space here for radical democratic politics that has serious substance. What we've seen in the last twenty-five years is the ideology of professionalism and specialization playing itself out within the privileged space of the academy. This is a site where certain anti-foundationalist and historicist discourses take place which are far removed from any serious analysis of the rule of capital, the interlocking network of corporate and financial elites, and their ways of making political elites subordinate to them.

RP Do you see any positive role for philosophical discourse here? The dominant movement in twentieth-century European philosophy has undoubtedly been a negative one. It's not scepticism as such, but it's an unpicking of the project: a particularistic kind of scepticism where philosophy is done in the mode of undoing itself. As you said, for some, like Cavell, that's all philosophy does. On the other hand, in the tradition of the forms of social theory to which you appeal, there's a sense of philosophy as a *reconstructive* discipline, continuing its historical role of totalization in a new form, in relation to the social sciences – not in a foundationalist way, but in a reconstructive way. Do you want to refuse it this role?

West That is a fast-hitting question, the metaphilosophical question. Like Cavell, I see philosophy as a quest for wisdom, as a desire to see how things hang together such that we can exercise critical judgements for the purpose of expanding possibility, democratic possibility, the creation of conditions such that individuals can flourish to the best of their abilities and capacities. But philosophy doesn't have a cognitive content for me, as a discipline. It is the name for a particular *desire*: the desire for wise deployment of various kinds of arguments, insights, visions, perspectives, and so forth. Now, it's true that there's a totalizing impulse behind this conception and this goes back to my Christian heritage, the Hegelian tradition, and to the Marxist tradition. I believe that the visionary aspect of philosophical discourse provides a synecdochic characterization of what the relations and connections are, but that doesn't mean that philosophy itself becomes some privileged discourse. It simply means that it tries to show how things are related, connected to one another, without itself having any kind of cognitive content.

RP So, to take the project you describe as prophetic pragmatism or prophetic criticism: it is defined by the values of individuality and democracy. What would be the form of your intellectual defence of those values?

West It would be an attempt to show the ways in which those particular traditions, among peoples that highlighted individuality and democracy, tend to be those that contribute most to the desirable forms of life. Now, that doesn't mean that arguments would not play a role. Argumentation is very important. One of the reasons why one reads philosophers is that they have tended to put a certain premium on argument. But I don't think argument exhausts the philosophical tradition. There are other forms of promoting understanding and broadening insight, although arguments do play an important role. One would still have to make arguments as to why individuality and democracy are better as opposed to authoritarianism and – I don't want to say fascism, that's too easy – truncated forms of democracy, I'll put it that way, limited forms of democracy. The defence of individuality and the defence of democracy still have to be put forward. There's no doubt about that. But I view these as values that are *already embedded* in particular traditions of struggle, traditions of political and social engagement, and I quite unabashedly view myself as part of those traditions, not just in the West, but in the world.

That's not a direct answer to your question, because in order to actually defend these values I'd have to engage in a much more detailed account of how one goes about showing these values to be desirable ones. But the main point is that for me it's never a matter of viewing the values abstracted from their enactment and embodiment within an ongoing tradition over time and space. That's my historicist mode and mood, which you would expect.

Intellectuals and Their Publics

RP Let's move from philosophers to intellectuals, or the philosopher as intellectual.

West That's my fundamental allegiance, as an intellectual.

RP You've written a lot about intellectuals, about the specificity of the black intellectual, but also about intellectuals more generally. There's been quite a debate about this in the US over the last few years, a highly politicized debate. Yet there is considerable common ground between the positions of people like Alan Bloom, on the Right, and Russell Jacoby, on the Left. They share a certain nostalgia. In your own work, you write of a 'crisis of vocation', but you don't seem to mourn the passing of the so-called public intellectual of the past. How do you view the prospects for effective intellectual activity outside the academy?

West Part of the problem here is that in the United States you have a racially bifurcated society, not simply due to the legacy of segregation, going back to slavery, but also due to the fact that different publics are often unacknowledged or uninterrogated by different intellectuals. So, for example, when I relate myself, as I often do, to a black intellectual tradition and highlight the role of the life of the mind within the public life of that community, it's something very different from what you find about the role of ideas in the public life of the dominant society. The kind of nostalgia that Russell Jacoby has for the 'New York intellectuals' concerns only a really minuscule sector of our society. *Partisan Review* was read by 3,500 people. It was fascinating, it was engaging – I get excited about it too – but once you historicize it and contextualize it, you see this nostalgia as very, very limited. Du Bois's *The Crisis* had 100,000 subscribers, more readers, but Russell Jacoby has no nostalgia for Du Bois's public intellectual activity, because it's not part of his world, unfortunately. That's part of the segregated life of the mind in our society. The same was true with James Baldwin. Baldwin sold millions of copies of *The Fire Next Time*, but these people have no nostalgia for James Baldwin's attempt to construct a public to talk about the most fundamental issue facing the country: namely, race. It may not be the most fundamental issue analytically – I think class and capital are, actually – but in terms of salient explosive issues, race certainly is.

I don't want to downplay the New York tradition. It's worth examining. I'm deeply influenced by New York intellectuals, especially the Jewish ones, who were concerned with the transition from a certain kind of parochialism of the ghetto and Brooklyn and Brownsville and other impoverished places to a more cosmopolitan space. This is what you get in Lionel Trilling and Alfred Kazin and Irving Howe and others. It's a very important move, but it's still a particular tradition, and there are other traditions from which to learn. Feminist intellectuals are teaching us this every day, and it's not only them. There are also issues of region. Southern intellectuals have different kinds of public. For me, the issue of the intellectual has to do with the relation between those who have a deep commitment to the life of the mind and its impact on public life, of all sorts.

Dewey's great text, *The Public and its Problems*, was very important to me here, in its treatment of different kinds of publics, and the relation of different intellectuals to those publics. These days, the larger public is much more shot through with the influence of the information and entertainment industries, mediated by electronic and printed media. New publics need to be constituted. One of the things that I've tried to do in the last few years is to play a role within these apparatuses, because one can shape very vague publics. They are going to be different kinds of publics than they were before. But those publics of the past will never come back, in the same way that the old public of the Greek city state is gone. We can be nostalgic about it all we want – there's nostalgia in Marx in that regard – but it's still gone. How do we reconstruct publics? Right now it's very difficult, not only because the private is cast as sacred, but because the public is something to be shunned across the board, with the exception of the spectatorial public: the virtual public that's produced and constructed by the network of information and entertainment media. That's the challenge for public intellectuals. It's a challenge that earlier public intellectuals had little sense of.

RP Your own category here – the intellectual carrier of prophetic prag-matism – is what you call the 'critical organic catalyst'. It obviously has a Gramscian dimension, a reference to some communality of interest between the intellectual catalyst and the social group on whose behalf he or she acts. Isn't there a contradiction between this idea and something which you stress very strongly in 'The New Cultural Politics of Difference': namely, the constructedness of all representation and the danger of the appeal to preconstituted notions of community? This takes us back to foundationalism in social theory, in a way. There's a point at which you say: 'We need to become more organic.' That seems to me a strange phrase, because surely the organic is that which is already so.

West Always-already so, yes, that's why we need to examine it. By 'organic' I don't mean to appeal to some pre-Derridean notion of representation that somehow leads toward a oneness or coincidence between the intellectual and the community. What I actually mean by organic is a much more fluid and constructed notion of participating in the organizations of people. So when I think of my own organic link with the black community, it's not that I am somehow thoroughly immersed in the black community, in some pantheistic way. Rather, I'm simply working in a particular organization or institution in which we are contesting among ourselves how we can best generate visions, analysis, and forms of political action. I want to say 'be organized', rather than 'be organic'.

Organic has a sense of being rooted, but this metaphor can be quite slippery. I want to preserve a certain notion of constructed rootedness, or constructed organic, in the sense that we are attempting to get beyond our own privileged sites, to get beyond our own professional sites, to be part of movements, even as we are critical of their leaders – in my own case, black organizations and institutions, from united fronts to churches. In terms of my own identity, I want to be viewed as someone who puts a premium on being part of those groups, even as I am a critic of those groups. That's what I have in mind with the critical organic catalyst. It may be problematic, but that's what I have in mind.

There's a tremendous need for multicontextualism, even more than multiculturalism, I think. Multicontextualism means moving between a variety of different contexts, from that of working people to very poor people, to the academy, as well as to other professions. I don't want to talk about being organic solely with masses, you see. I want to talk about being organized, or being part of organizations, with other professions as well. Tomorrow, I'm off to the Black Congressional Caucus, which is a group of political elites who are liberal, neo-liberal, a few progressive, two democratic socialists. But I have to organize with them. They have their organization. I am part of that organization. My voice is heard. If an intellectual is to be characterized as someone who tries to preserve a sense of the whole, who has a synoptic and synthetic vision and perspective, then being multicontextual will allow one to have a much more sophisticated and refined sense of the whole, and a much more convincing synthetic and syntactic view of things. In this, movements themselves contribute to the role of intellectuals, as I understand it.

Alliances, Conflicts and Disputes

RP Presumably, one goal of this kind of multicontextualism is the construction of alliances. How do you respond to the criticism that a generalized politics of alliances is too wishful about the compatibility of the social interests of those with an enemy in common?

West That's a very fair warning for persons like myself. But I'd come right back and say: 'Yes, perhaps, but don't we otherwise end up privileging a certain social interest (traditionally, class) which itself requires questioning?' But it isn't only class. One of the problems of a narrow black nationalism is that it downplays the class issues, and it downplays the gender issues. I think the major countervailing forces in the future, in addition to a weakening trade union movement, are going to be the forces against white supremacy, the feminist and womanist movements, the anti-homophobic movements, and the ecological movements. Ecological movements are much more international than any of the others, at this point, and we will need to speak globally if we're talking about effective countervailing forces.

RP Presumably, we will also have to talk about their relations to nation-states. What gave the labour movement its countervailing force in Europe during the period of its ascendancy was its particular relation to the state. Are these other forces likely to acquire such a weight within the state?

West Oh, in the United States they have already.

RP At one point in your recent book you identify Jesse Jackson's attempt to gain power at a national level as a *weakness* of the movement.

West That's right – because of the thinness of American electoral politics. There was a lack of the serious grassroots organizing necessary to mushroom into an effective and substantial candidacy. Jackson just leapfrogged over all of that and became a figure with very little social base, except through television. It was a sign of weakness. In stark contrast to Jesse Jackson, the Right had forces that were mobilizing deeply, organizing on grassroots levels, in ordinary people's everyday lives. They could generate a hegemonic presence.

RP Let's go back to the issue of the interests at stake in alliances and take last week's Cairo summit on population control as an example of the kind of conflicts which can arise. There, we seem to have articulated in a global way and in an exemplary manner a contradiction between a particular conception of individual rights – with historically specific consequences for questions of sexuality and abortion – and the beliefs

of certain religious traditions, Roman Catholicism and Islam in particular. This looks like a rather familiar kind of ideological conflict which
is resistant to contextual mediation; in fact, it is contextually produced.
Isn't there a point, which comes quite quickly, at which contextualism
isn't going to help you any more?

West That's true. And I must say, it's not just a danger for the vague
contextualism that is wishful about coalitions and alliances. It is inherent
in the dominant tendency in pragmatism itself, which believes that
conflicting views can somehow be adjudicated by appeals to conversation, or civil communication. I'm all for conversation and civil
communication, but the traditions from which I come teach me that
power and privilege are going to go far beyond that, and dialogue is
not always going to be the means for resolving conflicts. In the chapter
on Dewey in *The American Evasion*, I hit him very hard precisely
because, as C. Wright Mills pointed out, the issue of power goes deep.
It's the same problem with Du Bois and white supremacy. He's talking
about dialogue, and acquiring more knowledge of the issue and so forth;
and there's Sam Holes, around the beginning of the century, who was
cut in thirty two parts and 5,000 folk in Atlanta go to buy different
parts, with his penis getting the highest price. And Du Bois says, 'Oh
my God, I've been involved in a scientific investigation concerned with
knowledge, this enlightenment project that highlights ignorance as a
major impediment to freedom, but something else is going on here.'
Yes, Du Bois, you're right! There is a concern or desire for power that
flows far over and beyond the bounds of rational dialogue, even as we
argue that rational dialogue must be a central court of appeal. What
we see in Cairo is fundamental cleavages and conflicts which are not
so much incommensurable; they just clash.

RP They clashed there at the global level, but of course they're also
internal to the societies in which we live.

West That's true even within the Left, with issues of race and gender,
vis-à-vis class or ecology, and so on. Someone like myself, who wants
to put forth some holistic vision that would allow for a coming together,
can't be naive about the ways in which these clashes are rooted in
traditions which are deeply distrustful and suspicious of one another.
Dialogue in and of itself is not ultimately going to create the bridges;
but dialogue is a crucial element in creating a bridge. Dialogue is for
me a form of struggle. There are other forms of struggle as well, and
different historical conjunctures that throw people together; just as there
are different historical conjunctures that create these different conflicts.
They're very real.

RP Isn't this a point at which the libertarian and religious dimensions of
your own thought come into conflict? An old question arises here, the
question of secularism. Wasn't that what was at stake for the European

states at Cairo? Of course, famously, Edward Said's conception of the intellectual is as a secular figure.

West I disagree with brother Edward here. I would just say the 'critical intellectual' – that cuts across religious traditions as well as non-religious ones. But I agree with what he's getting at. When I say 'prophetic', I think I get at it: that is, someone who is critical of *all* forms of authority and highlights critical consciousness across the board. Religious authorities are included alongside economic ones, political ones, and so forth.

RP But isn't that itself a form of secularism? Isn't there something fundamentally secular about the universalization of critical judgement? For example, there are liberal theological traditions which, for this reason, don't really seem to be religious any more.

West That's right. There are elements of this in MacIntyre, the notion that somehow the processes of modernization, rationalization, commodification and nationalization have so thoroughly dissolved the kind of ties and communities requisite for genuine religious practices that the only things left are either these quasi-secular practices, under the name of liberal religion, or fundamentalist ones that are authentically religious. Now, MacIntyre's own view is deeply secular in content – there's no doubt about it – so he finds himself in great tension here. His Aristotle and his Aquinas are, in part, extensions of his own deeply historicist imagination. But what MacIntyre embodies is true for myself: this profound sense of living life on the boundaries, being religious and modern at the same time. He wants both and I want both. But you can't have both without this tremendous tension. The question is whether it's going to be creative or destructive. I can understand persons who would argue that the tension will always be destructive, because the religion that you're talking about is just so thin that it doesn't cut deep any more; that your only options are the thicker forms, which are dogmatic and fundamentalist. You don't want that, because your fundamental allegiance is to modern sensibilities, democratic ones. That's a real tension, but it's something that I try to deal with in my definition of the prophet.

When I talk about the prophet I'm not talking about some kind of revelation from on high, but rather of keeping a certain tradition of resistance and critique alive, in which the issues of the existential and the spiritual, as well as the political, the social and the economic, are in movement together. The question about secularism is a crucial one. But when I see the secular used as a marker, I juxtapose it with the prophetic as my marker, because for me the prophetic is a suspicion of *all* idols, including the secular ones. What Nietzsche and Wittgenstein tell me is distinctive about this particular slice of human history, the age of Europe, is that new kinds of idols are projected. For me, the secular falls too easily into the idol of science and scientific method, the idol of professionalism, the idol of the expert. I want to be anti-idolatrous across the board. That is why I criticize Said, who still wants to view the secular versus the religious in secular terms. I simply attempt to broaden it out.

The Church, the Family, the Democrats

RP I'd like to ask you about a certain conservatism in Afro-American culture which is related to the role of the Church as a site of resistance. It seems connected to the necessarily defensive character of so many of the struggles in which the black community has been engaged, given the extreme inequalities of power in US society. Once again, it concerns questions of individual rights. I'm thinking about the role of the family in relation to issues of sexuality and abortion. Even a film-maker like Spike Lee, about whom you've written, tends to show what I think of as a conservative conception of the family in a very positive light.

West That's true. But the family has played a fundamental role as a countervailing force against white supremacy and other forms of degradation and devaluation. I like to talk about it in terms of the *preservative* versus the *conservative*. You can preserve certain aspects of institutions that have played crucial roles in sustaining people, while subjecting them to democratic ideals and accountability. Yet it's true that the dominant role the black church has played vis-à-vis families has been a conservative one, because the family has been that 'haven in a heartless world' which Christopher Lasch talks about. It's ideally cast: families shot through with brokenness as well as connectedness, dysfunctionality as well as functionality.

It's a difficult issue because you don't want a progressive conception of the family that is not functional on the ground, in terms of how people are actually going to cope as they get about from day to day. On the other hand, you can't use how it functions on the ground as an excuse for accepting uncritically a conservative conception of the family. The black poor are very poor and they're living in a state of siege. A real war is going on, but under war conditions you must still preserve democratic values. This means that women, and gay brothers, and lesbian sisters must have the same status and the same rights that the others have. Yet, given the history of patriarchy and homophobia, the struggle against black patriarchy and black homophobia needs to be cast in the form of an argument for the survival of the black community *as a whole*, in terms of a practical and prudential strategy.

RP Not on the ground of individual rights?

West Exactly, on prudential and practical grounds. Morally, it can be made on libertarian grounds, but politically, prudentially and practically, it's got to be cast in terms of survival, or the real argument will never get off the ground in the black community. This is a struggle that we have daily, weekly, and I encounter it everywhere I go in black contexts.

RP Do you think this struggle has been constructive or destructive for the black community as a whole?

West In the end it must be constructive, because otherwise the black community will self-destruct, owing to the suffocating effects of black patriarchy and black homophobia. But it could also self-destruct if libertarian arguments become the sole grounds for strategic intervention, thereby highlighting cleavages and conflicts, given the prevalence of black patriarchy and homophobia.

RP Broadening the political perspective a little, how do you view the Clinton experience?

West Poor Clinton, he emerged at a deeply conservative moment. He tried to play both sides of the street and for the most part it doesn't work. At the same time, there's hardly any Left to put pressure on him. Most of the pressure has come from Ross Perot, or the conservative populace, or the old tradition's right-wingers – Dole, for example. So whatever progressive tilt he may have wanted, he's been unable to follow through on it: no minimum wage whatsoever, even though Robert Reich had been pushing for it; no serious talk about workers' right to organize, even though they know it's crucial. And the Left has been unable to put pressure on him to help him move in that direction.

RP Is the Democratic Party capable of functioning in that way any more?

West The Democratic Party is a schizophrenic party right now. It is in the process of disintegration. In another fifteen or twenty years it will probably no longer exist as a Democratic party, with a capital 'D' – it's never been democratic with a small 'd'. It's in the process of disintegration, slowly, but it's happening. We'll have to see what's left. It might be that, given the power of the Right, we'll need a Democratic Party just in order to keep some neo-liberals around who at least believe in some kind of accountability of the rule of capital. As the right-wing forces become even more powerful, some of the liberals end up being friends, neo-liberals can even become friends, just by preserving civil liberties and some liberal rule of law; even though we know the limitations of such liberalism. Things get that desperate. My hunch is that we're going in that direction.

In the elections in November, they're projecting that the Republicans will take over the Senate, that the Republicans will take over the House. Sad business. Clinton couldn't even get through a truncated liberal health care deal. Crime bills, as conservative as they can be, are touted as something liberals ought to be excited about. Clinton's bragging about it. We really are talking about some bleak times for progressive possibilities in the United States. Europe knows this better than we do, because we've never experienced the kind of wholesale right-wing takeover, when the fascist Right push everything farther to the right. We're in for a real ugly ride. There's no doubt about it.

It's a struggle on the Left just to keep a certain vision alive, an alternative vision, and to make it available to people. We need to link that vision to some concrete issues; then in the long run we need to create some institutional vehicles for it. Right now we're at the first stage. We don't have too many progressive vehicles beyond single-issue organizations. We don't have too many intellectuals who are trying to find an alternative vision that could gain some exposure to large numbers of persons. And the link between that vision and the concrete issues is a tough one. Single-payer health care was one example. It was crushed, but it was one example that we tried to push through. In Democratic Socialists in America, we tried to make health care a major public issue for nine years and we were unable to do it for the first six or so. Then boom, it just took off and we thought we had a real chance. The country missed the moment. Forget it.

We can work on a state level, because it's going to be federalized. States can enact it, Hawaii and Oregon maybe. But it's going to be difficult and that's just in relation to health, which is now at least an issue people are talking about. We're saying nothing about the right of workers to organize, or workers' power in the workplace, or any serious talk about redistribution of wealth, taxation on wealth, or restructuring of the wage system – all of those crucial strategies that are requisite for the maintenance and sustenance of American society in the next fifty years. Decomposition continues.

RP Is this how you see the medium-term future of American society?

West Well, it doesn't look good, does it? I think there's a good chance that we're in the early moments of a dying civilization, in the process of decomposition and disarticulation and disaggregation. On the other hand, it's never looked good for most working people and poor people. And it certainly has never looked good in America for most black people. So these larger questions of doom and gloom are not really part of my world-view, even though the issues of decline and decay are undeniable. One feels, though, as one gets older, this sense that American civilization as we know it is simply running out of gas.

Interviewed by Peter Osborne
New York, September 1994

8
Feminism, Deconstruction and the Law

Drucilla Cornell

Drucilla Cornell is Professor in the Departments of Law and Political Science at Rutgers University, New Jersey, and author of a series of books – *Beyond Accommodation* (1991), *The Philosophy of the Limit* (1992), *Transformations* (1993) and *The Imaginary Domain* (1995) – which work at the boundaries between feminism, European philosophy and legal theory. Best known for her advocacy of an ethical interpretation of deconstruction as the basis for a feminist critique of the law, her latest writings outline a programme of equivalent rights for a legal recognition of sexual difference.

RP Perhaps you could begin by saying something about the Critical Legal Studies movement in the USA. What is its relationship to feminism? And where do you see your own work as fitting in?

Cornell Regrettably there's very little organized presence of either Critical Legal Studies or what were called the 'femcrits' in the legal academy in the United States in 1994. In the late 1970s and early 1980s when I was a law student, there was something that was called the Conference of Critical Legal Studies, and it had the effect of being a movement. We had yearly conferences; there was a sense of political intervention in the academy, as well as academic discourse promoted by critical legal studies. The femcrits came out of a confrontation of feminists with critical legal studies over the impossibility of feminists being heard. In 1982 or '83, there was a conference run by women which led to the establishment of the femcrits. For several years the femcrits were an organized presence, but all that has been dispersed. There are still women who would consider themselves as writing in feminist juris-prudence, and there are still people who would consider themselves associated with the Conference of Critical Legal Studies, but the expe-rience of movement has disappeared. There was some repression, meaning that people were fired – myself and Clare Dalton being two examples, although there are many more.

RP From law schools?

Cornell Yes, Clare and I were denied tenure within one week of each other. It was seen by people in the Conference of Critical Legal Studies as a response to our association with them. I'm a leftist, so when I became a law professor I affiliated with the Left that was available to me, but my own intellectual and political history is very different from the Conference of Critical Legal Studies.

RP How did you come to be a lawyer?

Cornell I was a student radical and a feminist very early on. I was active in civil rights activities in high school from the age of 16. I went on to college, but I dropped out for a while and went to study Marxism in Germany, in 1969, when there was still a great deal of uproar at the Free University, which is where I went. I considered myself a Left Hegelian. Then I came back to Berkeley, briefly; then went to Santa Barbara. I went to study Heidegger in Freiburg and I ended up at Stanford, where I became involved in the student movement. I joined a Marxist-Leninist organization, since I had decided that if feminism was going to be a truly popular movement it would have to go into factories and organize.

RP What was the organization?

Cornell Venceremos. At the time, it was closely associated with the Black Panther Party. Anyway, we – that's me and the man in my life – joined Venceremos, and we were very involved in the organization. He was a conscientious objector and worked at Pacific Studies Center, and I went to work in a factory, staying in factory work, with a brief spell doing clerical work in New York, until I went back to graduate from college by correspondence from Antioch. So I have a very different trajectory from most academics.

RP Do you view this as a productive period?

Cornell I consider it one of the most productive periods of my life. As I look back now, it's one of the things that I'm most proud that I did, because I was a real union organizer. My entire experience, philosophically, of the question of race, and its relationship to gender, was influenced by relationships with African-American women of such overwhelming quality that they've marked me for life. I'm not the same white girl I would have been had I not had that experience. It was utterly transformative for me. It has shaped me in ways that I can't even describe, including giving me visions of loyalty and possibilities of solidarity between women that I have not experienced before or since. It probably even influenced the distinction I make in my writing between femininity and feminine sexual difference, because I was confronted with a richness of possibility of feminine sexual difference that I couldn't even dream of, as a white girl.

RP Does your critique of MacKinnon come out of this?

Cornell Very much so, and my critique of a certain strand of object-relations theory too. It made me understand that I am white. I live every day knowing I'm white now. Whatever I think of my femininity, my womanhood, it's white. I didn't know that before my union days. I came to understand that even the deepest recesses of how I had been scarred by the wound of femininity were inseparable from my whiteness. I also came to understand that there could be true solidarity between African-American women and white women based, paradoxically, on an understanding of that difference.

Obviously, since I was a union organizer, class was very much part of that experience too. We had a view that struggles between men and women in the community, and the need for women to take up struggles when necessary, should be done through direct organization, rather than through the intervention of the state. I'll give you an example from my consciousness-raising group. Muriel's man did not pay his child-care payments, and we knew that he worked at Harlem Hospital. So rather than proceed through law, we took our consciousness-raising group down to Harlem Hospital and passed out leaflets calling on all the women, our sisters, to join with us in expressing their extreme dissatisfaction with this man's behaviour. And we explained that we were doing this because we didn't want to join with the 'white man's' law, but this man's behaviour was extremely disruptive of any real solidarity. It was a huge success. The man was pelted with food in the cafeteria, he had smoke bombs put in his locker, and the last I heard he was still paying his child-support payments. So this experience involved the idea that there were other creative mechanisms than the legal. We certainly rejected the idea that law was the way to handle intercommunity conflicts.

RP So how did you end up a lawyer?

Cornell It must be the cunning of reason. I got very sick during the last years of my union work and I just burned out, physically. So I decided I would graduate from college. I intended to be a mathematician. I lost my nerve. I'd published some poetry by that time, so I decided to be a writer and support myself as a lawyer who worked for unions. It was the most practical I ever got. Twelve years later, I'm still a law professor. But I never saw feminism getting involved in legal reform as its main focus. Once I became a law professor I joined the Left that was present, but I didn't see that as my primary realm of political activity.

From Hegel to Derrida

RP So where did the Derrida come from? You are associated with a feminist application of deconstruction to legal theory. What is your philosophical background?

Cornell I am totally self-trained, but I started reading philosophy quite seriously in high school – to the point where I had read a great deal of Hegel by the time I entered college. I started taking German in high school so that I could read Hegel in the original and I continued German through college. But for me philosophy wasn't an academic enterprise; it was a deep and profound struggle to come to terms with the world, so that I could find a way to live in it. I didn't think 'I am a Hegel scholar'; I thought 'I am a Left Hegelian, with a particular take on Hegel' – to the point where a number of the women in my consciousness-raising group decided that they wanted to have a subgroup where we read *The Phenomenology of Mind* together. So for me Hegel was a living presence and our Harlem Hospital activity was very influenced by our collective reading of *The Phenomenology of Mind* – even in its rhetoric: the struggle for recognition. For me philosophy was about changing the world, and about how you came to terms with how the world could be changed. I have none of the elitist presuppositions about who can be a philosopher. Like I said, I read *The Phenomenology of Mind* in my consciousness-raising group and all of those women were working-class women.

RP And the Derrida?

Cornell I went the Adorno route. I was one of the very few law professors who focused on teaching Hegel's *Science of Logic*. Since I was a Hegelian, there was no escaping whether or not the logic was 'true'. That had to mean something. And in three years of teaching Hegel's *Science of Logic* I could not defend any workable concept of absolute knowledge as truth. I had already been deeply influenced by the Frankfurt School, by their notion of ideology critique, by negative dialectics. (One of my dreams had been to study with Adorno.) This was a possible trajectory for finding the truth in Hegel, because Adorno is very much within the problematic of Hegel's *Science of Logic*. I took negative dialectics as far as it could go. *The Philosophy of the Limit* opens with my reading of Adorno's *Negative Dialectics*. My interest in the ethical came way before I decided to become a law professor. These were ideas I was having in the late 1970s.

RP This is the piece called 'The Ethical Message of Negative Dialectics'? So your approach to deconstruction was anticipated there, as an ethical reading of Adorno? This is interesting, because *Negative Dialectics* is so often read, especially by Habermasians, as an impasse, the end of the road for the first generation of the Frankfurt School, a work with nowhere to go.

Cornell If there is one goal which has guided me throughout this period of my life, it has been taking the ownership, the appropriation, of Critical Theory away from Habermas and returning it to its radical underpinnings. I do not believe that negative dialectics leads us into the impasse. Philosophically, my interest in the ethical came out of my engagement with Adorno. It was there that I realized that what I had been struggling to articulate through Hegel was not ethics as *Sittlichkeit*, ethics as ethical life, but the concept of responsibility before 'what is not yet'.

I was still Hegelian at this time, so even if 'what is not yet' is there as a negative presence, or a messianic 'now', I was searching for a different way of understanding the emancipatory moment as it was historically produced in its different formations, but also inevitably there. That's what I call the *quasi-transcendental meaning of the limit*. So I was already struggling for something like 'the ethical' as I used it later on, when I read it through Levinas. Although I've backed off Levinas a bit now, because it's too sanctimonious for the radicalism of what I mean by the limit, and the idea of the thereness of the emancipatory moment as both impossible and, because it's impossible, always unerasable.

Regarding Derrida, I was initially concerned that the experience of deconstruction did not carry enough analysis of the force of the beyond as the ethical. So my first encounter with Derrida was quite critical. But later, reading Derrida and Benjamin and Adorno together, I came to see the absent presence of the ethical in Derrida's work.

RP There seem to be two things that are distinctive about your reading of Derrida. On the one hand, it is self-consciously opposed to the sceptical, nihilistic reading which is common in some parts of the American academy. On the other hand, it's much stronger than what others take to be the ethics of deconstruction, by which they often tend to mean little more than an ethics of reading. You want to claim something which is much more ethically substantive.

Cornell *Specters of Marx* – that is my Derrida: the force of the absence of a historicity that marks emancipation as 'something' that can't ever be either erased or fully actualized. He says there (p. 75) :

> It was then a matter of thinking another historicity – not a new history or still less a 'new historicism', but another opening of event-ness as historicity that permitted one not to renounce, but on the contrary to open up access to an affirmative thinking of the messianic and emancipatory promise as promise: as *promise* and not as onto-theological or teleo-escatological program or design. Not only must one not renounce the emancipatory desire, it is necessary to insist on it more than ever, it seems, and insist on it, moreover, as the very indestructibility of the 'it is necessary'.

As someone who was trying to struggle with the truth of Hegel's *Science of Logic*, I was looking for a way to justify the indestructibility of the 'it is necessary' of the emancipatory desire. If there is one theme that has guided me philosophically, it has been that search.

RP This sounds like a generalization of something which appears in Adorno only in relation to art: the promise of happiness. Your reading of Derrida, your Derrida, would recover that promise within the temporal structure of all experience. Is that right?

Cornell The difference between the negativity of Adorno's view of art and Derrida's understanding of impossibility as what always makes the 'it is necessary' indestructible is the difference between their understandings of time. On my reading of Derrida, time, or more precisely temporality, keeps open the 'not yet', but as part of experience. There is never any reason – there can't be – in this real world of ours, for us to give up on our emancipatory desire.

RP But in the Adornian context, isn't the affirmation in the act of producing the object?

Cornell But the production is always of an art. It absolutely rejects the world as it is. Adorno could only see the promise of happiness as a narcissistic return to some kind of imaginary fantasy of childhood, perhaps his own. The world that had denied the happiness had to be abjected. Art maintained the possibility of redemption in abjection, not in political action. For Adorno, the promise of happiness is only the promise of happiness, not the destiny of responsibility. Whereas Derrida's 'it is necessary' means that we are infinitely responsible before the other and, indeed, the otherness of the 'not yet'– a theme he sounds over and over again in the Marx book. In the way I read the philosophy of the limit, it is the quasi-transcendental moment which makes the messianic hope indestructible. That means there can be no reason for giving up. *Specters of Marx* is so powerful for me because it is as far as Derrida has come in putting the present absence of the 'not yet' before us.

Interestingly enough, in his 'two examples of the diverse spirits of Marxism' (and he wants to say we could live up to those spirits in many different ways), one is to intervene in constitutionalism, and fight for human rights. He sees that as a feasible way of being true to one of the spirits of Marxism. The ways we live out this emancipatory desire, and attempt fidelity to it, could be very diverse. What can't be legitimated is the idea that there is one truth to what the political can be, and that there are limits on political possibility which can tell us now that this emancipatory desire is unnecessarily utopian, in the bad, unrealizable sense.

Adorno's placement of the hope of redemption in the abjection of the artist's work was itself a capitulation to what, in a lovely phrase, he called 'the ideology of lesser expectations'. This led him away from the insight (which is so central to *Specters of Marx*) that because of the impossibility of there ever being a truth to the content of emancipation, the emancipatory desire is both necessary and indestructible

– because of the impossibility of a full actualization. This is a very different concept of impossibility from the one Adorno has.

The Philosophy of the Limit

RP Your renaming of deconstruction as a philosophy of the limit returns it to the Kantian tradition. Doesn't it thereby risk losing the measure of its philosophical specificity? You use the term quasi-transcendental, for example, but you also write about the immanence of alterity and iteration. Isn't it one of the advantages of Derrida's Heideggerianism that it gets rid of the whole problematic of the transcendental, which always produces an opposition to the empirical – all these dualisms – returning us instead to something like a pre-transcendental category of transcendence, read now as immanent, through the ecstatic structure of temporality? The idea of the quasi-transcendental doesn't seem complex enough to grasp that.

Cornell There are enormous problems with the idea of immanence in transcendence in any reading of Derrida, because it is almost impossible to articulate it without returning to Hegel, in a strong sense; without returning to the idea of actuality as possibility, to that sense of immanence. I believed that the truth of Hegel that had to be held on to was that actuality and reality had to be rethought. Let's start there, with Derrida and Hegel, and what Derrida says about 'hauntology': time is out of joint.

Temporality means that the very categories of immanence and transcendence are shaken up, because there is no concept of the here-and-now. When time is out of joint, the dislocale of the emancipatory desire, meaning its impossibility of ever being located, *is* its infinite possibility. Immanence and transcendence take us back to a relationship between actuality and the real which is, for me, inadequate.

RP But doesn't the idea of the transcendental take us out of temporality altogether?

Cornell Well, yes it does, in Kant, that's undeniable; but it depends what we do with Kant. For many years now, I've been struggling with Rawls's attempt to redefine Kantian constructivism in a way which is consistent with a certain Piercean critique of metaphysics. (I'm not sure that Rawls would put it that way, but this is me reading Rawls.) I'm interested in whether what I call the philosophy of the limit, and what Rawls calls Kantian constructivism, could have some kind of alliance. I've been struggling to articulate what that alliance might be via an engagement with Charles Pierce.

However, we're going to have to specify the political role Kantian constructivism plays, because for me feminism is very much about emancipatory desire and impossibility, and it goes way beyond what Rawls claims for the proper sphere of his Kantian project. What I see as the truth of the quasi-transcendental is that time is introduced, but not as what we think of as time. It's much closer to some of the conceptions of temporalization to be found in the new physics.

RP I found your essay on temporality and legal interpretation in *The Philosophy of the Limit* extremely interesting, but I wonder if there's anything specifically deconstructive about your position. Wouldn't Heidegger's notion of existential temporalization from *Being and Time* do just as well?

Cornell No, I don't think so at all. I agree with Derrida that sometimes what is most ancient is the only way to know what is most new: *différance*. The way that I read Derrida as a philosopher of the limit is that there could never be a system that could so self-enclose itself that it would not be delimited by its Other. The concept of delimitation, which is a way of thinking about the relationship of transcendence to immanence, is inherent in *différance*. A field of significance which frames itself will always delimit itself, and thereby produce, in that sense of what it means to be a delimitation, its Other. There's no simple return to Kantian metaphysics, but for me there is no simple getting rid of Kant either.

In the United States, Kantianism has gone in two interesting directions: the political constructivism of Rawls and the meta-notion of validity developed by Pierce. If there's such a thing as Piercean philosophy, it's this meta-view of validity. Now, there's a moment in *Specters of Marx*, when Derrida talks about living out the diverse spirits of Marx, when he evokes a concept of practical reason that's very close to Pierce. The concept of the limit of theoretical reason is extremely important for the way in which what is traditionally called practical philosophy has to be rethought, in all of its *theoretical* claims.

RP This raises a rather different question about limits: not the limit as the production of the possible, infinite possibility, but the limit of what you can do with deconstruction. It is connected to Derrida's use of the idea of the iterative as an opening up of possibilities. My problem is this: you have a philosophical argument for the fact that there is this space of infinite possibility (although no project can ever be fully actualized in it), but you don't have anything to put in it, since your sense of the limit warns that it is both erroneous and dangerous to try to fill the gap philosophically. So what goes in it? Politics goes in it. But what's the basis of the politics? What are the principles? What are the aims? How do we justify them? We seem to get into a kind of stalemate through the philosophical opening up of a practical space, the terms of which don't allow us to use philosophy to justify the way in which we occupy it.

Cornell I don't think that's true. This takes us back to my own trajectory. I read Derrida at a particular moment, as a Left Hegelian who'd gone out to actualize the ideal and found some major limits to the process of actualization! I had no intention of giving up on being a radical, but I needed to rethink the philosophical basis of my radicalism. Derrida has helped me elaborate the complexity that has to be part of any understanding of being that undermines the simple divide between being and non-being. Hegel's fundamental mistake in *The Science of Logic* is to start as if being, even as indistinguishable from nothing, could be the primary category for investigation. Instead, Derrida begins with temporalization. The result is a 'hauntology' that effectively undermines the traditional categories of transcendence and immanence, and demonstrates the experience of deconstruction as the experience of delimitation of the possibility of any coming together of philosophical presence.

If by philosophical principle you mean what Reiner Schürmann, I think correctly, reads the philosophical tradition to mean – a principle grounded in the truth of being – then of course there's no way to occupy the philosophical space left open by Schürrmann's brilliant reading of Heidegger, and his replacement of principle with anarchy. What I was left with at the end of *The Philosophy of the Limit* was this indestructible emancipatory desire, as it is necessary, and always possible, because it's impossible. So what does that mean, practically? We can't proceed through Hegel's *Science of Logic* to ground the principles of ethics in the truth of being. What can we do? This is where Charles Pierce comes in. We can begin to rethink the very idea of practice at the level of what we call law. This is a very Piercean project. What are the different fields of significance? What are the claims that can be made for objectivity, and validity, and reason, within those fields of significance? Knowing these fields of significance can never be philosophically totally bounded doesn't mean they can't be analytically distinguished. So the question becomes: How can you develop a practical philosophy that already assumes the distinction between theoretical and practical reason, as the basis of enlightened tolerance?

RP My worry is to do with the relationship between this philosophical discourse and the construction of social theory. The key term here is 'theory'. Can the idea of theory survive the rigours of a deconstructive pragmatism? Some people still use the term, but it seems peculiar to describe Derrida as having a 'theory' of any kind. One effect of Derrida's influence in the social sciences (marginal though it is, if growing) has been a certain liquidationism in social theory, a certain delegitimation of theory construction as philosophically naive. This may not be justified, philosophically, but it is very much a part of the intellectual culture of deconstruction in the Anglo-American context. What are your views about this?

Cornell Let me be very clear. A critique of the limits of theoretical reason, and of the possibility of uncovering principles in the ground of the truth of being, or some other notion of objectivity, does not mean that the field of practical reason is necessarily influenced in any particular direction. To fail to note that is to fail to note the disjuncture between registers of thought, and, more specifically, the distinction between theoretical and practical reason.

Habermas is trying to think a pure view of practical reason, theoretically; deconstruction tells you why you can't do that. Pierce already understood that there is no such thing as a pure view of practical reason. Derrida's delimitation of the possibility of such a project means that Habermas's project is no longer philosophically justified. That's true. Meanwhile, however, Rawls's Piercean Kantian constructivism need not be *touched* by this overarching critique of theoretical reason. To be honest, I never considered myself a deconstructionist. I read Derrida out of my Hegelian trajectory. My question is how to think difference as it's relevant to sexual difference, and the field of practical reason that I think has to be 'filled in' – the space of feminist legal reform.

Femininity and the Feminine

RP Let's get back to that. Could you explain your distinction between femininity and the feminine?

Cornell For me the feminine is identified with femininity as understood through Lacan's symbolic analysis of a cultural order based on patriarchal lineage, with a family triangle that dominates because of patrilineage. The feminine 'is' the paradox of being the objective other that does not have any adequate symbolization. In its place is the objectification of the psychical fantasy of woman. Women are forced to identify, or disidentify, with these fantasy structures. One problem for second-wave feminism was that we went back and forth between identification, non-identity and dis-identification. We were caught up with what it would mean to dismas-querade the masquerade.

RP So you accept the Lacanian masculinization of the symbolic?

Cornell Partially. For example, I see law as an example in which the masculinization of the symbolic is so close to being complete that feminist interventions have found it very difficult to avoid simply replicating the psychical fantasy of woman.

RP But isn't it *always* complete, for Lacan, in principle? And doesn't this have certain restrictive consequences for possible political strategies which run counter to your use of Derrida? In *Beyond Accommodation*, for example, following Irigaray's inverted Lacanianism, you say: 'Mimesis is the only strategy.' Yet if one accepts the Derridean critique of Lacan – which I take to be consistent with the ethical impulse of your work – a whole range of refigurations of gender becomes possible, beyond those confined by the concept of mimicry. There seems to be a tension here.

Cornell There is a tension, but I see my own work as much more involved in the tragedy. Let me clarify what I mean. I think there is a deep and profound engendering on the level of the work of culture; but I also think that reconfiguration is always possible within it. My reading of Derrida into Lacan is about the truth that cannot be true, the reverse of the truth, which is fiction. Unlike one reading of Judith Butler in *Gender Trouble*, I have much more militantly insisted that there is a *wound* of femininity, and that wound of femininity is something which has to be marked in its tragedy. So while I would now elaborate the possibilities of reconfiguration much more expansively that I did in *Beyond Accommodation*, I remain – at least for today – more Lacanian than some queer theorists. I want it both ways. My phrase to describe the normalization of heterosexuality as inseparable from imposed femininity is 'het hell' (maybe this is Judith Butler's 'heterosexual hegemony'). I believe there is such a thing as het hell. I believe that femininity is profoundly inscribed in het hell, and I believe that it has overwhelming cultural implications.

RP So het hell is a specific type of normative heterosexuality which is socially inscribed at the level of the psyche. But is it fixed in early life or can it be changed?

Cornell It can be changed but only with the greatest difficulty, because it is a materialization of the system of gender, and I do believe that it is a system. The system operates to enclose itself by materializing this reality of gender. You see it in law all the time.

RP But isn't this talk of system – your recent use of Luhmann's systems theory – quite different from the Lacanian symbolic? Doesn't it operate at a quite different level of analysis?

Cornell Absolutely. But Lacanianism has two advantages here: (i) it gives us a symbolic analysis while still allowing us to socialize a psycho-analytic critique (although it doesn't give us the tools to do it); and (ii) it enriches the concept of the field of significance with the play of unconscious fantasies, with a very different take on individual investment. The struggle to disinvest and make yourself truly unreadable in terms of gender categories is long and arduous. I think it's possible, and I think it's the only hope for everybody, in Adorno's sense of a promise of happiness. The more unreadable you become, the better. But it's a long struggle, and you don't know for sure when you're doing it and when you're not!

RP There are a couple of phrases that crop up a lot in your work which seem to mark an uneasiness about this. One is the 'feminine imaginary' – which is an odd expression because your theoretical position suggests that the imaginary is always feminine, so there seems to be a redundancy there; the other is 'feminine sexual difference' – which is a strange way of referring to sexual difference if the feminine is only one side of the difference.

Cornell Now I prefer the feminine *within* sexual difference. I believe that there is a system in which the feminine within sexual difference has been reduced through the psychical fantasy of woman. In Luhmann's sense, we have a field of observation in which we cannot even see the diversity of actual women. Look at bell hooks' books. Why are certain women seen as beautiful? This is a question that she returns to. For her that question is inseparable from something I started this interview with: the way in which the psychical fantasy of woman is coloured through all these notions of attractiveness, as white. What I want to try to do, what I'm struggling to do, within the feminine, within sexual difference, is to come up with words that separate femininity from the need to open up the field of significance that has marked us all as woman.

I don't think anyone escapes. I don't think there's anyone who started their life as the unreadable other. It's an achievement, and a big one. You need an account of what you are making yourself unreadable against; and paradoxically, the feminine within sexual difference is the affirmation of the feminine, so the category of the feminine as femininity would ultimately transform itself. This is a deconstructive moment. We can't leap over gender hierarchy without having to struggle within the wound of femininity. To erase the feminine is not only a philosophical mistake; it's a political mistake which will reinscribe the repudiation of the feminine, a repudiation inseparable from the reinscription of gender hierarchy.

RP How does this relate to gay and lesbian politics? One objection to the Lacanian underpinning of this affirmation of the feminine within sexual difference is that it is fixated with one dimension of sexual politics: the heterosexual dimension.

Cornell I am rethinking my answer to this question. For now, let me say that a classic example of the dephallicization of the familial triangle occurs when two lesbian mothers insist on the name mummy. I know several couples who have done that. I consider it both a demand for the restructuring of the family, a dephallicization of the way in which the triangle plays out, with the two parents and the child, a resymbolization of the mother, a resymbolization of the other lover, and a political challenge to the very idea of the feminine as designatable as the unsymbolizable other.

Two mothers is an impossibility in the symbolic oedipal scheme, but it's precisely that kind of imagined impossibility that I see as making this act so profoundly disruptive of the symbolic fantasy of heterosexual family life. Traditional Freudian ego psychology would say that there can't be two mothers. I completely disagree: and this is not just the case with a lesbian couple. An adopting mother is always in a relationship with another mother. You can deny it, you can repress it, but you're in a relationship with another mother.

Sexual Difference and the Law

RP Perhaps we could move on to the relationship between sexual difference and the law. In the case of abortion, you defend it in terms of the right to bodily integrity. Now, on the one hand, this seems to fall within a conventional liberal conception of the legal subject, in the sense that it's an ungendered right; but on the other hand, it's gendered in its application – it has specific consequences when applied to women because of their different bodies. Is this as far as legal theory can or should go in recognizing sexual difference?

Cornell Well, we have to ungender rights. Let's take the question of gay and lesbian rights before the law. For me, sexual difference is at stake in discrimination against any form of sexuality – transsexual, transvestite, whatever the person means to claim as their sexuality. There was the case of the pilot who decided to add breasts but not be castrated. This provoked a huge debate about whether or not he was a man or a women. But he was fired because he chose to imagine his sexual difference in a different way. I call for legislation against discrimination on the grounds of any form of sexuate being. The gender comparison through which sex discrimination law has been articulated so far is conservative of the very idea of sexual difference.

In the case of the pilot, the pleading had to be that he was 'really' a woman for purposes of the law in order to have standing to sue for sex discrimination. My argument is that part of the legal conservatism of feminism is indissociable from the conscious decision of legal feminists to separate feminism as a struggle for equal rights for women from sexual radicalism. We have to militantly deny that move within legal reform and call for equality for all forms of sexuate being. Otherwise, analysis of gender hierarchy will not only reinscribe symbolically limiting conceptions of feminine sexual difference, which won't allow its explosive power; it will also reinscribe the conservatism that there's a good feminism (meaning not queer feminism) and a bad feminism. That conservatism has been a conscious part of legal reform in the United States in my lifetime. It's a big thing for me. Feminist legal reform must go back and make up for the wrong direction that was taken.

Now, in terms of my position on abortion, I don't think the right of bodily integrity exists because we actually have bodily integrity. I think it exists because we need to have our imaginary projection of ourselves as a person protected. My concept of the imaginary is both psychoanalytical and phenomenological. What the right of bodily integrity means in the arena of abortion is that the woman has the right to imagine her own pregnancy, and the state has no right to impose any meaning on it. That means she can mourn, because she imagined it as a baby; or she can be indifferent to it. It's not the state's business to ask her. There is no inherent meaning to pregnancy. Of course, we have these fantasies associated with pregnancy – killing mothers and the like – but they should not be imposed by the state. The bottom line is that women have the right to have an abortion, in good medical facilities, fully paid for by the state all the way through to the cutting of the umbilical cord, and no one can stop them. In a way, it's 'liberally argued', within the concept of bodily integrity; but once you turn the meaning of maternity over to women you open up all kinds of different possibilities – including the legal recognition that Mamma Barbara and Mamma Patty are actually two mothers, and that it's wrong to make one the birth mother and one the adopting mother.

There should be no need for adoption for lesbian mothers, because the meaning they give to their act of maternity already makes this their baby. So if you really took it seriously, this argument wouldn't just affect straight women, and it wouldn't just affect abortion, it would affect the whole way that maternity is constructed and governed by the state. We have to take these issues away from the state and turn them back into the politics of our lives. Why does the child have to belong to only one mother? Where do we get all this from? We get it from the enforced patriarchal triangle. But as an adoptive mother I can imagine a different relationship with the 'birth mother'. I should be allowed to actualize it.

RP How does this fit into your notion of transformative legal interpretation? Given the existing legal tradition, are there not fairly strict hermeneutical constraints on how transformative your interpretations can be? What if you want legal interpretations that are more transformative than the hermeneutical resources of your legal tradition allow?

Cornell Law is inherently a conserving system; but the right of bodily integrity is an enormously powerful one in our culture. It will help women lawyers and women justices see pregnancy and maternity differently. You can take the right of bodily integrity, change the elaboration of its defence, come up with a much more radical articulation, and create a paradox within the hermeneutical field itself. Transformative interpretation elaborates the right in a disjunctive and paradoxical way, and that disjuncture, that paradox, opens up the field.

However, as somebody who's not arguing before the court, I also want to make a political point. What I'm ultimately saying is that all law can do is help zone out certain encroachments on our politics. When we look to law for the substantive transformation of this hermeneutical field, we are severely mistaken. Law is inherently limited: not just by the fact that it distributes force and coercion, but by the fact that its field of hermeneutical significance is by definition a conservative system. However, we can intervene in some of the traditional hermeneutical parameters offered to us, to protect an imaginary domain in which most of queer and feminist politics has to take place. I have written a book on legal reform, but what I hope is that it will get women back in the streets again, because the rights of abortion, and Medicaid for abortion, and good services for abortion, are not going to be won on the level of the courts. And they're certainly not going to be protected there. When we marched for it, we got it. When we stopped marching, we've seen nothing but curtailments. Legal reform is not at the heart of feminist politics.

RP But you still need a positive evaluation of the resources of the existing tradition.

Cornell Not really. The traditional legal resources turn on the backdrop of Lacan's symbolic: the absolute taken-for-grantedness of the heterosexual nuclear family. And the absolute taken-for-grantedness of the heterosexual nuclear family means that any call for women to have the governing power over their own maternity is a radical demand, even if it is liberally expressed. What it shows is that there's enormous tension in the liberalism that publicly articulates itself with its 'private foundations' in the heterosexual matrix. I'm actually very uncomfortable with the word 'liberal', because in the United States it really means law in economics. Dworkin's liberalism, Rawls's liberalism, do not dominate. What dominates is Hobbesian liberalism.

RP Despite your emphasis on interpretation, you never refer to hermeneutics in your books. But isn't transformative legal interpretation a kind of critical hermeneutics?

Cornell No. Interpretation has to proceed much more through what Habermas fears: paradox and performative contradictions. The legal field blocks off legal engagement as part of the public domain from the thoroughgoing challenge to the status of femininity. You can't simply enter the feminine internally. You can enter it from the standpoint of bodily integrity, yes, but when you plug the feminine into it the Right starts going haywire. It's like a television that doesn't work. It can't mean anything. For critical hermeneutics, on the other hand, there is a field of significance and everything is within it. (Maybe this is the Lacanian moment that I won't give up about the feminine.) The symbolization of the feminine within sexual difference is not within the hermeneutical field of legal significance at this time, yet feminist jurisprudence has continuously tried to operate within the encoded definitions of femininity that are part of that hermeneutical field.

RP So you associate hermeneutics with a Gadamerian sense of the given?

Cornell I don't think that you can take it away from that. Part of the reason I was attracted to Luhmann was that I wanted to talk about the systemization of meaning, the materialization of meaning, but I also wanted to talk about its violent bordering against certain forms of inclusion. What happens when you start to introduce the feminine as a legal subject in kinship systems is that you find there's no place for it in this field of meaning. There's no place for the articulation of the feminine Other as equal subject in the law, at this time, without utterly exploding the current conjuring of the heterosexual matrix, and the concept of the subject. It's that basic to our legal system.

Politics and Society

RP Perhaps we could move on to the question of the relationship between the law and society. There has been a wide-ranging debate in Britain over the last decade about the virtues of a written constitution. In Britain, at present, there's no distinction between constitutional and statute law. Partly in reaction to Thatcherism, there has been a growing Left–liberal movement in favour of a written constitution and a Bill of Rights: the suggestion being that if there had been a Bill of Rights, the Thatcher government could not have restructured the state in the way in which it did, because there would have been constitutional barriers to, for example, the removal of certain trade union rights. What is your view about such arguments?

Cornell Well, I've thought about it a lot in the course of my life as a union organizer, because I was quite an anarcho-syndicalist in my youth. I always had deep suspicions about relying on law as anything other than a practical weapon for political movements, particularly trade union movements. But overall in a long process of thinking about it, I've concluded that the consolidation which law offers can help prevent exhaustion. It's difficult to fight the same battle over and over again. However, I also think that constitutional history, as invested in by Federal Court judges, kept some of Reagan's economic 'reforms' at bay. I really do. At that time, the Left was very weak in this country, and keeping certain repressive measures at bay has left open a little more space. The legalization of feminism (its increasing concern with legislative reform) has to do with the sense of overwhelming powerlessness that took place in the United States during the Reagan period.

At the same time, there are serious weaknesses in the United States, because of the power of law in the popular imagination. People think that law does much more good to men and women on the street than it actually does. For example, in the fight against sex discrimination, the expense of a law suit makes it almost impossible for any ordinary woman, or man, to fight back legally.

RP What forms do you see radical social movements taking now, accepting the limitations and the conservative character of the law, and the connection of the whole US party system to big capital?

Cornell There is some discussion about trying to develop a third party, but it's never worked before in the United States, because this is such an entrenched tradition. Our union movement has been practically destroyed – that's a case where law did nothing to protect it. We don't really have, at this point in history, a popular place of mobilization. It's hard to tell whether a revival of the union movement is possible. Right now, every year the United States loses union members. It's down to 11 per cent of the workforce and falling. The unions are enormously conservative. The political unions I worked in never really succeeded in overcoming the anti-communism of McCarthyism. This is a really very powerfully reactionary country. Still, I believe we must continue to struggle. For example, as feminists, we should have backed the union effort by Una Zel Wiegers in the pornography industry, rather than focusing primarily on legal regulation of the industry. As a form of popular organization, the idea of a union is clearly not dead.

RP And do you think feminism exists as a social movement in the United States at this time?

Cornell Yes. It's such a profound phantasm that it's endlessly attacked! It may not be anything you can belong to, but we know who we are when we're attacked. We know the enemy. So yes, it exists but it's lost its organizational force. The legalization of feminism has now become the focus of the attacks: 'they're trying to control sexuality, they're trying to regulate pornography, etc.' It's affected what I call the long and arduous struggle to become unreadable. That's what Judith Butler and I share: the aim is to be so unreadable that what our gender is could, in fantasy at least, be untranslatable.

What happened with the decline of the solidarity of the 1970s is that many women reverted to traditional forms of normative heterosexuality. In my new life as a mother, in playgroup, I'm the only mother who works. There's no subsidization of child care in the United States. When it is not endlessly contested, and when alternative forms of the most basic sense of support are not provided, the engendering system reasserts itself. You can see how little feminism has reached into the cultural encodings of women. But I am commanded in my responsibility to my daughter to continue to hope and to affirm my political activism.

Interviewed by Peter Osborne
September 1994, New York

9
Setting to Work (Transnational Cultural Studies)

Gayatri Chakravorty Spivak

Gayatri Chakravorty Spivak is Avalon Foundation Professor in the Humanities at Columbia University, New York, and the author of several highly influential collections of essays in literary and cultural theory and the politics of criticism: *In Other Worlds* (1988), *Outside in the Teaching Machine* (1993) and *The Spivak Reader* (1996), published by Routledge. Spivak made her name in the 1970s as the translator of the English-language edition of *Of Grammatology*, by Jacques Derrida – a figure almost unheard of at the time in the Anglo-American academy – to which she contributed an extraordinary eighty-page Translator's Preface. Associated since then with the growth of deconstruction in North America, Spivak has been perhaps its most creative practitioner, extending its range far beyond that of its originator in a four-way exchange with Marxism, feminism and Subaltern Studies. A frequent exponent of the interview form (see her collection *The Post-Colonial Critics: Interviews, Strategies, Dialogues*, 1990), she is also the translator and interpreter of the fiction of the Bengali writer Mahasweta Devi; a collection of which, *Imaginary Maps: Three Stories by Mahasweta Devi*, appeared in 1995.

Notable in its early phase for both the tenacity and consistency of its anti-essentialism, Spivak's work has become increasingly concerned with the institutional sites of cultural agency, as the productive locus of signifying power. By thus attempting to read Derrida and Foucault through each other, Spivak has moved beyond the more purely textual deconstruction of her colleagues, towards the elaboration of a new theoretical approach to the study of power as cultural form.

RP Could I begin by asking you to situate your recent work within the field of deconstructive criticism in America? You once described yourself as 'a Marxist outsider in the deconstructive establishment'. Do you still see yourself that way? Somehow it doesn't seem to do justice to the specificity of your position any more.

Spivak Well, I am definitely an outsider, although 'Marxist' may now be a little inaccurate. In terms of my work, the way I am an outsider is very much influenced by the length of time that I've been reading Derrida. It's twenty seven years now, and I've read him with some care. I stopped reading the stuff as it was coming out in the middle, but then I started again, very carefully. So the importance of deconstruction to my way of thinking is a solid fact of my intellectual life. On the other hand, although I have always tried to work with these ideas I'm not interested in proving myself a Derridean. Meanwhile, a whole deconstructive circus has developed, to which I really don't belong, and I am bemused by this phenomenon.

RP I was thinking more in terms of what you have tried to do with the ideas. The thing that struck me most forcibly about your recent collection, *Outside in the Teaching Machine*, was the way it's held together, framed, by the interview about anti-essentialism at the beginning and the essay about transnationality at the end. It suggests a certain logic to your development, if that's not too strong a term, which goes something like this. First, there was the deconstructive critique of essentialism. This led a lot of people to a generalised anti-essentialist position, which was soon revealed to have problems of its own. (It is difficult to think its relation to practice.) Your way of dealing with this was to inflect the deconstructive understanding of anti-essentialism into a defence of 'strategic' essentialism. This was very popular with those wanting to combine their anti-essentialism with politics; specifically, a politics of identity. Next, however (in the interview with Rooney), came the critique of strategic essentialism. This was a political critique directed at the effects of generalizing strategy into theory. It's connected to your attempt to think about agency – institutional agency – in a new way. Now, there seems to be a lot more than deconstruction going on here, even the deconstruction of a 'Marxist outsider'. At one point, for example, you talk about 'complicating' both economic and philosophical theory by cultural material. How does that relate to your understanding of deconstruction?

Spivak Rather directly, I think, for I understand the word 'culture' in this context in a deconstructive, nominalist way: as a name lent to a complex strategic situation in a particular society.

RP And what is it about this situation which makes essentialism the wrong strategy?

Spivak I had something fairly simple in mind: namely, that US culture is so profoundly personalist and nationalist – a peculiar kind of nationalism,

I admit, but still a very nationalist culture – that the strategic use of essentialism was bound to become a simple convenience for identitarians. First it was a strategy, a repeated strategy, whenever the need arose, but still a strategy; then it became a theory. But my problem was with *what* it could strategically be used for and against. That's the thing that made me rethink it.

RP And the thinking of institutional agency which is to replace it? What is its theoretical form?

Spivak You have to remember that I'm taking the word *institution* in a very broad sense here to refer to something that is instituted, an instituted script within which one acts, acts in that robust sense where one interprets a sign or understands a role. And what I'm doing is learning to learn. I'm trying to learn from real subalternity, even as we keep in mind the question of democratic agency in countries where the largest part of the electorate is the rural subaltern. It involves an incredible spending of both time and money, and a giving of skill and so on, in order to have that opportunity. One has the most extraordinary series of experiences if one is trying to learn within this collision of two instituted scripts: a rights-based notion of democracy and the various responsibility-based ethical 'systems' that shore up subalternity. This provides the possibility of what, for the Derrideans, would be a situation of responsibility – with responses running from both sides.

Now, when you think about institution in that way, as something already in place which allows you to act as an agent, then you're not just thinking about institutions in the conventional sociological sense. That to me is more important than taming essences. Basically it's about learning the marks of the material essences in which agencies are located. I find the idea that something socially constructed is anti-essentialist boring. I would say: what is 'society' if not an essence?

And I'm not talking about masquerade. Getting into the skin of a role, learning the marks, is not a masquerade. It's a radical institution of another script in an already constituted agent. This is not very far from the notion of the instituted trace. Yet it is also very far, because the context is different. Remember where Derrida talks about *différance* never appearing outside its text, in the essay 'Différance'? In the first version, Allison translated it as 'context'. And he wasn't far wrong. It isn't the colloquial sense of context, of course, but that's what is meant by this instituted script.

RP In your own work, the context is some notion of the transnational, is it not? Could you say something about your use of the idea of transnationality, what it means for cultural study, and how it relates to ideas of the national and the international?

Spivak I took the word 'transnational' from the discussions of the structure of companies. I used it to get around both the word 'international' and the meretricious notion of the 'post-national' which is very trendy nowadays. It's part of radical chic, because the well-placed migrant community, the so-called hyphenated Americans, the real culture-wallas, think that what's happening to them is basically what's happening. It's an old mistake, but unfortunately it's being rehearsed once again. It goes along with the idea of globalization as a kind of a 'good thing'. Globalization is actually an alibi word to cover Americanization. If America is understood as the dominant force in the three main trans-national agencies (the IMF, the World Bank and GATT, now being supplanted by the World Trade Organization), and you call it 'global-ization', then for some reason it becomes a good thing. This is where post-nationality plays its game, because in the context of a First World space your migrants have no sense of nationalism old-style. It allows them to put a cap on the North–South divide. And when they go on their sol-idarity tourism binges, they don't spend enough time. So when they see these satellite dishes here and there in the restricted rural areas that they travel in (it's the same areas that are worked over by the World Bank), they find enough examples floating around. If you want to see global-ization, you'll see globalization. Nice. But you won't understand it.

What I am interested in is the *financialization* of the globe in terms of these three transnational agencies. If you want to be extremely formu-laic, you could say that the South (the new code name for the Third World after the fall of the Soviet Union) is assisting the North in sustaining its lifestyle, and this is managed in the name of aid coming the other way. This is 'development'. Now – I'm coming to culture – in the context of all this, what one needs to notice is how something called 'culture' (in many different ways, shapes and forms) is negotiated in order to take various kinds of positions on these issues. This use of 'culture' – use, not content – finds something like a description in Foucault's account of how he uses the word 'power'. This is what I was invoking earlier as nominalism: 'a name that one lends to a complex strategic situation in a particular society'. There is a loose set of *enoncés* which constitutes something like a cultural cluster. It is with them that the negotiations are undertaken. This is very different from claiming a cultural identity.

RP How does this approach relate to the transformation of comparative literature – to the idea of transnational cultural studies as an outcome of the deconstruction of comparative literature?

Spivak At its best, the notion of comparative literature is anchored in language learning, getting into the skin of a language. If this really could be operative in transnational culture studies, it would be great. Anthropological language learning, even at its best, does not get under the skin of language. You don't compute with the software of that language when you are working in that way. The anthropological is by definition not learning to learn, but learning enough in order to transcode for another audience, generally anthropologists. This last is mainly what comparative literature does in a literary way. I fear the received notion of comparative literature will explode in my kind of culture studies.

Post-Coloniality and Hybridity

RP What is the relationship of this kind of transnational cultural studies to the concept of the post-colonial? Does the post-colonial function as a unifying concept for the current historical moment here? This is increasingly how it appears to function for some – as a heuristic concept for redefining the field around a single point.

Spivak Namely?

RP Decolonization. It provides a periodization of history according to a colonial/post-colonial divide, as opposed to modes of production, for example, or political conjunctures.

Spivak 'Post-colonial' . . . I must say that this word, like 'subaltern', has really bitten the dust. I don't know what to do with it any more. I still use it, just as I use the word subaltern, but I feel a sense of the vanity of human wishes when I use those words. Do you want me to continue, since I seem so sad?

RP Yes, please . . .

Spivak I mean it quite seriously. Anything that's related to any kind of migrating skin colour is suddenly called post-colonial in some university curriculum or description of what someone does. In this country, it's distinguished from Afro-American, Native American and so on, but it really just means new immigrants. What bothers me is that it's taken up by so many as a kind of good work. It means we have survived colonialism. But when some of us used the word 'post-colonial' to begin with, we really meant the beginning of economic colonialism, fully-fledged. I'm not a Leninist, but that thing of Lenin's about capitalism turning into imperialism was a solid insight. In a certain sense, this transnational stuff is a reconstellation of Marx's object of study. In that context, post-colonial was used by us as a name for the inauguration of neo-colonialism in state contexts. Now it just means behaving as if colonialism didn't exist.

RP Nonetheless, even in your sense, in the sense that had a political edge, where it was a word for neo-colonial, might it not mark the inauguration of a new global period in economic relations, with a different political shape? Or is it too specific to national contexts? The periodization doesn't seem to work for Latin America, for example.

Spivak No, it doesn't and I've said that. I agree with you completely. Those of us who were thinking the post-colonial in the early days were taking the model of colonialism from the nation-state colonialism of Western Europe. In my Marx seminar, I'm reading Stalin's papers on colonialism and the national question; not because Stalin is so great, but because I want my students to see that all this talk about multi-national empires is not new. People thought about it before: the Russian, the Hapsburg, the Ottoman. Now, with the Commonwealth of Independent States and the Russian Federation, and all of the problems of ethnic cleansing which go back to unsettled debts in the Ottoman Empire (or rather, these three empires moving together), we can't think of post-coloniality in terms only of nation-state colonialism. We have to think of it in different ways. Otherwise, it becomes more and more a study of colonial discourse, of then rather than now. You can no longer whinge on about imperialism. We're looking at the failure of decolonization. That's why I find these new laments about imperialism really . . .

Bangladesh, South Africa, even these places don't fit the old model. The only three places that distinctly fit the model are India, Algeria, and maybe Nigeria. The differences are much more interesting. In the strict sense, the failure of decolonization has gone so far that it's almost no use calling these places post-colonial at all. Whereas if you follow the Lenin line, neo-colonialism is changing its shape constantly: with the new world order, the North–South divide, the collapse of non-alignment, and GATT playing a completely different role. During the GATT round, they waited and waited and waited and the Soviet Union fell and fell and fell. Now that was interesting. That's not post-coloniality. There you really saw how the transnational was moving. And what has happened as a result? Economic restructuring, economic underdevelopment, to use an old-fashioned term. One area is the super-exploitation of women: home-working, post-Fordist fax-based unorganized casual women's work. Even the export processing zones and international subcontracting are already a bit in the past. Even neo-colonialism has too old-fashioned a ring to it. There is space for a reconstellation of the Marxist project here.

I have just seen what happens when benevolent First World women are clueless about this in the farce of the Cairo conference. There was no concept of transnationality there. You have to get into it to see how much development is an alibi for exploitation, how much it's a scam: the responsibility for the entire world's ills is between the legs of the poorest women of the South. George Bush was reported as saying after the Rio conference: 'Our lifestyle is not negotiable.' So many stories in the mainstream media are based on sensationalist details and human interest, without any emphasis on the critique of international capital. But if that critique were attended to, and if these women were not reduced to untheorized producers of human interest stories and sensationalist details, there would be a much broader context for what one can call transnational culture studies. It would set it to work, so it could become a means rather than an end, rather than just a refurbishment of comparative literature. These are idiotically hope-filled words, I know, but there they are.

RP What about the attempt to rethink the concept of culture itself through the idea of colonial difference, in terms of some generic notion of hybridity? What do you make of that?

Spivak Well, if you take hybridity in the narrow sense, there is an implicit assumption that there is something which is pure. But if you consider the hybrid as general, so that you have a sort of non-exhaustive taxonomy of different kinds of hybridity, then the old problems still obtain. On the other hand, when the word culture is used in the same way as Foucault uses the word power (to give a name to a complex strategic situation in a particular society), there I see that you can use the idea of hybridization. Let me tell you what the complex strategic situation is, and what the particular societies are.

The particular societies are developed states. The complex strategic situation is where people have come hoping for justice under capitalism. They see that the dominant European cultures are saying that the rational abstractions of civil society (not in the World Bank sense, but in the old Enlightenment sense, *bürgerliche Gesellschaft*) have an appropriate cultural subject. They question this. That is the complex strategic situation. So one thing which may be suggested by the claim that culture is something that determines you beyond the principle of reason is that access to the rational abstractions of civil society should not mean having to fit the appropriate cultural subject, because there ain't really any such thing. No migrant community will or should ever give up the claim for civil rights. In those contexts there is sometimes even a demand for the acknowledgement of locatable so-called 'cultural practices', often on the bodies of women: clitoridectomy, the veil . . . But I think it is a mistake to transform that into a theory of hybridity, because then you have the two problems that I talked about before.

Everyone is a hybrid, good and fine. But if you take it in the narrow sense that some people are more hybrid than others, and then you talk about the hybridization of the globe, that's the narcissism of the new cosmopolitan academic. There is a hybridity from above and one from below. There is a situation where claims to hybridity are positive and a situation where claims to hybridity are negative. To use an example I've used a million times, it's like using weight loss as your analytical category when some people are starving and some people are dieting, when some people are anorexic and some people are on hunger strike. Others are doing penance. Some think this is fate. Some are being good women and allowing their men to be fed, etc. You can't use a generalized notion of weight loss to analyse how people are. It's a similar problem. The hybridity problem has something to do with the incredible error of demographic notions that take whole populations as examples. For that reason I find it less than interesting.

RP Isn't there a more general notion of culture at work in your essay 'Who Claims Alterity?'? There is a nice definition there of cultural politics as 'subject production'.

Spivak Yes, but that can be taken on board in looking at how situations are negotiated. What's the problem? Is it too neat? In a way the clarity of that essay has become muddied, because frankly I know a little more now. But I'm glad you like the piece.

Conference Culture

RP Let's switch topics slightly. You pass through a lot of different cultural spaces in your travels. I wondered how you thought about your own cultural function. Do you consider yourself an intellectual *as opposed to* an academic, for example? Or don't you accept this classical distinction between intellectuals and academics?

Spivak This distinction always raises my hackles. I just wrote a piece for *Frontier*, a Calcutta-based journal, about the radical chic elements in the academy and those on the fringes of the academy. The academy is much broader than just salaried university positions. Of course, there is a person who is very recognizably only an academic; and there is a person who is very recognizably, self-declaredly, non-academic and an intellectual – someone who writes for the *Voice*, as opposed to someone who's just teaching courses on Victorian prose. There is that sort of thing. But given the incredible proliferation of conferences, it's the conference culture that we have to think about. Given the international conference culture, the old distinction between the academic and the intellectual is beginning to waver a little.

RP How is the division of intellectual labour affected by the internationalization of the conference circuit? There seems to be a new level of mobility required these days to perform certain intellectual functions. Might it be that the public function traditionally associated with the intellectual is now, ironically, only open to certain academics?

Spivak If we were to sit down and look at who goes to speak at these conferences, we would find that there are plenty of people who are not attached to academic institutions.

RP Perhaps, but isn't the character of the discourse defined by those who circulate through them with greater regularity?

Spivak I'm not so sure, although there is certainly a regimentation there. There is a proliferation of establishment figures, radical or otherwise, producing foregone conclusions, like election polls. Recently I refused to bring one of my most interesting friends from activist circuits in the South to a conference on war, because I felt that there would be no way he could relate without loss of respect to its interminable analysis of videographic production of war. I felt that in the generalized conference culture, where intellectual and academic in the old dispensation sit down together and talk, this person would be an outsider. Outsiders stand out and quite often they are asked to give a flavour of 'real' internationality. The conference culture is peculiar. It has a life of its own. And it changes quickly.

RP How does all this relate to your conception of transnational culture studies? Are intellectual cultures becoming less national?

Spivak I don't think this has anything to do with transnational culture studies. The conference culture is an object of investigation for transnational culture studies. It's field work. Even at the so-called activist conferences to which I go the power of the conference culture takes them over. Transnational culture studies involves detail (conferences don't involve detail) and it involves knowing, among other things, the metastructures of conference production. Conferences are alibis of various kinds, and not only in university contexts.

RP How about the effect of the conference circuit on academic writing? In the USA, the talk seems to be the economic base of academic literary production. Books are series of essays which are actually collections of talks. Very few people write books as such, in the sense of sustained pieces of book-length writing conceived as a whole. You do a lot of interviews, for example.

Spivak I hate interviews. It's true. I am in the unhappy position of a person most of whose written work comes out of teaching, which is both like and unlike interviews, because it's not sustained. For example, today I was teaching *Jane Eyre* and a couple of the students had read an old piece I wrote called 'Three Women's Texts and a Critique of Imperialism' in which I discussed *Jane Eyre*. It made me think very seriously about how that article came to be. It was a great discovery for me because I'd read *Jane Eyre* as a child and not noticed the implicit imperialist presuppositions. But now it's come full circle. I spent two hours persuading the students how one must get under the skin of Jane Eyre, because they were just pointing fingers at Jane's imperialism. I finally had to say to them: 'Anyone who believes the Third World needs aid is an imperialist. Beware of just noticing imperialists in the last century!' The horror of the talk-essay is that it's read like a book. Subject changes and institutional-technological changes are not isotemporal. So it's a problem for me that I, like anybody else, cannot write books any more. They come out of essays and it's a problem.

RP Are you saying that the forms of reception don't change fast enough?

Spivak Yes. And the essay, as a form of donation, is close to ephemeral, at least situation-specific. Add this to the troublesome business of information-command substituting for learning; although I know it's supposed to be very much with the times, postmodern, and so on. For example, when you said, 'Let's switch' earlier, I could see that actually you meant 'Shift F3', at least on WordPerfect. More and more I think that's what I'm doing to myself, switching. Document 2 is coming up right now. It's both better and worse. One doesn't think this through carefully enough, because of the fear of being called old-fashioned. Mine is not the kind of old-fashioned complaint that American children watch TV too much, that they don't read enough, that kind of nonsense. I just think we're declaring a rupture too soon.

RP What about your experience of the visual art community? (I'm thinking of your involement in the Alfredo Jarr exhibition at the Whitechapel Gallery in London a couple of years ago, among other things.) It seems to be one of the few places outside the academy where explicitly philosophical ideas can be conveyed to wider audiences; albeit not without a certain pretension.

Spivak Let's just say it was a learning experience. In principle, it's a very good idea, but the culture of the museum is not so easily undone; although it's good to attempt to undo it. It's a mistake to think that it has been undone simply because you have wanted to undo it. The staging of a desire is not its fulfilment. There is a great deal to learn on both sides, and not enough effort to do so yet. Let me compare this to something we both know well: collections of so-called political essays. Look at the last paragraphs. See how, after a whole series of basically sensationalist details, last paragraphs talk about what should be done. If those changes were to come about, those vast systemic changes, divine intervention would be required. It's always in the last paragraphs.

Ethical Metaphysics and Derrida's Marx

RP You spoke earlier of a reconstellation of the Marxist project. Recently, along with his 'ethical turn', Derrida seems to have loosened his sense of the theoretical specificity of deconstruction in a way which brings it much closer to a Marxist sense of critique. (Yesterday, for example, at the New School for Social Research, he said, 'It's important that we criticize or deconstruct the UN Charter.') You have always upheld a very rigorous distinction between deconstruction and critique. How do you view these developments in Derrida's work, and his *Spectres of Marx* in particular?

Spivak I don't see these changes the way you do. Okay, so Derrida increasingly allows himself to use a popularized vocabulary of deconstruction when he is in certain crowds. Who am I to be a purist? People have quite often thought that I was a hopeless vulgarizer of deconstruction. But I wouldn't put that on the same level as the *ethicization* of deconstruction. I am much less troubled by this turn toward the ethical than you seem to be. I am interested in Derrida talking about the indeconstructibility of justice, the experience of the impossible, the notion of the gift and responsibility and so on. In the early days, there was a lot of junk spoken about deconstruction because people wouldn't read carefully enough. You know: it was like a paralysis, it was a nihilism, it denied that there was a subject, etc. The thinking of gift and responsibility has not become common currency, but it would change those received ideas; and in some ways it goes back as far as the thinking of *différance* in 1968.

Back then, Derrida was able to say rather nicely to the philosophical crowd, 'Listen here, if you want to avoid the classic error of philosophy, you can do this and this and this.' Whereas now, that you can do this and this and this has become much more complicated. The first phase was picked up by the free-playing deconstructors. This phase has been picked up by the heavy-handed smugglers, the ethical metaphysicians. They just love this stuff. In the old days, the game-playing, smaller surrealists loved that stuff too. I'm not worried by this and I don't relate it to the habit of somewhat loose speech in popular contexts.

RP But isn't there something irreducibly metaphysical about the indeconstructibility of justice? The last time we did an interview (in 1988) you said that there was a point at which it looked as if Derrida was going to become 'son of Heidegger', but he never did. Now, with the turn to ethics, it looks to me as if he might be taking up the mantle once again. The thing that strikes me, personally, about the Marx book is not what most people are getting excited about – the fact that Derrida has said that we ought to keep reading Marx: of course, big deal – but that it's really a counterpart to (a continuation of) his book on Heidegger.

Spivak No!

RP In the sense that it is involved in the development of a new kind of ethical ontology – an anti-ontology of the phantasm, if you like.

Spivak The connection is the ghost, yes, who could deny that? But more and more now Derrida distinguishes his position from Heidegger. Perhaps that's a sign of becoming the 'son of', perhaps it's the same thing. I wouldn't disagree. But I do disagree about the Marx book. I have a piece called 'Responsibility' in *boundary* 2, where I offer a very schoolmarmish reading of *Of Spirit* in which I suggest that Derrida is pulling out all the stops of his method in that book. It's a book that's extremely hard to understand if you are not one of his 'schoolmates'. It's a book where everything methodological has been brought to bear, including the famous use of typography, the relation of footnotes to text, all that side of it. Now, it is because the relationship between Derrida and Heidegger is one of such close critical intimacy that the book is like that. With the Marx book, it's exactly the opposite.

The relationship between Derrida and Marx is not that close. In the Heidegger book there is a distancing through an incredible intimacy; in the Marx book there is an invocation of intimacy where there is none. In fact, the Marx book is written almost in the language that we were talking about earlier, the one Derrida uses when he is playing the elder statesman. In the last chapter of *Spectres,* for example, when he talks about Marx's relationship to Stirner and how exchange value is the origin of capital, how the commodity starts jumping and how Marx really thinks that a disappearance of the ghost is right around the corner, how important the religious is in the ideological thinking of ideology and so on, every detail is fuzzy because Derrida is not sure of the detail. This appropriation of Marx within the religious is finally disappointing. I hope that it's an enthusiastic aberration in the direction of writing in that way. It does seem that it's not the tip of an iceberg, the Marx book. It's all there is in Derrida on Marx.

RP Nonetheless, more broadly, isn't there an increasingly positive content to Derrida's ethical concepts? Isn't he naming things which were previously never to be named?

Spivak Give me an example.

RP The messianic promise. Why is this the name for the utopian promise inherent in the temporality of every utterance? There seems to be a systematic project here – to give a new ethical content to what Heidegger says about ecstatic-horizonal temporality in *Being and Time* – and it looks rather like a traditional philosophical meta-ethics. Don't you lose the specificity of each engagement?

Spivak No, you don't and I'll tell you why: because of the constant reminder of singularity, the singularity of the *arrivant*. It is a peculiar singularity, because it is not specified in terms of identity. And, paradoxically, the choice of the 'messianic' is specific to Derrida's cultural production.

RP It sounds like a generic singularity.

Spivak No, definitely not. Derrida's thinking of the ghost, for example, is a catachresis of the ghost. The word is being used in such a way that you will not find a literal reference for it. It's not a generic notion of something ghostly. 'The ghost, *if there is any*'; 'the gift, *if there is any*' – he says it all the time. The people who think that I'm out to lunch when I talk about the nominalism of deconstruction, it is *they* who are committed to the old-fashioned ethical position that you're talking about. The singularity of the *arrivant* is different from the messiah. There are many singularities.

Oddly, I didn't get into all this talking about the ghost because of Derrida, but by reading James Mooney. He's a crazy late nineteenth-century anthropologist, who was enraged against the US functionaries in the West and went and talked to a lot of the Sioux. He wrote this extraordinary book on the Sioux ghost dance. This was how I became interested in this incredible desire to turn ancestors into ghosts that would haunt one, so that one could think of a future that would be like something that had been there before. Because of the collision with the whites, ritual was not sufficing any more. That's the central insight of the subalternist historians, as to what the subaltern does: religion comes to a crisis. That's what got me going on ghosts.

A New International?

RP What do you make of Derrida's gesture towards a New International?

Spivak I'm very sympathetic to him wanting to say something about the way the world is out of joint, but I must admit that I find this part of the book rather difficult to take, this notion of the International – the First, the Second, the Third, the Fourth and now the New. Especially since he says that he's not thinking of any organization. The old dream of the International, human rights becoming economically aware, but without any organizing?

Wallerstein says that the problem with the new social movements, which are the hope for the future, is that they want state power. So they're going to run into the same problem as nineteenth-century socialism: Second International, not New, but Second. Now, this does not hold with the non-Eurocentric new social movements of which I have good knowledge of two: the ecological movement and the women's movement specific to the South. They can't think about taking state power at this point in the new world order, when even if the state wanted redistribution, which it doesn't, its redistributive powers have been completely eroded, one by one, by all the economic constraints imposed upon them. In a situation like that, these movements are very far from the idea of an International, and yet they work globally, and they really are connected with the power of the subaltern. The Chipko movement made the World Bank take a step back from Narmada, although it doesn't mean that they have really succeeded, because transnational agencies are in place. It is a very different form of locational agency, when local self-management is a real threat globally. It runs interference. That's very different from any idea of a new International.

There are important new directions of resistance where Marxism has been reconstellated in various ways since the experiment of international communism showed itself to have certain kinds of problem. Derrida's readerly involvement with the text of *that* practice has not been very close. This shows up in his talk about technology. He brings in some of the slightly dated fashionable names like Virilio, just referring to them, but there is no mention of what electronification has meant to international capitalism. This is a huge gap. There's talk about how there is no real public space in telematic societies, therefore the state is not that important. But in economic restructuring one of the first things that's happening is the US-aided electronification of various developing countries' stock exchanges. The Bombay stock exchange was electronified in 1994 with 25 million dollars from the US. He talks about commodities, but one might have heard something, even something old-fashioned, about commodity futures, that kind of virtual space. The problem is the mode of political prediction, based on the experience of one generation in Europe, plus Kojève's trip to Japan. This, it does seem to me, betrays a superficiality in the engagement with the text. I say this in the friendliest possible way, because nobody can do everything.

RP A surprisingly broad section of the European Left seems to have invested in the hope that the UN and its subsidiary organizations might be developed into a benevolent international power. What are your views about that?

Spivak In some areas the UN does good things: WIDER (the World Institute for Development Economics Research), the recently established Institute for New Technology at Maastricht, the critical role played by development programmes – these are good things. So I'm not going to be completely negative about it. But I can't speak about the UN as a whole, so let me talk about the Cairo Conference on Population and Development, since I've just returned from there. What you had there was the extremely well-publicized business about the Imams and the Popes and the issue of abortion. Fine, but it is true *de facto* that almost all aid packages have population control as a part of them. This connection was not even entertained as a serious objection. It was considered as trouble-making and divisive. The elite Southern NGOs are very much in favour of this kind of thing. They provide endorsement. Here, you have an extremely crude notion of national identity at work in what is now called the new international civil society. The North says: 'Look, the Bangladeshis want it; look, the Indians want it; look, the Somalis want it,' etc. On that level, if you are talking about the new international role of the UN, you are certainly not thinking about hybridity.

On the other hand, you have the non-elite Southern NGOs.When paragraph 8.25 was written to the satisfaction of the North-dominated women's organizations, the enormous consensus among the activist non-elite NGOs was certainly that access to legal and safe abortion was a very important thing, but it was *society-specific* and *secondary*. In situations where increasing poverty and absence of social security mean children are the only social security, and there are no efforts under the so-called 'umbrella' of sustainable development to provide social security in any other form, it is not relevant to have reproductive rights defined at such a global level. If, under these circumstances, where they are the dumping ground for international pharmaceuticals, and not only their reproductive health but their general health is laid waste, women should choose not to contraceive, then the idea of access to legal and safe abortion might be irrelevant. In fact, in situations where the absence of resources makes the very idea of an equal future for male and female children impossible, and internalized gendering can masquerade as choice, the access to safe and legal abortion can lead to female feticide.

The whole idea of the Northern-based women's groups, endorsed by the elite NGOs from the South, was that having secured the wording of paragraph 8.25 we were ready to move to development. Some hip Indian family planner says, 'The best contraception is development.' But when they came to development, without having defined reproductive rights properly at a global level, the relationship of aid packages to population control was never raised. Development was just development. We were told that the World Bank had to readjust its priorities for restructuring. We could look forward to the Social Summit at Copenhagen and so on. Business as usual.

When the idea that there should be some sort of monitoring device for the accountability of pharmaceuticals finally came up – nothing. The International Women's Health Network offered some loosely worded stuff about how we must make sure that our governments and other institutions are accountable, but what does that mean? It was just a covering action. So as far as the experience of the Cairo conference goes, where the presence of the NGOs was supposed to be such an extraordinary new thing, I'm not hopeful for the future. There is no reason why capital should not now enter into a new stage of imperialism, given that there is no possibility of non-alignment any more. There is no bargaining point for the South. But that's no reason why we should be such fools as to say that the UN is going to move forward in a better direction.

This too is an example of the task of transnational cultural studies: to know the uses of 'cultural identity' in the production of a United Nations for the New World Order.

Interviewed by Peter Osborne
New York, September 1994

Index

nebulizer

Atlanta Allergy
and Asthma

TEACHING AND LEARNING

TEAM SPORTS

AND GAMES

Jean-Francis **GRÉHAIGNE**, Jean-François **RICHARD**,
AND Linda L. **GRIFFIN**

RoutledgeFalmer

NEW YORK AND LONDON

Published in 2005 by
RoutledgeFalmer
Taylor & Francis Group
270 Madison Avenue
New York, NY 10016
www.routledge-ny.com

Published in Great Britain by
RoutledgeFalmer
Taylor & Francis Group
2 Park Square
Milton Park, Abingdon
Oxon OX14 4RN
www.routledge.co.uk

10 9 8 7 6 5 4 3 2 1

Library of Congress Cataloging-in-Publication Data
  Gréhaigne, Jean-Francis.
    Teaching and learning team sports and games / Jean-Francis Gréhaigne,
  Jean-François Richard, Linda L. Griffin.
      p. cm.
    Includes bibliographical references and index.
    ISBN 0-415-94639-5 (hb : alk. paper) — ISBN 0-415-94640-9 (pb : alk. paper)
    1. Sports–Study and teaching.   2. Teamwork (Sports)—Study and teaching.
    3. Group games–Study and teaching.
  I. Richard, Jean-François, 1966–   II. Griffin, Linda L., 1954–   III. Title.

  GV361.G74 2004 2005
  796'.071—dc22   2004012244

DEDICATION

This book is dedicated to the memory of my father, Adelin Richard (1919–2003), whose simple and unselfish approach to life is the greatest education I could have ever received.

Jean-François Richard

This book is dedicated to teachers and coaches willing to embrace a constructivist approach to learning sport-related games.

Linda L. Griffin

CONTENTS

FOREWORD

As is the case for many physical education teachers, I spent hundreds of hours throughout my childhood, and even more during my adolescence, practicing various sports. In the fifties, playing informal hockey and skating for hours on outside ice rinks was to young Quebecers what playing football or basketball is to many young Americans. Personally, I skated a lot not only on outside ice rinks but also on frozen ponds and frozen parts of the St. Lawrence River. On many occasions, I also played with a hockey stick and a puck, either on skates or on foot. However, despite a reasonably high level of technical skills, I never truly excelled in playing real hockey matches. All the technical ingredients were there, but somehow there was something missing. In retrospect, I must admit that my game presented serious defects in terms of strategy and, even more so, in terms of tactics.

It was only at the university level, in Quebec City, that I was formally taught my first physical education courses as I enrolled in a physical education teaching program. There were many courses focused on the teaching of sports, including individual, dual, or team sports. But every time a particular sport involved playing against one or several opponents, whether it was badminton, tennis, basketball, football, hockey, or volleyball, priority in learning tasks was always given to the technical aspects of the sport involved.

As soon as I completed my bachelor's degree in physical education teaching, I enrolled in a graduate program at the University of Illinois at Urbana-Champaign. There, I was exposed to John Dewey's "Learning by Doing" theory but completed a master's degree in physiology of exercise. I had entered the world of kinesiology, or sports science. Five years later, I returned to the United States and enrolled in a Ph.D. program in educational research and design at Florida State University. One of the leaders in the department where I studied was named Dr. Robert Gagné, who had written, among other books, *The Conditions of Learning*. Understandably, the place was a stronghold of behaviorism applied to teaching. Given my past learning experiences in track and field, gymnastics, and team sports, this teaching perspective suited me perfectly. Throughout the following 15 years, I taught and researched first the measurement of motor skills and then their formative assessment; in doing so, I had to tackle the matter of tactical skills. Progressively, I shifted toward what one might call the "arts and science of physical activity." Nevertheless, the general sport pedagogy paradigm to which I kept referring was still that of a behaviorist and technical approach; moreover, it was in line with the teaching and assessment practices of most physical education teachers with whom I worked.

By the end of the eighties, I had the pleasure of directing the doctoral program of a colleague who was well acquainted with the work of Piaget and who was convinced of the value of a constructivist approach in the teaching of physical education. The various discussions we both had on the subject enhanced my awareness about constructivism, but I still was not convinced. Then in January 1991, I met Jean-Francis Gréhaigne during an AISEP congress in Atlanta. Since then we have discussed, on many occasions, the various aspects of constructivism as it applies to physical education in general and to the learning of team sports in particular. During the same period of time, I was involved with the revision process of two teacher education programs in my own university. One was concerned with general education at the secondary level, and the other was focused on physical education teaching at both the elementary and secondary levels. It was obvious to me that for members of both revision committees, the student remained at the center of the teaching-learning process, the teacher's task being to facilitate rapport between students and the subject matter. Similarly, each student was perceived to be, in some way, in charge of his or her own education. Moreover, one competency sought in each program was *reflexive thought*, that is, the ability to reflect back on previous experiences and to build from them in view of future practices. Such views were clearly in line with pedagogical principles put forward in recent publications from the Quebec Ministry of Education concerning not only public school curricula but teacher education programs as well. Several American research bodies have expressed the same ideas. It has become clear to me that in many countries, several researchers, teacher educators, and education governing bodies favor a constructivist view of learning.

On the other hand, our own research on professional practices in physical education shows that physical education teachers, when teaching team sports, keep presenting their students with technical solutions to be reproduced or tactical principles to be applied rather than technical or tactical problems to be resolved. And yet I do not recall meeting one single P.E. teacher who would refute the idea of putting the student at the center of the teaching-learning process. Hence, there seems to be a gap between the discourse and actual practices. Some of the reasons for that may be the following:

First, a majority of physical education teachers, particularly those who completed their teacher education many years ago, were given a sports education in which they were essentially taught the "do as I do" method. They then proceeded to apply this model in their own professional practice and do not know how to transform their practice for it to be more in accordance with a constructivist approach.

Second, the little time devoted to physical education at school likely bears on pedagogical choices. Physical education teachers, like all teachers, hope for their students to succeed. But given the time that they have at their disposal, they must proceed quickly. So as soon as students experience learning problems, they are said and shown what to do. Implementing a constructivist approach in the classroom requires assessment procedures in which students become active participants. While students observe peers or reflect on past actions, they are not practicing; therefore, according to many teachers, they are not learning.

Finally, many physical education teachers' reservations may originate from a too-narrow and rigid interpretation of the pedagogical implications associated with a constructivist approach. On the one hand, the construction of knowledge by students does not require that they reinvent the wheel every time they encounter a new learning task. On the other hand, even in a constructivist learning environment, there is room for practicing reproductions of solutions to consolidate students' constructions thought to be promising.

Teaching and Learning Team Sports and Games provides physical education teachers and student teachers with a working tool based both on theoretical aspects and practical considerations drawn from field experimentation. Therefore, it provides some answers to the difficulties and reservations discussed above. Beyond the epistemological debate about the transmission or construction of knowledge, this book also discusses the respective contribution of strategic and tactical components and technical aspects with respect to teaching and learning team sports. Of course, it is not a matter of applying the "all or nothing" rule. What is more at stake is determining which aspect will be given priority and a leading role in the learning process. The traditional approach, the one I was exposed to, consisted first in mastering a series of technical skills to be later exploited in game situations; at that time, tactical aspects were then introduced. Strategic aspects, for their part, were rarely considered. In the tactical approach, students engage in real play from the start. The teacher's strategy is to bring them either (a) to understand and apply predetermined tactical principles, which are still a behaviorist, although cognitive, approach or (b) to solve tactical and strategic problems and, therefore, construct new knowledge (a constructivist approach). As students feel the need while in action, appropriate technical skills become part of the learning tasks.

It probably is too soon to determine the outcome of this technical/tactical debate. Some authors completely advocate the tactical approach while other sport pedagogy specialists keep asking for more scientific evidence, arguing that studies conducted so far show conflicting results. Considering all the attention given to the Teaching Games for Understanding (TGfU) model over the last 10 years or so, the publication of this book appears timely. Clearly, the teaching strategies advocated in the following chapters resemble those of TGfU in the sense that tactical knowledge is given priority over technical skills and that much attention is given to the cognitive aspect of learning. Beyond that, readers will see that the book goes one step further, clearly putting the student at the very center of the teaching-learning process and making the student responsible for the construction of his or her knowledge.

According to an old saying, if we give a person a fish to eat, we nourish that person for one day. If we teach someone how to fish, we nourish that person throughout his or her entire lifetime. This is, I believe, what this book is about.

Paul Godbout, Ph.D.
Professor Emeritus
Laval University
Quebec City
Canada

ACKNOWLEDGMENTS

As you are all aware, the accomplishment of a project of this nature is not without great sacrifice. In such a time-consuming endeavour, family and friends are sometimes neglected. We want to thank our families and close friends for their understanding and support throughout the completion of this book.

Because this book required a significant amount of rewriting and translation, we want sincerely to thank Angela Clarke for her linguistic review of the first few versions of this manuscript. Her expertise helped us to establish a cohesive train of thought from one chapter to the next and greatly contributed to the overall clarity of the text. Her assistance with this project is greatly appreciated. We would also like to thank the Routledge Editorial Team for their support and patience with this book project.

Finally, we want to express our gratitude and recognition to our dear friend and colleague Dr. Paul Godbout, who has been the external conscience throughout the completion of this book. Dr. Godbout has been very instrumental in the evolution of this project by providing us his thoughts and opinions pertaining to content. Being himself an expert on this topic, we also want to sincerely thank him for setting the stage of this book by writing the foreword. Thanks again Paul, and in recognition of your contribution, we collectively raise our glasses from our own little part of the world and express a heartfelt "cheers!"

INTRODUCTION

Play is a privileged part of a child's and adolescent's world. From spontaneous play to traditional games to organized sport, games offer multiple avenues for self expression through a physical activity medium. A certain number of rules preside over the way games are played, and these rules are transmitted from generation to generation, which constitutes a society's cultural patrimony. Nevertheless, games and game play possess traits that are common in all societies. Typically, a child's game play can be characterized as being carefree and organized by rules based on his/her own reality. Caillois (1961) confirms that rules are inseparable from play, even more so when they are recognized institutionally.

At the origin of play, there exists a certain liberty that is characterized by distraction and relaxation but also by seriousness. As stated by Wallon (1941), play is an activity that liberates people from their habitual constraints: It is an opportunity to free the sensorimotor side of their persona to explore and express themselves. For Wallon, play is an excellent means to stimulate imagination because it permits not only one's personal development but also one's relationship with others.

From these different characteristics, play consists of a series of actions that are accomplished in a defined time frame and play space, that follow a set of rules, and that are often accompanied by sensations, tension, and jubilation (Huizinga, 1951). Consequently, what are the distinctive traits of play that lead to these feelings and sensations?

First of all, one of the main sensations that can be associated with play is *social adhesion*. Participants often value the feeling of belonging to a group. The second sensation is often linked to *jubilation*, which refers to the feelings of joy that playing a game should bring. As Huizinga (1951) points out, people play, not because it is cumbersome or perceived to be a burden, but because it brings them pleasure. Play can also bring a strong sensation in relation to *fiction*, which doesn't necessarily mean that there is a total escape from all contingencies of daily life. It is merely a pause from certain norms and obligations in the presence of another reality, which presents a different set of constraints and obligations. This reality is *game play*. These three sensations can result in a fourth sensation, which is the development of *immediate interest*. The development of interest through game play can be harnessed through learning and other external motivators such as competition and success.

In a school setting, play is first associated with recess: a short leisure period between two classes. Recess is a time to have fun doing different things that do not necessarily have an immediate goal. In physical education classes, play, and especially game play, is structured and based on specific learning outcomes. Game confrontation between students is often integrated to put into practice what has been learned.

In the past two decades, educational reform movements in many countries have been pointing toward more authentic learning experiences for students across the curriculum, which includes physical education. Sport-related games teaching in physical education provides the primary content that teachers use to attain specific learning outcomes. From a research perspective, there is an ongoing agenda that continues to grapple with the effectiveness of different available teaching strategies. From a practical perspective, several works have addressed how to integrate these strategies in classroom settings; however, most textbooks available today lack details about the theoretical foundations that underlie these different teaching strategies. *Teaching and Learning Team Sports and Games* focuses not only on how to teach sports and games via the use of different teaching strategies but also on the underlying theories which support these strategies.

Written as a resource for teachers (pre and in service) and coaches, *Teaching and Learning Team Sports and Games* is a *theory to practice* textbook that focuses on the foundations and applications of constructivism as applied to the teaching and learning of invasion team sports and games. This textbook retraces the evolution of games teaching from Mahlo (1974) to Deleplace (1979), to Bunker and Thorpe (1982), and it conceptualizes this evolution with respect to the modern theories of constructivism to aid teachers in developing more educational teaching-learning scenarios for their students in relation to invasion sports and games. More precisely, this textbook explores a tactical approach to games teaching beyond the work of Bunker and Thorpe (1982). Bunker and Thorpe proposed a Teaching Games for Understanding (TGfU) model to pose and answer critical questions regarding *what to teach* and *how to teach it* for students to develop a more complete knowledge in relation to the games they play.

Teaching and Learning Team Sports and Games goes beyond TGfU and proposes the Tactical Decision Learning model (TDLM), which is a more in-depth model for the teaching of sports-related games in a school physical education setting. In part 1, performance in team sports is defined, the different elements that influence performance are identified, and the methods to measure and assess performance are explained. In part 2, the focus is on the teaching-learning process itself. In this section, the underlying theories of games teaching and the learning process are thoroughly explained. The major focus of this section is to explore the notion of constructivism and how it can be used in games teaching and learning. Issues surrounding the development of students' critical thinking skills and construction of knowledge will be foregrounded as the different teaching strategies that emphasize tactical learning are examined.

Teaching and Learning Team Sports and Games will benefit pre-service and in-service physical education teachers, coaches involved in youth sports, and teachers in their development as games teachers through the use of a constructivist frame. *Teaching and Learning Team Sports and Games* provides teachers and coaches with a theoretical foundation aimed at improving their interventions (i.e., teaching) in relation to the teaching of invasion team games and sports. This foundation will enable these practitioners to better comprehend games teaching, permitting them to construct and offer more educational learning scenarios to their students.

Throughout this book we have used the terms "student" and "player." In many cases these terms are interchangeable; students often are, or will be, players and vice versa. As used in this book, the terms help situate knowledge about the teaching and learning of games. The use of these terms is not designed to be limiting in any way. Concepts, ideas, and information conveyed for "players" or "students" can be useful in the teaching of games whether the people receiving the information are players on a team or students in a classroom gaining information about physical education.

During a period when the value of physical education is continually questioned, *Teaching and Learning Team Sports and Games* will be an indispensable resource that contains detailed information no other source has yet to offer: a complete and comprehensible textbook on the theoretical foundations and applications of games teaching, which foregrounds a constructivist teaching-learning approach. Furthermore, this book is unique because it brings the perspectives and expertise of three individuals from three different cultures to a topic that is of interest to physical education teachers and coaches around the world.

I

Performance in Team Sports

1

CLASSIFYING, DEFINING, AND ANALYZING TEAM SPORTS AND GAMES

In this first chapter, we provide an overview of a classification system for games. We will specifically focus on team sports that are classified as invasion games and present different models for analyzing game play.

THE CLASSIFICATION OF SPORTS AND GAMES

Logic, tactics, and practice are three notions that involve two associated ideas: a) the reality concerning game play is intelligible; and b) the intervention in relation to this reality can be the subject of objective, rational inquiry. As several authors have stated, game play is essentially a player's personal property (ownership) (Deleplace, 1995; Wade, 1970). This idea emphasizes that through time, players have had a major influence on the evolution of game play because they are the ones actually applying game play concepts in practical contexts. Coaches, referees, and rules of play are also factors that influence game play.

Through time, the dynamics of game play and the essence of team sports and games prompt players to better use the potentialities reflected in the spirit of fundamental rules (Deleplace, 1966) or primary rules (Almond, 1986a). Deleplace (1979) considers that the traditional technical analysis model must be contextualized within actual game situations in which a "force ratio" between opponents is present. Hence, this tactical analysis model's primary function is to identify the different possible game configurations within this force ratio and also to iden- tify the pertinent indices that characterize them. Second, this model consists of extracting the principles that lead to a configuration's transformation. The extraction of these principles permits one access to the internal logic of a particular sport or game. This internal logic is the product of the game's continuous interaction between the game's main rules and the changing game responses produced by players.

The fundamental or primary rules are concerned with the means to an end, and to achieve the end by other means is not playing the game. Thus, primary rules supply the game with its essential character. Primary rules are what makes basketball, "basketball" not volleyball (Almond, 1986a).

Fundamental rules have a major influence on the relationship between opponents because they determine certain parameters in which players must function. A particular game or sport is organized around a nucleus of fundamental and complementary rules that evolve to try and adapt to the changes introduced by new techniques and tactics while still conserving the essence or "spirit" of that partic- ular game or sport. These fundamental or primary rules are charac- terized by:

- *The modalities of scoring*, which relate to the particular character- istics of the game's target and the necessary skills involved in order to score.
- *The players' rights* (both from an offensive and defensive stand- point), which are based upon the modalities of scoring that com- plete those rights with respect to the equality of chances.
- *The liberty of action* that players have with the ball to give the game a specific character.
- *The modalities of physical engagement* that ensure the respect of the three previous rules.

The knowledge of rules within their specific logic is necessary to bet- ter understand the logic of observed game play behaviors, both tech- nical and tactical. According to Almond in the book *Rethinking Teaching Games* (1986b), games can be classified in the following four categories: invasion, fielding/runscoring, net/wall, and target games.

For his part, Gréhaigne (1989) adds another dimension to the classi- fication of invasion games. He specifies that the target in invasion games

Invasion Games

1. | | | |
|---|---|---|
| Handball | American football | Stick-ball |
| Basketball | Soccer | Field hockey |
| Netball | Rugby | Lacrosse |
| Team handball | Gaelic football | Cycle polo |
| Korkball | Australian football | Shinty |
| Tchouk-ball | Hurling/Camogie | Roller hockey |
| Ultimate frisbee | Speedball | Ice hockey |
| Waterpolo | Touchball (Finnish rugby) | |

2. Games can have:
   a) either a focused target, like hockey.
   b) or an open-ended target, like football.

Fielding/Runscoring

Baseball
Softball
Rounders
Cricket
Kick Ball (football cricket)

Net/Wall

Net/Racquet	Net/hand	Wall
Badminton	Volleyball	Squash
Tennis		Handball (court)
Table Tennis		Paddle Ball
Paddle Tennis		Raquetball
Platform Tennis		Basque pelote

Target Games

Golf	Ten (or 5 or 9) Pin
Croquet	Duckpin
Curling	Pub skittles
Pool	Billiards
	Snooker

can greatly influence their particular characteristics. Typically, targets can be vertical or horizontal, big or small, high or low, and within the playing area or at its extremity. These characteristics can have different effects on the technical and tactical components of the game. He adds that games can also be characterized by being played either on a bigger or smaller playing surface. Finally, Gréhaigne mentions that the way players interact with the projectile can also define games. The interaction is a factor that either reunites or separates opponents as they fight to gain possession of the projectile.

THE NATURE AND DEFINITION OF TEAM SPORTS

Figure 1.1 illustrates the continuous and fundamentally reversible character of play. In a natural sequence of events in any invasion game, players are either defenders or attackers in connection with the configurations of play. One can note that we differenciate between the notions of "attack" and "offense". The offensive aspect of the attack is scoring or taking a shot on a goal. Conservation of the ball is the defensive aspect of the attack, especially when the ball circulates at the rear of the effective play-space. Recovering the ball or putting pressure on the opposing team to regain possession of the ball is the offensive aspect of the defense. Defending one's goal consists in the defensive aspect of the defense. We have already moved from a simple attack-defense model to a more complex model with the use of offensive and defensive notions.

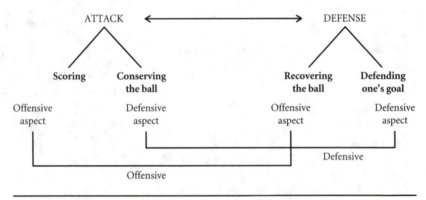

Fig. 1.1 Concepts related to the notion of opposition (translation from Gréhaigne, 1989).

As we examine a little closer, team sports offer certain closely interwoven characteristics within a given set of rules, focused toward winning the match (Gréhaigne, 1989, 1992; Gréhaigne & Godbout, 1995). These characteristics are:

- **A force ratio.** A group of players confronts another group of players, fighting for or exchanging an object (most often a ball)
- **A choice of motor skills.** Mastery of a certain range of motor responses—those of daily life or others that are much more specific and elaborate

- **Individual and collective strategies.** Implicit or explicit decisions, taken by the group, on the basis of a common frame of reference to defeat the opponents

The emphasis put on the inseparable character of the relationship among these three elements has consequences on the way one approaches or patterns team sports (Gréhaigne, 1994). The main challenge of team sports according to Deleplace (1979) is that in an *opposition relationship*, each of two teams must coordinate its actions to recover, conserve, and move the ball so as to bring it into the scoring zone and score.

Team sports are defined by Gréhaigne & Roche (1990) as the self-organization of a group confronted by another group with antagonistic interests. To score and prevent scoring players use common strategies:

1. To resolve anticipation-coincidence motor problems, that is, the preparation of responses before the arrival of the ball and the regulation of these responses as the ball arrives
2. To make informed choices among potential answers depending upon likely costs and benefits
3. To manage the varying courses of the players and the trajectories of the ball in urgent conditions of decision making

Brackenridge (1979) proposes a struggle for territorial dominance within a set of rules or structural parameters that includes significant cognition and technical aspects and in which coincidence-anticipation is paramount. The struggle for territorial dominance is decided by a system of scoring, which determines victory. The code of rules identifies the problems surrounding the achievement of territorial dominance and ensures that both teams or individuals meet and compete on equal and fair grounds. Gréhaigne (1992) indicates that this way of viewing team sports brings in three main categories of problems:

- **Problems related to space and time.** In an attack situation, one must find solutions to problems of individual and collective handling of the ball to overtake, use, or avoid varying mobile obstacles. In a defense mode, one must bring forward obstacles to slow down or stop the forward progression of the ball and of the opponents in view of an eventual recapture of the ball.
- **Problems related to information.** Players must also deal with problems related to the production of uncertainty for the opponents and of certainty for their partners in a situation that remains

fundamentally reversible. The reduction of uncertainty for the team in possession of the ball is a function of the quality of the communication codes and the choice of explicit tactics, thus allowing appropriate choices, understood by all teammates, according to momentary configurations of play.

- **Problems related to organization.** Players must accept the switch from an individual to a collective project. Each player must truly merge the collective project with their personal actions while giving the best of themselves to the group.

Generally, in team sports the main organization for a team is its "system of play." It is defined as

"The general form in which players' offensive and defensive actions are organized by establishing a precise arrangement of certains tasks in relation to positions and field coverage and certain principles of cooperation among them. The system of play is the basic structure of collective team tactics." (Teodorescu, 1965)

In the following section, we will share different game play analysis models with the goal of situating the conceptions and limitations related to teaching team sports and games.

GAME PLAY ANALYSIS MODELS

In this section, we present three different analysis models based on two reference frameworks: one based on pedagogical conceptions and the other based on the learner's conceptions.

Analytical Model

Traditional conceptions of a team's strength hold that it is equal to the sum of the individuals that make it up. We juxtapose quality individuals to make up a team. Game play is decomposed into simple elements that, when combined with quality players, result in a quality or high performance.

Pedagogical Conceptions of the Analytical Model The analytical model is heavily influenced by rational and mechanical theories. This approach analyzes game components (technical skills) outside the actual game context. Game components that are decomposed and analyzed individually are then associated with each other. Within this approach, which is based on a behavioral teaching approach, a major importance is attributed to imitation and repetition. However, it has often been noted that imitation and repetition is accomplished in a near-total absence of creative or critical thinking.

Structuralist Model

In contrast to the previous model, the team is perceived to be more than the sum of the individuals who compose it. The team is seen as a structured group of individuals or a "social microsystem" working together toward a common goal (Teodorescu, 1965). Within this microsystem, there exists a reciprocal coordination of individual and collective actions from which the group tries to draw general principles to better understand the game.

Pedagogical Conceptions of the Stucturalist Model The structuralist model relies on different factors of execution, such as speed, strength, and power, to develop team play. Its main goal is to organize team strategies and tactics through practice situations that put emphasis on ball circulation and player movement. These strategies and tactics are modeled in practice and then tried in actual matches. Game behaviors and actions are deduced from game situations, thus producing a wider array of possibilities and reflecting the different realities within a particular game or sport.

Systemic Model

In the two previous models, analysis of game play has focused on players of a same team without taking into consideration what actions the opposing team could be developing at the same moment. In the systemic model, there is a switch in the pedagogical focus because its aim is to explain game play from the oppositional relationship that constantly exists between two opposing teams. By looking at games through the analysis of the force ratio between opponents, one considers a game's reality in its entirety.

Pedagogical Conceptions of the Systemic Model When using this particular approach to analyze games, the focus is on trying to explain the oppositional relationship to develop better understanding of the game and to better execute actions during the game. Different aspects of game performance must be analyzed within this model, such as a player's combativeness in one-on-one confrontation, cognitive work, and the identification and comprehension of game play principles. Also, the perceptual elements of game play must be developed for a player to be able to apply them in the anticipation of future game situations.

Playing is a very important aspect of learning how to play. One of the major goals of games during childhood is to provide an outlet where the child can affirm him/herself in a context of self-actualization. A teacher or coach offers children game situations that permit them to satisfy their own desires and not the ones created by adults (teachers, coaches, parents, etc.). Essentially, the idea is to place the child in a game situation that is adapted to be relevant to different age and developmental levels. Thus the educator's challenge is to find or imagine situations that present players with challenges that must include a force ratio between opposing teams.

In conclusion, it is noteworthy that the systemic analysis model will provide the foundation and framework in which our exploration and explanation of teaching team games and sports will be based.

2

THE SYSTEMIC NATURE OF TEAM SPORTS

To better understand the principles at work in team sports, a pertinent approach could be to model the interactions between the players and the environment as a complex system. In team sports, environmental variables represent fluctuating conditions that momentarily constrain the organization of players' actions (Ali & Farraly, 1990; Bouthier, 1989; Caron & Pelchat, 1975; David, 1993; Davids, Hanford, & Williams, 1994; Gréhaigne, 1988; Gréhaigne & Godbout, 1995; Walliser, 1977). For example, according to the available space, the ball carrier's choices will dictate the success of an attack. In order to better understand such choices, this chapter examines, in the first part, the systemic nature of team sport. The second part presents a French analysis model based on the oppositional relationship.

EXPLORING TEAM SPORT THROUGH SYSTEMIC ANALYSIS

Since invasion team sports represent the interaction of two separate entities, it is essential to explore the analysis of these interactive systems through the various sub-disciplines (e.g., motor learning). Our study of team sport from a systemic point of view will center on the theory of dynamic systems.

Theory of Dynamic Systems

Systemic analysis was born in the last 30 years as a result of the union of various disciplines such as biology, information theory, cybernetics, and systems theory. According to Atlan (1979; 1992), it should not be considered a science, a theory, or a discipline but rather a new process allowing for the gathering and organization of knowledge in view of more efficient action. According to Walliser (1977), the systemic approach aims to find answers to three essential concerns:

1. The drive to come back (as a reaction to ultra-analytic tendencies of some sciences) to a more synthetic approach that would recognize properties of dynamic interactions between elements of a whole, giving it a totality of character.
2. The need, in order to conceive and control large and complex wholes, to put together a method that would make it possible to obtain and organize knowledge so as to better relate means and objectives.
3. The necessity, in face of fragmentation and the dispersal of knowledge, to promote a utilitarian language that could support the articulation and integration of theoretical models and methodological precepts scattered in various disciplines.

General Properties of Systems The analytical approach tries to break down a system to its simplest constituent elements. Then, modifying one variable at a time, it tries to deduce general laws that make it possible to predict the properties of the system in different conditions. For such predictions to be feasible, additive laws of elementary properties must come into play. However, in the case of highly complex systems, such as a soccer match, these additive laws do not work. Therefore, such systems must be approached with new methods, such as those gathered under the systemic approach. Studying a system's behavior over time leads to the determination of action rules that are used to influence or modify the state of the system.

A systemic approach relies on the notion of system or a whole made up of interacting elements. These elements include:

1. A whole in reciprocal rapport with an environment, whereby such exchanges provide the whole with some autonomy
2. A whole composed of interacting subsystems, such that interdependence ensures a certain coherence
3. A whole submitted to more or less important modifications over time while maintaining a basic permanence

Often in a classical approach, the only explanation of phenomena relies on linear causality; it is an explanatory mode based on a logical chain of causes and effects. With the systemic approach, movement replaces permanence, flexibility replaces inflexibility, and adaptability replaces stability. Notions of flow and flow balance join those of force and force balance. Hence, by integrating time, a systemic approach reveals the interdependence of phenomena and their gradual change. Causality has become circular and is now conceived of as a regulation loop (Bertalanffy, 1972; Caverni, 1988; Caverni, Bastien, Mendelsohn, & Tiberghien, 1988; Morin, 1986; Rosnay, 1975).

Two main categories of systems are defined: closed systems and open systems. A closed system exchanges neither energy nor matter with its environment; it is self-sufficient. On the other hand, an open system relates constantly with its environment. It exchanges energy, matter, and information useful for maintaining its organization. Its complexity takes into account variety and interaction between elements. Some liaisons may be studied either from a causal point of view (balance, stability, etc.) or from an end product point of view (adaptation and learning).

Systems and Subsystems A system is said to be quasidecomposable if it can be decomposed into semi-isolated subsystems, with some interaction between them and the environment (Walliser, 1977). With reference to a given system, one may consider the following in the context of team sports:

1. *Microsystems*, which are obtained by retaining only a few subsystems with all their interactions. For example, the confrontation between two teams at a given time, each possessing its own configuration of play.
2. *Infrasystems*, which represent few subsystems with some of their interactions (that is, 1 vs. 1 or 2 vs. 2) at some point in the match.

As was the case for general characteristics of systems, interactions between subsystems are energy based or information based. These subsystems may organize themselves into various types of networks, either superimposed upon or merged inside the system. Each subsystem in turn can generally be decomposed into other subsystems according to an interlocking order that reflects hierarchies or multiple sets of combinations. Relationships among elements of a given level differ in terms of nature and intensity from those among elements of subsystems pertaining to different levels. For example, one may not switch from 5 vs. 5 soccer to 11 vs. 11 without reorganizing one's knowledge and capacities. This situation is true even though relatively homogeneous subsystems may sometimes show up, as, for example, a three-player configuration of play at the periphery of the field between a defender, a midfield player, and the involved wing.

Systems and Time The temporal dimension is important for studying systems because it is the medium through which they operate and evolve. All things considered, nothing may be fundamentally understood about soccer if one does not shift from a spatial to a temporal reference system while processing information. The synchronous properties of a system relate to the relationships among various characteristics of that system at a given time. The diachronic properties relate to the relationships of those same characteristics through many successive moments in time. They make it possible to bring to light the system's evolutionary trends. In a quasidecomposable system, one may differentiate among modifications mainly related to the system's structure, functioning, evolution, or relationships to these three phenomena. The system's structure, in a strict sense, rests upon the whole set of its most unvarying characteristics; thus, the system's structure ensures its very existence and its permanence. In a larger sense, the structure is formed by all the system's characteristics at a given point in time, thus reflecting the state of the system at that moment. The system's functioning relates on the one hand to each subsystem's transformations and, on the other hand, to flows passing through linking channels between subsystems and between the system and its environment. The system's evolution is brought about, on the one hand, by a change in the subsystems' transformation laws and, on the other hand, by changes in the way the system organizes itself into subsystems and changes in the linking channels between the system and the environment.

For instance, in soccer, the structural dimension is characterized by:

1. A boundary that establishes the frontiers of the system (i.e. the play area)
2. Elements that may be counted and grouped into categories, such as the players, the attackers or defenders, the ball, and so on
3. "Containers" in which energy or information is stocked (the potentialities within a certain play configuration, the goalkeeper, players' energy potential, etc.)
4. A communication network that allows energy and information exchanges (the rules, the code of play, a common frame of reference to read and interpret plays in the same way, etc.)

The functional dimension is characterized by:

1. Flows of energy, information, or various elements that include players, the ball, replacements, state of fatigue, and so on
2. Gates controlling the rate of various flows, such the play leader, players' momentary tactical choices, the referee, rules of play, and so on

3. Delays resulting from flows moving at different speeds or from the gate response time, as in situations of creating open space, gaining an interval, restoring a defensive block, and so on
4. Regulation loops, either proactive or reactive, that play a large part in the system's behavior by managing all parameters, either taking information to adjust the game plan, setting a defensive reserve, or modifying the system of play.

Regulation: General Principle The information process uses a collection mechanism and makes use of information to modify the system. To characterize this process, one may consider five types of activity that intervene, in a cyclic way, in its functioning (see Mahlo, 1974).

- **Information activity.** Translating action into a conceptual form of observed real phenomena (perception)
- **Prospecting activity.** Constructing probable, possible, or desirable schemes about the future (planning)
- **Decision activity.** Translating intents and aspirations into actions on reality (programming and management)
- **Execution activity.** Transforming the system through voluntary and coordinated actions (execution)
- **Control activity.** Collecting information about the results of actions with a view to pursuing or transforming the current action or the upcoming one (regulation)

TEAM SPORTS: CONTRIBUTIONS OF SYSTEMIC ANALYSIS

To obtain more information about the structure and function of play, we will use a systemic approach, as presented in chapter 1, to discuss the modeling of team sports.

Some Concepts Related to the Notion of Opposition

In a soccer match or any other type of invasion game, structures and configurations of play should be considered as a whole, rather than be examined piece by piece. Systems with many dynamically interacting elements are capable of rich and varied patterns of behavior that are clearly different from the behavior of each component considered separately. The influence of general systems theory is now clearly evident, and one must analyze the performances of the players as a system in synergy with the environment.

Indeed, in a match, the opposition generates the unexpected, and there is a constant need to adapt to constraints brought about by the confrontation. A match rarely relies upon the simple application of schematics learned during practice sessions. Thus, most often during the game, one can foresee only probabilities of evolution for the attack and defense configurations; hence the importance of heuristics to quickly solve the problems inherent in specific interactions between two teams.

In a classic learning approach, one tries before anything else to teach students technical skills and to maintain order on the playing field by, for example, the use of formal groupings. However, it could be argued that it is just as important, and maybe even more so, to get the players to optimally manage disorder (Villepreux, 1987; Gréhaigne, 1989; 1992a). This type of approach, which puts forward "opposition" and "disorder management" as a base for any progress, brings to light new concepts that appear fundamental for a renewal of team sport teaching. Figure 2.1 identifies some concepts that come into focus when one points out opposition as a fundamental element of the modeling process in team sports.

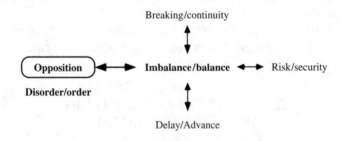

Fig. 2.1   Concepts related to the notion of opposition (translation from Gréhaigne, 1992).

The central notion of opposition leads us to consider the two teams as interacting organized systems. The structural characteristics of these systems consist of a program that can be modified according to acquired experience; their main functional property is learning. The operational conditions of such systems in team sports require that one manage disorder before anything else, while preserving a certain order and thus allowing decisions in a not completely *a priori*, foreseeable environment.

For instance, let us analyze a match, looking at its structural and functional characteristics. By structural, we mean the spatial organization of the constituent synchronic and topological elements of the system, while the functional aspect refers to the various time related processes such as exchanges, regulations, and reorganization of the elements, both the diachronic and kinetic properties.

In a match, from a structural point of view, the elements of the system are represented by the two opposing teams, and the communication network between the two is defined by the rules of the sport. At this level, the idea is to characterize, from a spatial standpoint, the opposition rapport and to analyze the relationships between the strong points of the attack system and those of the defensive system. Notions at stake here are "in block," "in pursuit," center of gravity, circulation of the ball, and so on (Gréhaigne, 1992b; Bouthier, David, & Eloi, 1994; Gréhaigne & Bouthier, 1994). From a functional point of view, one is dealing with the evolution in time of the opposing relationship between the two teams (advance, delay; breaking, continuity; etc.). In this case, each match provides phenomenological data—something original and unique—thus reducing the efficiency of ready-made motor or strategic solutions.

The Consequences

A match constitutes a complex system. Analysis of the game reveals the existence of a large number of interacting variables. On the playing surface, a nonhomogenous distribution of the players brings about a nonhomogeneous distribution of the energy state of the players. A certain type of homogeneous scattering characterizes the equilibrium state toward which invasion team sports systems always evolve. It corresponds, therefore, to homogeneity of the players' distribution on the different energetic states. The degree of homogeneity of the configurations of play can also be explained by the probabilities of the presence of the players at certain areas of the playing surface.

Another way to show the homogeneity of a system consists in defining the microstates of the system of attack and defense. Each microstate is defined by a distribution of the players on the playing surface's area according to their positions, orientations, and speeds. One can call this type of distribution a *dynamic configuration of play*. The apparent disorder indicates a more general homogeneity than the simple spatial distribution of the players on the ground because the latter distribution influences only two energy levels: potential and speed. In those situations of opposition, the kinetic interactions lead to the stabilization of the spatially nonhomogeneous states by other nonhomogeneous distributions, which appear homogenous if one looks for certain energetic states. It means that those states would seem to be more homogeneous for an observer who would be able to recognize the different kinetic states. Conversely, a classic observation would stress the heterogeneous aspects by dealing only with positions and geometric shapes. In our opinion, that is how the dialectic equilibrium/disequilibrium of the game operates. On the one hand, very stable structures make one think of a crystalline structure, defined as rigid and with few chances of evolution, as for example in set-plays. On the other hand, the dynamic configurations of play have within themselves a number of transformations limited according to the different possibilities of the continuous evolution of the game but nevertheless important if one chooses a break in modifying the movement during its process.

This group of elements forms a foundation for our framework of analysis. Dynamic systems are able to attain multiple patterns of stability in achieving a state of coordination with the opposition. A theoretical framework that focuses on the achievement of coordination within a dynamic system may be appropriate for the study of configurations of play.

A FRENCH MODEL OF ANALYSIS

In this section, we are going to present the Deleplace model, the tactical matrix of technique and team sport modeling.

The practice modeling presented in Deleplace's work (1966; 1979) gave birth to the school of "tactical approach" (Bouthier, 1984; Deleplace, 1992). These authors have demonstrated that the intervention of cognitive processes is decisive for the advanced organization of play and the control of motor responses (Bouthier, 1986). Their advocates hypothesize that this approach yields better results than two other pedagogical methods. One method, "the execution model approach," focuses on the player's repetition of efficient solutions produced by experts, while the other, "the self adaptive model approach," postulates that judicious variations in the setting are the most efficient for players to discover solutions and develop skills. The central strategy of the tactical approach calls for the presentation of essential information concerning the tactical advance and organization of actions during game play and then for the actual implementation of such actions in relatively self-sustaining and tactics-oriented patterns of play. These patterns, borrowed from actual game play, are not to be confounded with traditional drills. They are selected because they can be played out independently of a match situation, that they call for tactical decisions, and that the outcome remains open-ended.

Nevertheless, the amount of information provided to the player must remain limited, and it is the quality of the information that is determining. In that respect, prior analysis of the internal logic of the sport by a coach, a teacher, or some other expert provides useful data. Based on such analyses, one can draw the player's attention to typical patterns of play. This way, under time constraints, the player has at his or her disposal an already-worked-out mental picture for solving the problem at hand.

Thus, the tactical approach to team sports focuses on players' exploration of the various possibilities of game play and of their modeling based on defensive and offensive matrices. If one looks carefully, the internal logic of every team sport refers to a coherent system of representation—the matrices. In a general sense, a matrix, according to the *Oxford English Dictionary,* is a "place where something begins or develops." In this particular context, in a more figurative sense, the matrix is a shared frame of reference that makes it possible for players to interpret or even anticipate the general movement of the unfolding play. It constitutes a common origin of knowledge and responses for players. The defensive matrix, whatever its shape, deployment, or successive new developments, is at the same time the simplest and the most general matrix that will make it possible to counter the offensive movement attempted by the opponent in possession of the ball. For its part, the offensive matrix is first and foremost the choice of a way of penetrating into the defensive system, given its momentary configuration. Thus, in an invasion game such as soccer, as illustrated in Figure 2.2, the principle of the defensive matrix, which consists in circulating between the various defense lines in order to oppose attackers, is paired, for its offensive counterpart, with the principle of transformation of the initiated movement to maintain one's advance on the defensive replacement. At this moment, the notion of double-impact organization becomes very important because it emphasizes the immediacy of switching from attacker to defender in the event of losing possession of the ball.

Fig. 2.2 Relationship between technique, tactics, and athletic potential.

What is the connection between tactics and technique? The model presented in Figure 2.2 highlights the interdependent nature of tactics, technique, and athletic potential. The player also devises action plans in accord with strategic decisions and makes adjustments as effective action proceeds.

Any decision with regard to the context and theory of play becomes valid only if it can be efficiently translated into action. This implies that a player actually has at his or her disposal a range of corresponding responses (i.e., individual or collective technical skills). Although tactics make up the context that justifies technical skills, these skills should not be considered as secondary. Techniques constitute the tools for the execution of tactics (Mahlo, 1974). Thus, the educational setting should not oppose technical learning and tactical learning but rather should articulate them in a tactical matrix of technique.

It is well known that the motor execution of a tactical choice requires physical energy. Indeed, fatigue not only affects the quality of skill execution but also affects the lucidity of choices. Thus, athletic potential is another limitation factor for the activity.

TEAM SPORT MODELING

The task of a team sport player lies in the ability to detect, during game play, the incipient evolutions in the oppositional relationship. The player must infer or deduct the choices of appropriate successive actions for both offensive and defensive purposes to possible game situations that can develop on the playing surface at any moment.

The shape of a particular game play configuration, like the orientation of offensive or defensive action, has sense according to the characteristics of evolving action from the opposing team. In an offensive situation, the offensive team must consider the state of the defenders' movements and actions, both individually and collectively. In a defensive situation, the defenders must consider the state of the attackers' movements and actions, both individually and collectively. Understanding these reciprocal relationships between the states of movement on the two faces of the opposition and knowing how they operate in real game play constitutes, by definition, *tactical intelligence* in actual game play. At all levels of play, the problem is to reach an automated state of conscious-centered activity.

The reality of evolving game play presents a great multiplicity of different concrete game situations. One can say that there are practically never two game situations that are absolutely identical. Hence, it is almost impossible to re-create all of these situations during practice sessions, but if we consider their characteristics, they can be categorized to form patterns with a small number of categories or types of situations that constitute so many separable tactical units. For each of these units, it becomes possible to explain the foreseeable evolution in the particular oppositional relationship that characterizes it. This explanation constitutes what we can call the law of evolution of play in accordance with a particular tactical unit.

In constructing a model, the problem is therefore to reduce the whole complexity of the game to the smallest number of elements, articulated to a highly logical functional unit. On one hand, the player develops a clearly understood functional logic of game play; on the other hand, he or she understands that particular aspects depend on his or her perceptual-motor skills. In chapter 3 we will use the model and concepts present in this chapter to expand our focus on the internal logic of team sports.

3

THE INTERNAL LOGIC OF TEAM SPORTS

In relation to team sports, one can consider four notions that are central to the topic of this chapter: *opposition* to opponents, *cooperation* with teammates, *attack* on the opposing team's camp, and *defense* of one's own camp. Each of these four elements comes into play, however the complexity of each interaction may vary depending upon the category of sport involved (Almond, 1986b; Werner, 1989). For instance, in baseball, a fielding/run scoring type of team sport, attack and defense are two separate phases in a given inning while in invasion games, the four elements are at play simultaneously. The basic idea is for each player to cooperate with teammates to better oppose the opponents either while attacking (keeping one's defense in mind) or while defending (getting ready to attack) (Gréhaigne, Godbout, & Bouthier, 1997). Given that two teams play in opposition, a systemic view of team sports brings us to consider two main organizational levels: the *match*, related to the force ratio, and the *team*, related to the competency network.

THE FORCE RATIO (THE RAPPORT OF STRENGTH)

In invasion games, the internal logic of play has its source in the opposition relationship that generates, during each sequence of play, a dynamic of moving from one target to the other. We call this opposition relationship the *force ratio*. It refers to the "antagonist links existing between several players or groups of players confronted by virtue of certain rules of a game that determine a pattern of interaction" (Gréhaigne et al., 1997, p. 516). In all instances, the possession of the ball can change and the direction of play inverts. This fact imposes on both teams an organization whereby an answer to the reversibility comprises location and replacement of general movement generated by the opposition in relation to the depth of the playing surface (Gréhaigne, Bouthier, & David, 1997).

In this general movement, the ball carrier is faced with two interrelated decisions of play:

1. The first is centered around two possibilities: to go directly to the target to shoot or to move the ball closer to the target;
2. The second is linked to the rapport between the width of the playing surface and the number of players that each team can use in the specific part of the playing surface where the play is unfolding at that particular moment. This creates, the alternative of running or passing on one side or the other. The movements are in relation to the width of the playing surface in order to bypass coming opponents.

The target-oriented dynamics, which entail various shapes of movement or shooting according to the available depth and to the widthwise orientation of the play, constitute the essence or "soul" of play. This holds true whatever the particular structure of a sport that determines its primary rules; that is how the game is played and how winning can be achieved (Almond, 1986a), regardless of the surface of play or the characteristics of the targets. The potential for reversibility of general movement at any instance, either in depth or width, is a major characteristic of the internal logic of the force ratio. All players must be aware of their orginal frame of reference (i.e., starting point; home base). At the same time, all players must be capable of initiatives that each teammate can decode to react accordingly or can even anticipate. This double dimension of a collective frame of reference strongly linked to individual initiative is fundamental in team sports however, this aspect is often overlooked.

Different organizational levels can be identified. In fact, during a game, the global opposition relationship that we call "organizational level match" breaks down into partial opposition relationships. These opposition settings that momentarily involve a few players generate a particular shape of play representing the "organizational level partial forefront" (see Figure 3.1). At any moment of the match, this partial forefront contains a third-level opposition unit that links the ball carrier and his or her direct opponent. This is called a "primary organizational level" (Gréhaigne, 1992a).

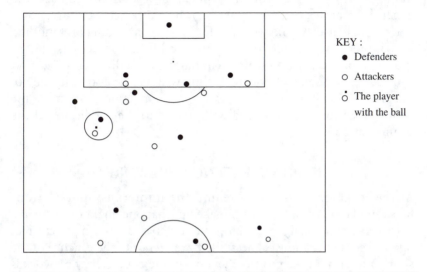

KEY:
● Defenders
○ Attackers
○̇ The player with the ball

Fig. 3.1 Match, partial forefront, and primary organizational levels. Reprinted, by permission, from Gréhaigne, Godbout, and Bouthier, 1997, pp. 500–516.

Figure 3.1 illustrates the last two organizational levels, whereas the representation of the whole field would show the "organizational level match." Thus the force ratio may be looked at as involving two teams, two sub-groups of players, or eventually two specific players. The continuity of opposition influences the opponents' movements not only at the one-to-one level, but at the partial forefront level and at the match level as well. These simultaneous interlocked opposition settings constitute the context of play (Deleplace, 1979). They evolve in reciprocal rapport in response to the evolution of any part of the system. At any specific moment, according to the evolution of play, this reciprocity relationship offers, for example, a specific problem to attackers but, at the same time, contains pertinent solutions for conducting the action. The solutions are:

- To continue the action at the one-to-one level
- To pursue the attack with the help of partners in the partial forefront
- To change general movement by transforming its shape, its orientation, or even both.

Thus the continual reciprocity relationship between the three organizational levels constitutes the second major characteristic of the internal logic of the force ratio (Deleplace, 1966). As one can see, the general dynamics of team sports can be expressed as a force ratio where, in a sense, two networks of forces are confronting one another. This implies the consideration of a second frame of analysis, that of the "organizational level team" (Gréhaigne & Godbout, 1995). If we consider only one team, we are dealing with the evolution in time of the players' distribution on the players' field or action zone and of the communication network used with regard to the conditions of the confrontation.

THE COMPETENCY NETWORK

At the "organizational level team," the numerous interrelations between players within the team make up what one might call a *competency network* (Gréhaigne, 1992b). Although based on each player's recognized strengths and weaknesses with reference to the practice of the sport, and also on the group's dynamism, the competency network is more a dynamic concept than a static one. The concept of a competency network refers, in general, to the student's game-related behaviors that one can identify in connection with the force ratio between the two participating teams, or with each player's functions within the team. Such behaviors vary depending upon players, moments, external factors, and the particular team sport involved. During play, in connection with behaviors, the notion of *role* is essential for analyzing the competency network. In this case, *role* refers to behaviors that convey what a player thinks he or she ought to do, given the way he or she experiences the rapport of forces or the competency network within the team, and how the player manages his or her resources in a system of constraints.

The function within the group, chosen by the player or assigned by the teacher or by the group, is another indicator of the player's position in the team's dynamics. At the interface of the player's logic, the team's logic, and the internal logic of the sport involved, the player's function in this competency network often is a reliable indicator of the reciprocal rapport between the player and the team. Contrary to what one might think, cooperation in team sports, as in other aspects of life, goes far beyond simple goodwill. For the competency network to be efficient, there is a need for both effort and restraint on the part of many players if not all of them.

In conclusion, from a systemic point of view, one could consider a team sport as the functioning of two competency networks involved in a force ratio. It should then be clear that the very existence of both the force ratio between opponents and of the competency network within each team makes it necessary for each team to try to anticipate the opponents' attacks and defenses and plan according to its offensive and defensive actions. It also becomes useful for each team and player to reflect upon the efficacy of decisions made during the encounter itself, depending upon one's partners' or opponents' behaviors. For this reason, it appears necessary to explore the notions of tactics and strategy.

TACTICS AND STRATEGY

Although found in a completely different context, the terms *strategy* and *tactics* have been used for a long time in the vocabulary of war. According to Von Clausewitz (1989) the strategist determines for the whole act of war a goal corresponding to the object of war. He sets up a war design compatible with the resources of the state, elaborates the plan of the different campaigns, organizes the engagements of each of them, and combines the actions of the military forces and organizes them into systems to preserve their coherence. Von Clausewitz adds that for the strategist, any conflict calls into play physical, mental, and moral factors. The problem then consists in maintaining reflection or theory at the center of these three tendencies as if suspended among three attracting forces or magnets. For his part, the tactician focuses on a more limited, concrete, and generally geographic objective, adapted to the strategic plans. The tactician conducts the battle or operation in sight by adapting the action, combining maneuvers, and deciding on the engagement of the different means of combat. Von Clausewitz points out the relative subordination of the latter to the former: The strategist takes time into account and accompanies the tactician on the field.

Similarly, the European school of team sports makes a distinction between strategy and tactics. For Bouthier (1988), strategy refers to all plans, principles of play, and action guidelines decided upon before a match to organize the activity of the team and the players during the game. The finalized strategy may either concern the most important general options of play or specify the intervention of players for different categories of play. For their part, tactics involve all orientation operations voluntarily executed during the game by the players to adapt to the immediate requirements of an ever-changing opposition, their spontaneous actions, or those organized through the predetermined strategy. Similarly, for Gréhaigne and Godbout (1995) strategy refers to:

> ...these elements discussed in advance in order for the team to organize itself. Tactics are a punctual adaptation to new configurations of play and to the circulation of the ball; they are therefore an adaptation to opposition. As discussed by Gréhaigne (1994) strategy concerns (a) the general order, that is, the outside order form resulting from the general strategic choices of the team (background play, team composition...), and (b) the positions to be covered according to particular instructions each player receives in training (assigned position). For their part, tactics relate to (a) the positions taken in reaction to an adversary in a game situation (effective position) and (b) the adaptation of the team to the conditions of play (flexibility). (p. 491)

There is a fundamental difference between strategy and tactics as far as their relationship with time is concerned. Strategy is associated with more elaborate cognitive processes because the decisions made are based on reflection without time constraints. Tactics operate under strong time constraints. During the learning process, one can use both strategic and tactical aspects of the game whenever temporal pressure is reduced. During regular play, tactics are of paramount importance for players near the ball defined earlier as the partial forefront and primary organizational levels. Thus, given an equivalent force ratio and similar configurations of play, progress in team sports may be seen as performing the same actions faster or solving problems brought about by a higher temporal-pressure type of play; or given identical time, progress in team sports may be seen as performing more complex actions.

Players can choose to perform only what they know how to do or what they can do. But performance in team sports appears to be determined by the most appropriate choice among the various solutions at the players' disposal and by the speed of this decision-making. In this context, it seems that play action is eventually determined by a strategy that needs to be specified, if not modified, during play. While strategic aspects rely on the conception of the game, tactical aspects are fundamental to regulation during play because they are based on successive decisions taken according to the evolution of the action. When players get away from action, they can focus both on the strategic and tactical aspects of their game because they have more time at their disposal.

Consequently, efficiency during play has nothing to do with a series of dissociated behaviors. It relies on efficient-action rules and play-organization rules (Gréhaigne & Godbout, 1995) that regulate strategic and tactical choices that are neither conscious nor directly observable. However, the existence of such rules appears to be confirmed by the fact that the player can adapt to many configurations of play and eventually state the rule or rules on which a solution was based. When teachers or researchers ask students, "What strategy did you use on that point?" (French, Werner, Taylor, Hussey, & Jones, 1996, p. 446), they are in fact trying to elicit the more or less explicit formulation of such rules. Coming back to play efficiency, one might say that tactical efficiency is a generative capacity likely to produce infinite tactical behaviors in response to infinite new configurations of play.

One must, however, differentiate between the unfolding of a static phase (a set-play) or the use of tactics in an unexpected play (Bouthier, 1988). A static phase is made up of one or many schemas of play that consist of preestablished sequences of action, linked in a specific order, and set in motion at a given signal. Thus, a set play is a program of actions. Tactics, on the other hand, build up during action, altering the players' perception of information and their considered moves according to the lessons they draw from the events of the game. Tactics imply, for the player, a capacity to use both determinism and random occurrences. On an individual basis, tactics may be defined as a subject's own operating system during play, and to fulfill his or her role, the player tries to submit as little as possible to the restraints, the uncertainties, and the hazards of the game while using them as much as possible.

A program is predetermined in its operations, and in this sense, it is automatic. Tactics are predetermined in their end result but not in all their operations, even though they must have numerous automatisms at their disposal to function properly. The program is put to use when there is little choice, little chance at play, or simply when it is necessary to play faster than the opponent. Tactics and strategy can emerge only at a conscious level where one finds available choices, faces unexpected events, and has the possibility of finding solutions to these new situations.

Tactical efficiency implies the capacity for deciding and deciding fast. This capacity rests upon the ability to conceive solutions. Thus, tactical decision-making requires knowledge. When tactics are operating, cognitive processes serve to extract information from play, to draw an adequate representation of the situation, to weigh contingencies, and to elaborate action scenarios. The resulting operative knowledge of configurations of play allows players to recognize restraints, regularities, and constants, and hence to capture and question the unexpected event to transform it into information. In a sense, tactical knowledge uses certainty, stability, and constancy to recognize and solve unexpected configurations of play.

Strategy and tactics encompass a vast number of potential decisions and actions regarding offense or defense, and it is not the intent of this book to analyze them at length. While discussing the teaching and learning of team sports, some authors have come up with categories of tactical and strategic knowledge (Gréhaigne & Godbout, 1995; Mitchell, 1996; Werner, 1989) that may be of interest to readers concerned with the substance of pedagogical content knowledge in team sports. In the present work, we have elected to consider some basic principles that may help focus the students' attention while they are discussing or considering a strategy to be implemented or are reflecting on successful or unsuccessful tactical choices. Those principles may also guide a coach when preparing the team for a match, or help a teacher plan a teaching unit.

SOME PRINCIPLES UNDERLYING STRATEGY AND TACTICS

None of the principles presented in this section relates to specific maneuvers on the part of the players. In a way, one might say that they emerge from the internal logic of invasion team sports discussed earlier. Some are linked to the force ratio; others are linked to the competency network, but all serve the same general purpose—overcoming the opponents in view of victory. For the sake of clarity and generalization, the principles are examined separately and in general terms in relation to the reality of the game. Essentially, it is their combination and contextualization that generate success. At times, certain principles may apply more to strategy and others to tactics, but each of them should be seen as eventually bearing consequences for both aspects of the game.

- **The deception principle.** This principle relates to trying to deceive and trick the opponent into making a bad move or a poor response. In team sports, this principle is used at all levels, on a collective or individual basis. Everyone knows that on an individual basis, numerous players make use of fakes to outwit their direct opponent. Deception is also possible on a collective basis, however it requires a great deal of involvement among players.

The organization of the defense to force the ball carrier to an area on the playing surface where he or she will be faced with a bad angle for shooting on goal is a good example. When a team can collectively organize their defensive actions to produce this result, the defending team's goalkeeper can easily foresee the chain of events potentially leading to a shot on the goal, knowing that this shot will be coming from a bad angle.

- **The surprise principle.** This is the most-used principle when a team attacks with several interlocked sequences of play. A winger who progresses on the outskirt on the opposite side of the ball, at the opponent's back, is obviously counting on a surprise effect. This principle is closely related to the mobility and opportunity principles. Whereas the surprise principle implies using unexpected actions, the deception principle, which may seem similar, leads opponents to act wrongly or to misinterpret the configurations of play.

- **The mobility principle.** Positional attack, based on continuity of play, requires preparation before the attack can be launched. Through fast shifting and good circulation of the ball, attackers may induce, in a given area of the attack zone, a breaking-down point in the state of equilibrium between the two teams and thus facilitate a shot on goal.

- **The opportunity principle.** Taking advantage of the opponents' mistakes is such an obvious principle that it does not deserve further development. But still, one must see the mistake and seize the occasion.

- **The cohesion principle.** For a team's objective to be achieved, there is a need for coherence of action from its conception through its execution. This requires the application of the cohesion principle on the team's part. All players must play in harmony, with everyone playing his or her part. Consequently, the logical, rational aspects of thoughts and actions cannot ignore the affective counterpart of the cohesion principle, that of adhesion. Depending upon teams and pursued objectives, this enduring cohesion may bear a higher or a lesser energy cost for maintaining the group. At times, this maintenance cost may be at the expense of the productive energy required by the confrontation with the other team.

- **The competency principle.** Coherence and cohesion are obtained, in part, through the competency network that entails different roles and functions among players. This way, the whole acquires a certain homogeneity that makes it possible to lower the maintenance energy cost. Indeed, competency at all levels and at all positions brings about, in the relationships between players of a same team, a feeling of trust based on mutually recognized capacities.

- **The reserve principle.** As an example, a support organization of play is based on this principle. A support player is a player by whom the attack may be immediately restarted when a sequence of play including certain maneuvers has failed. In soccer, having the forwards carry the ball makes it possible to distribute other players and constitute a reserve along the longitudinal axis of play.

- **The economy principle.** The dynamics of reciprocal attacks, linked to scoring or to the loss of the ball, leads sometimes to a result, for example a goal, that may call for a change of objective in the case of both the winning and the losing team. For instance, simply keeping ahead in the score, instead of increasing one's advantage, brings about a change in the spirit of the play and in the attack principles. It is no longer a matter of taking initiatives in view of scoring, but rather of taking initiatives in view of keeping the ball without denying the play. This is what we call the economy principle. Whether the use of this principle is desirable in physical education classes is another matter related to the teaching-learning process per se. It should be noted that applying the economy principle forces a team, a group of players, or a specific player to think over strategic, tactical, or technical choices, as well as their cost. In this perspective, one may also think that, all things considered, it is better not to change one's game and that the cost of the successive opponents' offensive maneuvers will be enough to make their actions less and less efficient.

- **The improvement principle.** Before a match, on the basis of a subjective estimate of the force ratio, players select or elaborate consistent systems of play that they will implement with whatever tactical and technical abilities they possess at the time. At this level, technical progress is subordinated to the systems of play, in relation to the estimated force ratio and the selected strategic principles. A deeper knowledge of and a higher degree of integration to the implemented systems of play may make it easier for a player to decode opponents' and partners' play and, thus, to act faster. But this gain, obtained through automation, may be counterbalanced by the opponents' knowledge. Indeed the opponent may in turn, through a similar fast decoding of the play, offer a more attuned opposition to the player's actions. Then, a progress dynamic sets in whereby players attempt to surpass the present stage of execution to outwit the opponents.

In the present chapter, fundamental features of team sports and games, the notion of oppositional relationship, the force ratio, and the competency network have been presented. The notions of strategy and tactics have been differentiated, and various principles related to the force ratio and underlying strategy and tactics have been examined. In the next chapter, the goal will be to define and refine the notion of *configuration of play* and show how it can be used to analyze team sports.

4

DECISION-MAKING IN TEAM SPORTS

Game play intelligence is the result of a combination of flair, resourcefulness, vigilant attention, a sense of opportunity, and so on. Based on this description, emphasis is always put on "practical efficiency" to attain success during game play. A player's practical efficiency must be flexible to adapt to constant, varying game situations. Instead of developing one model that will constitute a norm for his or her game play action, a player should focus on the flow of play and the play configuration at hand to detect its coherence and to profile its evolution. One has to detect favorable factors within a given configuration of play and base oneself upon the situation's potential to try and take advantage of it.

CONFIGURATION OF PLAY

In a broad sense, a configuration is a list or a schematic providing the nature and the main characteristics of all elements of a given system. In relation to team games and sports, the notion of configuration of play refers to the relative positioning of players on both teams in relation to the possession and the location of the projectile ball, puck, and so on and in relation to the various players' movements. At times, it is also referred to as a pattern of play (Ali, 1988), a situation of play (McPherson, 1993), or a display (McMorris & Graydon, 1997). During the game, players need to study the shift from one configuration of play to another to better understand the evolution of play. In soccer, for instance, attackers who have moved the ball to the center of the field and who realize that the defenders have spread themselves across the field may elect to go on with an attack, exploiting the depth of the field to get closer to the goal. In basketball, once a team realizes that they are facing a zone defense, attackers can choose to shoot from the periphery. Another choice could be to pass the ball to a player located behind the defenders in the front of the play space, where players are effectively engaged in the action.

During the game, a configuration of play evolves from state 1 to state 2 and so on to state N as long as the ball remains in play. There are two ways of looking at this situation. First, the configuration of play may be defined by the positions of the players at a certain moment (Gréhaigne, Bouthier, & David, 1997). This would lead to a static, two-dimensional study of the spatial distribution of attackers and defenders and of the position of the ball. Considering several successive configurations of play at this point, like a series of still photographs, one could determine the reasons for attackers' and defenders' choices of action.

Another way of considering the problem in a more dynamic manner consists of defining the microstate of the attack/defense system on the basis of location, direction, and the possible speed of all players, including the ball carrier and the ball itself, involved in the confrontation system at this moment. Then, each microstate is determined by a distribution of the players and the ball on the playing surface with regard to their respective locations, orientations, and speed of displacement (Gréhaigne et al., 1997). Considering such dynamic configurations of play represents a more elaborate means for describing the reality of the game. In connection with perceptual and decision-making skills, the construct of configuration of play appears crucial because it makes it possible for the players to optimize their activity during play.

One can think that, to detect pertinent clues in a given configuration of play, a novice needs to be guided with precise landmarks. These precise and simple reference elements are probable indicators of the evolution of the game play situation, and they make it possible for the novice to ignore many parameters useless for adequately dealing with the configuration of play. Configurations of the game vary because players' actions bring in purposeful or random changes. Dealing adequately with a configuration of play means that a player makes a pertinent analysis of its characteristics and potential and makes an appropriate decision. However, there may be more than one pertinent analysis applicable to a configuration of play. As the opposition evolves, new relations are created between elements of the game and others are destroyed; thus there is always a production of endless, instantaneous states of equilibrium. From a player's point of view, all these relations that constitute the whole set of configurations are not equally interesting. Some are not at stake, and the player can ignore them; others must be recognized because they are the ones that must prompt the production of an adequate response in the shortest possible time.

Two notions are at the centre of the game analysis process:

1. **Game play configuration** as it actualizes itself and takes form in the force ratio between opposing teams
2. **The situation's potential** that a player or team has to take advantage of

Consequently, a player must base him or herself on the situation's potential to make a decision and formulate an adequate response (the notion of "cascade of decisions" from Deleplace, 1979). Hence, the idea of determining the course of game play events based on a predetermined plan is excluded. Evaluation and even prognostication are at the forefront of decision-making and replace the idea of a predetermined plan.

From a precise reference framework, the opposition relationship can be assessed to detect a situation's potential that can, in turn, be exploited. The assessment of the force ratio between opponents in the presence of a game situation's potential represents a key moment in a player's reflection. The player must consider the promising factors in the game play configuration that he or she has concluded could play favorably. Within an antagonistic process, interaction is continuous. Also, a player can perceive, at any moment, what is profitable to his or her team and reciprocally, what can be damaging to the opposing team. A situation's potential is determinant in a team's profit or loss since it is the factor that permits players to reorient a game situation. To conceive game efficiency in this manner, a player's game behaviors or responses must be considered not as an application of a preconceived plan but as an exploitation of the potential in a given game situation.

Instead of elaborating game plans that are projected for use in future game situations and defining the different means to effectively use these game plans, the teacher or coach must help players adequately assess the factors within a given game play configuration that will lead to positive game responses. These are often unforeseen, novel circumstances that require game-related wisdom for a team to effectively profit from them. A good player's tactics should consist of influencing the evolution of a game configuration by exerting pressure on the play. By doing this, the goal is to create a game configuration that will be advantageous to the offense. Once exploited, a game situation's potential should lead to a favorable configuration of play.

DECISION-MAKING IN SPORTS

Any voluntary action involves not only some level of motor skill—to ensure efficient execution—but also the choice to perform the action. In some instances, the choice may be simple, based on a yes-or-no context. In other more complex situations, there may be a need not only to decide whether to act, but also to choose among different courses of action. For instance, once one has made the decision to move a heavy object, one might pull, push, roll, or carry the object; place it in a wheelbarrow; and so on, depending upon the form of the object, the characteristics of the surroundings, one's strength, and so on. One's daily life is filled with decision-action dyads of this nature.

Among the various types of activity humans engage in, sports offer a unique context: Whether for the sake of leisure or profession, one competes against oneself or against others with the intent of winning. In individual sports, decisions will be made to ensure that one goes faster, jumps higher, throws further, and so on. Most of the time, such decisions are made well in advance. When the time comes to perform, the action is conducted accordingly. In sports where two people confront each other, the object is to "play" against somebody else and to perform better, knowing that the other is trying to do the same. Although general plans of action may have been established prior to the encounter, each player is faced with many decisions during the match as each one tries to outwit the other.

In this respect, team sports offer an even more complex situation, providing a bigger challenge in terms of decision-making. Thus for each player on both teams, playing well means choosing the right course of action at the right moment, performing that course of action efficiently, and doing this over and over throughout the match. To illustrate the complexity of team sports, Bouthier (1993) has presented a model (shown in Figure 4.1) that helps put decision-making and efficient action into perspective.

This model highlights the interdependent nature of all identified components. As one can see, the choice of pertinent solutions and decision-making are heavily related to the remaining components. During game play, the player must make decisions about actions to be undertaken. The player devises plans in accordance with strategic decisions and makes adjustments as effective action proceeds. Adjustments are based on tactical decisions (Bouthier & Savoyant, 1984; Gréhaigne & Godbout, 1995; Gréhaigne, Godbout, & Bouthier, 1999).

The two types of decisions are very much influenced by the social values of the group that the player is part of and by the player's personal

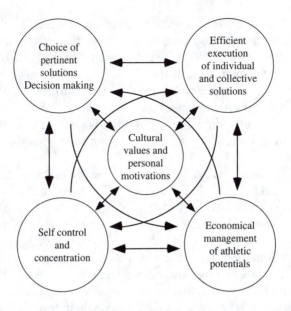

Fig. 4.1 Analysis of the complexity of team sports (translation from Bouthier, 1993).

motives regarding the activity (Nuttin, 1985; Leontiev, 1976; Bouthier, 1993; Bouthier, Pastré, & Samurçay, 1995). Cultural and motivational factors play an important role in the choice of solutions and in the degree of engagement in the action. Reciprocally, the development of decision-making competencies reinforces motivation. It is thus critical that in educational settings, students be put into situations where they can relate to real life contexts, which should help them to give significance to their learning activity.

Any decision with regard to the context and theory of play becomes valid only if it can be efficiently translated into action. This implies that the player actually has at his or her disposal a range of corresponding responses (i.e., individual and collective technical skills and tactics). However, players tend to favor, among possible answers, those valued by the group to which they belong. Reciprocally, the mastering of technical and tactical skills reinforces motivation. Thus, although tactics make up the context that justifies the use of particular technical skills, these skills should not be perceived as secondary. Technical skills constitute the tools for tactics (Mahlo, 1974). Thus, the educational setting, instead of opposing technical and tactical learning, should rather articulate them in a "tactical–technical" education.

It is well known that the motor execution of a tactical choice costs energy. For some 10 years, it has been noticed that mental activity consumes energy as well. The athletic potential of a player is therefore important not only in view of the physical requirements of game play, but also in view of its mental requirements(Bouthier, 1989a). Indeed, fatigue affects not only the quality of skill execution but also the lucidity of choices. Thus, the athletic potential is another limitation factor for decision-making in sport, and its use in turn is modulated by the player's motivation.

Decision-making is also influenced by the player's concentration and awareness and by his or her degree of self-control in the face of stress and pleasure associated with the game. These factors influence the lucidity of choices, though they can at the same time interfere with skill execution and limit or stimulate the access to the athletic potential.

In educational settings, critical aspects and moments of the game to focus on must be pointed out, as well as modalities of self-control. Depending upon sport activities, educational objectives and students' characteristics, teachers will need to choose their entry point and their intervention levers among the various components of sport action presented in the model.

RESEARCH ON DECISION-MAKING AND SPORTS

Most of the research on decision-making in sports appears to have been conducted in connection with expertise (McMorris & Graydon, 1997; Ripoll, 1991; Tennenbaum, 1999). As will be discussed later, it is not our intent to strictly apply all the conclusions reached in this type of research. However, it is of interest to note that some constructs considered in research on expertise in sport should be considered when teaching decision-making in physical education or recreational and competitive sport. In the context of this book, we will refer to children and adolescent learners involved in these types of programs as *novices*.

Although research results are not unequivocal as to differences between experts and novices (McMorris & Graydon, 1997), it is generally agreed that experts make faster and more accurate decisions when predicting an opponent's response (Chamberlain & Coelho, 1993; McPherson, 1993; Williams & Grant, 1999). Thus, they display greater anticipation skills. Chamberlain and Coelho (1993) recognized that experts make more accurate decisions based on earlier-occurring information. At the same time these authors stated that, in general, experts tend to have an advantage in the speed of decisions made, but not necessarily in the accuracy of their decisions. However, this advantage is context specific, meaning it is related to the expert's area of expertise.

> The superior decision-making capabilities of the experts appears to be due not only to a more extensive declarative knowledge structure (factual knowledge, consisting of if–then statements) but to a well developed procedural knowledge base (actions plans, the "do" statements). The disadvantage for the novice, then, is the lack of context-specific declarative and procedural knowledge base leads to a more generalized approach to problem solving, resulting in slower access to information needed for arriving at accurate decisions (Chamberlain & Coelho, 1993, p. 148).

There appears to be agreement in the literature with reference to experts' superior knowledge base both declarative and procedural, as opposed to experts' superior visual characteristics or aptitudes (e.g., French & McPherson, 1999; McPherson, 1993; McPherson, 1999; Nevett & French, 1997; Williams, Davids, Burwitz, & Williams, 1993; Williams & Grant, 1999). As pointed out by French and McPherson (1999), experts also display better problem representation in the sense that they are better at accessing the right portion of their knowledge base to perform specific sport tasks.

Thus, research findings acknowledge that anticipation, prediction, and decision-making are key elements for performance in sports. In both cases, speed is critical (Steinberg, Chaffin, & Singer, 1998), whereas accuracy is a necessary but insufficient condition.

It has also been recommended that perception and action be coupled for the analysis of experts' performance (Bouthier, 1989b; Chamberlain & Coelho, 1993; Williams et al., 1993; Williams & Grant, 1999). This suggests that when considering the development of decision-making skills, anticipation, decision-making, and effective action should be associated whenever reflection on action is sought.

Selective attention (McMorris & Beazeley, 1997; Ripoll & Benguigui, 1999) and attention orienting (Nougier & Rossi, 1999) have been evoked in connection with decision-making and should therefore be considered in learning activities in light of students' concentration capabilities. As suggested by Magill (1998), attention can then be oriented toward information-rich aspects of the game as opposed to specific cues. This is very much in line with a constructivist view of the teaching-learning process.

Deliberate systematic and long-term practice is considered essential for the acquisition of expert performance skills (Ericsson & Charness, 1994; Ericsson, Krampe, & Tesch-Römer, 1993). Many authors acknowledge that it may take as many as 10 years of practice to develop expertise (Ericsson & Simon, 1993; French & McPherson, 1999; Helsen, Starkes, & Hodges, 1998; Thomas & Thomas, 1999). In connection with deliberate practice, simulation techniques have been tried (Williams & Grant, 1999) as well as other learning activities more closely related to the actual practice of sport (Helsen et al., 1998).

Given the objectives pursued by school physical education programs and the time constraints imposed on regular physical education programs, many research findings on deliberate practice may appear irrelevant for the teaching of decision-making in sport. However, one can at least assume that if a minimal level of performance is to be achieved, some form of deliberate practice ought to be put in place, as opposed to play sessions (McMorris, 1999) and should display ecological validity, that is, guided direct practice and experience with the task should be allowed (Williams et al., 1993).

Finally, verbal reports are seen as an important strategy to obtain information on the thought processes of experts and novices (French & McPherson, 1999; McPherson, 1993). We view overt verbalization as a means to focus one's, overt verbalization will be discussed not as a measurement strategy per se, but as a mean to focus one's attention on one's thought process, to exchange information with one's partners, and to stimulate critical thinking.

ELEMENTS INVOLVED IN DECISION-MAKING

Faced with some event, one interprets reality and gives it meaning. In team sports, what is happening during a sequence of play actions? What interacting elements can one identify? Discussing the complexity of decision-making in team games, McMorris and Graydon (1997) write:

> Knowing which cues to process, however, does not guarantee successful decision making. The cues must be perceived accurately. The inter-relationship between attackers and defenders and, in particular, the space behind, between and in front of them, must be determined. This information will tell players what options are open to them in that particular situation. This

can be compared with past experience of similar situations and, based on that comparison, a decision of what action to take can be made. In making a decision, however, the players should, also, take into account their own abilities, the abilities of the opposition, the physical conditions in which the game is being played, the score at that particular moment and the area of the field in which the action is taking place (McMorris & MacGillivary, 1988) Furthermore, the situation is exacerbated by the fact that players often have to make decisions quickly, if the initiative is not to be lost (p. 71).

In Figure 4.2, a selected number of elements that are likely to influence each player's successive decisions during sequences of action are identified. As illustrated in this model, decision-making may be seen as triggered by a play action that offers a given configuration of play. As discussed earlier, this configuration of play will likely be perceived and interpreted differently by the various players involved in the action, and by outside observers as well, and may thus lead to differentiated decision-making. Both perception, related more or less to selective attention, and subsequent decision-making may be influenced by a series of elements. Some of these elements, listed on the right side of the figure, depend upon each player considered individually. Others, listed on the left side of the Figure 4.2, reflect the collective aspect of the game, which each player must also take into account.

Fig. 4.2 Some elements of the decision-making process in team sports (translation from Gréhaigne & Godbout, 1999a).

INDIVIDUAL ASPECTS OF DECISION-MAKING

While team sports imply the presence of teammates, choices of action rest ultimately upon each player. Decision-making elements related to each individual player are as follows:

- **Individual strategy.** Individual strategy is a type of advanced planning based on one's hypotheses of likely actions undertaken by one's opponents and partners (Gréhaigne, Godbout, & Bouthier, 1999); this prior planning may well influence the player's selective attention, and it gives a particular orientation to decisions that will be taken during the game before play has even started.
- **Player's cognitive map or knowledge base.** The declarative and procedural knowledge accumulated through past experience influences the player's interpretation of a configuration of play perceived in connection with efficient action rules (Gréhaigne & Godbout, 1995).
- **Tactical knowledge.** This type of knowledge may rest on some theoretical concepts but remains mostly experiential, based on notions extracted from practice. Once the configuration of play has been perceived, the player may make sense of it or not. The recall of successful or unsuccessful solutions helps players assess the relevance of such responses. Thus, strategic and tactical knowledge orients decision-making. The recall may rest on long term memory, involving some action plan profile, and on short term memory, focusing on events related to the unfolding game at hand and involving some current event profile.
- **Players' resources.** Knowledge about and consciousness of one's present resources serve as a filter, allowing the player to consider or reject certain action hypotheses offhand. Such resources may concern the player's level and range of general motor skills, motor competencies, and sport specific motor skills. In many cases, especially in invasion type team sports where attackers must invade the defenders' camp to score and thus cover much more ground, such resources will also concern the player's physiological response capacity, considering the energy cost of hypothesized courses of action. Although not necessarily at a conscious level, other variable characteristics of the player, such as concentration level and motivation, may also enhance or hinder perception and decision-making.
- **Player's location and posture.** A player's location and posture determine the possibilities of the player's responses given his or

her resources; a wrong perception of one's position and posture may negatively affect decision-making.

COLLECTIVE ASPECTS OF DECISION-MAKING

Collective aspects of the game may also influence each player's perception and decision-making. Gréhaigne et al. (1999) present three aspects that must be considered in efficient collective decision-making.

- **The collective strategy.** The collective strategy refers to the various plans, principles, or action guidelines selected prior to the match in view of organizing the activity of the players and the team as a whole during the competition. The strategy put together may either concern major general play options, or specify the players' behavior for various categories of play situations. Thus, collective strategy may direct, in advance, a given player's attention toward specific aspects of the game and orient the general trend of one's decision-making process.
- **The force ratio.** The force ratio refers to the antagonistic links that exist between several players or between the two groups of players brought together in an opposition relationship by virtue of certain rules of the game that determine an interaction mode. Advanced hypotheses about the force ratio and the actual perception during the encounter may well orient, in part, the player's individual strategy and tactical adaptation throughout the match.
- **The competency network.** The competency network is made up of the various relations between the players within a team. As discussed by Gréhaigne et al. (1999), it influences the players' play actions and behaviors depending upon their status within the team and the force ratio encountered. In a sense, the competency network may not directly influence a player's decision-making, but its weight is implicit since it is taken into account in the collective if not the individual strategy. Thus, the competency network will normally orient the attribution of specific roles to each player; hence its influence on decision-making.

Although considered separately for the sake of the discussion, the various individual and collective elements presented above are somewhat interwoven. For instance, the blending of each player's cognitive map, tactical knowledge, and resources leads to the recognition of a given competency network, and both the force ratio and the competency network orient the planning of collective and individual strategies. More stable elements, such as the competency network, the force ratio, the cognitive map, part of the tactical knowledge or action plan profile, and part of the player's resources (e.g., motor skills), constitute a meshed background that filters the perception–interpretation–anticipation–decision sequence. As the play action unfolds, more changing elements such as the player's location and posture, the level of one's fatigue and motivation, and the current event profile add their weight and ultimately determine a more or less stable chain of relevant and irrelevant decisions.

The whole set of elements can come into play only at a superior cognitive level where one can make choices, face unexpected events, and find solutions for new situations. At this point, cognitive processes serve to extract information from play, to make up an adequate representation of the situation, to assess potential events, and to draw up action scenarios.

There appear to be two theories at hand. According to supporters of one theory (Bayer, 1979; Famose, 1996; Parlebas, 1976), the larger a player's knowledge base, the more this player can recognize constraints, regularities, and constants, and the more the player can take notice of and question unexpected, unforeseen events. Knowledge, from a decision-making point of view, must rely on both certainty and fixed and stable references to confront and solve uncertainty. Thus, at the level of perceptual and decision-making mechanisms, learning consists of an increase in the amount of memorized knowledge and an improvement in the process of structuring perceptual knowledge into procedural knowledge (Famose, 1996).

Concerning the management and the organization of play, supporters of a second theory (Deleplace, 1979; Gréhaigne, 1989) contend that an expert can clearly seize a larger amount of information useful for the solving of problems brought about by the game compared to novices. Nevertheless, this amount of information remains relatively limited, and it is the quality of the information that is determining. In that respect, prior analysis of the internal logic of the sport by a coach, a teacher, or some other expert provides useful data. Based on such analyses, one can draw the player's attention to typical patterns of play. This way the player has at his or her disposal an already-worked-out mental action picture instead of being burdened by a mass of information not useful for the solving of the problem at hand.

The problem for a player is to succeed in encompassing the entire complexity of the game within a system made of the smallest possible number of fundamental action axes interrelated in a strong logical and functional unit. Tactics are based on successive decisions, taken according to the evolution of the action. The development of tactical capacity implies the development of a capacity for quick decisions. In turn, this capacity relies on one's capacity for conceiving solutions. In a word, the development of a capacity for choosing requires the development of knowledge and routines. Consequently, the player, through cumulative experience, builds up an actual action matrix by always assimilating and refining the data collected into a personal mental action picture that allows him or her to act and react faster.

One can use an operative model of decision-making that emphasizes the contributions of some of the elements discussed earlier. Such a dynamic model reflects the reality of a game played under strong time constraints. One hypothesis is to consider that the player's analysis of play action under strong time constraints is conducted with reference to a few typical configurations of play and to related forerunner cues that allow a player to anticipate upcoming play. Knowing the essentials of appropriate responses to given configurations of play facilitates fast decision-making (Bouthier, David, & Eloi, 1994).

This chapter exposed how an accurate analysis of the configurations of game play allows a player to identify components of decision-making. In chapter 5, a few ideas on the notion of *tactical knowledge in team sports* will be presented.

5

THE PLAYER'S TACTICAL KNOWLEDGE

In a study on the formative evaluation practices of physical education teachers, Gréhaigne, Billard, Guillon, and Roche (1988) registered and analyzed the didactic communications of teachers during sequences of play. They noted that these communications contained orders and rules given from the edge of the playing surface during game situations. However, in the teachers' comments at the end of the sequence, nothing was said in connection with such rules or advice. Gréhaigne and his colleagues believe that rules and advice constituted declarative knowledge about the game at hand but that such knowledge had to be more systematically and formally identified (Marsenach & Mérand, 1987).

In this chapter we will concentrate on the fundamental components which constitute tactical knowledge as this knowledge is critical to overall game performance.

THE CONTENT OF TACTICAL KNOWLEDGE
IN INVASION TEAM SPORTS AND GAMES

To identify tactical knowledge, Gréhaigne (1996) systematically collected action rules that were stated during game situations either by the students or by the teachers. Then, through content analysis, categories of rules were progressively identified. The categories were regularly validated in two ways: The categories were submitted twice to groups of experts on team sport and to a group of physical educators. They tested this tactical knowledge while teaching team sports to secondary school students and submitted suggestions and corrections based upon the relevance or the lack of relevance of various action rules (Gréhaigne & Laroche, 1994).

From our perspective, tactical knowledge is fundamentally "knowledge in action" because for a player, tactical awareness and performance are strongly linked. According to Gréhaigne (1992) and Malglaive (1990), knowledge in team sports rests upon action rules, play organization rules, and motor capacities. Action rules define conditions to be enforced and elements to be taken into account if one wants to ensure efficient action (Goirand, 1993; Gréhaigne, 1989; Gréhaigne & Guillon, 1991; Marin, 1993; Vergnaud, Halbvacks, & Rouchier, 1978). Such rules, which are basic to tactical knowledge about the game, and their use, whether isolated or in connection with other rules, provide an answer to a given problem. They represent a momentary truth, and some rules can become obstacles to progress on other occasions. For instance, to *create open space, one must tighten up the defense in one zone and swiftly pass the ball to another zone.*

Table 5.1 and Table 5.2 present a nonexhaustive list of action rules and related principles of actions for the attack and the defense. Action rules constitute an interesting notion in relation to learning and can be used as a theoretical tool for elaborating curricula in relation to the teaching-learning process of team sports.

ACTION RULES

Vergnaud, Halbvachs, & Rouchier (1978) define action rules as rules that permit a player to generate actions based on certain situational variables. These variables can evolve through time, from one situation to another. One rule, or a set of rules, however, can be applied to or associated with a class of game play problems. Gréhaigne et al. (1988) state that action rules define the conditions to be respected and the elements that need to be considered to produce efficient action. For example, when trying to free oneself from a marker, a player must be available and accessible to the ball carrier. The rules can be characterized in the following manner: They are conscious, they contribute to comprehension and selection in relation to motor competencies, and they contribute to the execution of action. Action rules also contribute to the explanation of action.

From a functional point of view, action rules constitute one of the principal sources of tactical knowledge. They permit teammates to exchange ideas among themselves or with the teacher or coach. From this perspective, action rules serve as irreplaceable support for communication. They lead players to verbalization and game play awareness and, hence, increase the players' precision in the analysis of a game situation.

TABLE 5.1 Offensive Action Rules and Related Principles of Action

Keeping the ball[4]

Having at one's disposal a maximum number of potentials receivers or increasing the possibilities of exchange

Protecting the ball (using one's body as an obstacle)

Keeping the ball away from the opponent and close to oneself

Directing passes into space behind the defender and in front of the attacker

Moving to be at passing distance, seen by the ball-owner, away from the defender

Playing in movement

Reducing the number of exchanges required to reach the scoring zone

Reducing the time used to bring the ball into the scoring zone and shoot

Varying the rhythm and the intensity of the moves

Moving when space is free

Creating passing angles

Passing the ball ahead of the receiver

Favoring instantaneous passes

Continuing movement after having released the ball

Receiving the ball while moving

Exploiting and creating available space

Using the depth and the width of the field or court

Locking the defense in one zone and playing in another

Alternating direct play, indirect play, short passes, and long passes

Locking opponents to free some partners

Changing the direction of play

Using spaces not occupied by opponents

Moving away from opponents, into the intervals or to the back of the opponents

Creating screens or blocks and exploiting them

Using speed and temporal advantages

Creating uncertainty

Keeping the alternative direct play/indirect play

Changing one's rhythm (slow/quick)

Luring opponents into one zone to conclude in another

Increasing the number of players involved in the action

Faking or combining the change of rhythm, space, and orientation

Moving in one direction and releasing the ball in another

Adopting a posture or an orientation that allows various actions (i.e., disguising one's intentions)

Adapted and reprinted, by permission, from Gréhaigne & Godbout, 1995, pp. 490–505.

TABLE 5.2 Defensive Action Rules and Related Principles of Action

Defending the target

Initiate pressure in the area of the ball in the few seconds following a loss of possession

Putting as many players as possible between the ball and the target

Reinforcing and covering constantly the axis of the goal

Organizing the team along lines of strength

Putting the attack off center, towards the outskirts

Moving the ball away

Covering one's partners

Preventing shots

Withdrawing quickly while looking at the ball to recreate the defensive lines

Regaining possession of the ball

Recovering the ball as close as possible to the opponents' goal

Increasing the numerical density in the middle of the field and in the attack area

Impairing the progression of the ball

Challenging every opponent

Looking for the interception

Putting immediate pressure on the player with the ball—harassment

Positioning oneself on likely ball trajectories to isolate the ball carrier from his or her teammates

Challenging the opponents' progression

Reducing uncertainty

Reducing the number of potential receivers

Foreseeing opponents' actions

Understanding quickly the opponents' system of play to stabilize the perception

Having an explicit communication within the defense. (A player must coordinate the defense)

Evaluating the capacity and skills of one's direct opponent

Keeping both the attackers and the ball in view

Sticking to agreed rules and to one's task

Impairing the opponent through one's placement and movements

Faking to trick one's opponent

Reducing the time, space, and options

Modifying rapidly one's defensive system to adapt it to the game

Adopting an optimal position on the field

Reducing available space

Keeping the attack away from the target

Defining everybody's rules on set plays

Spotting the favorite sector of one's direct opponent's actions

Reducing the effective space available to one's opponent

Delaying the attack whenever the defenders are outnumbered

Reprinted, by permission, from Gréhaigne & Godbout, 1995, pp. 490–505.

Action rules can be contradictory and even opposite depending on the oppositional relationship within a particular configuration of play. For example, when a team is faced with a situation where it needs to maximize the number of available and accessible players for potential ball exchanges and to cover adequately the axis of their own goal, the specific action rules that a team has to respect differ greatly. Practically speaking, when facing certain problematic configurations of play, the confrontations, which require contradictory action rules, force players to reason in a dialectic way. Players must be able to interpret action rules, test them, and if needed, infringe on or redefine them. In a sense, a player must rely on theoretical knowledge in relation to action rules but not be dependant on it. Thus, a player must be critical, pragmatic, and opportunistic to profit from a configuration of play. Hence, through inference, we find that decisions made during game play leave a mental trace due to their use, evolution and their evaluation. This type of analysis is not always easy because action rules that are well integrated become, over time, *habitus* (Bourdieu, 1972, 1980; Gréhaigne, Richard, Mahut, & Griffin, 2002). Bourdieu (1972) defines *habitus* as:

> A system of durable, transposable arrangements that, while integrating past experiences, functions like a perception matrix that can make the accomplishment of different tasks possible thanks to the analogical transfer of schemas that permits one to resolve problems of the same nature. (pp. 178–179)

Based on this definition, *habitus* is simply a player's singular experience and constitutes a nonconscious mode of functioning during game play.

Finally, action rules that are associated with a class of game play problems can be centered on a principle of efficient action, for example "playing in movement" when trying to move the ball into the offensive zone and effectively score.

THE EMERGENCE OF ACTION RULES

To achieve success during game play, the learner gathers information during action and then tries to apply it when facing different play sequences. Through experimentation, he or she can define tactical and technical responses to be used in different situations. After using these responses, the learner can then verify the gap between the expected outcomes of these responses and what actually happens. The learner can then redefine his or her action plan, if necessary, or find other alternatives for efficient action. For example, if players notice that from their 16 ball possessions, their team recovered 5 balls close to the opposition's goal, which resulted in 3 of their 4 goals, then this team should realize that ball recovery closer to the opposition's goal must be emphasized to maximize offensive potential. When these efficient action means are used successively over time and become constant, they basically become action rules. When defined, action rules become a reference framework from which a player can "actively regulate" (Piaget, 1974) him or herself to produce more efficient motor responses. However, it must be noted that the emergence of action rules does not necessarily mean a transformation in motor responses. A particular motor response can be defined as being the sum of, or the juxtaposition of, action rules. A motor response is always original and often complex and represents a player's organization when facing a particular game situation.

THE USE OF ACTION RULES

To better position game play problems in context, we will group together knowledge about game play and knowledge within game play in one category, which we will call "knowledge in action." This new category of knowledge emphasizes our concern in relation to the development of a player's game knowledge and skills, both tactical and technical, to be more efficient during game play. In regard to action rules, their use in an isolated situation or in combination with other rules (i.e., play organization rules) constitutes a response to a particular problem. Action rules represent a momentary truth, which can be inoperative at times and can even be an obstacle to a team's progress in other instances.

During game play, the notion of action is not only associated with the player's execution of action but also with a player's exploration of game-related knowledge through reflection on different game situations. Through this mental process, a player can analyze compatible and contradictory responses to different game situations. The goal of this experimental process, which requires effort from the player, is for the player to find coherent and economical ways of responding to game play constraints.

During the development of such knowledge, novices employ general and isolated responses, whereby the conditions in which the action is unfolding are examined partially, successively, and in a hierarchical way. Their game knowledge having evolved, intermediate players' responses are more refined, sophisticated, and discriminative; hence, they have a more tactical connotation. Intermediate players are more aware of the possible confrontational conditions between two teams. They consider explicit and implicit characteristics of play configurations that are often brought back to a few simple characteristics of game play.

It seems that learning action rules during a player's developmental phase is extremely important. During this phase, game situations are often modified (i.e., time constraints, smaller playing surface, smaller equipment, etc.), which can help players, through action rules, develop an action plan in advance based on the game situation's various elements. For example, in a 3 vs. 3 modified practice situation, where the emphasis is for a team to keep possession of the ball for three successive passes to score a point, the offensive team will apply previously learned action rules to develop efficient action within the parameters presented by this situation. Though this game situation is based on previously learned action rules, new action rules can also be learned. In a learning situation of this type, a player's cognitive activity is different from a real match situation because it permits the learner to develop awareness through experimentation and verbalization without hampering actual performance.

Play organization rules cover a certain number of themes related to the logic of the activity, the dimensions of the play area, the distribution of players on the field, and a differentiation of roles. These rules also cover a few simple organizational principles that may facilitate the elaboration of a strategy. For instance, due to the shape of the target, defenders in soccer and hockey must constantly maintain a defensive configuration protecting the central axis to throw the attackers off center. Table 5.3 presents a series of examples of such organization rules.

MOTOR CAPACITIES

Motor capacities refer to two large categories of problems related to the perceptual and decision-making activity of the player in close connection with the motor competencies that he or she possesses or must develop. Indeed, if they are to be applied, action rules require the development of motor capacities; thus rules and motor capacities can hardly be disassociated. A player's motor competencies are his or her resources from a skill execution point of view. The motor competencies that a player has at his or her disposition have a major influence on a player's repertoire of possible game play decisions. The speed of play will also greatly influence a player's decisions, even if he or she does possess a wide repertoire of motor competencies. For instance, for the ball carrier to effectively deal with a ball request from a teammate, the open player must be available and accessible.

TABLE 5.3 Play Organization Rules

Prior to the Game

Adopting a given plan of defense

Adopting a given system of play, a general framework

Assigning an optimal position on the field (or on the court) for each player

Identifying one's strength and weaknesses and those of the team

Constructing a game plan

Assigning roles and tasks within the team

During the Game

Creating imbalance in one's favor

Coordinating and connecting the various actions of the team

Playing into weak axis of the opponent's defense

Maintaining movement in the game

Gaining and keeping an advance on defensive replacement

Positioning everyone optimally along the axis and at the outskirts of the field or the court

Leaving the ball to the opponents and choosing the right moment to regain possession

Adapting rapidly to the specific details of the opponent's attack and defense

Reprinted, by permission, from Gréhaigne & Godbout, 1995, pp. 490–505.

PRINCIPLES OF ACTION

Based on a number of related action rules, efficient principles of action—each defined as a theoretical structure and an operative instrument—orient various actions, making it possible to act on reality (Gréhaigne et al., 1988). Principles of action constitute a kind of macroscopic frame of reference that makes it possible for the teacher and eventually for the student to isolate and classify noted facts. An example of this would be to observe the different elements that are necessary to move the ball effectively into the offensive zone to bring the ball in the scoring area and score.

To improve tactical knowledge players must establish guidelines on which they can base their decisions. The rules presented earlier (in Tables 5.1, 5.2, and 5.3) conceptualize goals and objectives for attacking and defending that can aid players in developing their cognitive processes, which, in turn, will be beneficial to player's' development of action rules, motor competencies, and the play organization rules needed for efficient game play responses. As stated by Giordan and De Vecchi (1987), knowing beforehand is being capable of using what we have learned to resolve a problem or clarify a situation.

In this chapter, the notion of tactical knowledge has been analyzed. From our standpoint, tactical knowledge is fundamentally "knowledge in action" because, for a player, tactical awareness and performance are strongly linked. Three general categories of knowledge that have been examined are action rules that lead to principles of action, play organization rules, and motor capacities.

In the next three chapters, different strategies will be presented to better analyze the state of game play performance. More specifically, different assessment strategies will be discussed to help players and students better understand their play in the perspective of improving performance.

6

THE ANALYSIS OF PLAY IN TEAM SPORTS

Observing game play is a key element of team sport "didactics." Due to the complexity of the environment, the temporal and spatial characteristics of players' locations and movements, as well as those of the ball, game play must be analyzed in a systematic way if one wishes to obtain dependable, reliable, and useful information. This type of analysis takes into account fixed elements such as the playing surface, but also considers other variables that are controlled by players, such as the ball, play organization rules, tactics, and so on (Gréhaigne & Godbout, 1995). The meaning of players perceptions is directly linked to the force ratio.

In addressing force ratio among players, the concept of "perceived configuration of play" is an interesting one because it makes it possible to optimize the player's activity in confrontational situations. A beginner needs a precise and advanced frame of reference to pick up relevant clues within the configuration of play. This picture or mental schema, which is a functional reflection of game play, is put together by and for the player's activity. It is by definition variable and short lived since the player's actions constantly bring about purposeful modifications.

From the standpoint of the player's activity, all relations that make up the whole perceived configuration of play are not equally interesting for analysis. Some are not relevant, and the player ignores them. Others must be acknowledged, for they are the ones that orient the production of an appropriate response within a limited time span. Often, several responses will allow the completion of the task by solving the problem at hand, but the most appropriate and most dependable response will frequently be the simplest because it is the most economical from a mechanical, energetic, emotional, and informational standpoint. A good solution implies picking up a few characteristics of the configuration, and a partial arrangement of elements that will include only the ones that are essential. By giving *a priori* precedence to certain elements of game play, the player processes these data more rapidly whenever they appear in configurations of play. At the same time the player has a limited frame of reference (i.e., in the game moment) from which to collect and interpret information.

To this end, we will describe in this chapter a few observational approaches that make it possible to analyze game play from a holistic perspective because knowing what players can and cannot do is indispensable to teaching and coaching.

OBSERVATIONAL APPROACHES IN THE ANALYSIS OF GAME PLAY

For the sake of illustration in this chapter, the approaches presented will be used in reference to soccer, but they could as well be used for European handball, basketball, field hockey, and other invasion sports.

Static Approach to Observation of Game Play

The simplest observational approach that can be used consists of considering, on one hand, the defensive zone and, on the other hand, the offensive zone. If one divides each zone, one obtains four observation areas: (a) defensive, (b) pre defensive, (c) pre offensive, and (d) offensive, as illustrated in Figure 6.1.

One could also consider the central corridors of the pitch and the two bordering corridors, as presented in Figure 6.2. This would make it possible to note play actions conducted in the "attacked goal–defended goal" axis and others carried in the peripheral corridors.

A third type of grid might consider the direct play-space with a vertical target as in soccer or handball (Figure 6.3). Due to the verticality of the target, the apparent target area varies according to the shooting angle. If one combines all previous grids, one obtains the observational grid presented in Figure 6.3.

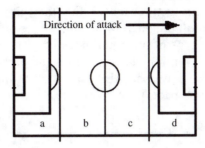

Fig. 6.1 Four observation areas.

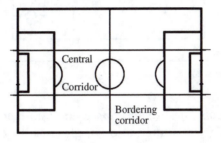

Fig. 6.2 Central and bordering corridors.

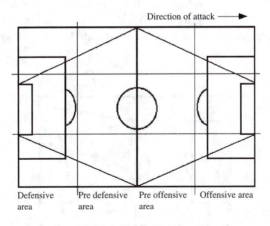

Fig. 6.3 Static observational grid.

An important feature of these tools is that they give some idea on the players' placement on the pitch, which illustrates different configurations of play. This type of information can be very useful to coaches and players in the evolution of a team's play and performance. Now we discuss the effective play-space (EP-S), the main dimensions of play, and the covered play-space (CP-S).

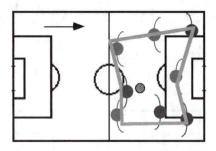

Fig. 6.4 Effective play-space.

Location of the Ball, Effective Play-Space, and Dominant Distribution If one considers a given configuration of play like the one illustrated in Figure 6.4 and Figure 6.5, one can summarize it using the notion of effective play-space (Mérand, 1977; Gréhaigne, 1989; Gréhaigne, Billard, & Laroche, 1999). The effective play-space (EP-S) may be defined as the polygonal area that one obtains by drawing a line linking all involved players located at the periphery of the play at a given instant. In the example illustrated in Figure 6.4, the ball is located at the rear of EP-S, in the central corridor (Figure 6.2), and is situated in the pre offensive area (Figure 6.1).

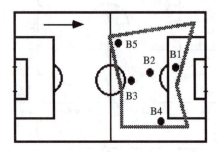

Fig. 6.5 EP-S and the location of the ball.

Due to the fact that the ball can be in different positions in relation to the effective play-space, we shall assign it to one of five categories. By convention:

1. B1 is a ball located in a central position, which is in the corridor defined by the "attacked goal/defended goal" axis, ahead of the effective play-space represented by the principal axis.
2. B2 is a ball located in a central position, in the middle of the effective play-space.
3. B3 is a ball located in a central position, at the rear of the effective play-space.
4. B4 is a ball located in a flank position either on the left or right periphery of the pitch, ahead of the effective play-space.
5. B5 is a ball located in a flank position either on the left or right periphery of the pitch, at the rear of the effective play-space.

At school, in relation to soccer in a physical education or competitive sports setting, the regular and specific player distribution on the pitch, which we call dominant distribution, presents certain constants, shown in Figure 6.6.

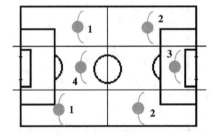

Caption

1 : player at the rear periphery

2 : player at the forward periphery

3 : player forward, a scorer

4 : leader of play

Fig. 6.6 Dominant distribution of the players.

One can use the dominant distribution to assess how players interpret the force ratio and position themselves, based on their resources, when confronting another team. Most of the time, the best players perform in the central corridor (i.e., lane), which is in the "attacked goal/defended goal" axis. More specifically, in *space-limited games*, better known as small-sided games, the best player usually stands at the rear of the effective play-space and assumes the role of the leader. The second best player is most often located at the front of the effective play-space and is given the role of scorer. The other players perform at the periphery, at the front or rear of the play-space. One can differentiate among them by noting that the more skillful player is at the forward periphery.

Indeed, players are often faced with more complex tasks, especially with regard to action on-the-ball within limited space and time. In contrast, the role of those who play at the rear periphery consists most often in clearing the ball away to keep it far from the scoring zone. Of course, one must conceive of this set of intentions and roles in a dynamic fashion. Players move around on the pitch and are led to deviate from their typical line of conduct, but generally speaking, they abide by this distribution.

Dynamic Approach to the Observation of Game Play

Movement of the Ball and Force Ratios The two analytical tools presented in this section are based on the different locations of the ball in relation to the effective play-space at the origin of the ball movement. In the rear-ball play (shown in Figure 6.7), the origin of ball movement is always at the rear with respect to the future receiver of the ball. Play usually starts with the recovery of the ball and continues until its loss to the opposition for whatever reason. In the forward-ball play, at some point during the movement of the ball, it travels backward towards a supporting player.

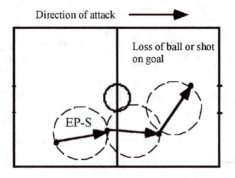

Fig. 6.7 The rear-ball play.

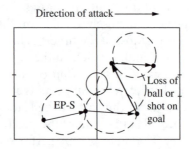

Fig. 6.8 The forward-ball play.

The transformation of the movement of the ball is the consequence of a defensive organization that creates a great difficulty for the offensive team to move the ball forward. With respect to the effective play-space, one can see a diversification of the movement of the ball (Figure 6.9).

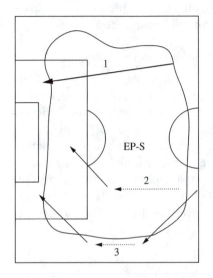

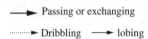

Passing or exchanging

Dribbling   lobing

Movement of the ball in relation to the effective play-space

1. Over the effective play-space
2. Into the effective play-space, dribbling or exchanging the ball
3. Around the effective play-space, dribbling or exchanging the ball

Fig. 6.9 Movement of the ball regarding effective play-space.

Covered Play-Space The covered play-space (CP-S) is the area representing the space occupied by attackers and defenders during an attack. It defines the maximum space used by players throughout a sequence of play, with a succession of distortions that eventually shows the way this space has been traveled through (Figure 6.10).

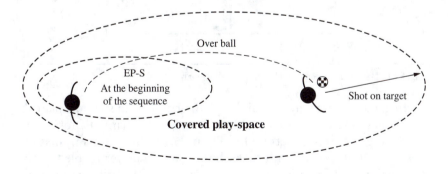

Fig. 6.10 Example of covered play-space.

SIGNIFICANT POSTURES AND BEHAVIORS

In this section, a player's level of play will be analyzed by examining his/her the postures and how he/she manipulates the ball. In this case the range of manipulation is often used as an indicator of the level of game play. For instance, a beginner mainly uses a little part of the space located in front of them, which we will call "close-space."

The Range of Manipulation

Because of gravity, players function according to a vertical plane. Players use perception to structure space on the basis of posture, or they structure it on the basis of their location with respect to a fictitious horizontal plane crossing at eye level.

The small cylinder illustrated in Figure 6.11 defines a manipulation range close to one's body. The large cylinder defines the maximum manipulation range when a player outstretches his or her arms (see Cam, Crunelle, Giana, Grosgeorge, & Labiche, 1979). These data make it possible to characterize the way a player handles the ball. A beginner uses essentially quadrants 1 and 2.

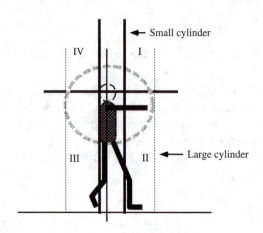

Fig. 6.11 Manipulation range in relation to the upper body.

In games where players mainly use their feet, as in soccer, a player's immediate space is constructed by increasing the manipulation range following the steps illustrated in Figure 6.12. From a manipulation restricted to the space in front of both feet, the player is able to gain possession of the ball in all positions, even with the ball coming from all directions.

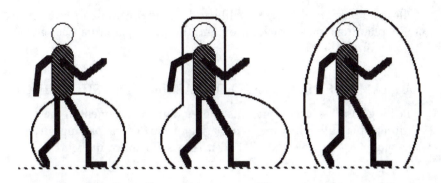

Fig. 6.12 The immediate space in soccer.

With respect to game play situations, the notion of immediate space can be specified further with the use of the following parameters: (a) the intimate-space that represents a space volume very close to the player (like a bubble); (b) the immediate-space that refers to the range of manipulation; (c) the safety distance that represents the space needed by the player to act without restraints; and finally, (d) the confrontational distance that is determined by the distance of opponents (Figure 6.13). Criteria such as the ones discussed in the

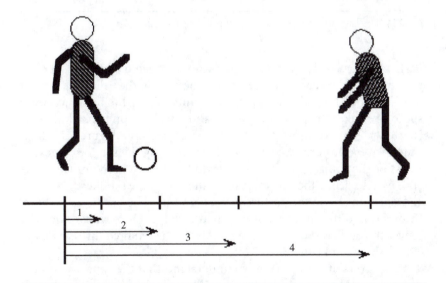

Fig. 6.13 1: Intimate space; 2: Immediate space; 3: Safety distance; 4: Confrontation distance.

following paragraph offer a viable and pertinent frame of reference for explaining a player's evolution and the way a player handles game play confrontations.

A FRAME OF REFERENCE FOR PASSING AND SHOOTING

The long pass in soccer represents one fundamental element in the evolution of play, allowing one to use a major part of the playing surface for long play (Amicale ENSEP, 1977). This is illustrated in Figure 6.14.

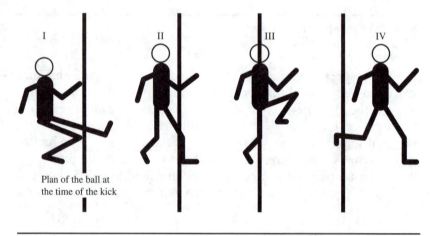

Fig. 6.14 Players' typical postures for a pass or a shot on a goal in soccer.

Part I of Figure 6.14 shows a beginner who stays behind the plane defined by the vertical line corresponding to the location of the ball at the time of the kick. A higher skilled player who wants to give the ball maximum speed overtakes the plane of the ball and falls back on his kicking foot (part IV). This requires both strength and precision. Figure 6.15 illustrates players' postures according to their throwing skills in the context of a pass or shot on goal in basketball, team handball, and so on. The reference used to define the vertical plane is the axis of the shoulder.

Depending upon the posture that a player uses, he or she may achieve throws that differ in terms of length and shape. One critical rule: The longer the desired shot, the more important the required throwing path. This is shown in Figure 6.16.

For players, it is important to understand that the capacity to produce a long throw is an asset for the ball carrier. In fact, in games where the ball is handled with the hands, players are quick to identify the kind

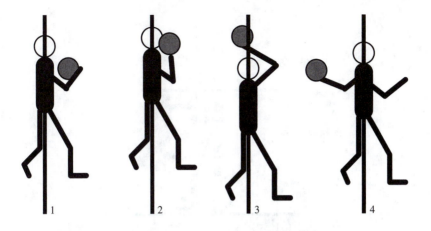

Fig. 6.15 Players' postures with reference to hand throwing.

of posture used by the throwing player and thus to foresee where the ball is likely to be thrown. The main postures that one can see on the playing surface are illustrated in Figure 6.17 along with the different shapes of the ball trajectory and related estimated distances.

If we combine the manipulation range in relation to the upper body with players' postures with reference to throwing, we obtain an excellent frame of reference for analyzing the capacities of the player in possession of the ball.

Players' location on the field at the time of throw-ins is in direct connection with the estimated thrower's capacity, and this yields different

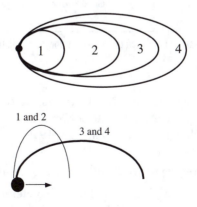

Fig. 6.16 Lengths and shapes of throws according to the postures illustrated in Figure 6.15.

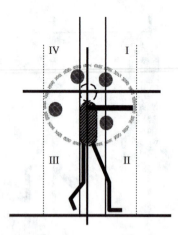

Fig. 6.17 An illustration of the manipulation range in relation to the upper body.

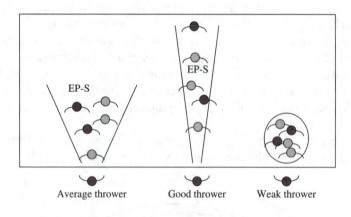

Fig. 6.18 Effective play-space in relation to a player's throwing capacities in restarting a game of soccer, basketball, handball, and so on.

effective play-spaces. Figure 6.18 illustrates the results obtained in a basketball experiment conducted at the Department of Physical Education in Dijon (Gréhaigne, Billard, Laroche, 1999).

Exchanging the Ball with Growing Complexity

Various ways of exchanging the ball are also elements that one must carefully observe because they yield accurate information on the level of play in a given force ratio. From the easiest to the most difficult ball

Face to face

Caption ——▶ Passing or dribbling

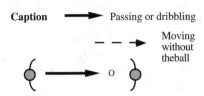

— — ▶ Moving without the ball

Beginners' classical positioning: Players are generally face to face, still, and 3 or 4 meters apart.

Using the depth of the playing surface

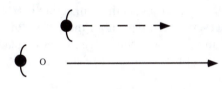

The ball carrier is still and the intended receiver is running in the depth of the playing surface. The ball is passed forward in the player's running axis.

Orthogonal pass

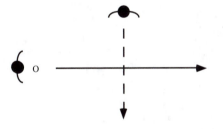

The orthogonal pass consists in passing the ball at the right time in an open space where the intended receiver will be shortly.

Interval attack

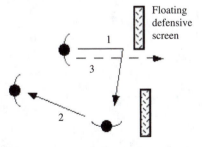

Floating defensive screen

After moving the ball, it is thrown in an open space where the player will be shortly. This requires an accurate temporal adjustment.

Fig. 6.19 Exchanging the ball with growing complexity.

exchange, we will examine some features: speed, location, and the direction of a player's movement according to the movements of the ball. These analyses are shown in Figure 6.19.

The analysis of players' paths, ball trajectories, and ball circulation constitutes valuable indicators for obtaining information about the actual play level and its evolution from previous matches or lessons.

In a physical education school setting, teachers and student observers collect information based on personal observations and will interpret reality according to a personal frame of reference (Gréhaigne, Godbout, & Bouthier, 2001). The role of the teacher is to provide feedback to students, describing and explaining the players' actions. Based on qualitative or quantitative indicators, the teacher favors the connection between objective data collected by observers and the result of the action. In the next two chapters we will examine the assessment of game performance and its role in the teaching-learning process of sport-related games.

7

PERFORMANCE ASSESSMENT IN TEAM SPORTS

The first element that comes to mind when one considers the analysis of a player's performance concerns his or her ability to apply motor responses to the resolution of game play problems. This notion limits a player's knowledge of typical skills and behaviors that are organized and presented based on their difficulty from simple to complex. Based on our explanation of the different components that constitute game play, the assessment of a player's performance provides a broader view. Game performance must be accomplished in a real life context and must reflect the different components that are important to a team's performance. The instruments presented in chapter 6 offer teachers and coaches a qualitative approach for the analysis of a team or an individual's play based on selected criteria.

In the current chapter, we will present different assessment strategies that can be used in the analysis of game components, either on a team or at the individual level. Also, we will examine in more detail the particular contexts and challenges of assessing performance in a team sport setting. The assessment strategies discussed in this chapter will then lead us to the description and explanation of two assessment instruments examines an individual's global performance. These two instruments will be presented in chapter 8.

PERFORMANCE ASSESSMENT IN TEAM SPORTS

There appears to be agreement among researchers in sport pedagogy as to the importance of authentic assessment in the teaching-learning process of team sports. As showed by Veal (1988); Cardinet (1986); and Allal, Cardinet, and Perrenoud (1985), assessment can take the form of preassessment, formative assessment, or summative assessment depending upon the phase at which it occurs and the reason for which it is implemented. If assessment is to be truly integrated with the teaching-learning process, it must meet at least two requirements. The first is ecological validity (Gardner, 1992), which refers to the relationship of measurement with what is taught and to the fact that the assessment is done in context so that it does not disturb the normal functioning of the classroom. The second requirement is the active participation of students in assessment as it is integrated into the teaching-learning process (Wiggins, 1993; Zessoules & Gardner, 1991).

Thus, problems with the assessment of any given player in team sports are those related to the assessment of any complex system, that is, the intervening elements are not only numerous but also interacting; the force ratio plays an important role, and it may vary in different opposition situations or even during one given situation; the interdependence of the members of a given team; and the assessment of a single player within a coherent system (that is, within the team).

FACETS OF PERFORMANCE ASSESSMENT IN TEAM SPORTS

Authentic assessment of performance in team sports offers a special challenge to physical education teachers and coaches. Beyond the usual motor fitness components, it is generally agreed that performance in team sports results from the interaction of strategy efficiency, tactical efficiency, and specific perceptual and motor skills (Gréhaigne & Godbout, 1995). In an effort to take into account the various facets likely to be of concern in the assessment of motor performance, Godbout (1990) has proposed a two-dimensional model (see Figure 7.1) that leads to the identification of four general categories of information or objects of measurement. All four categories of information may be considered to be of interest in the case of team sports performance assessment. On the one hand the model recognizes that an assessor may wish to consider the technical aspects or the tactical aspects of a player's performance. On the other hand the assessment may be focused on the result or the end product of the player's actions or on the way those actions are conducted, (the process). The distinction between product and process with reference to the assessment of motor skills has been briefly explained by Brown (1982) and has been described in greater details by Veal (1995) and may apply to the tactical aspects of sport performance (Werner, Thorpe, & Bunker, 1996). It may also be associated with the notions of *knowledge of results* (KR) and *knowledge of performance* (KP) used by motor learning researchers with reference to augmented or extrinsic feedback (Schmidt, 1991). Combining both technique versus tactics and product versus process, one can identify four facets of performance assessment in team sports:

1. Information relative to a *technical product*: For instance, is the player able to reach a partner when passing the ball?
2. Information relative to a *technical process*: For instance, how does the player proceed to pass the ball?
3. Information relative to a *tactical product*: For instance, player B is responsible for covering player C; does player C manage to receive a pass anyway or does player B effectively succeed in eliminating player C from the play?
4. Information relative to a tactical process: For instance, how does player B proceed to cover player C and prevent him or her from receiving a pass?

Figure 7.1 illustrates these facets of performance.

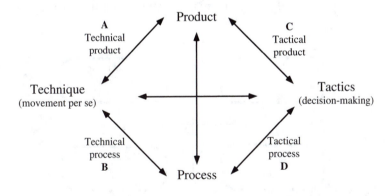

Fig. 7.1 Facets involved in the assessment of performance in team sports (Godbout, 1990).

CURRENT ASSESSMENT PRACTICES IN TEAM SPORTS

To collect information relative to these facets of performance, physical education teachers and coaches have developed various measurement strategies. In an attempt to summarize these practices, Godbout (1990) has proposed the two-dimensional model illustrated in Figure 7.2. On one hand, the model recognizes that in some instances the measurements are done in standardized set-ups, whereas in other cases, the information is collected in real life situations (that is, during regular matches). On the other hand, the measurement procedure may be quantitative in nature (low inference), relying on physical units of measurement, or it may be qualitative (high inference), relying on the use of rating instruments. By combining both dimensions of the model, one can identify four general strategies for collecting information with regard to a player's performance in team sports:

1. **Standardized tests.** For instance, asking a student to shoot a basketball into a basket as many times as possible over 20 trials from a given position.
2. **Statistics derived from competition.** For instance, computing the average number of controlled rebounds over a certain number of games.
3. **The rating of performance in standardized set-ups.** For instance, having every student execute five volleyball or tennis serves on an empty court and rating the quality or form of the serves.
4. **The rating of performance during the game.** For instance, observing a player during a match and rating the way he or she proceeds to penetrate in the scoring zone or observing a defensive player and rating the quality of his or her individual defense.

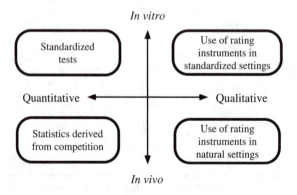

Fig. 7.2 Measurement strategies for assessing performance in team sports (Godbout, 1990).

Whether one consults Barrow, McGee, and Tritschler (1989), Baumgartner and Jackson (1991), McGee (1984), Safrit and Wood (1995), or any other measurement and evaluation textbooks in physical education, there is little doubt that testing efforts related to team sport performance have been focused on standardized tests. Typically, with reference to the model presented in Figure 7.2, such tests are focused on the *technical product* aspect of the student's performance. Without necessarily using published standardized tests, teachers do use similar home-made skill tests (Desrosiers, Genet-Volet, & Godbout, 1997; Veal, 1992). Although not widely used by teachers in physical education classes, observational instruments have been devised by coaches to register the frequency or number of various events occurring during a match (that is, the number of goals, penalties, percentage of successful shots, etc.). Such statistics focus on the result of performance. It is, however, impossible to determine whether these statistics reflect the technical aspect of performance, its tactical aspect, or both.

Over the last 15 years, there has been a growing interest in assessment procedures that address the process aspect of performance. Pinheiro's (1994) work illustrates the use of rating scales to assess the quality of motor skills; they may be used in standardized set-ups or in game contexts as well. McGee (1984) has provided examples of rating scales used to assess the tactical performance of children during games. More recently two authentic assessment instruments have been designed, the Game Performance Assessment Instrument (GPAI) (Griffin, Mitchell & Oslin, 1997; Oslin, Mitchell & Griffin, 1998) and the Team Sport Assessment Procedure (TSAP) (Gréhaigne, Godbout & Bouthier, 1997) to provide researchers, teachers and students with a means of observing and coding performance behaviors in game play context. Observations of secondary physical education teachers' assessment practices nevertheless show that some of them do consider tactical aspects of game play in teacher-made assessment instruments (Desrosiers et al., 1997). The work accomplished by Mitchell and his colleagues (Mitchell, Griffin, & Oslin, 1994; Mitchell, Oslin, & Griffin, 1995; Oslin, Mitchell, & Griffin, 1998), the University of South Carolina Group (Taylor et al., reported by Werner et al., 1996) and Blomquist and colleagues work with game-understanding test procedures (Blomquist et al., 2000) is an indication of a growing interest in this area.

Deciding what aspect of a given team sport ought to be assessed depends upon teachers' views as to what students should learn. As pointed out by Bailey & Almond (1983), Gréhaigne & Godbout (1995), Turner & Martinek (1995), and Werner et al. (1996), it is common in the teaching of team sports for teachers to start by working on a series of technical skills; then, when these skills appear to be reasonably mastered, more emphasis is put on playing the game and on related tactical skills. Such an approach to teaching team sports leads to motor skill–oriented assessment practices. It has been suggested by Mahlo (1974); Bouthier (1988); Bunker & Thorpe (1986); Turner & Martinek (1995); Gréhaigne, Billard, & Laroche (1999); and Butler, Griffin, Lombardo, & Nastasi (2003) that a greater emphasis should be put sooner in the learning process on understanding the game and on tactical efficiency. Such an approach would then make it all the more important to consider strategic and tactical efficiency in an assessment procedure.

USING NUMERICAL INDICES FOR FORMATIVE ASSESSMENT PURPOSES

If we return to the notion of formative and authentic assessment presented earlier in this chapter, we realize that these assessment characteristics are very important to a player's construction of team sports knowledge and skills. In education as a whole, there is also this growing interest for authentic formative assessment. This does not mean that we are now dealing with a new kind of formative assessment; the connotation of "authenticity" is intended to put the focus on the central nature and purpose of formative assessment (Allal, Cardinet, & Perrenoud, 1979). In 1992, Veal presented the main characteristics of authentic assessment in connection with physical education and sport:

a) "... it is regular and ongoing ...

b) ... [there is] a connection between daily instructional tasks and assessment ...

c) ... the teacher can 'see the skill' that is being evaluated, and there is a connection between skills and real-life situations as learning indicators ...

d) ... it accounts for student effort, improvement, and participation." (p. 90)

Formative Assessment and the Teaching-Learning Process

Formative assessment must be seen as a complement to teaching and coaching; it is and must be understood as an essential part of the teaching-learning process. Thus, if it is to be implemented, teachers must include the following steps in their teaching procedures:

1. **Communication of expectations.** Before getting into practice, players should know what it is they are trying to achieve. At what

point, expressed in concrete terms, can they consider that they have mastered the learning objective? This goes beyond stating the general objective and describing the learning task for them; unless they are given some type of success criteria, students will never know by themselves whether they have succeeded.

2. **Collection of information.** At some point during practice, players should know whether they have succeeded. Thus information regarding their performance must be collected either formally or informally. This can be done through observation by the teacher or peers, through self-assessment (with or without observational grids or through questionnaires), and so on. The idea is to get information that can be interpreted in light of the expectations or success criteria put forward by the teacher or even initially selected by the students themselves.

3. **Regulation of learning.** Only a few students succeed on their first trial. The real challenge and one wonders whether they need teaching at all. The true challenge of teaching is the management of success and failure. What is the use of telling students they have not succeeded if one does not do anything about it? A regulation scenario often used by teachers consists of providing students with feedback and then having them resume practice. The teacher may also encourage the students to put forward hypotheses for solving some tactical or motor problem, either through teacher-guided discussions (Rauschenbach, 1996), free discussions within teams, individual questioning, and so on. Other types of regulation scenarios may include an adaptation of learning tasks; going over an earlier, insufficiently mastered learning task; and so on.

The regulation of learning, which is a process that teachers rightly associate with teaching, requires that some information be obtained to start with, but getting information is not sufficient. Indeed, any collected information that does not help the teacher and students make decisions remains worthless as far as learning is concerned. This is why formative assessment cannot really be considered separately from teaching. It follows that a discussion about formative assessment cannot ignore the underlying teaching-learning process.

Authentic Formative Assessment in Team Sports

Authentic assessment of performance in team sports offers a special challenge to physical education teachers and coaches. For the information to be useful, it must be collected in real life situations. To accomplish this, French sport pedagogy researchers tried out various procedures to assess game play in context. The basic idea was to take into account players' specific behaviors during the game and to summarize the information through numerical data. In some cases, the final result takes the form of a score attributed to the team as a whole (for example, the number of times the team got possession of the ball); in other cases, the observation focuses on individual players' performance.

Assessment Indices

On the basis of objective data, students construct and learn tactical knowledge in relationship to motor skills. As discussed by Gréhaigne (1992), tactics relate to a) the effective positions taken in reaction to an opponent in a game situation and b) the adaptation or flexibility of the team to the conditions of play. Tactics are therefore momentary adaptations to new configurations of play (that is, the particular distribution of the players and moving of the ball on the field at given moments) and to the circulation of the ball; they are adaptations to opposition. Numerical data make it possible to examine the outcome of such tactics. When mastered, the problem solving of configurations of play indicates that tactical knowledge learning that is linked to motor skills is taking place.

To understand the progress students are making in terms of tactical skills and the offensive efficiency of each team, the teacher and students should register certain significant occurrences seen as indicators of an adaptation to problems brought about by the configurations of play (Mérand, 1984). The following sections discuss some occurrences that could be used on a collective or individual basis in various team sports.

Team Indices Teachers and coaches should focus the students' attention on three combined team indices throughout a match: number of possessions of the ball, number of shots, and number of goals. When recorded during intervals ranging from 7 to 14 minutes in short matches involving balanced teams, each one of those parameters will yield valuable formative information to each team, to each student, and to the teacher. For instance, a greater number of possessions of the ball as compared to that of a previous match, or a greater number of shots for the same number of possessions, will indicate collective progress on the part of the students. A simple data sheet can be used by each team to compare information relative to the indices (see Figure 7.3).

Again in relation to ball possession, in high-level soccer, a team gains possession of the ball between 100 and 110 times during a 90-minute match. In a school physical education setting, experiments by Gréhaigne et al. and Richard et al. have been conducted using 7-minute observation periods. In such a time frame, a team typically gains possession of the ball 12 times (± 1). In the context of European handball, between 16 and 18 ball possessions (± 1) have been observed with 12–16-year-old students.

It should be noted that the difference of ball possessions between the two teams can never be larger than one. This is a simple way to verify whether the student observers did their job correctly. For a basketball team after a 7-minute match, a total of 20 possessions of the ball resulting in four shots and one goal shows too large a number of lost balls. The students can be asked to solve this problem before worrying about improving their shooting skills.

Team _____	Match _____	
Indices	Occurences	Total
Possessions of the ball		
Shots		
Goals		

Fig. 7.3 Data sheet for each team (translation from Gréhaigne, 1992).

For more complex assessment situations, including time constraints or a smaller playing surface combined with a larger number of players in reference to the principle of "playing in movement," all one needs is to tally the number of positive responses after a player has gained possession of the ball. For example, three positive responses—either passes or shots on the goal—out of 12 played balls is sufficient to observe a transformation in a player's behavior.

Yet another way of obtaining game play data in a small-sided game context is to analyze game play sequences (Dugrand, 1989). These sequences are defined as the ball is exchanged among teammates from the time they gain possession of the ball to the time they lose it. In this assessment context, we note all ball exchanges within a team and we also note which players are putting the ball back into play and which are taking free or penalty kicks (or throws and shots in basketball, handball, etc.).

Game play sequences provide important information like the number of ball exchanges and ball possessions within a certain time frame. The former number is often linked to the confrontational level. We can also detect who is putting the ball back into play, who is giving the ball away to the opposition, and so on. It is also possible to construct a graph of all the exchanges to illustrate player relations and consequently to obtain a graphic representation of the competency rapport and the typical ball circulation that exists within a team when facing a given type of opposition.

Single-Player Indices   For individual players, one can note some numerical data that are indicative of their adaptation to the opposition encountered. The use of some or all of the following indices can be very useful.

Figure 7.4 presents an observational grid that can be used to register one or many performance indices. While planning formative assessment, the teacher can choose one or several indicators, depending upon the feedback that he or she wants to put at the children's disposal. For instance, a teacher may have the students analyze their number of played balls (PB), conquered balls (CB), and lost balls (LB). For an equal PB result of 18, two students should come to very different conclusions if one has 7 CB and 2 LB while the other has 1 CB and 9 LB. The first one brings the ball to the team while the latter loses it 50% of the time (9 lost balls for 18 played balls). If both students belong to the same team, it is a problem to be solved within the team. Thus, once the assessment results are communicated, each player and each team is faced with problems of some sort: how to reduce the number of lost balls and increase the number of shots, how to improve the movement of the ball, what strategy to adopt, and so on.

The Volume of Play   Another way to envision this assessment problem consists of analyzing the volume of play. This analysis is based on the postulate that in the context of a small-sided game, the more a player is in contact with the ball, the more he or she is involved in the game, and the more he or she participates in a team's performance.

The volume of play expresses a player or a team's involvement in the game and takes into account the force ratio. As expressed earlier, the volume of play is defined simply as the number of balls played by an individual or a team. It is not a coincidence if a player receives or conquers the ball frequently or infrequently. His or her availability, tactical ability, and fatigue level depend directly upon his or her game play intelligence and ability to communicate with teammates. As previously explained, when a teacher respects the principle of balance, the notion

Elements assessed	Criteria	Name : ——————— Team : ——————— Match : ———————		
Availability during play	Received balls (RB)	1st half	2nd half	Total
Defensive capacities	Conquered ball (CB)			
Offensive capacities	Passess to the partner (PP)			
	Shots (S)			
	Goals (G)			
Adaptation to the play	Lost balls (LB)			
Volume of play	Total number of played balls (PB) = (RB+CB)			

Fig. 7.4 Example of data sheet for a player (translation from Gréhaigne, 1992).

of game intensity can be assessed by computing the number of played balls by both teams (Gréhaigne, 1989; 1992).

An Illustration of Assessment Using the Volume of Play Through different work accomplished with physical education classes, Gréhaigne (1995) has looked at the number of played balls in 5 vs. 5 soccer (4 players + 1 goalkeeper). The analyzed matches were played on a 50 m × 30 m field with 6 m × 2 m goals. Pertaining to specific rules, there is no offside, throw-ins are done with the feet, and corners are done by hand. During the matches, student observers tallied the number of played balls for each of the players on the field.

The students involved in this project were 36 graduating high school (*Lycée*) students (17–18 years old). Eight teams of four players were formed, and a three-game tournament was played. The extra players served as observers or goalkeepers.

First of all, we will take a look at the number of balls played by each team (Table 7.1), and then we will analyze the repartition of balls within each team (Table 7.2).

TABLE 7.1 Total of Played Balls per Game Between Two Teams

A1- B1 = 152	E2 - G2 = 130
C1 - D1= 172	F2 - H2 = 161
E1 - F1 = 137	A3 - D3 = 171
G1 - H1 = 152	B3 - C3 = 134
A2 - C2 = 149	E3 - H3 = 138
B2 - D2 = 169	F3 - G3 = 143

In matches where teams played more than 160 balls in a 14-minute time frame (2 × 7-minute halves), it was noticed that play was fast, leading up to many shots on goal situations. A game at this intensity level reflected a high skill level (i.e., one-touch passing). Teams playing around 140 balls a match reflected slower play, often characterized by one or two players keeping possession of the ball. Weaker teams seemed to be playing around the 120-ball level. These teams' play was characterized by numerous balls lost to opponents.

The number of played balls is not necessarily divided by half between the confronted teams. Hence, we can compare the number of played balls to the final score. Team C1 (Table 7.1) played 82 balls and won 2–1, even though team D1 played 90 balls. Team F3 played 78 balls and easily won 5–2 against G3, who played 65 balls.

During a match, one can also study the way teammates exchange the ball. In the current sample of students, we observed the following

TABLE 7.2 Ball Possessions Among Individuals Players Across Teams

Team	P1	P2	P3	P4	Total	Team	P1	P2	P3	P4	Total
A1	21	26	21	14	**82**	E1	15	19	15	12	**61**
A2	22	20	16	17	**75**	E2	19	15	10	15	**59**
A3	28	19	21	15	**83**	E3	18	14	15	16	**63**
B1	22	11	14	23	**70**	F1	22	24	12	18	**76**
B2	20	12	24	12	**68**	F2	21	20	17	25	**83**
B3	20	11	20	13	**64**	F3	22	14	18	24	**78**
C1	22	20	25	15	**82**	G1	12	13	20	19	**64**
C2	17	13	27	17	**74**	G2	15	20	15	21	**71**
C3	16	23	17	14	**70**	G3	11	12	22	20	**65**
D1	17	24	25	24	**90**	H1	16	19	23	30	**88**
D2	25	24	18	34	**101**	H2	24	16	19	19	**78**
D3	21	20	20	27	**88**	H3	27	15	18	15	**75**

breakdown with teams that played more than 80 balls: team leader: 25–30 balls; players 2 and 3: 19–24 balls; worst player: approximately 15 balls. In the game in which there were 101 played balls (team D-1), the same ratio of played balls was observed (34; 25–24; 18). In the rest of the matches of different intensity levels, there was always at least one player who dominated play, while two others were involved moderately, and one seemed to be weaker than the rest.

Figure 7.5 illustrates that to obtain clear and reliable information, one must compute a team's number of played balls both collectively and individually. Two distribution percentages can effectively represent very different realities in terms of game play performance.

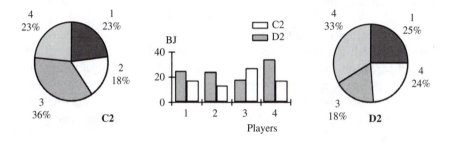

Fig. 7.5 Number of played balls for teams C2 and D2.

The use of these numerical data based on certain components of game play is not to be taken as a universal approach. This assessment strategy is based on a holistic approach to better analyze the end results in an opposition relationship. To be used effectively, statistical transformation of raw data is often required. From this transformation, tables and graphics can be constructed for a specific population. This type of data can also help to determine player difficulties or lack of comprehension pertaining to game concepts.

If a team played 80 balls during a match, one can formally analyze a match by decomposing how each teammate contributed to the outcome of the game. The following breakdowns exemplify possible scenarios:

a. 38 played balls for the best player, 17 and 17 for players 2 and 3, and 8 for the weakest player
b. 31 played balls for each of the two best players and 9 played balls for each of the two weakest players
c. 23 played balls for each of the two best players and 18 played balls for each of the two other players

One or two players seem to be dominant in this 4 vs. 4 game structure. Globally, the results that emerged from this experiment provide valuable information on the competency and rapport within a team. In a context where teams were divided in a random fashion, it was noticed that 90 played balls in a 14-minute time frame was a good result, and playing less than 60 balls was considered a weak performance. With a result of approximately 70 balls, another variable must be taken into consideration to better discriminate performance among teams: this variable is the number of shots on goal.

Game play behaviors can vary among players due to external factors (e.g., size of playing surface) and the team sport being played. This ensemble of behaviors and the variability associated with them are what makes team sports didactics in a physical education context so original.

To better appreciate the participation and accomplishments of all students within a group, a teacher can choose a game component that can discriminate performance to obtain an interesting photograph of what is happening within a team and the existing rapport between team members. Beyond the notions of played balls and shots on goal mentioned earlier, other game play variables can be used for game play assessment:

Exploited balls = Played balls − Lost balls

Neutral balls = Exploited balls − Attack balls (Passes, Shots on goal, so on)

These variables and indices represent interesting ways of assessing performance. However, they must be verified and refined to develop an objective strategy of assessing team sport performance.

LEARNING TO OBSERVE

Watching game play and observing specific students' behaviors are two different things. Students must learn to observe and focus their attention on specific occurrences during a match, sometimes sharing satisfaction or frustration with teammates but never forgetting to register whatever information they are supposed to collect.

Observational training should start with team indices. They are easier to register since there is no need to discriminate among players of the same team. Depending on whether teams are made up of several players playing on rotation or fewer players playing all the time, observers will be teammates not involved in game play or players of another team not involved in a particular match. At first, each of the three team performance variables may be observed by a different student, but eventually a single student can take charge of two and then of all three variables. Also, more than one student may be asked to assume the same task, with the possibility of comparing notes at the end of the period of play. Another way of familiarizing students with the observational task is called the "reporter game" (Dugrand, 1985) and has been used with students as young as eight years old (Gréhaigne & Guillon, 1990). In the reporter game, one student observes both teams involved in game play and describes the action as someone on the radio would. Another student plays the role of the reporter's secretary, registering the information provided by the reporter under the appropriate form, usually a team performance occurrence (e.g., possession of ball, shot, goal, etc.). Variations of the reporter game may call for a reporter and secretary to be assigned to each team, or two secretaries to be assigned to one reporter and having to compare notes, and so on. Also, at times teachers will involve students who attend the physical education class but cannot participate in the game because of injuries or health problems.

Once students are familiar with the observation of team indices, teachers may gradually introduce observations focused on single players. To do that, simply have as many observers as there are players involved in the game, which means dividing the class group into an even number of balanced teams and pairing students, with members of each pair assuming in turn the roles of player and observer. Observers lacking attention will soon realize that the players they are paired with often keep count of their own behaviors and are willing to question false results. When student observers are focused on single players' performance, the teacher should make sure that the teams involved in game play are not only balanced but also stable; if there is a rotation of players, results may be misleading since players are likely to spend different lengths of time on the court.

Finally, one important aspect for the teacher to remember while introducing students to peer observation is to make it clear from the start that their involvement in such observational tasks does not mean that they are doing the teacher's work. Far from that, it means that they are learning to take charge of their game and that, while observing, they are also reflecting on the requirements of the game.

In the first part of our exploration on assessment practices in a team-sport setting, we have presented some philosophical and theoretical notions as well as practical assessments related to the whole team's performance. In chapter 8, we will present two assessment instruments developed for the assessment of a player's individual performance.

8

AN INTRODUCTION TO THE TEAM-SPORT ASSESSMENT PROCEDURE AND THE GAME PERFORMANCE ASSESSMENT INSTRUMENT

In this chapter we continue to address the role of assessment in the teaching and learning of sport-related games. When implementing a tactical games model (i.e., game sense, conceptual-based games, TGfU) the teachers' goal for students is to focus on successful game play, which means that assessment should focus on game play (Veal, 1992). In other words, if the goal of games teaching is to improve game performance, then it is essential that assessment measures take into consideration two critical components. First, assessment measures should consist of all aspects of performance. A player's game performance includes concepts related to tactical awareness and understanding (i.e., what to do?) and skill execution (how to do it?). Second, assessment needs to measure game play in context (i.e., actual games or game forms).

Currently, when physical education teachers assess, they rely on skill testing to assess student performance. Using skill tests to assess game performance is problematic for several reasons: (a) skill tests do not predict playing performance; (b) skill tests do not take into account the social dimensions of sport-related games; (c) skill tests are out of context in situations not related to game play; and (d) skills test do not reflect a broader view of game performance (Griffin, Mitchell, & Oslin, 1997; Oslin, Mitchell, & Griffin, 1998). Two assessment instruments, the Team Sport Assessment Procedure (TSAP) and the Game Performance Assessment Instrument (GPAI), have been designed and validated to assess players' individuals performance in real-life learning scenarios—the game. The purpose of this chapter is twofold. First, we will introduce the major features of the TSAP and the GPAI. Second, we will provide the pedagogical and practical implications for using the instruments in sport-related teaching and learning.

THE TEAM SPORT ASSESSMENT PROCEDURE (TSAP)

The Team Sport Assessment Procedure (TSAP) was developed by Gréhaigne, Godbout, and Bouthier (1997). It provides information that quantifies an individual's overall offensive performance in selected invasion sports, such as basketball, soccer, and so on, and in net team sports, such as volleyball. It reflects both technical and tactical aspects of game play (Gréhaigne et al., 1997). The information provided by the individual variables, performance indices, and performance score are all macroindicators of both technical and tactical performance (Table 8.1). These indicators are all related to successful game play (Gréhaigne et al., 1997).

TABLE 8.1 The Relationships Between Observation Items and Types of Information Collected

Observation Items	Information Collected
Received balls (RB)	Involvement of the player in the team's play (availability, accessibility to receive a pass)
Conquered balls (CB)	Information related to the player's defensive capacities
Offensive balls (OB)	Player's capacity to make significant passes to his or her partners (offensive capacities)
Successful shots (SS)	Information related to the player's offensive capacities
Volume of play (PB = RB + CB)	General involvement of the player in the game
Lost balls (LB)	A small number reflects a good adaptation to the game

Source: Gréhaigne, Godbout, & Bouthier, 1997.

The TSAP is based on two basic notions: (a) "How a player gains possession of the ball" (2 variables) and (b) "How a player disposes of the ball" (4 variables). According to these notions a player's specific behaviors are observed and coded during game play on an observation grid such as the one presented in Figure 8.1. Two performance indices and a performance score are then computed from the collected data (Table 8.2).

Team Sport Assessment Procedure for Invasion Games

Name _____

Class _____

Observer _____

Date _____

Directions: Observe student's game play and place a tally mark in the appropriate box.

Gaining possession of the ball

Played Balls (PB)

Conquered Ball (CB)   Received Ball (RB)

Disposing of the ball

Lost Ball (LB)   Neutral Ball (NB)   Pass (P)   Successful Shot (SS)

Fig. 8.1 Observation grid for the TSAP – Invasion games.

A primary feature of the TSAP is that the data collection process is accomplished by students. A recent study demonstrated that students as young as 10 years old (grade 5) were capable of using the TSAP with a good deal of precision and reliability (Richard, Godbout, & Gréhaigne, 2000). The use of this assessment procedure combined with a TGfU model can offer an efficient means to develop students' learning of game concepts (Gréhaigne & Godbout, 1998).

TABLE 8.2 Observational Variables, Performance Indices, and Performance Score Computation Formula for the Team Sport Assessment Procedure—Invasion Games

Observational Variables: Operational Definition
A. Gaining possession of the ball
1. Conquered Ball (CB)
A player is considered to have conquered the ball if he or she intercepted it, stole it from an opponent, or recaptured it after an unsuccessful shot on goal or after a near loss to the other team.
2. Received Ball (RB)
The player receives the ball from a partner and does not immediately lose control of it.

B. Disposing of the ball
1. Lost Ball (LB)
The player is considered to have lost the ball when he or she loses control of it without having scored a goal.
2. Neutral Ball (NB)
A routine pass to a partner who does not truly put pressure on the other team.
3. Pass (P)
Pass to a partner that contributes to the displacement of the ball towards the opposing team's goal.
4. Successful Shot on Goal (SS)
A shot is considered successful when it scores or possession of the ball is retained by one's team.

The computation of performance indices and performance score:
Volume of play index = CB + RB

$$\text{Efficiency Index (EI)} = \frac{VP}{10 + LB}$$

Performance score = (volume of play/2) + (efficiency index × 10)
Source: Gréhaigne, Godbout, & Bouthier, 1997.

Using the TSAP in Sport-Related Teaching and Learning

A major feature of the TSAP is its adaptability to different teaching scenarios. What has been explained up to this point is a procedure that possesses six different observational variables that have been shown to reflect a student's global offensive performance in invasion games. When teaching more complex tactical problems at a higher grade level—for example, high school—the integral version of the TSAP is recommended. A teacher might, however, not want to use the integral version of the TSAP if the learning outcomes he or she is pursuing do not require such a complex procedure (i.e., upper elementary and middle school programs) or if, not having experimented with peer assessment very much, a teacher might feel that the students would need to be initiated with a simpler instrument. These are legitimate concerns, as observational complexity and cognitive maturity are definitely factors that need to be considered when integrating students in the peer assessment process. With regard to the use of the TSAP, Richard, Godbout, and Picard (2000) have developed, experimented with, and validated simpler versions of the TSAP to offer teachers alternatives for their assessment practices in relation to games education. The following pages offer a rationale for these modified versions in relation to their use in games education at lower grade levels (i.e., grades 5 to 8). For the purpose of this book, the TSAP will be presented pertaining to its use in relation to invasion games.

Invasion Games: 1st Modified Version

Volume of Play (VP) = # of possessions Conquered Ball (CB) + Received Ball (RB)

$$\text{Efficiency Index (EI)} = \frac{VP}{10 + LB}$$

Performance Score = (VP/2) + (EI × 10)

In this first modified version, the number of observational variables is reduced by half. With regard to the volume of play, no distinction is made between CB or RB. Only the total number of possessions is taken into consideration along with the number of lost balls. The reasoning behind this decision is twofold. First, we have noticed through different experiments with the TSAP that younger observers have a tendency to indicate most ball possessions as received, even if they are conquered or intercepted. Second, the nuance between these two variables are not so important in relation to game concepts taught at the lower grade levels.

The modified version of the TSAP is simpler than the original version. The modifications permit teachers to progressively integrate students in the observation of game play behavior without having an overly complex instrument to use. Also, the variables that were retained for this first modified version allow teachers and students to still make nuances about game play concepts such as getting away from a defender (represented by the volume of play) or ball circulation, which are mostly taught at the upper elementary level (grades 5 and 6) in most physical education programs. Through the efficiency index, we want students to realize that from their volume of play—the number of possessions—the goal is to lose as few balls as possible, which reflects a good contribution to team success whether it be passing the ball or shooting on goal.

Invasion Games: 2nd Modified Version

Volume of Play (VP) = # of possessions (CB + RB)

$$\text{Efficiency Index (EI)} = \frac{\text{Pass} + \text{Successful Shot}}{10 + \text{LB}}$$

Performance score = (VP/2) + (EI × 10)

Like the first modified version, this second version lets the teacher put a certain pedagogical emphasis in relation to the lesson objectives. In this case, the efficiency index's numerator is composed of the number of passes and successful shots on goal. In this version the pedagogical emphasis is on both gaining possession of and disposing of the ball in a successful manner (e.g., pass to teammate or shot on goal). The efficiency index helps the teacher guide the student to know whether he or she should pass the ball or shoot on goal. This second modified version of the TSAP increases the number of observational variables to four. Consequently, this second version could be considered an intermediate version of the original TSAP.

THE GAME PERFORMANCE ASSESSMENT INSTRUMENT (GPAI)

The Game Performance Assessment Instrument was developed to be a comprehensive assessment tool for teachers to use and adapt in assessing a variety of games. Teachers can use the GPAI for different types of games across the classification system (e.g., invasion, net/wall) or within a particular classification (e.g., basketball, soccer). The different observational variables included in the GPAI permit the coding of behaviors that demonstrate the ability to solve tactical problems in games by making decisions, moving appropriately (off-the-ball movement), and executing skills (Griffin et al., 1997).

Seven observable game components have been identified and formulated in the initial development of the GPAI (Oslin, Mitchell, & Griffin, 1998). These are shown in Table 8.3. Game components can be coded on observation grids (see Figure 8.2). All components are related to game performance, but not all of the seven components are applicable to a particular game (Oslin et al., 1998). For example, all components except "guard" are important for field/run/score/games, such as softball. On the other hand, all components except "base" are important for successful soccer performance (Oslin et al., 1998).

TABLE 8.3 Components of Game Performance

Base	Appropriate return of performer to a recovery (base) position between skill attempts
Decision-Making	Makes appropriate decisions about what to do with the ball (or projectile) during a game
Skill Execution	Efficient execution of selected skills
Support	Provides appropriate support for a teammate with the ball (or projectile) by being in position to receive a pass
Guard/Mark	Appropriate guarding/marking of an opponent who may or may not have the ball (or projectile)
Cover	Provides appropriate defensive cover, help, or backup for a player making a challenge for the ball (or projectile)
Adjust	Movement of performer, either offensively or defensively, as necessitated by the flow of the game

Reprinted, by permission, from Griffin, Mitchell, & Oslin, 1997, p. 220.

The GPAI was designed to be a flexible observation instrument that can be used to assess students' performance either in a live setting or from videotapes. Teachers can choose to observe any or all components related to a particular game, depending on the context of the instructional environment (Oslin et al., 1998). Simplification of the GPAI in the number and particular components to be observed is especially useful when students are involved in peer assessment.

The GPAI has been shown to be a valid assessment instrument. Content, construct, and ecological validity have all been established during its preliminary development (Oslin et al., 1998). Furthermore, instrument and observer reliability have also been established (Oslin et al., 1998).

Using the GPAI in Sport-Related Teaching and Learning

The appeal of the GPAI is that teachers can adapt the instrument for use based on the aspects of the game taught and the type of game being played. There are two basic scoring methods for using the GPAI: (a) the 1–5 scoring system (see Figure 8.2) and (b) the tally scoring system (see Figure 8.3).

Game Performance Assessment Instrument

Invasion Games

Class_____   Evaluator_____ Team_____ Game

_____

Observation Dates (a) _____ (b) _____ (c) _____ (d) _____

Scoring Key: 5 = Very effective performance

4 = Effective performance

3 = Moderately effective performance

2 = Weak performance

1 = Very weak performance

Components/Criteria

1. Decision made—

   a. Student attempts to pass to an open teammate

   b. Student attempts to shoot when appropriate

2. Skill Execution—

   a. Reception—control pass

   b. Pass—ball reaches intended target

   c. Dribble—control and adjust and move position

3. Support—

   a. Students attempt to move into position to receive a pass from teammates (i.e., forward toward the goal)

Name	Decision Making	Skill Execution	Support

Fig. 8.2 GPAI for invasion games. (Reprinted, by permission, from Griffin, Mitchell, and Oslin, 1997, p. 225.)

Mitchell and Oslin (1999) pointed out that the 1–5 scoring system is efficient for two reasons: First, observers who are primarily teachers do not have to record each time a player is involved in the game. In invasion games and some net/wall games, it is impossible to keep track of players' complete involvement because of the tempo, flow, and unpredictability of those games. This is especially so with players who have a wide range of skill levels. Second, the 1–5 scoring system makes consistency of scoring possible. Teachers need to create criteria for the 5 indicators (i.e., very effective performance to very weak performance), and the indicators should be based on lesson, unit, and curriculum objectives, as well as student abilities.

The tally system can be used with fielding (e.g., softball) and some net/wall games because they are played at a slower pace, which gives the observer an opportunity to tally every event. The tally scoring system provides an explicit game performance measure.

The GPAI can also provide students with a view of the bigger picture of their game play by calculating "game involvement" and "game performance." Game involvement can be measured by adding together all responses that indicate involvement in the game, including inappropriate decisions made and inefficient skill execution (see Griffin et al., 1997). One should not, however, include inappropriate guard/mark, support, adjust, and cover because an inappropriate response in these components indicates that players were not involved in the game. Game performance is a more precise measure and is calculated by adding scores from all components assessed and dividing by the number of components assessed.

Both teachers and students who have used a version of the GPAI in live settings to assess game performance have been considered reliable. In other words they have been consistent with a fellow observer in their assessment of performance approximately 80% of the time (Oslin et al., 1998; Griffin, Dodds, & James, 1999). The key to establishing reliability is in the quality of the criteria slated for observation. The criteria should be specific and observable (Mitchell & Oslin, 1999).

PEDAGOGICAL IMPLICATIONS

Because assessment should be an integral part of the teaching-learning process, there are certain considerations and implications that should be addressed to help teachers systematically implement the proposed instruments into sport-related games instruction. Both instruments provide information that can help guide teachers toward effective sport-related games instruction. Pedagogical implications focus on two primary considerations: (a) the process for yearly unit and lesson planning and (b) the construction of knowledge and skills.

First, teachers need to consider the notion of planning and in particular the notions of alignment between learning outcomes, teaching strategies, and assessment (Cohen, 1987). Teachers need to understand that planning what to teach is the same as planning what to assess and that there should be a strong link between these two facets of the teaching-learning process. The TSAP and GPAI can help teachers organize a *planning cycle* within and across lessons to help make the teaching-learning process more congruent. This cycle has three phases:

- First, students are confronted with a situation or problem to solve
- Second, students are in action (i.e., practice or game); and
- Third and last, students reflect on their action (i.e., critical thinking and problem solving).

For example, in a soccer lesson, students are asked to solve the tactical problem of creating space during an attack. Students are placed in an initial game with the goal of solving the tactical problem. After the initial game, students are asked to reflect through questions about their success in reaching the goal. Students are then placed in a situated practice that helps them practice creating space during an attack. Finally, students play another game similar to the initial game to modify and improve their game performance. Using a version of the TSAP or the GPAI can help teachers and students reflect about students' abilities related to an isolated objective such as the one described above or toward a more global performance that essentially reflects the sequence of a series of game objectives.

The second pedagogical implication builds upon the first and involves the construction of knowledge and skills. Constructivism is a theory about learning that describes learning as a building process by active learners interacting with their physical and social environment (Fosnot, 1996). A principle derived from constructivism that can and should guide games instruction is *reflective thinking*. By using either instrument, students are given time to reflect on such aspects of game play as choice of motor skill, individual and team decisions, and team strengths, which help them make meaning and connections across their experiences (Gréhaigne & Godbout, 1995). As mentioned earlier, to get the most out of the teaching-learning process, these instruments must be used appropriately. To this end, participating teachers who have used either instrument cannot stress enough the importance of using appropriate variables reflecting pursued objectives instead of always using the integral form of the instrument (Griffin et al., 1997; Richard, Godbout, Tousignant, & Gréhaigne, 1999).

CONCLUSION

Assessment can and should be a part of everyday teaching. The information that different assessment strategies can give students and teachers is critical to the regulation of the teaching-learning process. As authentic assessment instruments, the TSAP and the GPAI offer teachers the opportunity to promote the construction of game knowledge and skills. Authentic assessment procedures can help teachers teach and students learn about how to make connections within and among games (both intra- and intertransfer). Students clearly articulate that playing a game is a meaningful activity to pursue in physical education. Why? Playing a game provides structure and outcomes that gives meaning to performance. Students want to play games well.

The TSAP and the GPAI provide students with the opportunity to reflect and learn, through formative assessment, about themselves as game players. Both instruments provide students with both means and ends that are interrelated. Through game performance assessment students will learn that not only does each small element have a value but that each element is also a part of a coherent whole. Authentic assessment instruments such as the TSAP and GPAI can help teachers plan developmentally sound game experiences that can lead to more sport-literate learners and can help students better appreciate the playing of games.

II

The Teaching-Learning Process
in Team Sports

9

UNDERLYING THEORIES
IN THE TEACHING-LEARNING PROCESS
OF GAMES AND SPORTS

In the present chapter, the evolution of the teaching-learning process from a behaviorist approach to a constructivist approach will be presented. Technical versus tactical approaches to teaching games will also be discussed to show the evolution of frames of reference in the teaching of team sport-related games.

The observation of current practices in the teaching of games shows a series of highly structured lessons. The first part is dedicated to a warm-up with or without a ball. The second part is based on the teaching of techniques, and at the end of a sequence of learning activities, games are played to integrate learned skills. Bailey and Almond (1983) state that such an approach, which stresses the need for developing motor skills before getting involved in the game, puts more emphasis on physical capacities than on the understanding of the game. Before them, Hughes (1980) indicated that understanding requires knowledge and perceptions. Despite the importance of decision-making and knowledge in effective game participation, there appears to be, at least from a constructivist perspective, little research in the area of student decision-making during game play either in physical education lessons or in organized sport. Researchers need to find ways of describing cognitive processes as they occur during a match. As a result, they would better understand those mechanisms that influence the interplay of knowledge acquisition and skillful performances.

The cognitivist perspective is intended for teachers who want to place their students in the center of the teaching-learning process and is based on a constructivist learning perspective (Piaget, 1967). Constructivism recognizes that awareness, although at first focused on the results of activity, must reach the inner mechanisms of such activities if true learning is to occur. This transformation of the learner in team sports takes place when the player meets and solves problems related to the configuration of the game in school and to motor performances. The player "constructs" their knowledge from a strong subject–environment interaction. This game-centered perspective leads to a "learner" rather than a content-based teaching style.

A CONCEPTION OF APPRENTICESHIP

Pedagogically speaking one uses the opposition relationship as a basis for all progress in the teaching of team sports in school physical education and sport settings.

Teaching-Learning Settings

One solicits students' affective and cognitive processes to foster an understanding of the principle of play and the mechanisms of game play. Tactical decisions and decision-making are favored for the construction of the player's capacities to anticipate the evolution of play configurations. The playful aspect also constitutes an important dimension. Indeed, one of the main functions of games in childhood is to develop a child's sense of identity and self-accomplishment. Nevertheless, a primary objective for a teacher is to create an instructional setting that will include a rapport of strength within a problem-solving environment.

To better understand the use of games at school, Figure 9.1 presents principles to analyze different approaches to games teaching.

This model is organized on two intersecting axes: on the horizontal axis, from specific to general; on the vertical axis, from simple to complex. Each of the four quadrants has particular characteristics.

1. **Simple/Specific.** This 1st quadrant represents the classical approach, with lessons centered on the learning of motor skills. The teachers work with a technique focus in their game teaching and offer a skill progression based on a preexisting list of motor competencies.
2. **Simple/General.** The 2nd quadrant represents the use of traditional games or innovated games as a subset of team sports. Traditional games are used as application tasks for reinforcing the

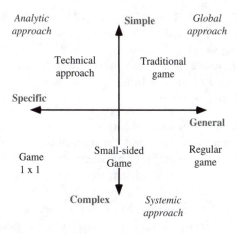

Fig. 9.1 A game analysis model (translation from Gréhaigne, 1994a).

subskills necessary to play a particular game: running with the ball, long and short passing, shooting, and so on.

3. **Specific/Complex.** The 3rd quadrant refers to the use of a small-sided game or modified game. Students are introduced to a mini game form close to the adult version of the game to preserve the meaning of game play.

4. **General/Complex.** The 4th quadrant refers to the utilization of the social-reference practice—the complete adult version of the game.

This diagram of principles for team sport analysis is not intended to put some normative value on teachers' practices. Rather, it makes it possible to establish a macroscopic assessment of a teacher's dominant conception. Depending upon class groups (age, motivation, number, coeducation, etc.), a teacher could use one approach or another.

As for other curriculum content in physical education, teaching practices for sport-related games may differ considerably depending upon one's views regarding the student's learning process. The ideas developed in this chapter are based on a cognitivist and constructivist perspective of learning. Also, at school, the learning of tactics and strategies in team sports is given priority over the learning of technical skills. This position is similar to the one put forward recently by many advocates of the Teaching Games for Understanding model (TGfU). Discussing what it means to teach for understanding, Good (1996) makes it clear that "teaching for student understanding" is associated with a constructivist view of the teaching/learning process. He writes:

"In the 1980s and 1990s, researchers have become interested in constructivist perspectives and in more detailed accounts of how students integrate and understand content" (p. 629). But, as mentioned by Cobb (1986), there are different constructivist perspectives. In general, one may identify two main teaching strategies while applying a teaching-for-understanding approach:

1. To propose to students the discovery of *the* tactical skill that applies in a specific situation. Such an option would be associated with an indirect teaching approach, combining both a subject matter–centered and a student-centered perspective. It could be referred to as an *empiricist constructivist* approach to teaching (Cobb, 1986), which considers that knowledge is an external reality and exists independently of the student's cognitive activity.

2. To propose to students the construction of suitable personal tactical skills that apply in a specific situation in which there may be more than one from the student's point of view. Such an option, also referred to as *indirect teaching*, would be associated with a radical constructivist approach (Cobb, 1986), which contends that the knowledge constructed by the student is the result of the interaction between his or her cognitive activity and reality (Gréhaigne & Godbout, 1995; Piaget, 1971, 1974a, 1974b).

The construction of sport skills by the students is therefore a process that requires:

1. That the students be presented with problems to solve or that they be put into situations favoring the recognition of such problems

2. That following the students' trials, they be presented with the result of their actions

3. That given these results, the students be invited to appreciate them and decide whether they are satisfactory

4. That following unsatisfactory results, the students be given the opportunity to experiment further and search for a better solution

Before going any further, it seems appropriate to summarize the postulates that underlie the view presented here concerning the construction of tactical knowledge.

1. **The learning process implies interaction.** The development and maturation of any individual take place through an adaptation to an environment perceived as a system of constraints and resources. At the outset, there is no formal object of learning defined as a

given set of solutions to be reproduced as is. The analysis of this adaptation necessarily includes the reciprocal action of a subject over the environment and of the environment over the subject.

2. **The learning process implies cognition.** Action regulation, particularly in the learning phase, occurs through mental activity whereby consciousness is but one aspect (Richard, 1990). Resort to conscious or nonconscious cognitive processes is essential for constructing knowledge. It is not sufficient for the teacher to state rules; the students must make them theirs. In a learning activity, the learners develop a self-regulation activity that consists of comparing the goal aimed for with the obtained result and analyzing the reasons for failure or success. This comparison allows an evolution of the ability to plan the selection of action and of the motor resources solicited.

3. **The learning process implies construction.** Faced with whatever situation, learners' knowledge, their ability to do certain things, and their development rest upon former learning. This development occurs through a new coordination of blocks of knowledge under the influence of internal or external constraints, forcing an adjustment of the learner's activity. In this sense, there is no novice at level 0.

4. **The learning process implies plasticity.** Plasticity represents a system's capacity for durably modifying its own structure and acquiring new skills. In the face of unusual situations, it is an organism's response capacity for developing new resources that will allow a better adaptation of the subject to the situation.

Given this frame of reference, we submit that *observation*, *critical thinking*, and *transformation* are three key elements to be considered in a constructivist perspective of the learning process in team sports.

AN OBSERVATIONAL APPROACH OF THE GAME PLAY

In the visual domain, to perceive implies decoding, putting different perceptions in order, and organizing information. In this sense, observation represents a critical moment in the teaching-learning process. Indeed, it allows information retrieval for both the student and the teacher. It provides for a simplified model of reality, but at the same time, it reveals which clues the observer gives priority to over reality.

One of the basic assumptions of qualitative research states that people develop various constructions of reality (Andreewsky, 1991; Bouthier, 1989; Gréhaigne, 1997; Gréhaigne & Godbout, 1995). We believe that the same phenomenon prevails in a classroom when many students and a teacher observe any given moment of the teaching-learning process. In such situations, observation may be looked at as a dynamic process involving the teacher, the student(s), and the action (the unfolding of the learning setup). This is shown in Figure 9.2. In the teaching and learning of team sports, we will more specifically refer to action as *game play*.

From a pedagogical point of view, one may view the observational situation from different perspectives. For instance, Figure 9.2 illustrates what might be considered a teacher-centered observational approach.

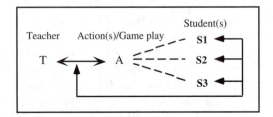

Fig. 9.2 A teacher-centered observational approach.

In this kind of approach, the teacher observes the action involving various students and then, on the basis of his or her frame of reference, provides feedbacks to the students, describing, explaining, justifying, recommending, and prescribing. What the students have perceived is thus confirmed if it fits the teacher's discourse or is put aside if it differs. In a learner-based teaching style such as that of constructivism, we perceive that the observational situation should be illustrated as shown in Figure 9.3.

While involved in the action or after its completion, each student is asked to collect or recollect information based on personal observations. Eventually, additional information may be provided by the teacher or by other student observers. We stress the word *additional* because the prime observer should be the player involved in the action. This is all the more critical because each observer reads action according to a personal frame of reference. Thus it is doubtful that an outside observer could duplicate the performer's perception of action. One could argue that in many instances an outside observer stands a better chance to perceive a picture closer to reality. Whether this is true or not

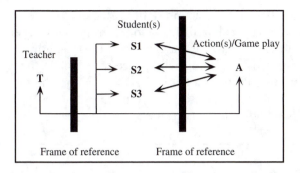

Fig. 9.3 A learner-based observational approach.

is, to a certain point, irrelevant. As stated earlier, the learning process, from a constructivist perspective, implies interaction between the subject and the environment. Augmented feedback is presented as additional information that can be processed differently by the learner depending upon his or her perception of the completed action and upon the learning stage exploited by the teacher (exploration, construction, consolidation).

If one argues that the learner cannot be replaced but can only be supported and complemented in his/her observational process, this does not imply that the learner possesses an innate and final observational frame of reference. As skill learning goes, so does observation learning. Therefore, the learner is also confronted with the construction of a frame of reference with the help of the teacher and other students. However, different decisions may be taken by the learner depending upon what the observations are focused on. Consequently, although constructed by each learner, the frame of reference must reflect the objectives pursued in the classroom. In team sports, we submit that the observation of game play encompasses four basic interacting elements. At an abstract level, one might say that they concern the static, dynamic, individual, and collective aspects of the game. At a more operational level, we shall identify them as location, movement, player, and configuration of play.

Figure 9.4 illustrates how one could perceive the observational situation and the ensuing communications in such an arrangement. At the center of the figure, one can see the action setting, involving a given number of students (e.g., 3 vs. 3; 5 vs. 5) in interaction with the subject matter; this interaction should eventually include reflection *in* action. Representing the observation setting, we have the teacher and student observer(s) observing the action setting, each one on the basis of a personal (maybe partly shared) frame of reference. A thicker line at the bottom indicates that the teacher also observes how each student observer proceeds, providing help if necessary. Finally, the various lines connecting members of a team (S1, S2, S3) and the team with the teacher and the student observer(s) illustrates the debate-of-ideas setting, involving reflection *on* action.

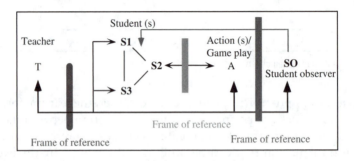

Fig. 9.4 Observational setting for the teaching and learning of team sports.

Finally, we wish to stress the fact that problem-solving learning and the construction of personal knowledge require reflection on the part of the students. Without it, the learner can only stumble blindly from one trial to another, hoping for random success, or wait for an outside observer to tell him or her what to do next. There is no understanding in either case. While verbalization may facilitate reflection, through informal (observation) and formal (TSAP; GPAI) observation will provide the basic data on which to reflect (Brechbuhl, Bronckart, & Joannisse, 1988). After many years of research and discussion in teacher education there is a common belief that important objectives of our teacher education programs is to develop *reflective practitioners* is an essential component of teacher preparation. If we follow the logic one step further, we should eventually come to the conclusion that a major objective of our school programs should be the development of *reflective learners*. Then, teaching for understanding will have taken on its full meaning, at least from a radical constructivist point of view (Cobb, 1986).

A SET OF SITUATIONS IN A LEARNING PROCESS

From a constructivist perspective, we perceive that the learning process in team sports may involve the successive use of three types of settings, shown in Figure 9.5.

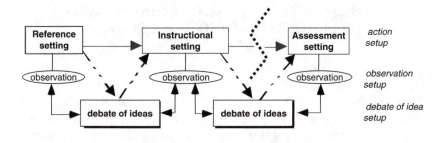

Fig. 9.5 Teaching and learning settings and setups (translation from Deriaz, Poussin, & Gréhaigne, 1998).

The settings are as follows:

- **Reference settings.** In which students are confronted with the actual practice of the sport or of some modification of that sport at the beginning of the learning sequence
- **Instructional settings.** Where students are asked to construct different tactical skills in response to problems brought about by play action
- **Assessment settings.** For providing students and teacher with information regarding progress achieved (i.e., summative and formative).

In connection with these settings and to facilitate learning, students may be involved in three different kinds of setups, as was illustrated in Figure 9.5:

- **Action setups.** In which students are engaged in the actual practice of a team sport
- **Observation setups.** In which students not engaged in the action setup are asked to observe peers and to collect information (usually with reference to performance criteria)
- **Debate-of-idea setups.** In which students are invited to exchange facts and ideas, based on observations collected or on personal activity experienced (Deriaz et al., 1998).

In all three types of setups, the teacher should keep in mind the importance of eliciting critical thinking. Teachers and students need to understand that the action steps during physical education lessons are designed for learning and constitute an authentic learning activity.

THE DEBATE OF IDEAS—A TEACHING STRATEGY FOR UNDERSTANDING AND LEARNING IN TEAM SPORTS

In recent years, several authors have discussed the development or use of critical thinking in physical education (McBride, 1991; Schwager & Labate, 1993; Tishman & Perkins, 1995). For some authors, the use of critical thinking is considered as an end in itself (McBride, 1991; Tishman & Perkins, 1995). Critical thinking is viewed as a learning objective, and the purpose is to improve thinking abilities, as illustrated by statements such as:

1. "Critical thinking is not and should not be limited solely to motor skill acquisition. The physical education environment is rich in opportunities for critical thinking" (McBride, 1991, p. 121).
2. "The nature of physical education offers a concrete context for exploring the payoffs of critical thinking that other subjects often lack: one can apply a useful exercise strategy, a plan for the game, or a new maneuver for a play" (Tishman & Perkins, 1995, p. 29).

Others, like Schwager and Labate (1993), views critical thinking as a useful tool that can help physical education teachers achieve their goals.

There are many ways of defining critical thinking. Given the purpose of this presentation, we will go along with McBride (1991) who "cautiously posit that critical thinking in physical education be defined as reflective thinking that is used to make reasonable and defensible decisions about movement tasks or challenges" (p. 115). Considering Tishman and Perkins' (1995) operational definition of critical thinking, we might add that in this presentation it involves particularly causal and evaluative reasoning as well as planning and strategic thinking. These authors have stated that "effective physical performance involves reasoning, reflecting, strategizing, and planning, all parts of the critical thinking process" (p. 24). Critical thinking is central to a constructivist view of learning (Good, 1996), but how is it to be used in the learning and teaching of team sports?

Let us consider four broad strategies that may be used by teachers at various stages of learning:

1. **Letting students explore.** At an early stage, students are put in play contexts, chosen so that they should present the students with problems or difficulties. After some exposure to play, students may fail to perceive any problem, and the teacher may then

let them pursue further exploration with or without modification of the play context.

2. **Asking open-ended questions.** Once students have perceived and possibly identified a problem, the teacher may bring them to debate among themselves or with him or her by asking open-ended questions that do not direct them toward specific and predetermined answers.

3. **Taking part in the students' debate and asking specific questions.** After asking open-ended questions, the teacher must be vigilant in moderating the students' debate by discussing the ideas and issues presented by students and asking them more specific questions.

4. **Having students reutilize suitable solutions.** Once students have come up with solutions that satisfy selected performance criteria, the teacher may then have them practice these solutions to stabilize their use.

While this last strategy is more routine oriented, the first three strategies all solicit critical thinking one way or the other. Strategies 2 and 3 are significant in view of constructivism and teaching for understanding and even more so when applied to tactical learning in team sports. General discussions, debates within groups of students, and debriefings (Dassé, 1986; Plummer & Rougeau, 1997; Tsangaridou & Sidentop, 1995) can complement one another in enhancing critical thinking and learning. In the field of general education, Good and Brophy (1994) have profiled some characteristics of a social construction view of teaching and learning. Among several of these characteristics one finds:

Knowledge [is seen] as developing interpretations constructed through discussion ...

Teacher acts as discussion leader who poses questions, seeks clarifications, promotes dialogue, helps groups recognize areas of consensus and of continuing disagreement.

Students strive to make sense of new input by relating it to their prior knowledge and by collaborating in dialogue with others to construct shared understandings ...

Students collaborate by acting as a learning community that constructs shared understanding through sustained dialogue (Good, 1996, p. 639).

We might say that what is sought is both reflection in action and reflection on action.

Evidently, discussions and debates among students or between students and the teacher involve overt and shared verbalization. Caverni (1988) has discussed verbalization as an observable source of information about cognitive processes. Considering the moment of its occurrence with regard to task performance, he distinguishes three types of verbalization: prior verbalization, which is considering what will be or ought to be done; concurrent verbalization, which is considering what is being done; and consecutive verbalization, which is considering what has been done. But why involve verbalization? It appears that verbalization settings should provide information about obstacles encountered by students in their effort to solve the problem at hand; such information can be used by the teacher or can be shared among students while debating about proper ways to perform a task at hand. As stated by Schunk (1986), studies demonstrate that verbalization can improve children's learning of information, modeled actions, and strategies, as well as their efficiency at performing tasks. Collectively, these findings support the notion that verbalization is a key process that can help develop self-regulated learning among children (Schunk, 1986, p. 362).

Gréhaigne and Godbout (1998) have coined this type of debate in physical education the debate-of-ideas. They defined it as situations in which, following game play action, students exchange ideas, based on observation or on personal experience. The debate may concern aspects such as the results obtained during the game action situation, the process involved, the tactics applied, and so on. What are the components of thought activity that one can identify in analyzing students' debate-of-ideas? According to Ericsson (1996) we can identify the following components in a general way:

- Intents or intentions referred to a purpose or a future state of the game
- Cognitions underlying a special attention to particular aspects of the setting
- Planning representing moves or states of game play mentally explored
- Evaluations expressing similarities among different possibilities

For their part, Hoc and Leplat (1983) differentiate the following:

- Verbalization about execution, which is the expression about a purpose or a state; expression about an assumption or a questioning about a purpose or a state

- Verbalization about the procedures (the subject expressing his or her way of doing)
- Verbalizations about assessment and justification
- External verbalizations about the general state of the subject; redefinition of the tasks

Figure 9.6 presents the relationship among settings, observation, and debate-of-ideas setups. The target is to do an alternation during a program of instruction to progress from the reference setting to the instructional setting and finally to the assessment setting.

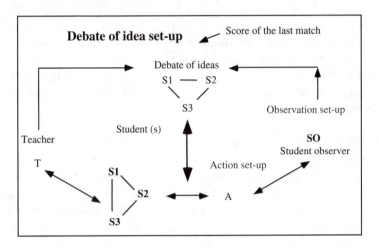

Fig. 9.6 The relationship between the debate-of-ideas and the instructional setting.

Depending upon the orientation of the debate, these debate-of-idea set-ups can be oriented toward different objectives, presenting some similarities with situations pertaining to the "setting theory" proposed by Brousseau (1986). Indeed, the debate-of-ideas may offer features similar to:

- Formulation settings, where knowledge plays a rational function
- Validation settings, where knowledge plays a solving function
- Generalization processes, where knowledge plays a reference function

Depending upon the level of conformity of students' responses regarding expected results, there is a change of plans to reduce the gap between the expected and the actual responses. One can consider, too, a stabilization of the responses, or an increase of the difficulty of the instructional setting to bring students to a higher level of performance.

Using verbalization in the teaching of team sports may help meet various needs, such as:

- Putting together a common frame of reference
- Acknowledging, conceptually, action rules (Gréhaigne, 1996) and management rules for the organization of the game
- Developing critical thinking skills that can be reinvested during the action in game settings

CRITICAL FEATURES OF THE DEBATE-OF-IDEAS

The use of the debate-of-ideas is an emerging pedagogical practice that needs to be examined attentively. Within this perspective, two axes are proposed to study this pedagogical strategy a little more deeply. The first axis concerns the choice of exchange modalities among students. The moment the debate-of-ideas is present, the teacher's and students' roles are of primary importance:

- What is the best moment for this debate to be beneficial in the teaching-learning process?
- Is the debate under the teacher's total control (Does the teacher ask all the questions and dictate the orientation of the discussion)?
- Is the debate interactive? Does the teacher assume the role of mediator?

The second axis corresponds to the types of questions to be asked in the debate:

- Are the questions open ended? Does the line of questioning pose certain problems that force students to refer to prior game responses?
- Does the line of questioning need to be closed until the desired response is discovered and given?
- Does the line of questioning need to be open ended until the desired response or responses emerge?

Teachers will adopt a way of proceeding based on the characteristics of their class-groups. In dealing with a difficult group, a teacher may be more concerned with keeping their classes busy and conflict-free and thus cannot foresee anything else in terms of learning. However, it is often easy to integrate a debate-of-ideas based on very practical notions. With other class-groups, it is easy to envision the debate-of-ideas in a variety of scenarios and different forms.

As stated by Janis and Feshbach (1953), communication often produces tension among students who do not use language very well. In the beginning stages of a debate-of-ideas, students expressing their thoughts often try to rupture the communication process. Their objective, although unconscious, is to escape the potential conflict of ideas that may arise by communicating in an aggressive manner (e.g., "Yeah, but Joey couldn't even hit the side of a barn by shooting like that.") or by trying to end the debate (e.g., "I don't understand nor do I care."). At the end of a learning process when students have been exposed to the debate-of-ideas, the discourse pertaining to learning evolves positively, notably due to the fact that students seem to engage themselves in the debate in a positive manner. Students center their attention on the theme of the debate and try to formulate arguments instead of trying to find ways of rupturing the debate or fleeing from it (Mahut, Nachon, Mahut, & Gréhaigne, 2000).

On occasion, it might be profitable to foresee a period of dialogue between student-observers and players instead of a debate-of-ideas. Discussions between students like "You lose too many balls" or "You are never available for a pass" can be very beneficial to a player's self-regulation in future game situations. Student observers often forget to tally certain game behaviors. Remarks on the player's behalf like "You forgot to indicate a shot on goal; I had 4 not 3" can lead students to a higher level of consciousness in relation to their game behaviors and responses. Hence, approaches like these, which solicit student engagement, are characterized by a process of guided discovery through a certain line of questioning (e.g., How can you move the ball effectively to maximize our chances of shooting on goal?) By exploiting dialogue, students are encouraged to analyze the problem or the obstacle to be surmounted and test out different solutions.

In conclusion, the time spent confronting ideas and reflecting on different solutions permits students to develop cognitive reflexes that bring them to higher levels of consciousness in relation to their performance. Deriaz and Poussin (2001) insist that these periods of confrontation and reflection should be an integral part throughout the whole learning process.

- In the **appropriation** and **exploration** phase, when students are presented with a game play problem and must find appropriate solutions that they already possess in their repertoire or build new solutions
- In the **validation** phase, when students are asked to show the pertinence of their solutions in action

- In the **integration** and **generalization** phase, when students are asked to exploit and integrate their learning in new game situations or more complex situations (Brousseau, 1998).

When faced with the production of a motor response, these attitudes must lead students to better plan game play behaviors and responses before and during play. The links between the indicators used for observation must be made obvious to students to be used for their reflection on their game play performance. The debate-of-ideas is founded upon verbal exchanges about game play to make decisions for future game play situations. We views it from a perspective where the appropriation of knowledge and the development of aptitudes are the main focus, with the goal of positively influencing practice based on sound reasoning and understanding. This perspective poses a problem: What is the connection between saying, doing, and understanding?

THE CONNECTION BETWEEN DOING AND UNDERSTANDING

French & McPherson (1999) and McPherson (1993a) have stressed the importance of the verbal reporting technique as a tool to obtain information on thought processes of experts and novices when one wants to better understand how players perform. In our case, the purpose of the debate-of-ideas among students is to learn about action rules and decision-making through the use of verbalization in a social-cognitive-conflict setting. With respect to the doing/understanding duality, our work with physical education teachers has led us to distinguish four main stages of evolution in the learning of team sports. The teachers' awareness of such stages might help them plan learning sequences.

In a team sport lesson, at the *first learning stage*, students are able to take note of a result to analyze numerical indices and code what others do by analyzing, such as displacements and occupied spaces (Gréhaigne, Billard, & Laroche, 1999; Richard, Godbout, & Gréhaigne, 2000). In this learning stage the student codes the action of the performer which is a type of learning by doing experience.

A *second learning stage* consists, for the students, in describing their specific actions once the game is over. They get into a regulation process from one learning setup to another, provided that obstacles remain of the same kind. For instance, players will use long passes in European handball and basketball to outmaneuver a blocking defense located in front of the ball. Starting with questions from the teacher, players may also consider their former strategy or planning for this action in relation to the result of their action and thus construct an explanation for the results achieved (e.g., I succeeded because I did this or that). It is a learning stage that consists of *doing again* or repeating the action and following a series of trials, to use an explanatory description to begin extracting action rules.

In a *third learning stage* students can, while analyzing their actions, describe their peculiarities, provide reasons for their success, and generalize results obtained to eventually formulate action rules. Starting with questions from the teacher, players seek from their knowledge the available repertoire of answers and, from the results of their actions, the reasons for changes in their conduct. Hence, students are invited to formulate hypotheses about success requirements and to construct links between action and reflection on action. It is a learning stage that consists in *succeeding* and *understanding*, with the beginning of generalizations.

Finally, in a *fourth learning stage*, students can start questioning themselves on the basis of proposed learning situations, formulating hypotheses about the problem to be solved and about the way to respond. So, they are able to analyze the constraints of the task at hand and to determine specific related objectives. At the same time, they can formulate action rules and even associate them with principles of action. This self-questioning may lead to more complex or simpler planning. It is a learning stage that consists in *understanding* for *succeeding* and in *succeeding* for *understanding*, allowing student self-questioning whenever necessary *before* and *after* action (Piaget, 1974b; Wallon, 1941).

The four-stage model presented above is a hierarchical model but not necessarily a linear one. A learner may well move from stage 2 to stage 4 or move back to stage 3 when faced with too easy or too unbalanced an oppositional relationship. Nevertheless, concerning stage 4, one hopes that succeeding and understanding will be followed by a real improvement during the game and will not remain merely a discourse.

TECHNICAL/TACTICAL DEBATE

Research has been conducted on the technical/tactical debate, and little, for lack of sufficient time for experimentation and appropriate tools, has provided convincing conclusions on the tactical approach's superior influence on game performance (Turner & Martinek, 1992; Allison and Thorpe, 1997; Harrison, Preece, Blakemore, Richard, Wilkinson, & Felligham, 1999). The following section presents the results of an unpublished study in which the focus was to try to shed some light on the technical/tactical debate.

The Avallon Project

To control for a significant difference between both types of learning approaches on the development of students' game performance, an experiment was set up with sixth grade students (n = 24) chosen at random among all the sixth graders at Avallon school (France) assessment. Each of the 24 students was assigned to one of two heterogeneous groups based on results provided by using the TSAP (Gréhaigne, 1994; Gréhaigne and Godbout, 1995; Laroche and Gréhaigne, 1995; Richard et al., 2000) to assess performance in a modified basketball setting. The choice of basketball for this work corresponds to the desire to examine the effect of learning scenarios on students' decision-making skills in contexts where urgency is often called for. For this purpose, it was necessary to use a continuous invasion-type game rather than a game characterized by frequent starts and stops like volleyball, thus giving a period of time to plan the following game sequence. All the participants had had some physical education at elementary school, but very few had been significantly exposed to basketball.

Methodology

The Technical Approach The technical approach considers the technical requirements of the game of basketball as the central focus of what and how things are going to be taught. A typical lesson in this type of approach is made up of three phases: (1) a warm-up, (2) the learning of skills, and (3) a short game at the end the lesson. The main goal in these lessons is primarily the development of offensive skills. The skills taught during the 10-week experiment were the basics of ball handling, passing, receiving, and shooting.

The Tactical Approach In the tactical approach, the emphasis is put on tactical aspects of the game in relation to modified game situations (e.g., 3 vs.3, 4 vs.4). At the beginning of every lesson, the teacher sets up different learning situations, presenting a tactical problem to the students. In this approach, offensive aspects of the game are emphasized. The teacher guides the students in this process by helping them to get organized, read game configurations, and decide on appropriate responses. The teacher then helps students to regulate their learning.

Data Collection To assess students game play performance, the TSAP was used (Gréhaigne & Roche, 1993). Consequently, every student was estimated on the basis of:

$$\frac{\text{Attack Balls (AB)} + \text{Conquered Balls (BC)} = \text{Played Balls (PB)}.}{\text{Lost Balls (LB)}}$$

Through the different phases of experimentation, students were tested periodically, and a performance score was given to provide them with feedback on their adaptation to game play.

Organization of the Experimental Context After a few lessons of discovering basketball, the experimental part was conducted from weeks 3 to 13. Each group had 10 lessons of 75 minutes each. During weeks 9 and 15, a tournament was organized to assess students' evolution. During these tournaments, students were assessed using the TSAP performance indices. Players were assessed by 9th grade students who had observed at the beginning of the project for player classification purposes. All players were filmed during one match.

Results Of the 24 students, 9 improved their performance score between lesson 1 and lesson 6. Of these 9 students, 8 were from the tactical approach group, while only one was from the technical approach group. Eight students improved their performance score between lesson 6 and lesson 12. Of this group, 5 students were from the tactical group. Only 9 students improved their performance score between lesson 1 and lesson 12. Among these 9 students, 6 were from the tactical group. The results of the study are detailed in Table 9.1.

TABLE 9.1 Avallon Project: Game Performance Scores Throughout the Different Phases of Experimentation

	Lesson 1	Lesson 6	Lesson 12	Results 5 months later
Tactical approach group				
Mean performance score	11.48	12.74	13	12.22
Standard deviation	4.35	3.81	3.94	4.02
Technical approach group				
Mean performance score	11.35	11.33	10.90	10.28
Standard deviation	3.89	3.68	6.22	5.32
Average mean	11.41	12.03	11.94	11.25

As illustrated in Table 9.1, mean performance scores increased during the experimental phase, from 11.41 to 11.94. Many students progressed. However, it is of note that the highest mean appeared in lesson 6 (12.03). During the pretest in lesson 1, the mean for both groups was almost identical. At lesson 6 a rather important difference between the groups already appears in favor of the tactical approach group (1.41 difference between means). This difference was maintained itself through lesson 12, with the tactical group improving its performance level from 11.48 in lesson 1 to 12.99 in lesson 12. A slight but constant decrease was noticed in the technical group from lessons 1 to 12. However, game performance was again assessed 5 months later without any team sport instruction between the end of the project and this assessment period. The investigators in this project wanted to see whether any learning had been stabilized and was still present. Again all students were assessed with the same instrument used in the investigation, and it was noticed that both groups' performance level had diminished. Nevertheless, it was noticed that the tactical group had a lesser decline in performance due to the durability of learning created by the teaching context. When comparing means between the two groups, it was obvious that the tactical approach seems to have had a more lasting effect on performance over time (12.22 vs. 10.28) than the technical approach.

In light of this experiment, the tactical approach seems to create better results in terms of game performance if adequate time is spent. This approach provides students with a surer and more durable education pertaining to decision-making when faced with different tactical problems.

CONCLUSION

In this section we have presented the major theories that underlie the teaching and learning process of sport-related games. First, we examined the concept of apprenticeship in the learning setting (i.e., learning by observing and doing). We view the observation, critical thinking and transformation as key elements to implement a constructivist perspective to learning. Second, we presented the major ideas that underlie an observational approach to teaching and learning in game play. Third, we proposed a set of situations (i.e., reference, instructional, assessment) that comprises the learning process. Fourth, we present the notion of the *debate of ideas* which, we believe is a vital teaching strategy to help promote critical thinking in game performance. Finally, we examined the technical and tactical debate through the presentation of specific research.

10

CONSTRUCTING TEAM SPORT KNOWLEDGE

In chapter 10, we will examine the contribution of the Teaching Games for Understanding, explore the various contributions of the German and French of schools of thought to tactical approaches in games teaching, and present a new model for the teaching and learning of team sports. This new model will emphasize learning on the students' part, with their representations of the game, and teaching on the teacher's part, with the implementation of settings and strategies using observation, enhancing critical thinking, and thus allowing students to transform previous answers. The regulation of learning through formative assessment will also be discussed.

THE LEARNING PROCESS IN TEAM SPORTS: PRIOR AND CURRENT MODELS

In the evolution of team sport didactics, there were progressive changes between 1965 and 1985. In France, the Vichy congresses of 1964 and 1965 initiated an important change in the teaching of team sports (Amicale des Anciens Élèves de l'ENSEPS, 1966). At the time, three major problems were tackled from a new angle; these were (a) skill execution, (b) force ratio, and (c) changes to be considered in players' actions.

   a. Skill execution would be considered as a perceptual-motor system in which perceptions play a major role.

b. The game, conceived as a force ratio, would be analyzed in a dynamic perspective to identify the structures at work with regard to team organization.

c. The player would be considered a member of a structured set, the team, which was organized in view of achieving some objective.

In line with these changes, learning consists of modifying the organization of the player's motor behavior based on his or her internalization of the structure of game play. Training loses its cumulative characteristic and, especially, leans on cognitive processes—perception and acknowledgment of signals—for internalizing structures. Subject matter is not *a priori* defined but rather is elaborated from a precise observation of the different games by the teacher.

With the emergence of structural analysis, the team is now considered different from the simple sum of the players who constitute it. The team becomes a structured set for achieving common aims (Teodorescu, 1965). There exists a reciprocal coordination between individual and collective actions. Our purpose is to show that team sports proceed from common tactical principles.

Mahlo's Model and the Tactical Approach

Mahlo (1974; originally published in German in 1969) studied game play phases and showed the complex character of "tactical action in play." He identified its components as follows (also illustrated in Figure 10.1):

- Perception and analysis of game play (resulting in knowledge of the evolution of the setting)

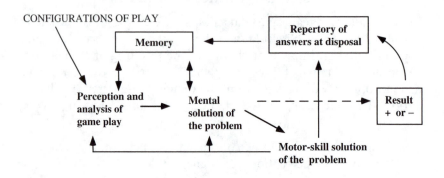

Fig. 10.1 The phases of game play according to Mahlo (1974).

- Mental solution to the problem (involving knowledge of the likely evolution of the setting and the representation of some plan of action)
- Motor skill solution to the problem (resulting in the practical solution)

The player determines distances, intervals, and speeds (hence, determining a subjective time to accomplish the task in accordance with his or her own motor skill). Mahlo put forward the notion of common referential and advance-organization in game play from perceptive aspects of the play. To gather information relative to this problem, he studied the answers of players and trainers from various levels of play who confronted different configurations-of-play pictures.

The modeling of practice presented in Deleplace's work (1966; 1979; 1995) gave birth to the school of *tactical approach* (Bouthier, 1984; Diaz, 1983; Reitchess, 1983; Stein, 1981); this school of thought postulates that "the intervention of cognitive processes is decisive for the advance organization and motor control of actions" (Bouthier, 1986). Its advocates hypothesize that this approach yields better results than two other pedagogical methods. One method, the *execution model* approach, focuses on the repetition, by the player, of efficient solutions produced by experts, while the other, the *self adaptive model* approach, postulates that judicious variations in the setting of the environment provide the most efficient means for the player to discover solutions and develop skills. The central strategy of the tactical approach calls (a) for the presentation of essential information concerning the tactical advance-organization of actions during game play and then (b) for the actual implementation of such actions in relatively self-sustaining and tactics-oriented patterns of play. These patterns of play, borrowed from actual game play, are not to be confused with traditional drills. They are selected on the basis that they can be played out independently of a match situation, that they call for tactical decisions, and that the outcome remains open-ended.

The Revisited Teaching Game for Understanding Model

In England in 1983, another model for teaching games, Teaching Game for Understanding (TGfU), was presented by Bunker and Thorpe (1983) and Kirk (1983). In relation to TGfU, the *Journal of Teaching in Physical Education*'s January 2002 issue presents two contributions concerning the evolution of the model. Holt, Strean, & Bengoechea (2002) note that in the debate concerning TGfU, the learner is at the center of the process, but the experience of the learner and his or her affective dimension have received only little attention within the English sport pedagogy literature. Pertaining to this topic, one can find contributions in the German or French literature (see Barth, 1994; Davisse & Louveau, 1991; etc.). Holt et al. stress that Thorpe et al. (1984) introduced four fundamental pedagogical principles aimed at developing physical education practices. These principles are sampling, modification-representation, modification-exaggeration, and tactical complexity. They are based on the concept of the transferability of key technical elements involved in games and the progression in apprenticeship. These four elements do not provide new information on the teaching-learning process in team sports. Research on transferability and linear progressiveness have provided very little evidence on the transfer of learning and the legitimacy of the use of progressions (in relation to skills and game situations) in the learning process. Using motor skills or knowledge in a new game or sport requires a certain reconstruction of skills and knowledge (Durand, 1989). Between transfer and reconstruction there is a gap that is characterized by the required time to learn.

After Bunker and Thorpe (1983) and Kirk (1983), Kirk and MacPhail (2002) present a new version of the TGfU model that draws on a situated learning perspective. This model is shown in Figure 10.2.

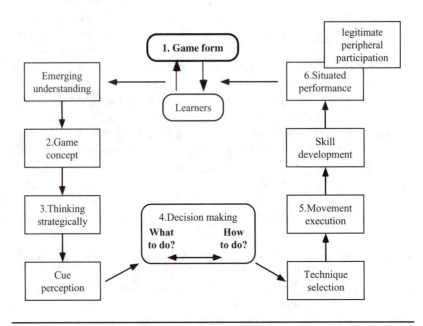

Fig. 10.2 The Bunker and Thorpe (1983) model revisited (Kirk and MacPhail, 2002).

A situated perspective assumes that learning involves the active engagement of individuals with their environment (Rovegno, 1999; Rovegno & Kirk, 1995). The notion of situated performance in the revised model provides one way of understanding the relationship between the game form and the players' representations.

However, these two new contributions to the TGfU body of knowledge fail to clarify the main problem with the TGfU model: What do students actually learn and understand from team sport instruction?

To better comprehend the reason for considering the "understanding" component in the TGfU model, let's briefly examine the relationship between theory and practice in physical education. Linking action to knowledge is a critical component of inquiry and reflective practice. In doing so, students do not apply theory in a learning setting but generate their own knowledge by questioning their practice based their own frame of reference. Thus, students have opportunities to connect practice to theory and theory to practice, enhancing their level of reflective thinking and broadening their scope of reflection in the pursuit of developing and improving motor competencies. The model resulting from this process brings us to conclude that in the learning process, approximate knowledge can help one make progress since it is because the model is approximate that it is likely to evolve. This being said, how are knowledge and motor competencies constructed by students?

The classical analysis model of the rapport between theory and practice proceeds from a *deductive logic*. Faced with a complex problem, it is tempting to adopt such logic, but there are limits to simplification. For instance, the simple learning of passing, dribbling, and shooting rarely produces an efficient performer.

A second model is based on an *inductive logic*. It is through practice, its meaning for the beginner, and the questions he or she is faced with that come first. Theory or knowledge is questioned following this practical phase. Within this perspective, practice and theory are intimately linked and interact constantly. The student's ability to extract knowledge from practice, relate this information to theoretical models, and return to practice constitutes the most certain way for avoiding a rigid theorization that would dictate game play.

The teaching strategies illustrated in this paragraph have been developed on the basis of theoretical choices and postulates about learning and on the basis of options about the function of the school. There is a strong link (filiation) between all of these prior and current models—the role of cognitive processes and tactical awareness. The part of understanding to anticipate on the following configurations is also crucial. In next section, we will present, in connection with the French tactical approach, a new model for the teaching and learning of invasion team sports

TACTICAL DECISION LEARNING MODEL (TDLM)

The use of the tactical approach (Rink, 1996) as framework, along with the contribution of a constructivist and cognitivist perspective and the accomplished work on tactical knowledge in team sports, has led us, in the context of school physical education, to put forward the "Tactical Decision Learning Model" (TDLM) (Gréhaigne & Godbout, 1995; Gréhaigne, Godbout, & Bouthier, 1999; Gréhaigne, Godbout, & Bouthier, 2001). This model focuses on the students' exploration of the various possibilities of game play and on the construction of adequate responses in small-sided games.

Figure 10.3 illustrates an operational teaching model that should enhance students' construction of tactical knowledge and the development of their decision-making skills. At the very onset of the learning sequence, students are put in action in some form of adaptation of the

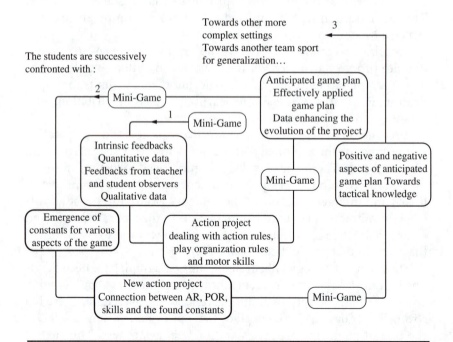

Fig. 10.3 A model for students' construction of knowledge in team sports.

game. For instance, fewer players should simplify the configuration of play. The use of smaller play areas however calls for some caution and should be balanced against the number of players involved since this may cause an increase in the time constraints, which are a limiting factor for decision-making (Gréhaigne & Godbout, 1998).

After appropriate observation, augmented feedback of a different nature can complement the intrinsic feedback experienced by each player. In the ensuing debate-of-ideas, each team puts together a first action project, which is then tried out in play. Following observation, the team's capacity for implementing the game plan or action project can be assessed and there may be proposals for an evolution of the plan. After a new exposure to play, students may perceive the emergence of constants for various aspects of the game. This in turn can lead to the development of a new action project with the introduction of connections between action rules, play organization rules (Gréhaigne & Godbout, 1995), and required skills on the one hand, and the constants that have just been identified on the other. After testing the new action project, the team may use the results of observations to appreciate positive and negative aspects of their anticipated game plan. In doing so, players are progressively putting together tactical knowledge and refining their decision-making skills. Once stabilization appears to be taking place, learning settings may be complex and, eventually, players may be exposed to another team sport to initiate a generalization process.

As one can see from this tactical-decision learning model, evolving from a first exposure to the pedagogical content to a state of stabilized knowledge of that content requires time. Thus, for students to truly construct new knowledge (i.e., knowing and doing) teachers need to provide more time and more progressions in their units.

MAKING SENSE OF LEARNING

For students to achieve and have success in relation to team games and sports, it is necessary to take into account the usefulness and appropriateness of the knowledge and competencies that need to be developed so that students can make sense out of the learning activities that are presented to them. Trying to make sense of a task implies that a learner will refer to his or her implicit or explicit formulation of the task, observable behavior, and cues before actually engaging in the task. How can we characterize the sense that students attribute to learning scenarios in physical education and sport? This notion can be defined as a particular evocation of the situation by the student, which is partially connected to his or her sociocultural background, by being in touch with his or her conceptions and representations of the content being taught, and by his or her intrinsic motivation. Furthermore, students' affective and intellectual resources must be taken into consideration to present learning tasks that have significance to them and that are accessible to them from a cognitive perspective. Hence, when presenting students to a new learning situation, a first step is to be aware of students' personal reference models to the task or activity being presented to develop adequate tasks.

A reference model can vary from student to student based on previous exposure to the activity. At the interface of a student's logic, the group's logic, and the logic of the game, a *reference model* establishes the conceptions conveyed by students. From this point of view, it is necessary to find a common ground between the teacher and the students with regard to the learning outcomes related to team sports and games. Is it not a simple question of making passes and scoring more goals than the opponents? The answers to these questions depend on the efficiency of learning.

There are three main categories of motivation:

- Play is perceived to be of relational interest: Students want to have fun; they want to be affiliated with a group. The end result or learning is of little interest.
- Play is an occasion for students to measure and prove themselves. Students are motivated on the basis of competition for social comparison purposes.
- Play is motivated by students' desire for improvement in the acquisition of knowledge and skills.

Often students analyze activities and distinguish among them the possibilities to satisfy that the activities offer them to satisfy the purposes for which they play. There are always students who have nothing to learn from the teacher or those who do not especially want to learn. All eventually agree very fast by refusing to actively engage in the learning activities. Nonetheless, students are in school to learn and thus progress and the conquest of "making sense" of what is being learned should generate interest and consequently pleasure.

TOWARD THE MODELING OF STUDENTS' PLAY IN TEAM SPORTS IN SECONDARY SCHOOL

In the present section, observation of practice and typical problems that students must solve to make progress will be discussed. The description of students' typical conduct makes it possible to model three characteristic stages for the "construction" of the confrontation by the students (Gréhaigne, Billard, & Laroche, 1999). With regard to the attack, these three stages are the *over-ball play*, the *relay play*, and the *forward-ball play*. Defense focuses on the *ball carriers*, the *potential ball receivers*, and the *stabilized space*.

First Stage

The first step is often observed in high school students whenever they have understood what is at stake in team sports: Their movements are oriented on the playing surface, and their actions lead them closer to the target under attack.

Organization Mode Selected descriptions of students' conduct deal only with successful setups that is, those that lead to a shot on goal. We think it more constructive to take into account positive aspects of success instead of analyzing hypothetical reasons for failure. In a match where both teams offer a comparable level of play, one often sees the setting of a first type of organization that focuses on two players. One player stays at the rear of the covered play-space (CP-S), playing the role of a distributor, and a second player plays at the front of the CP-S, attempting to score goals. Successful setups operate as follows: The rear player sends forward a long pass, over the group of players, toward the teammate occupying the role of scorer. The potential scorer takes control of the ball, gets as close as possible to the goal, and shoots; in doing so, he is hindered little by the players who eventually go after or accompany him.

In over-ball play, the ball is kicked forward, beyond the covered play-space, on behalf of a player who has broken away. Such a configuration of play favors a shot on goal. The distributor uses the long ball. The scorer has "constructed" (mastered) the catching-dribbling and dribbling-shooting coordination skills in movement and in game situations.

Evolution of the Pattern One can also observe for a given player the use of dribbling at the periphery of the play-space to make a pass or to shoot on goal. This type of organization appears when, for motor reasons, a player encounters technical difficulties performing the long ball pass. This is often the case in soccer.

At this stage, one observes numerous losses of the ball, but these organizational modes are always displayed every time an attack is successful with at least one shot on goal.

By the end of the first stage, a voluntary hindrance on the ball distributor forces players to adapt, and one begins to observe the use of relays. The teacher should make use of this new behavior because it foretells the functioning modes of the second stage.

Second Stage

The typical behaviors described in stage 1 being stabilized, the noticeable and lasting decrease in ball losses becomes a reliable indication of an evolution of the play. Still, without a real or apparent change in the number of played balls, one may observe, at times, a significant increase of lost balls. Does this indicate a sudden behavioral or learning regression? It is preferable to focus on the nature of the observed relations between attack and defense. These states of balance are changing, moving from the over-ball play to the use of a relay player.

Organization Mode The ball carrier is now subjected to a more efficient marking as soon as he or she gets possession of the ball, and the efficiency of the rear-distributor/forward-scorer system decreases significantly. The distributor-player's advance is hindered, or even impeded. The player often finds him or herself incapable of making a long pass forward. The player must construct a new solution for the problem he or she is faced with. The use of a proximate teammate, playing the role of relay, allows the ball carrier to get rid of the opponent and to find him or herself again in a situation close to that of stage 1. A player can then perform a long pass or advance alone toward the opponent's goal. But soon enough, the defense puts together an anticipation strategy on relays and potential ball receivers. Little by little, one observes a more rational occupation of the playing surface. This considerably slows down the progression of the ball and facilitates its recovery.

When observing the situation mentioned previously (the appearance of the relay player), one can quite often see two or three players taking charge of the progression of the ball toward the attack zone through a series of exchanges. This way of progressing toward the target offers the advantage of increasing both players' mobility and the speed of ball exchanges. This results in a significant increase of the covered play-space, particularly in relation to the width of the playing surface. For their part, given their placement between the ball carrier and the target, defenders display a deliberate will to recover the ball as soon as possible.

Interpretation Defenders' efficiency on the ball carriers greatly hinders their individual progression. Attackers must construct new solutions, most often by spreading themselves out or getting away from one another and from opponents. The play-space thus becomes noticeably enlarged (wider and longer), and one can observe a decrease in ball losses. Attackers have now mastered catching, kicking, and long accurate passes.

Following a first stage where focusing on the ball is paramount, the ball appears elusive, hard to control, and hard to pass along. Thus one observes, in the second stage, the appearance of a stronger focus on the opponent.

Third Stage

In stages 1 and 2, the attack–defense relationships are as follows: Attackers try to reach the target as fast as possible; defenders are anxious to display an increasing efficiency in hindering the potential ball-holder in his or her efforts to recover the ball. What is then happening on the pitch when game play reaches the third stage?

Organization Mode Defenders settle and organize themselves in the scoring zone (or the offensive zone, from the attackers' point of view). This is a fundamental characteristic of stage 3; to make it simple, we shall call it *zone defense*. This setup forces the attacker to find a different scoring-action space. Progression of the ball may be like that encountered in previous stages, but the main difference is that the scorer no longer has free access to the scoring zone. She finds herself hindered by an organized and efficient defensive blocking. The attacker must therefore modify her usual way of doing thing: She resorts to relays. A new scoring zone, off the general axis of play, must be constructed between the attacked target and the defended target.

This defensive setup, intentionally organized in the scoring zone, results from the defenders' backing-off stopping maneuver observed in the previous stage (e.g., defenders floating so as not to be outflanked or run over). Defenders are positioned in a blockade between the target and potential receivers. They back off while facing the ball carrier. Once again, game play must be transformed since backing off is no longer possible once the ball carrier gets close to the target. It is no longer a matter of slowing down the ball carrier's progression; she must be stopped within the statutory limits, and above all, any scoring action must be countered.

The previous stage is both preliminary and yet essential for putting together a stabilized defense. Indeed, the defender's new task is all the more simple if he has been efficient during the previous stage, where his motor competencies underlie the results of his actions.

Later Evolution Faced with a new problem to be solved, attackers are forced to switch from a fast and linear offensive progression to a different management of their conduct, shown in Figure 10.4. They must rely on a variety of runs and also on the speed of exchanges to neutralize defenders. The objective is then to free a shooter in the scoring zone by providing her with a time advance on defensive repositioning.

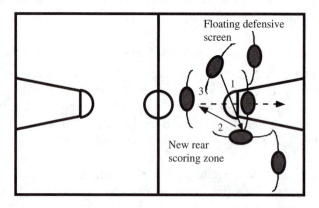

Fig. 10.4 Typical configuration of play for the new attack setup.

The new pattern for circulation of the ball is a convenient reference for an observer: From an almost exclusive circulation from the rear toward the front, one now witnesses a circulation ahead, laterally, and also from the front to the rear. This transformation results from the defensive setup, which, anticipating the generation of likely new scoring zones, comes between the attackers and the goal to defend the goal. On the attackers' side, game play typically displays a triangular circulation of the ball; this appears very rapidly in basketball and soccer. Its appearance in handball depends upon the players' construction of motor competencies that will allow them to perform long shots and over-the-defense (jump) shots with some chance of success.

In summary, the evolution of collective conduct always results from an interactive and adaptive solicitation on the part of the opponents (Bouthier & Durey, 1994; Gréhaigne, Bouthier, & David, 1997). Playing team sports is learning to manage positions and varying ball movements and trajectories. It is also learning to construct a rapport of strength with other players in conditions of decisional urgency in view of bringing the ball into the scoring zone and effectively scoring. Success requires the recognition or the generation of appropriate configurations of play that will make it possible to unbalance the opponents' setup.

These theoretical models of play are intended to help teachers better analyze what happens during team sports encounters. They are based on the theory of the construction of the players' strategies in play and by the play, as long as players are truly confronted with their opponents' adaptive logic. This teaching approach through game play questions the team sport coaches' *a priori* descriptions that use these stages as set stages for developing teaching content. The team sport model that we put forward works as long as one rests on a constructivist approach in which the confrontation dynamics with partners and against opponents remains paramount. This implies that the teacher, rather then applying high-level play observations to school situations, focus on the student's personal activity, with his or particular resources and cognitive functioning, trying to solve problems brought about by game play. In this respect, taking into account the specific context of school play is a determining factor in the teacher's analysis of typical conduct performed by his or her students in a particular situation (Van der Maren, 1999). It is only in action and in confronting a new situation brought about by the action that the student will be able to interpret and plan his action. In doing so, he brings in a new situation for the opponent and forces him to counter with original adaptive conduct, which, in return, enriches the dynamics of play.

Another model to help the analysis of the passes between players is shown in Figure 10.5.

The analysis of the different areas that a teammate can occupy in relation to the ball carrier permits us to define various categories of ball exchanges based on:

- The topological rapport between the ball carrier and teammates
- The direction in which players solicit a pass
- The position of the ball carrier in relation to the opposing team's goal
- Definition of support: A player is supporting the attack when he or she is available and accessible in an area in front of or behind the ball carrier
- Definition of calling a pass: To solicit a pass by initiating a run.

In our view, three conditions must be met for an effective call:

- A teammate must be in the ball carrier's field of vision
- A teammate must be at an adequate distance for a pass (accessibility)
- A teammate must be open to receive a pass (availability)

In short, attacking players should have teammates to support them who are in a good position, at an angle to receive the ball, at an angle

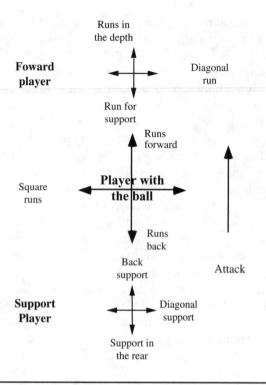

Fig. 10.5 A model to analyze ball exchanges among teammates.

that makes a forward pass possible, and at a distance that gives them time to make the pass.

In an attempt to characterize exploited game behavior at different performance levels, we can state that at a beginner level, the calling of a pass is often executed in inadequate or ruptured game conditions (e.g., calling pass in double coverage). At an intermediate level, the calling of a pass is often oriented forward or toward the opposing team's goal. Finally, at an advanced level, one can observe the exploitation of a variety of situations where players call for a pass. This exploitation will be based on the analysis of the rapport of strength in relation to the opposing team.

TRANSFORMATION

Students have truly learned if, when faced with a problem that is new but compatible with the resources at their disposal (inner resources), they have transformed their initial behavior and have identified and verbalized the action rules that made their success possible. "Action rules define conditions to be enforced and elements to be taken into account if one wants to insure efficient action" (Gréhaigne & Godbout, 1995, p. 496).

Transformation implies not only the appearance of new answers to a given problem but also a stabilization of such answers. Indeed the appearance of a new answer by the student does in no way mean that it will thereafter be used all the time. Under pressure, as in a time-constraint setting, a student may well reverse to a former and inadequate pattern of play. For new answers to be recognized as stabilized, they must meet three criteria: systematicity, durability, and generalization. *Systematicity* refers to a reduction in the range of the answers and a stability of performance over successive trials (i.e., the student will succeed 8 times out of 10). Durability means that after an interval of time without being exposed to the teaching and learning of a skill (for example, after a 2-month interval), the student can still perform at the same level. It should be clear that durability must not be mistaken for permanence. Durability ensures access to stabilized new knowledge until a new type of problem is encountered, calling for a solution pertaining to a higher level of performance or for a completely different type of solution. New answers must then be found, and the cycle starts all over. Finally, generalization refers to the student's recognition of a similarity between several situations and the subsequent utilization and reorganization of previously learned action rules; the reorganized rules are then applied in a given set or category of problems (Gréhaigne & Cadopi, 1990).

During game play, the teacher may conclude that new answers are being transformed into stabilized answers, therefore becoming a part of the student's resources in the following situations:

1. During game play, particular adaptations to the usual rules, like the use of a support player (i.e., joker) (Gréhaigne & Godbout, 1997), are no longer necessary and have been removed.
2. When confronted with a greater number of players during the game, for example, from 3 vs. 3 to 5 vs. 5, students keep using the same behavior developed during previous learning settings, such behavior indicating that newly acquired skills and action rules are getting stabilized.
3. When new teams are organized, players still resort to newly acquired behavior. This demonstrates that such behavior is part of the player's resources rather than associated with specific teammates and can therefore be called upon in play whenever necessary.

The construction and stabilization of new behaviors, then, rest upon the use of one or more of the following mechanisms:

1. **Sudden awareness.** It is an operation that brings to conscious level facts or events that were either usually managed by routines or had been previously processed by the student.
2. **Verbalization.** As mentioned earlier, it brings the student to describe orally what he or she has just done and, eventually, what he or she wants to do.
3. **Construction of automatism.** It consists in putting together motor or cognitive routines, most of the time through successive reiterations of the task.

To set these mechanisms on students, the teacher may have the students work on different types of tasks, such as:

- **Problem solving tasks.** They allow access to a superior level of understanding.
- **Nonautomated-performance tasks.** They correspond to situations for which general procedures are stocked in memory but must be adapted to the specific case at hand.
- **Automated-performance tasks.** They represent the performance of specific procedures, where reiteration remains the central feature.

During automated performance tasks, it should be noted that teaching for understanding does not exclude, at times, the construction of routines. These routines become "pre-established programs that put forward an automatic regulation in order to economically face relatively stable situations" (Gréhaigne & Godbout, 1995; 1997). Some of the problems brought about by a given configuration of play may then be managed rapidly as a background task without solicitation of the cognitive channel.

A routine is an internal operation used by a player that becomes automatic and is based on principles of economy and speed. When a routine is established, it works as a background application. The acquisition of cognitive routines not only results from repetition but can also be developed through adequate learning conditions. Several modes of acquiring routines have been identified by Leplat (1995) and Barbier (1996).

Acquisition through action involves intentional learning for which goals and objectives are developed but without any indication or operational means to attain them; controlled acquisition is common in formal scholastic or professional settings where acquisition of learning is based on knowledge and guidance is provided to the learner; and acquisition through osmosis involves nonintentional learning acquired without any formal instruction.

The modes of acquisition are not independent of each other; rather they interact with each other. In physical activity and sport, different types of information can provide feedback to a learner, such as the number of played balls in a certain time frame. Computer programs and simulators offer different possibilities for the development of more complex cognitive routines by offering players problem-solving situations in which they can learn proper responses to specific game situations (Blomqvist, Luhtanen, Laako, & Keskinen, 2000).

Routines have limited validity, depending on the variety of conditions in which they are acquired. They become inadequate when situations change. This limitation is, however, a favorable condition in their acquisition because these routines are simple and specific. What is important to know is what happens when a routine looses its validity due to unforeseen conditions. This failure, which interrupts a player's activity, forces a redefinition of the activity and thus a return to a conscious cognitive activity and to a state of lucidity. For example, experienced players have routines in their repertoire that allow them to consider other aspects of the game while executing specific tasks in game play. If a player is then confronted with an unforeseen situation, a different repertoire of possible solutions is put forth. The player's focus shifts to problem solving, which in turn permits the problem to be resolved.

When a routine is ingrained and becomes rigid, a player can continue his or her play. However, his or her responses are not valid to the game situation. The player does not obtain what was wanted, however, and his or her action, not taking into consideration the variations in the situation, leads to error. Moreover, the player does not necessarily perceive this error, as no other solution is available except the repetition of the same action. The player has automated the processing phase of possible cases and current incidents. For example, while attacking the opposing team's goal, the attacking team might be in advance on the defending team's repositioning, which represents an advantage in relation to time. A forward pass in an available lane, thus using the depth of the field, would help the attacking team take advantage of this situation. However, the player making a lateral pass to a partner will essentially lose the potential advantage created by his or her team's attack. Consequently, while the offensive team still has possession of the ball, the decision of using the width of the field instead of the depth in making a pass is not the best decision for the situation at hand.

When an exceptional situation arises, the player doesn't have the processes to find an original solution. Consequently, it can be affirmed that it is sometimes difficult to conserve the advantages of routines without loosing the advantages related to conscious mental processes. This game conflict is well illustrated using the notion of motor skills. Sport-specific skills have to be automated to meet game play requirements related to the speed of play. This automated process reduces the availability of more complex skills, which are needed to deal with and process different game play incidents (i.e., players who can adapt to the speed of play).

Nevertheless, it is true that competencies that are put forward to control a complex task suppose the acquisition of routines (Gréhaigne et al., 2001; Gréhaigne et al., 1999). These routines constitute the acquisition of higher-order cognitive competencies (Resnick, 1987). The situation has often been treated as the relation between skill and automated response. To this effect, Shiffrin and Dumais (1981) stated: "We think that automated response is a major component in the acquisition of a cognitive or motor skill, and we suggest that this factor be accorded a particular importance" (p.138).

Routines supply ready and available action units for higher-order activities. Routines and planned sequences define action blocks, which are used in regular game situations that have a foreseeable result.

In order to promote the players' construction of game competencies teachers and coaches need to create conditions and environments that consider factors that directly relate to the teaching-learning process. We will address some the critical factors in chapter 11.

11

CRITICAL ISSUES IN THE TEACHING OF TEAM SPORTS

In chapter 11, our aim is to explore different factors that are critical to the teaching-learning process. In the first part of this chapter, our goal is to study in more detail team sports' and games' common traits without neglecting their distinctive and unique characters. Within this analysis, we do not want to distance ourselves from the regular social practices of sport but want to try and have a better understanding of these social practices to:

1. Try and maximize learning time in a school physical education setting
2. Avoid seeing students as perpetual beginners
3. Go beyond regular sporting practices that seem to hamper learning at the novice and intermediate stages by distorting the true learning objective, which is the development of game sense

COMMON TRAITS IN GAMES AND SPORTS

Transversality/Specificity

The notion of specificity relates to a linear evolution or progression in motor competencies ranging from simple to complex and from kindergarten to high school. In our view, however, we question this linear progression of motor competencies because of probable moments of stagnation due to students' biological and psychological evolution and the learning conditions that we present to students. Also, one can note that the evolution of action rules and motor competencies can be efficient and eventually be stabilized at a certain speed of play but can totally deteriorate as soon as the speed of play is increased. From an ideal learning perspective, the idea would be to be to integrate a few adapted similar and different action rules from a student's first exposure to team sport learning to the end of scholarship. However, the learning of action rule knowledge should be detached progressively from the objects from which this knowledge was originally constructed. The underlying hypothesis resides in the fact that action rules, grouped as guiding principles, can be reinvested in other games or sports with similar characteristics.

In relation to *transversality*, we put forward three postulates that we consider to be of importance in relation to the teaching-learning process of games.

1. Transversality is cognitive in nature. A student's development of knowledge and motor competencies is greatly influenced by a maturation process.
2. From the perspective of a specific learning outcome, transversality is relative to a specific classification of problems and must be understood as being in an indissociable dialectic with specificity.
3. Transversality must effectively be reinvested when a student is faced with a new learning situation. Transversality does not concern sensory motor skills, which are, in our perception, the necessary tools to put in place action rules.

Different action rules and principles of action have been presented in this book using these three postulates as guiding principles in the teaching-learning process. The presented action rules and principles of action can be exploited in different invasion games. Furthermore, it seems possible that, with certain modifications, they could be used in team sports of a noninvasive nature. We extended this conception to the construction of reference situations, learning situations, and success criteria that have common characteristics. In turn, this conception suggests that we should possibly limit the diversity of games when integrating children and adolescents into games to avoid disparity, thus having a focused vision on true and durable learning. This conception does not exclude the possibility that the specificity of different team sports can enrich a student's construction of new game responses. The end result of learning should be that students be able to consciously and more quickly construct more appropriate game responses.

Reproducing/Constructing

In the teaching-learning process, we make a strong distinction between reproducing solutions and constructing new answers. For the player, reproducing solutions involve the learning of a program of actions that is composed of a series of schemas of play. Theses schemas consist in preestablished sequences of action with singular technical skills, linked in a specific order and set in motion when certain specific game play events occur. On the contrary, constructing new responses implies, for the student, a capacity for using both determinism and random occurrences. The knowledge and motor skills constructed during action alter players' perceptions of information and their considered responses according to the lessons they draw from the events of the game. Progressively, players build up the capacity of quickly deciding, and this capacity itself rests upon the ability to conceive responses. In this case, cognitive processes serve to extract information from game play, to draw an adequate representation of the situation, to weigh contingencies, and to elaborate action scenarios. The resulting operative knowledge of configurations of play allows players to recognize restraints, regularities, and constants.

Theory and Practice: Toward a Practice–Theory–Practice Model

Educators have long been concerned with the separation between practical and theoretical aspects of teaching. Linking action to knowledge is a critical component of inquiry and reflective practice. In the case of physical education teachers, they do not apply theory in teaching settings but generate their own knowledge in questioning their practice based on a frame of reference. Thus, teachers have opportunities for connecting practice to theory and theory to practice, enhancing the level of reflective thinking and broadening the scope of reflection to multiple aspects of teaching.

The model that arises from this work allows one to assert that in didactics, approximate knowledge can help one to get ahead, and it is because the model is approximate that it is able to evolve. The classical analysis model of rapport between theory and practice adopts a top-down logic. Facing a complex problem, the temptation is often to adopt deductive and reductive logic; nevertheless, simplification has limits. For example, the learning of passing, dribbling, and shooting rarely produces an efficient performer.

A second model is based on a bottom-up logic. This model is based on the sense that a novice player makes out of the initial contact to different game play situations. Theories or scholarly knowledge are integrated into this practical process. In this perspective, practice and theory are intimately linked and function with constant interactions. Extracting knowledge from practice, confronting these data to theoretical models, and returning to the practice constitute the most certain means of avoiding a theorization that prescribes game play.

Reversibility/Stability

The notions of reversibility and stability are based on the idea that in a complex setting, there exist several solutions or attitudes that constitute an adapted response for a given situation. Several distinct situations also exist, where a same or similar solution or attitude can constitute an adapted response. For students, a good adaptation to a similar problem in different classes depends on a combination of different factors. Hierarchy and the importance of each solution can vary considerably for each player, with apparently similar results.

The state of equilibrium is precarious, and its main feature is reversibility. An experienced player, because of a temporary failure or stress, can reverse, for a moment, to behaviors associated with novices. The dispersion of the elements that constitute a behavior is more important in a complex setting than in simple tasks. This idea suggests that the organization of elementary processes in more complex procedures introduces variations particular to this organization. We are confronted with a system of variables whose interrelations can explain the variations or stabilities observed. Consequently, the expression "adaptable procedure" means that the random aspect of certain behaviors has been selected. This process makes it possible to constitute routines that offer the player the possibility to function with economic schema in many settings (Houdé, 1992). The schema present the possibility of being at the interface between awareness and automatic regulation.

ADAPTATION AND LEARNING IN RELATION TO TEAM GAMES AND SPORTS

The second part of this chapter proposes to focus on the learning of adaptability and decision-making rather than presenting ready made "recipes." In sports, there is always a need to adjust for the active opponent trying to interfere with one's skill execution. In soccer, rugby, or similar invasion games, where continuous play is ensured by the rules of the game, resorting to play schema is rarely appropriate since, as the game unfolds, disorder settles rapidly. Tactical knowledge, then, comes into play.

To facilitate the learning of such tactics, we propose a combination of two teaching procedures. The first way to bring about game situations requiring adaptation and decision-making is to use, in various ways within the same sport, a *joker* playing the role of a support player. By analogy with card games, we call the "joker" a player to which specific roles have been assigned, after due transformation of the usual rules of the game. Pedagogically, the use of a joker is very significant for two reasons: First, beyond the simple change of rules, the specific location and role assigned to the joker force a subtly oriented adaptation on the part of the students for them to solve a new problem requiring both a strategic and tactical solution. Second, depending upon the specific role assigned to the joker, the teacher may choose to select a good or a poor player to play that role. In cases where the joker's role does not require good motor skills, assigning a poor player will do a lot of good to the student's ego and give him or her a chance to improve passing skills as well as decision-making. It should be clear for the reader that the expressions "joker" and "support player" will be used interchangeably; in the classroom, however, teachers should systematically use the expression "support player" since it is the joker's function within the team.

The second teaching procedure, aiming at getting students to recognize the similarities among different sports in term of tactical skills, consists in moving, in a short time interval and sometimes during the same class period, from one sport to another to facilitate a reappropriation of the tactical skills in a different context (i.e., other required motor skills, different rules, etc.) and therefore avoid too close an association between given tactical skills and one given sport.

One may wonder why so much emphasis is put on the development of decision-making and adaptation skills. If what is learned in physical education is to have any carry over value, though, one must recognize that a life-long practice of team sport calls for continuous adjustment:

- To various levels of one's ability over the years
- To different levels of players
- Sometimes, to different sports

Using a Joker in Different Team Sports During P.E. Classes

To illustrate the teaching process and the learning strategies resulting from the use of the teaching procedures described above, we now present a series of four exercises involving three team sports: European handball, soccer, and basketball. As alluded earlier, one way of increasing the learning outcomes is to provide opportunities for the students to articulate several sports. The players can analyze how they play the game from one sport to the other and can discuss tactical choices among themselves.

For each exercise, the reader will first find the principal action rule to be used or to be acquired by the students. Action rules (Gréhaigne, 1989; Gréhaigne & Godbout, 1995) refer to conditions to be looked for and to the elements of the game to be taken into consideration if one wants to ensure efficient action. Tactical knowledge about team sports basically rests upon such rules; their use allows a player to solve problems encountered during the game. Focusing on action rules is a choice that clearly favors the understanding of the action. After having stated the principal action rule at work, we will provide details about the organization for practice, about specific instructions, and about points for the teacher to observe.

The reader will note that the intent of such exercises is to have the students experience the advantages and difficulties inherent to each specific condition of play and to progressively discover which condition appears more efficient; eventually, in the regular practice of the sport, the search for such a condition will allow the application of the action rule. As proposed here, the use of such exercises is intended for the students to discover which condition of play works better and which tactics or strategy ought to be favored when a problematic condition of play is encountered.

Exercise 1: European Handball

Action rule: To score, the team must bring the ball rapidly ahead of the effective play space (a play space is any area where a group of players are effectively engaged in the action).

Organization for Practice The practice takes place on a 40 m × 20 m European handball field. Inside this area, there are six players against six players, with each team consisting of a goalkeeper, four regular players, and a support player (the joker).

Specific Instructions To force the action ahead to the effective play space and in open space, the support player is placed inside the 6-meter area. The ball must be given to the joker before a goal can be scored. The support player cannot score, and the goalkeeper must stay on the goal line.

Points for the Teacher to Observe When a team regains possession, the ball should reach the support player as quickly as possible.

Observe the quality of the first pass because it will determine whether the team stays in advance of the opponents. The players moving into open spaces should plan their run so as to receive the ball in front of them.

Exercise 2: European Handball This is the same exercise as exercise 1, with the same action rule, but now the goalkeeper is allowed to move and defend in the 6-meter zone with the usual rules for defense in European handball. The teacher will observe especially the counterattack when a team regains possession. Then, when the students appear to have learned and used this first action rule (bringing the ball rapidly ahead of the effective play space), the teacher can introduce other action rules, such as:

- Reducing the time to bring the ball in the scoring zone
- Moving away from opponents
- Moving into available intervals (free space between opponents)
- Moving behind the opponents' backs
- Using speed and temporal advantages (temporal advance)

By doing so, the teacher initiates tactical learning on the players' parts. Students are not given recipes to apply but are invited to consider the problem brought about by the specific setting, to discuss it within the team, and to decide upon some solution, thus constructing a collective action project.

Exercise 3: Soccer Then, in a second part of the class period, the teacher continues to focus on the learning of efficient action rules. The players apply the first action rule mentioned above but in connection with a different sport.
Action rule: To score, the team must bring the ball rapidly ahead of the effective play space.

Organization for Practice Outdoors, the practice takes place on a 50 m × 30 m surface with 6 m × 2 m goals. Inside this area, there are five players against five players, each team consisting of a goalkeeper, three regular players, and a support player (joker). Indoors, the game can be played on a European handball court but without goalkeepers (four players against four players).

Specific Instructions The teacher places the joker within the 6-meter area. The ball must be given to the support player before a shot at goal. The joker cannot score. When a team regains possession, the ball should reach the support player as quickly as possible.

Points for the Teacher to Observe

1. The quality of the last pass should be noted because the strikers must have time to adjust their location to shoot. Any player moving into an open space should arrive at a "favorable receiving angle" (Hughes, 1980, p. 76) with respect to the defender by outrunning him or her or by falling back.
2. The pass should be directed behind the defender and in front of the attacker.
3. The direction of the ball passed by the joker should be to the better foot of the striker in a face-to-face fashion (that is, in line with the player's run).

The interactions between teammates and opponents are numerous, and the role of the support player is critical. This third exercise should lead to a beginning of generalization with a positive transfer.

Exercise 4: Basketball
Action rule: Playing the ball ahead.

Organization for Practice The practice takes place on a basketball court. There are four players against four players, each team being made up of three regular players and a support player.

Specific Instructions To obtain a play located ahead of the effective play space, the teacher places the support player in a small area at the top of the key. The other players are not allowed to enter that area. The ball must be given to the support player before points can be scored, except in the case of an offensive rebound. The joker is not allowed to score.

Points for the Teacher to Observe.

1. The quality of both the first and the last passes.
2. The students should be shooting while moving forward.

The Management of a Class for Optimal Learning

Beyond some obvious differences, like attitude and morphology, a class of students is made up of unique and original individuals.

Teachers have to manage the learning of such a class-group, in which, at each moment, interactions between the individuals can modify individual or group behavior. The management and proper functioning of a class-group supposes that certain particularities be taken into consideration.

In relation to the teaching of team games and sports, one the first encountered problems resides in the constitution of work groups or teams. Not everybody is interested or wants to actively participate in the content being presented. This can be the result of girls and boys being in the same class, bad experiences in previous physical education classes, and so on. In teaching team games and sports, the grouping of students into different teams presents contradictory requirements, between stability and adaptability. One thing remains certain: When grouping students, the result of a confrontation shouldn't be determined by the teams' composition. How can a teacher use the diversity of his or her students as a positive element instead of perceiving it to be an obstacle? What are the principles of forming work groups that will promote the learning process of team games and sports? How does a teacher manage a classgroup composed of boys and girls in a games education setting?

To answer these questions, different perspectives from the physical education literature in relation to the grouping of students are presented, and an analysis of the advantages and disadvantages is put forward. Finally, the qualities, weaknesses, and potentials of student groupings will be discussed in light of specific confrontational problems in games education.

Team Dynamics The notion of *team dynamics* is presented based on the contributions found in international literature on sport pedagogy.

Contributions from Anglo-Saxon Literature "Team work is the essence of life" (Riley, 1993, p. 15). One of the most gratifying and exciting experiences for a team sport player or coach is to be part of a team that has cohesion and is successful. However, building an efficient team takes time and effort to achieve success. It is always a paradox to see a talented team performing with mediocrity because they cannot exploit their resources adequately when less-talented teams perform better because of a greater cohesion within the group. If too much energy is focused on developing and maintaining a group's cohesion, this energy expenditure is often unavailable for constructing a team's game play performance. Teammates must interact, work together toward common goals, adapt to various demands, and equilibrate personal aspirations to group objectives. This particular theme has not been addressed extensively in the sport psychology literature. Hence, there is a need to improve our comprehension of a team's functioning to have a better grasp of what types of systematic interventions can be developed in the early stages of team building.

Although all teams are considered to be composed of a group, all groups cannot be considered teams (Parker, 1990). Generally speaking, a team represents a certain type of group. Carron (1988, p. 7) explains that teams, in a sport setting, are characterized by a collective identity, an acute sense of collective objectives, structured interaction procedures, structured methods of communication, and personal and collective independent tasks.

Teams are in constant evolution, changing to adapt to internal and external factors. These changes can be minor and not perceivable or major and necessitate significant modifications. Carron (1988) suggests that the development of a team can be described by linear, pendular, or cyclic models. When a team develops itself, it can take different courses in relation to these models.

All teams want to be efficient and perform well. Efficiency can have different meanings, depending on the composition of a certain team. It depends on the prescribed task, resources, and the state of development of the team in question. The prescribed task could be related to game rules. The available team resources rest upon the knowledge and motor competencies of each team member. The variable "resource" specifies the type and the cost of available resources, while the prescribed task defines the team's needs in terms of resources and how these resources should be used. A group's state of development consists of the existing interpersonal relationships among the group's members and their influence on the group's performance (Sherif & Sherif, 1979). In particular, Hanson and Lubin (1986) insist on the engagement of team leaders for a team to be successful.

This relatively linear and continuous perspective of team development is somewhat different from a dialectical perspective that is more predominant in certain European schools of thought. The next section will address some of the predominant French perspectives.

The French Tradition To better situate a discussion on team building from a French perspective, different elements from the literature will be presented in relation to complexity, required variety, and opposition rapport. Finally, the team as a social organization will be the object of a distinct presentation.

The Notion of "Team" in a Team Sport Setting The psychosocial approach to the investigation of team dynamics was inspired by Lewin and his collaborators in the 1950's. From this approach, numerous studies on team dynamics, and its various components (its genesis, cohesion, climate, communication networks, psychological preparation, leadership styles, etc.) have been accomplished. Based on the abundance of accomplished work, here are but a few examples of authors and their main research interests:

- Rioux and Chapuis (1967; 1976) studied team cohesion.
- Anzieu and Martin (1968); Carron (1986): studied team cohesion.
- Mérand (1977) studied team sports as an original modality to study group dynamics. The dynamics within a group where individuals oppose each other is often characterized by the complexity of problems or obstacles put forward to hinder the opposing team's performance while trying to resolve the problems put forward by the opposing team.
- Gréhaigne (1989) studied the force ratio between two teams in a teaching-learning context. The force ratio, as defined previously in this book, is the antagonistic links that exist between players of opposing teams, which are due, in part, to the application of certain rules of play that determine interaction between teams. The essential elements in this research topic have provided the foundation of future study of the teaching-learning process in team sports.

Modified Games: A Case of Presenting Minimal Complexity A common theme in much of the team sport literature is related to the *collective dimension*. In his definition of team sports, Gréhaigne (1992) mentions that the force ratio is characterized by two groups confronting each other. In light of creating a teaching-learning context that is adequate in the construction of tactical competencies, it is proposed that modified games should be 3 vs. 3, which Gréhaigne considers to be the minimal number of players for a game to be considered a team game. Below this number of players, modified game situations represent various incomplete configurations of play when considering the confrontational aspect of team sports. Constructing complexity in team sports involves much more than going from a 1 vs. 1 situation to a 2 vs. 2 situation and so on. Three vs. three situations allow a teacher to construct learning scenarios where students have to go beyond binary choices—keeping the ball or passing it to his or her partner—to preserve an important aspect in team sports, which is playing without the ball. The ball or projectile confers to its handler a particular status composed of responsibilities concerning tactical choices.

Group Stability: A Question of History and Permanence In trying to understand a team sport player's behavior, one must assess this player in relation to the rest of the members of the team. A player's game responses are often the product of a situation's characteristics and the constraints and opportunities as he or she sees them. Taking into consideration a player's responses as pertinent is to rediscover a game situation and the unforeseeable responses it can generate. This process can help analyze the player–game interaction. The analysis of this interaction, through observation, can aid in determining how members of a given team can structure their cooperation for both offensive and defensive purposes.

Bernard (1963) described a team as a totality under construction. Both time and history are important elements in the genesis and life span of a team. In relation to physical education, Plummer and Rougeau (1997) insist on the necessity of analyzing the repartition of status and tasks within a group while systematically reserving adequate time for a group's regulation.

SPORT ETHICS

From an ethical point of view, succeeding in team sports means that rules must be considered a key element for game play. They are essential for advancing, yet also ensure the security of students. We must conceive of refereeing as an indispensable help to the understanding of play mechanisms.

Efficiency is an unavoidable aspect of the game and plays a central role in team sports, as in any sport. Most of the time, the result of a match determines winners and losers. Team sports must nevertheless remain a courteous and codified assault in which the presence of a referee, through its regulative function, reduces considerably the hazardous nature of a warlike confrontation. The very notion of "courteous assault" may force a smile. But in this case, an important aspect concerns the distinction between competition and emulation. The competition can introduce hostile relationships with other players when opponents are perceived as people to be dominated. Emulation represents a means to compare oneself to another player and to exchange with that player in considering who he or she is. Emulation is a source for success because it allows a comparative approach with the other to discover the similarities, the differences, and the progress one has made. Also, in educational contexts, the search for fair conditions of play, such as reasonably balanced teams, should constitute a background on which to select the learning objectives and the teaching procedures. Looking for the most efficient strategies and tactics should not lead to a victory-at-all-cost attitude because for the school it becomes a Pyrrhic victory. In this sense, the rightful place of ethics in the teaching of team sports and games needs to be considered.

The content in the first 11 chapters of this book has focused on the underlying theories that support a constructivist learning perspective in team sports and games. Our beliefs, knowledge and convictions regarding the teaching-learning process of sport-related games bring us to the presentation of the Tactical Decision Learning Model (TDLM). The TDLM promotes a student-centered model to games learning. In the present chapter we present factors to help you maximize the implementation and effect of the TDLM. Chapter 12 will focus on various aspects of research that need to be considered in order to continue our collective work relative toward building a better games theory for sport-related games teaching and learning.

12

RESEARCH AND DEVELOPMENT: WORKING TOWARD EVIDENCE-BASED PRACTICE

There is a gap between research on teaching and learning sport and teacher and coach practices and development. This gap between the institutional and scientific discourse and professional practices shows how difficult it is for knowledge to penetrate into the fields and courts where physical activity is taught. What are the specific and essential game knowledge structures that ought to be taught? How do teachers and coaches adapt the content in light of the development of efficient tactical and motor skills and movements in their students? On which precise basis is a given progression proposed, and more specifically, are the articulated levels determined by teachers? These types of questions go beyond the classical thoughts about the relationship between social practice and school practice.

Thus far we have examined the teaching of team sports in the light of a new team-sport didactic approach at school with a constructivist and cognitive approach. We have provided an overview of historical aspects concerning conceptions of teaching in team sports, and presented the *Tactical-Decision Learning Model* (TDLM) with reference to French and German literature. We also have provided you with a model of players' activity using invasion games. We have argued that the TDLM, the modeling of the practice, the team sport assessment procedure, and the observation tools discussed in this book appear to produce an objective, reliable, and valid indication for interpreting the player activity.

The purpose of this chapter is twofold. First we will argue for research and development work (i.e., data-based not data-free development) that should be pursued to develop the knowledge on a team sport learning-teaching system. From a novice status to that of an experienced player, there is a qualitative transformation. Rather than resting on incidental learning, we should seriously study this transformation process and strive to better understand how learners construct their competencies and their motor skills to make appropriate action during play. Second, we will present two theoretical frameworks that hold strong possibilities for more closely examining the strength of the TDLM. To accomplish this we need to consider the following:

1. We (i.e., teachers, coaches, teacher educators, and researchers) need to value field-based research. Field-based research, while messy and trying at times, needs to be an essential part of good development work, thus leading us toward evidence-based practice.
2. We should consider more programmatic research (that is, a plan under which small steps can be taken). This might involve a couple of institutions following a particular theoretical framework, each carrying out a shared but separate research agenda. We are not advocating that we all take this on, but this type of research could lead to more robust findings.
3. We must ground our research questions in a theoretical framework that can help lead to strong research designs and thus more robust findings.

Similar to the Teaching Games for Understanding (TGfU) model, the TDLM is centered on getting students engaged in a game-like manner and thinking about the tactical problem on which instruction is focused and designed to develop tactical awareness (i.e., decision-making) (Griffin, Mitchell, & Oslin, 1997). As with all teaching methodology TGFU makes some assumptions about how students learn (Rink, 2001).

To further our understanding of the TDLM, it is important to employ multiple theoretical perspectives in the design and interpretation of sport-related games research. We advocate two theoretical frameworks for information-processing theory and situated learning theory to investigate how individuals learn and how prior knowledge of subject matter (i.e., games) that learners bring to instruction influences the teaching and learning process.

EXPLORING THE DEVELOPMENT OF LEARNERS' GAME KNOWLEDGE

As research on games teaching and learning evolves, and as the debate concerning technical-versus-tactical approaches to games instruction subsides, sport pedagogues must begin to move forward and explore new and important avenues of study. As Rink (2001) argued, "when you spend all of your effort proving that a particular kind of teaching is better than another kind of teaching, you limit what you can learn about the very complex teaching/learning process" (p. 123). Grounding work in learning theories that underlie different teaching methods and approaches to teaching will enable researchers, teachers, and curriculum experts to create a knowledge base that extends beyond identifying direct links between what a teacher does and what a student learns to begin to test the assumptions of different methodologies. For instance, in the case of TDLM, application of a theory of learning may enable researchers to ask questions that examine the assumptions the model. For example, does the constructivist nature of this model lend itself to more motivated learners? How do learners construct knowledge of games, strategies, tactics, and decision-making in games?

Sport pedagogy researchers have argued that instructional strategies should be based on learning theory because without a clear understanding of how students and teachers learn, one cannot expect to achieve intended learning outcomes (Kirk & MacPhail, 2002; Rink, 2001). Researchers with a learning orientation put an emphasis on understanding what students know, can do, and bring to sport-related games (prior knowledge) and how their knowledge changes as a function of games instruction (Griffin & Placek, 2001).

Information-processing theory from cognitive psychology provides a theoretical framework for investigating domain-specific knowledge and contributes to ideas of what learners know and how they learn cognitive aspects of movement activities. Information processing suggests that humans represent the world through knowledge structures stored in long-term, intermediate, and short-term memory (Shuell, 1986). These knowledge structures are formed by gathering and combining forms of new information and then by relating the newly acquired information to prior knowledge already stored as representations in long-term memory (Sternberg, 1984). These knowledge structures consist of nodes that represent particular concepts, facts, or theories and relate hierarchically to other nodes in an array of relationships (Anderson, 1976; Dodds, Griffin, & Placek, 2001).

Information-processing research reports that complex knowledge structures internally represent the outside world and can be changed under various conditions over time (Dodds et al., 2001). Further, knowledge can be broadly characterized as declarative, procedural, conditional, and strategic (Alexander & Judy, 1988; Anderson, 1976). Sport pedagogy research reveals that individuals may simultaneously be highly knowledgeable about some aspects of sport and physical education while far less knowledgeable about others. For example, individuals in a physical education setting in the same class in school will differ greatly in their knowledge structures of sport-related games. A student could be highly knowledgeable about the tactics involved in invasion games while their knowledge structures relating to the tactics of net/wall games may contain many gaps.

From a perspective related more directly to instruction, Gréhaigne and colleagues' theoretical papers have explored players' acquisition and use of knowledge, expanding our views of how to teach strategic and tactical knowledge in the context of game play. Drawing on the motor learning and control research, Gréhaigne & Godbout (1995) proposed that games involve teams operating as competency networks engaged in high strategy sports (e.g., invasion or net/wall games) against opponents in a contest and that learning occurs for both individuals and teams.

Four components of games (cooperation with teammates, opposition to opponents, attacking opponents' space, and defending a team's own space) can be taken as highly sophisticated goal structures using forms of declarative and procedural knowledge (Gréhaigne, Godbout, & Bouthier, 1999). Gréhaigne et al. reiterate the importance of strategic and tactical knowledge as key components of expert game play. They assert that these can be taught by carefully structuring learning environments to facilitate use of players' knowledge structures when representing and solving problems related to game play, thus expanding their knowledge structures. They also explored more specifically the role of decision-making during game play (Gréhaigne, Godbout, & Bouthier, 2001), concluding that decisions are grounded in dynamic, fluid configurations of game play related to player positions and the location of the ball. These concepts are amenable to an information-processing interpretation in that players use appropriate cues from the environment (e.g., game play) to activate portions of their knowledge structure so that appropriate responses are selected and executed.

Motor learning researchers have used the information-processing perspective to study expert–novice sport performance. The following is a summary of their research findings.

- Expert performers plan, while novice performers "wait and see."
- Expert performers continuously monitor relevant current and past responses and build and modify their game status. Novice performers react to game events rather than plan for response selection (McPherson, 1999a; McPherson, 1999b).
- Expert performers use a specific approach to problem solving that is highly contextual while novice performers use a global approach to problem solving (McPherson & Thomas, 1989).
- Expert performers process information at a deeper, more tactical level, while novice performers process events in the environment or surface features of a game situation (McPherson & Thomas, 1989).
- Expert performers make faster and more accurate decisions, while novice performers have slower access to the information needed to make accurate decisions.
- Expert performers have specialized search and retrieval abilities (if-then-do statements) from game situations and long-term memories, while novice performers do not have these abilities or the game experiences to draw from in their long-term memories (Rink, French, & Tjeerdsma, 1996; McPherson & Thomas, 1989).
- Expert performers will (a) have high success at performing skills correctly during games, (b) perform effortlessly and more automatically (i.e., make it look easy), (c) show greater consistency and adaptability in performing movement patterns, and (d) be better at monitoring their own performance as well as detecting and correcting errors (Rink et al., 1996).
- In early work Thomas, French, and McPherson suggested that knowledge and decision-making processes may develop faster than motor skills (French & Thomas, 1987; McPherson & French, 1991; McPherson & Thomas, 1989). They believe now that this assertion is wrong in that knowledge and the decision-making develop much more slowly (French & McPherson, in press).
- Different instructional approaches produce different knowledge representations that influence the performers' views and interpretations of game events (French & Thomas, 1987; French, Spurgeon, & Nevett, 1995; Werner; Rink et al., 1996; French, Werner, Taylor, Hussey, Jones, 1996; McPherson & French, 1991; McPherson, 1994).

We believe that the understanding and development of learners' domain-specific knowledge provides us, as teachers and researchers, with an additional means to facilitate learning and to find out what children know about physical education at the outset of instruction and as instruction unfolds over time (Griffin & Placek, 2001). This strategy acknowledges that learners are active participants in the teaching-learning process (Weinstein & Mayer, 1986) and come to every new learning experience with some knowledge about the topic already established. In a physical education context, players' knowledge is important in building overall game skills, knowing what to do and under which conditions to do it, knowing how to perform particular motor skill components of the game, and knowing how to apply these skills tactically and strategically during game play.

Viewing the learning process with information-processing theory and research demonstrates just how complex the instructional environment is and the difficulty teachers are faced with to facilitate learning (Dodds et al., 2001). Thus, researchers need to continue to explore the various kinds of knowledge that learners hold and the interactions and relationships among those kinds of knowledge as they study various pedagogical approaches.

SITUATED LEARNING THEORY

Situated learning has also emerged as a framework to theorize and analyze pedagogical practices in physical education (Kirk & Macdonald, 1998; Kirk & MacPhail, 2002). Individuals are considered part of a holistic learning enterprise, not as acting or participating in isolation. The assumptions and organizing structures of the TDLM allows for participation to occur in a student-centered "learning curriculum" as opposed to a teacher-centered "teaching curriculum" (Lave & Wenger, 1991, p. 97). This view of a learning-centered curriculum moves the teacher off center stage and provides an opportunity for the student (i.e., learner) to help other students learn. Situated learning theory can be used to explore the potential of the TDLM as a valuable system for invasion games learning. As set forth by Kirk and Macdonald (1998), situated learning theory is conceptualized as one component of a broader constructivist theory of learning in physical education. Lave and Wenger (1991) posit that in this mode of learning, the mastering of knowledge and skills requires that novices move toward more advanced participation (full participation) in the sociocultural practices of the community.

Perkins (1999) emphasized three tenets of constructivism: the active learner, the social learner, and the creative learner. As active learners, students are not passive recipients of knowledge but are involved in tasks that stimulate decision-making, critical thinking, and problem solving. As social learners, students construct knowledge through social interaction with their peers, facilitated by their teachers. As creative learners, students are guided to discover knowledge themselves and to create their own understanding of the subject matter. Individuals draw on prior knowledge and experiences to construct knowledge.

Situated learning provides an authentic framework in which to position teaching and learning in physical education. Situated learning theory investigates the relationships among the various physical, social, and cultural dimensions of the context of learning (Lave & Wenger, 1991). Social and cultural contexts contribute to and influence what is learned and how learning takes place. Lave and Wenger (1991) discuss "legitimate peripheral participation within a community of practice" as a key concept for situated learning theory. They refer to legitimate peripheral participation as participation that occurs within sets of relationships in which "newcomers" can move toward "full participation" by being involved in particular experiences or practices, and this develops new sets of relationships. Learning is not the reception of factual knowledge or information, but rather the legitimate (genuine) peripheral (complex interplay of persons, activity, knowledge, and the social world) participation (activity toward a specific task/goal). Lave and Wenger (1991) state that legitimate peripheral participation "obtains its meaning, not in a concise definition of its boundaries, but in its multiple, theoretically generative interconnections with persons, activities, knowing, and world" (p. 121).

Kirk & Macdonald (1998) provide a useful explanation of community of practice. "We understand the notion of community of practice to refer to any collectivity or group who together contribute to shared or public practices in a particular sphere of life" (p. 380). The social and cultural situation of the teaching environment contributes significantly to what is learned and how learning takes place (Kirk & Macdonald 1998). We argue that TDLM can provide structures for situated learning to occur within a community of practice based on the meaningful, purposeful, and authentic tasks presented and practiced by students. Legitimate peripheral participation is intended to convey the sense of authentic, meaningful, and purposeful participation by students in an activity. Learning takes place in the interactive social world within social practices or interpersonal relationships that are in the process of production, reproduction, transformation, and change (Lave & Wenger, 1991). Kirk and Macdonald (1998) have argued that "school physical education may regularly and consistently *fail* to provide young people with the opportunity for legitimate peripheral participation in a community of practice of exercise, and physical recreation" (p. 382).

Constructivist and situated learning perspectives have been endorsed as providing a potentially useful reconceptualization of existing approaches to teaching and learning in physical education (Chen & Rovegno, 2000; Dodds, Griffin, & Placek, 2001; Ennis, 2000; Rovegno & Bandhauer, 1997; Kirk & Macdonald, 1998; Rovegno & Kirk, 1995). TDLM has the potential to represent situated learning within a social constructivist theoretical framework.

Guiding Pedagogical Principles

Practitioners need to take into account several pedagogical considerations when implementing the TDLM: (a) The teacher/coach is a facilitator, (b) students are active learners, (c) students work in small groups and with modified games, (d) learning activities are authentic and developmentally appropriate, (e) learning activities are interesting and challenging, and (f) students are held accountable (Dyson, Griffin, & Hastie, 2004).

- **The teacher or coach as a facilitator.** As the facilitator, the teacher sets problems or goals, and students are given an opportunity to seek solutions to these problems. Solutions to the problem are identified through a questioning process, and these solutions then become the focus of a situated practice. The teacher also facilitates the practice by either simplifying or challenging students based on their abilities. In this way the teacher is working with the students' prior knowledge to develop new knowledge. The teacher guides the instruction and curriculum as a facilitator of learning.
- **Students are active learners.** In TDLM students have a high rate of engagement. Students take responsibility for organization and management and take on leadership roles. Teachers delegate responsibility so that more students can talk and work together on multiple learning tasks. Therefore students have positions of responsibility. The teacher is not at the center of instruction and students are active learners, creative learners, and social learners (Perkins, 1999).

- **Students work in groups or modified games.** Grouping is usually heterogeneous in small groups or teams. The behaviors required in cooperative small groups are radically different from those required in traditional classroom settings (Cohen, 1994). Modifying the games allows students to practice their skills and decision-making in "real," game-like situations. Having the teacher emphasize authentic performance puts students in an active learning situation (Darling-Hammond, 1997). For an activity to be considered authentic in physical education, it must involve some form of observable performance (Wiggins, 1993).
- **Learning activities are interesting and challenging.** When learning activities are either interesting or challenging to students, they are more likely to be satisfying or even enjoyable. The discovery of solutions to various learning activities requires that students contribute to the group or team task.
- **Students are held accountable.** Assessment is an ongoing part of instruction, and students are provided with continuous feedback for reflecting on and problem solving about games or physical activity experiences. Assessment should be authentic and aligned with specific tactical problems to be solved.

IMPLICATIONS FOR LEARNING AND INSTRUCTION

From the research base using the information-processing perspective, French and McPherson (2004) provide what they refer to as "best guess approaches" to sport-related games learning. First, teachers and coaches should design game play situations so that students must make decisions that should be repeated many times. Second, teachers and coaches should use questions to gain insight and information from students about what they are processing or not processing. Finally, we have argued that situated learning, a community of practice based on the meaningful, purposeful, and authentic learning activities presented and practiced by students, also provides a strong theory from which to explore a games learning teaching system (Kirk & Macdonald, 1998; Kirk & MacPhail, 2002; Lave & Wenger, 1991).

Much more research and development work is needed to understand how to facilitate the development of game knowledge. A challenging but important question is to explore what types of learning situations (i.e., games or practice) elicit what types of improvement in game performance (i.e., decision-making and execution) (French & McPherson, 2004).

Application of a better theory for games learning has implications for sport pedagogy researchers, teachers, and coaches and for the students. First, application of theory may add to the limited knowledge of how teachers, coaches, and students learn games and will aid in curriculum development and better ways of teaching games.

Teachers and coaches who know more about the prior knowledge their students or players bring to class have better opportunities to provide a quality learning environment that extends and deepens that knowledge during instruction. When teachers and coaches understand students' knowledge structures, which include nodes and relationships among them, they can build on what students already know, making bridges to new learning. Physical educators and coaches, whose curricula largely rely on games in various forms (Rovegno, Nevett, & Barbiarz, 2001), could thus design learning tasks that challenge students to increase and better connect their knowledge of rules, strategies and tactics, motor skill selection and execution, and decision-making in games contexts.

Physical education teachers and coaches can consider students' prior knowledge to identify gaps in students' knowledge structures so that instruction and practice opportunities can be tailored to address these. For example, teachers who know students lack a particular aspect of tactical knowledge might design and cater instruction to fill this knowledge void.

Finally, a better theory for games learning has implications for students and players. As physical education teachers and coaches learn how to access students' prior knowledge structures, they will have a more complete picture of where gaps exist within groups of students' knowledge, and they may become more adept at providing challenging learning environments that will facilitate students' learning and skillfulness. As students gain expertise in games, they are more likely to enjoy the activity and to include participation outside school contexts in their daily lives, thus strengthening the possibility of lifelong participation in games and other physical activities.

Bibliography

AEEPS (1977). Sports co n° 3. Paris : Amicale ENSEPS.

Alexander, P., & Judy, J. (1988). The interaction of domain-specific and strategic knowledge in academic performance. *Review of Educational Research, 58*, 375–404.

Ali, A. H. (1988). Statistical analysis of tactical movement patterns in association football. In T. Reilly, A. Lees, K. Davids, & W. J. Murphy (Eds.) *Science and football* (pp. 302–308). London : E. & F.N. SPON.

Ali, A.H., & Farraly, M. (1990). An analysis of patterns of play in soccer. *Science and football, 3*, 37–44.

Allal, L., Cardinet, J., & Perrenoud, P. (1979). *L'évaluation formative dans un enseignement différencié* [Formative assessment in a differentiated teaching]. Berne: Peter Lang.

Allison, S., & Thorpe, R. (1997). A comparison of the effectiveness of two approaches to teaching games within physical education. A skill approach versus a game for understanding approach. *British Journal of Physical Education*, Autumn 1997.

Almond, L. (1986a) Primary and secondary rules in games. In R. Thorpe, D. Bunker, & L. Almond (Eds.), *Rethinking games teaching* (pp. 73–74). Loughborough, England: Loughborough University of Technology.

Almond, L. (1986b) Reflecting on themes: A games classification. In R. Thorpe, D. Bunker, & L. Almond (Eds.), *Rethinking games teaching* (pp. 71–72). Loughborough, England: Loughborough University of Technology.

Amicale des Anciens Élèves de l'ENSEPS. (1966). Des colloques de Vichy 1964–1965. *Éducation Physique et Sport, 78*, 19–73.

Anderson, J. R. (1976). *Language, memory, and thought*. Hillsdale, NJ: Erlbaum.

Andreewsky, E. (1991). *Systémique & cognition* [Systemics & cognition]. Paris: Dunod.

Anzieu, D., Martin, J. Y. (1968). *La dynamique des groupes restreints*. Paris: PUF.

Atlan, H. (1979). *Entre le cristal et la fumée*. Paris: Seuil.

Bailey, L., & Almond, L. (1983). Creating change: By creating games? In L. Spackman (Ed.), *Teaching games for understanding* (pp. 56–59). Cheltenham, England: The College of St. Paul and St. Mary.

Barbier, J. M. (1996). *Savoirs théoriques et savoirs d'action*. Paris: PUF.

Barrow, H. M., McGee, R., & Tritschler, K. A. (1989). *Practical measurement in physical education and sport* (4th ed.). Philadelphia: Lea & Febiger.

Barth, B. (1994). Strategie und Taktik im Wettkampfsport. *Leistungssport, 3*, 4–14.

Baumgartner, T. A., & Jackson, A. S. (1991). *Measurement and evaluation in physical education and exercise science* (4th ed.). Dubuque, IA: Wm. C. Brown.

Bayer, C. (1979). *L'enseignement des jeux sportifs collectifs* [The teaching of team sport games]. Paris: Vigot.

Bernard, M. (1963). Une interprétation dialectique de la dynamique de l'équipe. *Éducation Physique et Sport, 62-63*, 7–11.

Bertalanffy, L. V. (1972). *Théorie générale des systèmes*. Paris: Dunod.

Blomquist, M.T., Luhtanen, P., Laakso, L., & Keskinen, E. (2000). Validation of a video-based game–understanding test procedure in badmitton. *Journal of Teaching in Physical Education, 19*, 325–337.

Boudreau, P. (1987). *L'évaluation par les pairs. Une étude de sa justesse et de son influence sur l'apprentissage d'une activité physique (hockey)* [Peer assessment. A study on its reliability and its impact on the learning of a physical activity (hockey)]. Unpublished master's thesis, Université Laval, Québec, Canada.

Bourdieu, P. (1972). *Esquisse d'une théorie de la pratique*. Genèva, Switzerland: Droz.

Bourdieu, P. (1980). *Le sens pratique*. Paris: Minuit.

Bouthier, D. (1984). *Sports collectifs: Contribution à l'analyse de l'activité et éléments pour une formation tactique essentielle. L'exemple du rugby* [Team sports: Contribution to the analysis of the activity and elements of essential tactical learning]. Paris: INSEP.

Bouthier, D. (1986). Comparaison expérimentale des effets de différents modèles didactiques des sports collectifs [Experimental comparison of the effects of different didactic models in team sports]. In *E.P.S.-Contenus et didactique* (pp. 85–89). Paris: SNEP.

Bouthier, D. (1988). *Les conditions cognitives de la formation d'actions sportives collectives*. [Cognitive conditions for learning in team sports]. Unpublished doctoral dissertation, Université Paris V, Paris, France.

Bouthier, D. (1989). Les conditions cognitives de la formation d'actions sportives collectives. [Cognitive conditions for learning in team sports]. *Le Travail Humain, 52*(2), 175–182.

Bouthier, D. (1993). *L'approche technologique en STAPS; représentations et actions en didactique des APS*. [Technological approach in STAPS; Representation and actions in sport and physical activities]. Habilitation à diriger les recherches, Université de Paris 11, Orsay, France.

Bouthier, D., & Durey, A. (1994). Technologie des APS. *Impulsion, 1*, 95–120.

Bouthier, D., & Reitchess, S. (1984). *Contenus et évaluation en sports collectifs*. Paris: C.R.D.P.

Bouthier, D., & Savoyant, A. (1984). A contribution to the learning of a collective action; The counter attack in rugby. *Journal of Sport Psychology, 15*(1), 25–34.

Bouthier, D., David, B., & Eloi, S. (1994). Analysis of representations and patterns of tactical decisions in team games: A methodological approach. In J. Nistch & R. Seiler (Eds.), *Motor control and motor learning* (pp. 126–134). Sankt Augustin: Academic Verlag.

Bouthier, D., Pastré, P., & Samurçay, R. (1995). Le développement des compétences. Analyse du travail et didactique professionnelle. [The development of competencies. Analysis of work and professional didactics]. *Éducation Permanente, 123*.

Brackenridge, C. (1979). *Games: Classification and analysis*. Conference presented to the Kirkless Teachers.

Bransford, J. D., Brown, A. L., & Cocking, R. R. (Eds.). (2000). *How people learn—Brain, mind, experience and school*. Washington, D. C.: National Academy Press.

Brechbuhl, J., Bronckart, J. P., & Joannisse, R. (1988). Contribution à une didactique du sport [Contribution to sport didactics]. *Université de Genève. Cahier de la section des sciences de l'éducation-Pratiques et théorie, 49*, 1–145.

Brousseau, G. (1986). *Fondements et méthodes en didactique des mathématiques*. Grenoble, France: La Pensée Sauvage.

Brown, E. W. (1982). Visual evaluation techniques for skill analysis. *Journal of Physical Education and Recreation, 53*(1), 21–26, 29.

Bunker, D. & Thorpe, R (1982). A model for teaching of games in the secondary schools. *Bulletin of Physical Education, 10*, 9–16.

Bunker, D., & Thorpe, R. (1983). A model for the teaching of games in secondary schools. *Bulletin of Physical Education, 18*(1), 5–8.

Bunker, D., & Thorpe, R. (1986). Is there a need to reflect on our games teaching? In R. Thorpe, D. Bunker, & L. Almond (Eds.), *Rethinking games teaching* (pp. 25–33). Loughborough, England: Loughborough University of Technology.

Bunker, D., & Thorpe, R. (1986a). The curriculum model. In R. Thorpe, D. Bunker, & L. Almond (Eds.), *Rethinking games teaching* (pp. 7–10). Loughborough, England: Loughborough University of Technology.

Butler, J., Griffin, L., Lombardo, B., & Nastasi, R. (2003). *Teaching for understanding in physical education and sport.* Oxon Hill: AAPHERD Publications.

Caillois, R. (1961). Man, play and games. New York: Free Press of Glencoe.

Cam, Y., Crunelle, J., Giana, E., Grosgeorge, B., & Labiche, J. (1979). *Basket-ball. Mémento du CPS FSGT.* Paris: Sport et Plein Air.

Cardinet, J. (1986). *Évaluation scolaire et mesure.* Brussels: De Boeck.

Caron, J., & Pelchat, C. (1975). *Apprentissage des sports collectifs, hockey et basket* [Learning of team sports, hockey and basketball].Québec : PUQ.

Carron, A. V. (1988). *Group in sport: Theoretical and practical issues.* London, Ontario: Spodym.

Caverni, J. P. (1988). La verbalisation comme source d'observables pour l'étude du fonctionnement cognitif [Verbalization as an observationable source of information about cognitive process]. In J.P. Caverni, C. Bastien, P. Mendelsohn, & G. Tiberghien (Eds.), *Psychologie cognitive: Modèles et méthodes* [Cognitive psychology: Models and methods] (pp. 253–273). Grenoble, France: Presses Universitaires.

Caverni, J. P., Bastien, C., Mendelsohn, P., & Tiberghien, G. (1988). *Psychologie cognitive: Modèles et méthodes.* Grenoble, France: Presses Universitaires.

Chamberlain, C. J., & Coelho, A. J. (1993). The perceptual side of actions: Decision making in sport. In J. J. Starkes and F. Allard (Eds.), *Cognitive issues in motor expertise* (pp. 135–157). Elsevier Science Publishers B.V.

Chen, W., & Rovegno, I. (2000). Examination of expert teachers' constructivist-orientated teaching practices using a movement approach to physical education. *Research Quarterly for Exercise and Sport, 71*, 357–372.

Cobb, P. (1986). Making mathematics: Children's learning and the constructivist tradition. *Harvard Educational Review, 56*, 301–306.

Cohen, E. G. (1994). Restructuring in the classroom: Conditions for productive small groups. *Review of Educational Research, 64*, 1–35.

Cohen, E. G., & Lotan, R. A. (1997). *Working for equity in heterogeneous classrooms: Sociological theory in practice.* New York: Teachers College Press.

Corbin, C.B. (2000). Physical activity for everyone: What every physical educator should know about promoting lifelong physical activity. *Journal of Teaching in Physical Education, 21*, 128–144.

Darling-Hammond, L. (1997). *The right to learn.* San Francisco, Jossey-Bass.

Dassé, B. (1986). *Étude sur la capacité d'élèves à mesurer des habiletés motrices de leurs pairs et influence sur l'apprentissage.* [A study of students' capacity of assessing their peers' motor skills and impact on learning]. Unpublished master's thesis, Université Laval, Québec, Canada.

David, B. (1993). *Place et rôle des représentations dans la mise en oeuvre didactique d'une activité physique et sportive: L'exemple du rugby.* Thèse (nouveau régime). Université Paris-Sud, Paris, France.

Davids, K., Handford, C., and Williams, M. (1994). The natural alternative to cognitive theories of motor behaviour: An invitation for interdisciplinary research in sport science? *Journal of Sports Sciences, 12*, 495–528.

Davisse, A., & Louveau, C. (1991). *Sports, école, société: La part des femmes.* Paris: Actio.

De Montmollin, M. (1986). *L'intelligence de la tâche: éléments d'ergonomie cognitive*. Bern, Switzerland: Peter Lang.

Deleplace, R. (1966). *Le rugby* [Rugby Union]. Paris: Armand Colin Bourrelier.

Deleplace, R. (1979). *Rugby de mouvement—Rugby total* [Rugby in movement—Total rugby]. Paris: Éducation Physique et Sport.

Deleplace, R. (1992). Phases statiques: Lancement du jeu par les lignes arrières. In AEEPS, Marciac 91 (Ed.), *Les forums du rugby* (pp. 11–27). Paris: AEEPS.

Deleplace, R. (1995). *Logique du jeu et conséquences sur l'entraînement à la tactique*. Communication orale "Colloque sport collectif," Paris: INSEP.

Deriaz, D. & Poussin, B. (2001). Plan d'Études: Éducation physique. Genève: cycle d'orientation de l'enseignement secondaire, département de l'Instruction Publique.

Deriaz, D., Poussin, B., & Gréhaigne, J. F. (1998). Le débat d'idées. *Éducation physique et sport, 273*, 80–82.

Desrosiers, P., Genet-Volet, Y., & Godbout, P. (1997). Teachers' assessment practices viewed through the instruments used in physical education classes. *Journal of Teaching in Physical Education, 16*, 211–228.

Diaz, J. C. (1983). *Problèmes posés par l'apprentissage du rugby chez de jeunes enfants, l'exemple d'une situation de un contre un*. Mémoire de Maîtrise en STAPS. Université Paris V, Paris, France.

Dodds, P., Griffin, L. L., & Placek, J. H. (2001). A selected review of the literature on the development of learners' domain-specific knowledge. *Journal of Teaching in Physical Education [Monograph], 20*, 301–313.

Dugrand, M. (1985). Approches théorique, expérimentale et clinique de l'enseignement du football. L'exemple au Sénégal. Thèse de troisième cycle, Université de Caen, Caen, France.

Dugrand, M. (1989). *Le football: De la transparence à la complexité* [Soccer: From transparency to complexity]. Paris: PUF.

Durand, M. (1989). Transversalité et progressivité des apprentissages en Éducation Physique et Sportive. *Actes de l'Université d'Été de Dijon*, September 1989.

Dyson, B., Griffin, L. L., & Hastie, P. (in press). Theoretical and pedagogical considerations for implementing sport education, tactical games, and cooperative learning instructional models. *Quest*.

Ennis, C.D. (2000). Canaries in the coal mine: Responding to disengaged students using theme-based curricula. *Quest, 52*, 119–130.

Ericsson, K. A. (1996). *The road to excellence: The acquisition of expert performance in the arts and science, sports, and games*. Mahwah, NJ: Lawrence Elbaum.

Ericsson, K. A., & Charness, N. (1994). Expert Performance. Its structure and acquisition. *American Psychology, 49*, 725–747.

Ericsson, K. A., & Simon, H. A. (1993). *Protocol analysis: Verbal reports as data* (rev. ed.). Cambridge, MA: MIT Press.

Ericsson, K. A., Krampe, R. T. & Tesch-Römer, C. (1993). The role of deliberate practice in the acquisition of expert performance. *Psychological Review, 100*, 3, 363–406.

Famose, J. P. (1996). Les recherches actuelles sur l'apprentissage moteur [Present research on motor learning]. *Dossier EPS, 28*.

French K. E., & McPherson, S. L. (1999). Adaptations in response selection processes used during sport competition with increasing age and expertise. *International Journal of Sport Psychology, 30*, 173–193.

French, K. E., & McPherson, S. L. (2004). The development of expertise. In M. R. Weiss (Ed.), *Developmental Sport and Exercise Psychology: A Lifespan Perspective*. Morgantown, WV: Fitness Information Technology.

French, K., & Thomas, J. (1987). The relation of knowledge development to children's basketball performance. *Journal of Sport Psychology, 9*, 15–32.

French, K., Spurgeon, J., & Nevett, M. (1995). Expert-novice differences in cognitive and skill execution components of youth baseball performance. *Research Quarterly for Exercise and Sport, 66,* 194–201.

French, K. E., Werner, P. H., Taylor, K., Hussey, K.,& Jones, J. (1996). The effects of a 6-week unit of tactical, skill, or combined tactical and skill instruction on badminton performance of ninth-grade students. *Journal of Teaching in Physical Education, 15,* 439–463.

French, K., Nevett, M., Spurgeon, J., Graham, K., Rink, J., & McPherson, S. (1996). Knowledge and problem solution in youth baseball. *Research Quarterly for Exercise and Sport, 67,* 386–395.

Gardner, H. (1992). Assessment in context: The alternative to standardized testing. In B.R. Gifford, & M.C. O'Connor (Eds.), *Changing assessments-Alternative view of aptitude, achievement and instruction* (pp. 77–119). Boston: Kluwer Academic Publishers.

Giordan, A., & De Vecchi, G. (1987). Les origines du savoir. Neuchâtel: Delachaux & Niestlé.

Godbout, P. (1990). Observational strategies for the rating of motor skills: Theoretical and practical implications. In M. Lirette, C. Paré, J. Dessureault, & M. Piéron (Eds.), *Physical education and coaching—Present state and outlook for the future* (pp. 209– 221).

Goirand, P. (1993). Règles ou principes d'action en EPS [Rules or principles of action in physical education]? Lyon, France: *Spirales 6,* 143–159.

Good, T. (1996). Teaching effects and teacher evaluation. In J. Sikula, T.J. Buttery, & E. Guyton (Eds.), *Handbook of research on teacher education* (2nd edition, pp. 617–665). New York: Simon & Schuster.

Good, T., & Brophy, J. (1994). *Looking in classroom* (6th ed.). New York: Harper Collins.

Gréhaigne, J. F. (1988). Game systems in soccer. In T. Reilly, A. Lees, K. Davids, & W. J. Murphy (Eds.), *Science and Football* (pp. 316–321). London: E. & F.N. SPON.

Gréhaigne, J. F. (1989). *Football de mouvement. Vers une approche systémique du jeu* [Soccer in movement. Towards a systemic approach of the game]. Unpublished doctoral dissertation. Université de Bourgogne, Dijon, France.

Gréhaigne, J. F. (1992). *L'organisation du jeu en football* [The organisation of play in soccer]. Paris: ACTIO.

Gréhaigne, J. F. (1992a). Modélisation pondérée de l'attaque du but en football. In M. Laurent J.F. Marini, R. Pfister, & P. Therme (Eds.), *Les performances motrices: Approche multidisciplinaire.* (pp. 521–529). Paris: Actio/Université d'Aix—Marseille II.

Gréhaigne, J. F. (1992b). Les représentations du jeu en sport collectif et leurs conséquences sur l'apprentissage [Representations of play in team sports and their consequences for learning]. In J. Colomb (Ed.), *Recherche en didactique: Contribution à la formation des maîtres* (pp. 148–158). Paris: INRP.

Gréhaigne, J. F. (1994). Analyse comparative de deux types d'enseignement des sports collectifs : approche centrée sur la technique et approche centrée sur le jeu. *Rapport de Recherche.* IUFM de Franche-Comté.

Gréhaigne, J. F. (1994a). Quelques aspects bibliographiques concernant l'enseignement des sports collecifs à l'école. *E.P.S., Dossier 17,* 12–15.

Gréhaigne, J. F. (1995). Des exemples de pratiques d'évaluation pour les jeux sportifs collectifs [Examples of assessment practices in team sports]. *Revue de l'Éducation Physique, 35,* 125–134.

Gréhaigne, J. F. (1996). Les règles d'actions: Un support pour les apprentissages [Action rules: A support for learning]. *Éducation Physique et Sport, 265,* 71–73.

Gréhaigne, J. F. (1997). *Modélisation du jeu de football et traitement didactique des jeux sportifs collectifs* [Modeling of play in soccer and didactic treatment of team sports]. Habilitation à diriger les recherches, Université de Paris 11, Orsay, France.

Gréhaigne, J. F., & Bouthier, D. (1994). Analyse des évolutions entre deux configurations du jeu en football. *Science et Motricité, 24,* 44–52.

Gréhaigne, J. F., & Cadopi, M. (1990). Apprendre en éducation physique. In AEEPS (Ed.), *Éducation physique et didactique des APS* (pp. 17–24). Paris: AEEPS.

Gréhaigne, J. F., & Godbout P. (1995). Tactical knowledge in team sports from a constructivist and cognitivist perspective. *Quest, 47,* 490–505.

Gréhaigne, J. F., & Godbout, P. (1997). The teaching of tactical knowledge in team sports. *Journal of Canadian Association for Physical Education, Recreation and Dance, 63*(4), 10–15.

Gréhaigne, J. F., & Godbout, P. (1998). Formative assessment in team sports with a tactical approach. *Journal of Physical Education, Recreation and Dance, 69*(1), 46–51.

Gréhaigne, J. F., & Godbout, P. (1999). Observation, critical thinking and transformation: Three key elements for a constructivist perspective of the learning process in team sports. In R.S. Feingold, C.R. Rees, G.T. Barrette, L. Fiorentino, S. Virgilio, & E. Kowalski (Eds.), *Education for life* (pp. 109–118). Garden City, NY: Adelphi University.

Gréhaigne, J. F., & Godbout, P. (1999a). La prise de décision de l'élève en sport collectif. In J.F. Gréhaigne, N. Mahut, & D. Marchal (Eds.), *Qu'apprennent les élèves en faisant des activités physiques et sportives ?* [CD-ROM]. (Dossier Symposia, 2). Besançon: IUFM, Université de Franche-Comté.

Gréhaigne, J. F., & Guillon, R. (1991). Du bon usage des règles d'action [Making good use of action rules]. *Echanges et controverses, 4,* 43–66.

Gréhaigne, J. F., & Laroche, J. Y. (1994). Quelques fondements et présupposés théoriques d'une démarche [Some theoretical bases and assumptions of an approach]. *E.P.S., Dossier 17,* 12–15.

Gréhaigne, J. F., & Roche, J. (1990). Quelques questions à propos du football [A few questions concerning soccer].In AEEPS (Ed.), *Education physique et didactique des APS* (pp. 63–72). Paris: AEEPS.

Gréhaigne, J. F., & Roche, J. (1993). Les sports collectifs au bac [Team sports in "baccalauréat"]. *Education Physique et Sport, 240,* 80–83.

Gréhaigne, J. F., Billard, M., & Laroche, J. Y. (1999). *L'enseignement des jeux sportifs collectifs à l'école. Conception, construction, évaluation.* Brussels: De Boeck.

Gréhaigne, J. F., Bouthier, D., & David, B. (1997). Dynamic-system analysis of opponent relationships in collective actions in soccer. *Journal of Sports Sciences, 15,* 137–149.

Gréhaigne, J. F., Godbout, P., & Bouthier, D. (1997). Performance assessment in team sports. *Journal of Teaching in Physical Education, 16,* 500–516.

Gréhaigne, J. F., Godbout, P., & Bouthier, D. (1999). The foundations of tactics and strategy in team sports. *Journal of Teaching in Physical Education, 18,* 159–174.

Gréhaigne, J. F., Godbout, P., & Bouthier, D. (2001). The teaching and learning of decision making in team sports. *Quest, 53,* 59–76.

Gréhaigne, J. F., Billard, M., Guillon, R., & Roche, J. (1988). Vers une autre conception de l'enseignement des sports collectifs [Towards an other view of the teaching of team sports]. In G. Bui-Xuan (Ed.), *Méthodologie et didactique de l'éducation physique et sportive* (pp. 155–172). Clermont-Ferrand, France: AFRAPS.

Gréhaigne, J. F., Richard, J. F., Mahut, N., & Griffin, L. (2002). Reflections on player competencies in team sport. *Journal of Sport Pedagogy, 8* (2), 22–37.

Griffin, L., & Placek, J. (2001). The understanding and development of learners domain-specific knowledge: Introduction. *Journal of Teaching in Physical Education, 20*(4), 299–300.

Griffin, L., Mitchell, S., & Oslin, J. (1997). *Teaching sport concepts and skills: A tactical games approach.* Champaign, IL: Human Kinetics.

Hanson, P. G., & Lubin, B. (1988). Team building as group development. In W.B. Reddy, & K. Jamison (Eds.), *Team building: Blueprints for productivity and satisfaction* (pp. 76–78). Alexandria, VA: National Institute for Applied Behavioral Science.

Harrison, J. M., Preece, L. A., Blakemore, C. L., Richards, R. P., Wilkinson C., & Felligham, G. W. (1999). Effects of two instructional models—skill teaching and mastery learning—on skill developpement, knowledge, self-effcacity, and game play in volleyball. *Journal of Teaching in Physical Education, 19*, 157–171.

Helsen, W., Starkes, J., & Hodges, N. (1998). Team sports and the theory of deliberate practice. *Journal of Sport and Exercise Psychology, 20*, 12–34.

Hoc, J. M., & Leplat, J. (1983). Evaluation of different modalities of verbalization in a sorting task. *Journal of Verbal Learning and Verbal Behavior, 3*, 187–198.

Holt, N. L., Strean, W. B., & Bengoechea, E. G. (2002). Expanding the teaching games for understanding model: New avenues for future research and practice. *Journal of Teaching in Physical Education, 21*, 162–176.

Houdé, O. (1992). *Catégorisation et développement cognitif*. Paris: PUF.

Hughes, C. (1980). *The football association coaching book of soccer tactics and skills*. London: Queen Anne Press.

Huizinga, J. (1951). Homo ludens, essai sur la fonction social du jeu. Paris: Gallimard.

Janis, I.L., & Feshbach, S. (1953). Effect of fear-arousing communication. *Journal of Abnormal and Social Psychology*, 48.

Kirk, D. (1983). Theoretical guidelines for "teaching for understanding." In L. Spackman (Ed.), *Teaching games for understanding* (pp. 80–83). Cheltenham, England: The College of St. Paul and St. Mary.

Kirk, D., & Macdonald, D. (1998). Situated learning in physical education. *Jounal of Teaching in Physical Education, 17*, 376–378.

Kirk, D., & MacPhail, A. (2002). Teaching games for understanding and situated learning: Rethinking the Bunker-Thorpe model. *Journal of Teaching in Physical Education, 21*, 177–192.

Lambert, N. M., & McCombs, B. L. (Eds.) (1998). *How students learn—Reforming schools through learner-centered education*. Washington, D.C.: American Psychological Association.

Laroche, J. Y., & Gréhaigne, J. F. (1995, October/November). *Utiliser un nomogramme avec des groupes mixtes. Quelle validité pour une évaluation en volley-ball*. Communication affichée: Journées d'automne de l'ACAPS, Guadeloupe.

Lave, & Wenger. (1991). *Situated learning: Legitimate peripheral participation*. New York: Cambridge University Press.

Leontiev, A. (1976). Le développement du psychisme: Problèmes [The development of psyche]. Paris: Éditions sociales.

Leplat, J. (1995). A propos des compétences incorporées. *Education Permanente, 123*, 101–123.

Mahlo, F. (1974). *Acte tactique en jeu* [Tactical action in play]. Paris: Vigot. (Originally published in German in 1969.)

Mahut, N., Nachon, M., Mahut, B., & Gréhaigne, J. F. (2000, October). *Illettrisme et apprentissage en E.P.S. L'acte moteur en débat*. Symposium conducted at the Colloque sur l'illettrisme, Reims, France.

Malglaive, G. (1990). *Enseigner à des adultes* [Teaching to adults]. Paris: PUF.

Marin, J. C. (1993). Règles d'action, histoire d'une notion [Action rules, the story of a notion]. Lyon, France: *Spirales 6*, 103–109.

McBride, R. E. (1991). Critical thinking—An overview with implications for physical education. *Journal of Teaching in Physical Education, 11*, 112–125.

McGee, R. (1984). Evaluation of processes and products. In B.J. Logsdon, K. R. Barrett, M. Ammons, M. R. Broer, L. E. Halverson, R. McGee, & M. A. Roberton (Eds.), *Physical education for children: A focus on the teaching process* (2nd ed., pp. 356–421). Philadelphia: Lea & Febiger.

McMorris, T. (1999). Cognitive development and the acquisition of decision-making skills. *International Journal of Sport Psychology, 30*, 151–172.

McMorris, T., & Beazeley, A. (1997). Performance of experienced and inexperienced of soccer players on soccer specific tests of recall, visual search and decision-making. *Journal of Human Movement Studies, 33*, 1–13.

McMorris, T., & Graydon, J. (1997). The contribution of the research literature to the understanding of decision making in team games. *Journal of Human Movement Studies, 33,* 69–90.

McMorris, T., & MacGillivary, W. W. (1988). An investigation into the relationship between field independence and decision making in soccer. In T. Reilly, A. Lees, K. Davids, & W. J. Murphy (Eds.), *Science and Football* (pp. 552–557). London: Spon.

McPherson, S. L. (1993). Knowledge representation and decision making in sport. In J.J. Starkes and F. Allard (Eds.), *Cognitive issues in motor expertise* (pp. 159–188). Elsevier Science Publishers B.V.

McPherson, S. L. (1993a). The influence of player experience on problem solving during batting preparation in baseball. *Journal of Sport & Exercice Psychology, 15,* 304–325.

McPherson, S. L. (1994). The development of sport expertise: Mapping the tactical domain. *Quest, 46,* 223–240.

McPherson, S. L. (1999a). Expert-novice differences in performance skills and problem representations of youth and adults during tennis competition. *Research Quarterly for Exercise and Sport, 70,* 233–251.

McPherson, S. L. (1999b). Tactical differences in problem representations and solutions in collegiate varsity and beginner women tennis players. *Research Quarterly for Exercise and Sport, 70,* 369–384.

McPherson, S., & French, K. (1991). Changes in cognitive strategies and motor skills in tennis. *Journal of Sport & Exercise Psychology, 13,* 26–41.

McPherson, S., & Thomas, J. (1989). Relation of knowledge and performance in boys' tennis: Age and expertise. *Journal of Experimental Child Psychology, 48,* 190–211.

Mérand, R. (1977). *L'éducateur face à la haute performance olympique* [The educator faced with high olympic performance]. Paris: Sport et Plein Air.

Mérand, R. (1984). Contribution à l'évaluation des connaissances et des capacités d'analyse des activités pratiquées [Contribution to the assessment of knowledge and of analysis capacities of physical activities]. In *L'évaluation en E.P.S.* (pp. 206–207). Paris: SNEP.

Mitchell, S. A. (1996). Improving invasion game performance. *Journal of Physical Education, Recreation and Dance, 67*(3), 30–33.

Mitchell, S. A., Griffin, L. L., & Oslin, J. L. (1994). Tactical awareness as a developmentally appropriate focus for the teaching of games in elementary and secondary physical education. *The Physical Educator, 51*(1), 21–28.

Mitchell, S. A., Oslin, J. L., & Griffin, L. L. (1995). The effects of two instructional approaches on game performance. *Pedagogy in practice—Teaching and coaching in physical education and sports, 1,* 36–48.

Morin, E. (1986) *La connaissance de la connaissance.* Paris: Seuil.

Nevett, M. E., & French, K. E. (1997). The development of sport-specific planning, rehearsal, and updating of plans during defensive youth baseball game performance. *Research Quarterly for Exercise and Sport, 68,* 203–214.

Nougier, V., & Rossi, B. (1999). The development of expertise in the orienting of attention. *International Journal of Sport Psychology, 30,* 246–260.

Nuttin, J. (1985). *Théorie de la motivation humaine: Du besoin au projet d'action* [Human motivation theory: From need to action project]. Paris: Presses Universitaires de France.

Oslin, J. L., Mitchell, S. A., & Griffin, L. (1998). The Game Performance Assessment Instrument (GPAI): Development and preliminary validation. *Journal of Teaching in Physical Education, 17,* 231–243.

Parker, G. M. (1990). *Team players and teamwork: The new competitive business strategy.* San Francisco: Jossey-Bass.

Parlebas, P. (1976). Les universaux du jeu sportif collectif, la modélisation du jeu sportif. *Éducation Physique et Sport, 141,* 33.

Piaget, J. (1967). *Biologie et connaissances* [Biology and knowledge]. Paris: Gallimard.

Piaget, J. (1971). *Biology and knowledge: An essay on the relations between organic regulations and cognitive processes*. (B. Walsh, Trans.). Chicago: University of Chicago Press.

Piaget, J. (1974a). *Réussir et comprendre* [Succeeding and understanding]. Paris: PUF.

Piaget, J. (1974b). *La prise de conscience* [Sudden awareness]. Paris: PUF.

Pinheiro, V. (1994). Diagnosing motor skills—A practical approach. *Journal of Physical Education, Recreation, and Dance, 65*(2), 49–54.

Perkins, D. (1999). The many faces of constructivism. *Educational Researcher, 57*, 6–11.

Plummer, O. K., & Rougeau, D. (1997). Team building magic for all. *Strategies, 10*(6), 22–24.

Rauschenbach, J. (1996). Charge! and catch coop. Two games for teaching game for play strategy. *Journal of Physical Education, Recreation and Dance, 67*(5), 49–51.

Resnick, L. B. (1987). *Education and learning to think*. Washington, D.C.: National Academy Press.

Reitchess, S. (1983). Problèmes posés par l'apprentissage d'actions collectives en rugby en utilisant une pédagogie des choix tactiques avec de jeunes enfants. Mémoire de maîtrise en STAPS. Université Paris V.

Richard, J. F. (1990). *Les activités mentales. Comprendre, raisonner, trouver des solutions* [Mental activities. Understanding, reasoning, finding solutions]. Paris: Armand Colin.

Richard, J. F. (1998). La mesure et l'évaluation de la performance en jeux et sports collectifs: La participation des élèves du primaire dans une perspective d'évaluation authentique. Unpublished doctoral dissertation. Université Laval, Québec, Canada.

Richard, J. F., Godbout, P., & Gréhaigne, J. F. (1998). The establishment of team sport performance norms for grade 5 to 8 students. *Avante, 4*(2), 1–19.

Richard, J.F., Godbout, P., & Gréhaigne, J. F. (1998a). *The precision and reliability of a performance assessment procedure in team sports*. From an unpublished doctoral dissertation. Université Laval, Québec, Canada.

Richard, J. F., Godbout, P., & Gréhaigne, J. F. (2000). Students' precision and interobserver reliability of performance assessment in team sports. *Research Quarterly for Exercise and Sport, 71*(1), 85–91.

Richard, J. F., Godbout, P., Tousignand, M., & Gréhaigne, J. F. (1999). The try-out of team-sport performance assessment procedure in elementary school and junior high school physical education classes. *Journal of Teaching in Physical Education, 18*, 336–356.

Riley, P. (1993). *The winner within: A life plan for team players*. New York: G.P. Putman's Sons.

Rink, J. E. (1996). Tactical and skill approaches to teaching sport and games [Monograph]. *Journal of Teaching in Physical Education, 15*(4).

Rink, J. E. (2001). Investigating the assumptions of pedagogy. *Journal of Teaching in Physical Education, 20*, 112–128.

Rink, J., French, K. E., & Tjeerdsma, L. (1996). Foundations for learning and instruction of sport games. *Journal of Teaching in Physical Education, 15*, 399–417.

Rioux, R., & Chapuis, G. (1967). *L'équipe dans les sports collectifs*. Paris: Vrin.

Rioux, R., & Chapuis, G. (1976). *La cohésion de l'équipe*. Paris: Vrin.

Ripoll, H. (Ed.). (1991). Information processing and decision making in sport. *International Journal of Sport Psychology, 22*, 3–4.

Ripoll, H., & Benguigui, N. (1999). Emergence of expertise in ball sports during child development. *International Journal of Sport Psychology, 30*, 235–245.

Rosnay, J. de (1975). *Le macroscope*. Paris: Seuil.

Rovegno, I. (1999, April). *What is taught and learned in physical activity programs: The role of content*. Keynote presentation at the AIESEP Conference, Besancon, France.

Rovegno, I., Nevett, M., & Babiarz, M. (2001). Learning and teaching invasion-game tactics in 4th grade: Introduction and theoretical perspective. *Journal of Teaching in Physical Education [Monograph], 20*, 341–351.

Rovegno, I., & Bandhauer, D. (1997). Norms of the school culture that facilitated teacher adoption and learning of a constructivist approach to physical education. *Journal of Teaching in Physical Education, 16,* 401–425.

Rovegno, I., & Kirk, D. (1995). Articulations and silences in social critical work on physical education: Towards a broader agenda. *Quest, 47,* 447–474.

Rumelhart, D. E., & Norman, D. A. (1978). Accretion, tuning, and restructuring: Three modes of learning. In J. W. Cotton & R. L. Klatzky (Eds.), *Semantic factors in cognition* (pp. 37–53). Hillsdale, NJ: Erlbaum.

Safrit, M. J., & Wood, T. M. (1995). *Introduction to measurement in physical education and exercise science* (3rd ed.). St. Louis, MO: Times Mirror/Mosby College Publishing.

Salmela, J. H. (1997). Détection des talents [Talent detection]. *Education Physique et Sport, 267,* 27–29.

Schmidt, R. A. (1991). *Motor learning and performance: From principles to practice.* Champaign, IL: Human Kinetics.

Schunk, D. H. (1986). Verbalization and children's self-regulated learning. *Contemporary Educational Psychology, 11,* 347–369.

Schwager, S., & Labate, C. (1993). Teaching for critical thinking in physical education. *Journal of Physical Education, Recreation and Dance, 64* (5), 24–26.

Sherif, M., & Sherif, C.W. (1979). Les relations intra et inter groupes: Une approche expérimentale. In W. Doise (Ed.), *Expériences entre groupes* (pp. 1–58). Paris: Mouton.

Shiffrin, R. M., & Dumais, J. T. (1981). The developmemnt of automatism. In J.R. Anderson (Ed.), *Cognitive skills and their acquisition* (pp. 111–139). Hillsdade, NJ: Lawrence Erlbaum.

Shuell, T. (1986). Cognitive conceptions of learning. *Review of Educational Research, 56,* 411–436.

Stein, J. F. (1981). *Sports d'opposition, éléments d'analyse pour une pédagogie des prises de décisions* [Opposition sports, elements of analysis for a decision making pedagogy]. Paris: INSEP.

Steinberg, G. M., Chaffin, W. M., & Singer, R. N. (1998). Mental quickness training—Drills that emphasize the development of anticipation skills in fast-paced sports. *Journal of Physical Education, Recreation and Dance, 69*(7), 37–41.

Sternberg, R. J. (1984). A theory of knowledge acquisition in the development of verbal concepts. *Developmental Review, 4,* 113–138.

Tennenbaum, G. (Ed.). (1999). The development of expertise in sport: nature and nurture. *International Journal of Sport Psychology, 30*(2).

Teodorescu, L. (1965). Principes pour l'étude de la tactique commune aux jeux sportifs collectifs [Principles for studying tactics common to team sport games]. *Revue de la S.I.E.P.E.P.S., 3,* 29–40.

Thomas, K. T., & Thomas, J. R. (1999). What squirrels in the trees predict about expert athletes. *International Journal of Sport Psychology, 30,* 221–234.

Thorpe, R., Bunker, D., & Almond, L. (1984). A change in focus for the teaching of game. In *Olympic Scientific Congress Proceedings, 6* (pp.163–169). Champaign, IL: Human Kinetics.

Tishman, S., & Perkins, D. (1995). Critical thinking and physical education. *Journal of Physical Education, Recreation and Dance, 66*(7), 24–30.

Tsangaridou, N., & Sidentop, D. (1995). Reflective teaching: A literature review. *Quest, 47,* 212–237.

Turner, A. P., & Martinek, T. J. (1995). Teaching for understanding: A model for improving decision making during game play. *Quest, 47,* 44–63.

Van der Maren, J. M. (1999). *La recherche appliquée en pédagogie. Des modèles pour l'enseignement.* Brussels: De Boeck.

Veal, M. L. (1988). Pupil assessment perceptions and practices of secondary teachers. *Journal of Teaching in Physical Education, 7*, 327–342.

Veal, M. L. (1995). Assessment as an instructional tool. *Strategies, 8*(6), 10–15.

Vergnaud, G., Halbvacks, F., & Rouchier, A. (1978). Structure de la matière enseignée, histoire des sciences et développement conceptuel chez l'enfant [Structure of the subject matter, history of sciences and conceptual development of the child]. *Revue Française de Pédagogie, 45*, 7–18.

Villepreux, P. (1987). *Rugby de mouvement et disponibilité du joueur* [Rugby in movement and player's readiness]. Paris: Mémoire, INSEP.

Von Clausewitz, C. (1989). *De la guerre* [About war] (Rev. ed.). Paris: Lebovici.

Wade, A. (1970). *The football association guide to training and coaching*. London: EP Publishing LTD.

Walliser, B. (1977). *Systèmes et modèles. Introduction critique à l'analyse de systèmes*. Paris: Seuil.

Wallon, H. (1941). *L'évolution psychologique de l'enfant*. Paris: Armand Colin.

Weinstein, C. E., & Mayer, R. E. (1986). The teaching of learning strategies. In M. C. Wittrock (Ed.), *Handbook of research on teaching* (3rd ed., pp. 315–327). New York: Macmillan.

Werner, P. (1989). Teaching games—A tactical perspective. *Journal of Physical Education, Recreation and Dance, 60*(3), 97–101.

Werner, P., Thorpe, R., & Bunker, D. (1996). Teaching games for understanding: Evolution of a model. *Journal of Physical Education, Recreation, and Dance, 67*(1), 28–33.

Wiggins, G. P. (1993). *Assessing student behavior: Exploring the purpose and limits of testing*. San Francisco: Jossey-Bass Publishers.

Williams, A. M., & Grant, A. (1999). Training perceptual skill in sport. *International Journal of Sport Psychology, 30*, 194–220.

Williams, M., Davids, K., Burwitz, L., & Williams, J. (1993). Cognitive knowledge and soccer performance. *Perceptual and Motor Skills, 72*, 579–593.

Wrzos, J. (1984). *La tactique de l'attaque*. Bräkel: Broodcoorens.

Zessoules, R., & Gardner, H. (1991). Authentic assessment: Beyond the buzzword and into the classroom. In V. Perrone (Ed.), *Expanding student assessment* (pp. 47–71). Alexandria, VA: Association for Supervision and Curriculum Development.

Endnotes

CHAPTER 1

1. Uncertainty and certainty are related to the quantity and quality of available information. Uncertainty is the information that we do not possess about the state of the system (Atlan, 1979).

CHAPTER 3

1. For more details on the systemic analysis of team sports, see Gréhaigne & Godbout (1995).

CHAPTER 4

1. See French & McPherson (1999) and McPherson (1999) for more details on the recent development of the *action plan profile* and *current event profile* constructs.

CHAPTER 5

1. A class of game play problems is defined by the similarity between the practical knowledge involved the problem solving modes in which the student/athlete must rely upon in order to respond to the different problems faced in different game situations.

CHAPTER 8

1. For information on the TSAP-volleyball, refer to Richard, Godbout, & Griffin (2002).

Index